MY ENEMY'S ENEMY

AVINASH PALIWAL

MY ENEMY'S ENEMY

INDIA IN AFGHANISTAN FROM THE SOVIET INVASION TO THE US WITHDRAWAL

HarperCollins *Publishers* India

First published in the United Kingdom in 2017 by
C. Hurst & Co. (Publishers) Ltd.

First published in hardback in India by
HarperCollins *Publishers* in 2017

Building 10, Tower A, 4th Floor, DLF Cyber City, Phase II,
Gurugram Haryana – 122002, India
www.harpercollins.co.in

2 4 6 8 10 9 7 5 3 1

P-ISBN: 978-93-5277-268-1
E-ISBN: 978-93-5277-269-8

Book design by Brooke Koven

Printed and bound at MicroPrints India, New Delhi

For Nina, Amma, and Baba

CONTENTS

PART III
DEBATING ENGAGEMENT

ACKNOWLEDGEMENTS

'Sometimes we have to do a thing in order to find out the reason for it. Sometimes our actions are questions, not answers' [John le Carré, *The Perfect Spy*]. Taking up an unfunded doctoral position in London on a topic requiring expensive (and sometimes scary) fieldwork, especially after quitting a journalism job in India, is insane. Working on this book explained to me why I did so. Finding answers to bothersome questions needed time and effort that academia afforded best. Though the idea of this book emerged during my stints of (f) unemployment and chasing stories as a young journalist, it flourished as a doctoral dissertation at King's College London under Harsh Pant's stellar supervision. A master of the trade, Harsh entertained my (various) ideas with patience and helped develop the reasonable ones into what you see here.

Christophe Jaffrelot and Chris Ogden's encouragement and constructive feedback as examiners helped sharpen my arguments, whereas Srinath Raghavan's interventions at key moments offered breakthroughs. In their own ways Tracey German, Wyn Bowen, Sunil Khilnani, Theo Farrell, and Rudra Chaudhuri taught me a lot about academia and writing, whereas Geraint Hughes allowed me to steal the title of his book for my own. Lynda Hobbs, Lyn Reynolds, Lucy Fisher, and Karen Crouch at the Defence Studies Department made this journey an administrative breeze.

Giving it financial legs, the King's Continuation Scholarship, the Defence Studies Research Studentship, and various small grants offered by the King's Graduate School ensured sustainability and progress of this project. The UK-India Education Research Initiative's Trilateral Research in Partnership (UKIERI-TRIP) grant enabled field travels to India, Afghanistan, US, and within the UK, whereas the Defence Academy Postdoctoral Fellowship allowed me to rewrite my PhD thesis into a book. As chairperson of the

Afghanistan Studies Group I had the opportunity to meet and learn from Afghan experts and enthusiasts from across the world.

I could not have capitalised on these opportunities and learned from these experiences without the emotional, practical, and intellectual support from (mentioned in no particular order): Apra Vaidya, Saumyajit Bhattacharya, Mark Erbel, Swapna Kona Nayudu, Tajjamul Hussain, Sarita Sharma, Stefan Schilling, Rahul Prakash, Jill Russell, Sonali Mittra, Johann Chacko, Andy Gawthorpe, Bhanu Gupta, Aditya Bisen, Shafi Rahman, Nikos Daskalakis, Alexandre N Pereira, Megha Kumar, Kamaldeep Singh Sandhu, Raphaelle Khan, Kapil Gupta, Claire Yorke, Shankar Jayaram and Pawan Gupta. A special thanks goes to Martin Bayly, Hugo Meijer, Arvind John, Karthik Nachiappan, and Aryaman Bhatnagar all of who not only humoured my rants on South Asian politics, but generously took the time to read parts or all of the manuscript and offer critical feedback.

I am thankful to all the interviewees who took time out to share their experiences, thoughts, and ideas with me. During my fieldwork in India, Afghanistan, and the US, a host of wonderful people and institutions helped me. In New Delhi, the Observer Research Foundation (ORF) played an important role in cultivating my interest in Afghanistan and Pakistan at the outset, and then in offering a Visiting Fellowship in 2013. I am indebted to C. Raja Mohan and Samir Saran for their guidance during my stint at the ORF and afterwards, and to Wilson John, with whom I had many long and fascinating conversations about the region. At the Ministry of External Affairs (MEA), I am thankful to brilliant officers such as Virander Paul, Smita Pant, Amandeep Singh Gill, J P Singh, Mukul Arya, and Sriparna Pathak Raimedhi for helping in myriad small and big ways. I am also grateful of P, R, J, A, and Benoy Khare for allowing me a glimpse into the shadowy world of Indian intelligence.

Fieldwork in Afghanistan would not be possible without the hospitality of Zuhra Bahman and Jawed Ludin. Zuhra's eye for detail, contacts across the country, and knowledge of Kabuli politics kept me in excellent stead. Luke Beer's charisma and grasp of Kabul's expat networks and Khalid Nadiri's impressive (encyclopaedic) knowledge of Afghanistan made my trip truly enjoyable and fruitful. Sanaullah Tasal's insights from the ground, Zaki Ludin and Yama Nasir's help with arranging interviews, and Samim Sarem's translations where English, Hindi/Urdu failed, saved the day. In Herat, Toryalai Yaqoobi, Attaullah, and Amarjit Singh made my stay safe and productive. In the US, Walter K. Andersen and Khalid Nadiri (again) kindly hosted me as an exchange scholar at Johns Hopkins University's Paul H Nitze School of Advanced International Studies (SAIS).

The anonymous reviews organised by Hurst and Oxford University Press (OUP) helped finessing the shape and form of this book considerably. Michael Dwyer and his team at Hurst—Jon de Peyer, Alison Alexanian, Kathleen May, Daisy Leitch, Jane Eagles, and others—supported this project with professionalism, care, and enthusiasm. Similarly, at HarperCollins India, Bidisha Srivastava and her team ensured timely delivery in India. This book is dedicated to the three pillars of my life: my wife Nina Kaysser, and my parents, Renu Sharma (Amma) and Vimal Paliwal (Baba). Nina's love, patience, and encouragement gave me the confidence to write this book. She graciously read the manuscript and gave critical feedback at various stages of its development. Finally, Amma and Baba's selflessness, compassion, and faith in the value of education made the impossible, possible.

ACRONYMS

ACF	Advocacy Coalition Framework
AIA	Afghan Interim Administration
AI	All India Radio
ANP	Awami National Party
ANSF	Afghan National Security Forces
ASEAN	Association of Southeast Asian Nations
AWACS	Air Warning and Control System
BBC	British Broadcasting Corporation
BJP	Bharatiya Janata Party
BLA	Baloch Liberation Army
BPLF	Balochistan People's Liberation Front
BRP	Baloch Republican Party
BSA	Bilateral Security Agreement
CAR	Central Asian Republics
CCIT	Comprehensive Convention on International Terrorism
CCS	Cabinet Committee on Security
CENTO	Central Treaty Organization
CIA	Central Intelligence Agency
CII	Confederation of Indian Industry
CIS	Commonwealth of Independent States
COAS	Chief of Army Staff
COIN	Counterinsurgency
CPI	Communist Party of India
CPI (M)	Communist Party of India (Marxist)
CPSU	Communist Party of the Soviet Union
DFID	Department for International Development

DIA	Defence Intelligence Agency
DNI	Director of National Intelligence
DRA	Democratic Republic of Afghanistan
EAM	External Affairs Minister
EIC	East India Company
FAR	Foreign Affairs Records
FATA	Federally Administered Tribal Areas
FCO	Foreign and Commonwealth Office
FICCI	Federation of Indian Chambers of Commerce and Industry
FS	Foreign Secretary
GRU	Glavnoye razvedyvatel'noye upravleniye
GTR	Grand Trunk Road
GWU	George Washington University
HPC	High Peace Council
HM	Hizbul Mujahideen
HN	Haqqani Network
HuA	Harkat-ul-Ansar
IAEA	International Atomic Energy Agency
IB	Intelligence Bureau [of India]
ICCR	Indian Council for Cultural Relations
IDCR	Indian Development Cooperation Research
IDSA	Institute for Defence Studies and Analyses
IFS	Indian Foreign Service
IPS	Indian Police Service
IRGC	Islamic Revolutionary Guard Corps
Il-76	Ilyushin II-76
IUML	Indian Union Muslim League
INC	Indian National Congress
INF	Intermediate Range Nuclear Force Treaty
INR	Indian Rupee
IR	International Relations
ISAF	International Security Assistance Force
ISI	[Directorate of] Inter-Services Intelligence
IUML	Indian Union Muslim League
ITBP	Indo-Tibetan Border Police
J&K	Jammu and Kashmir
JeM	Jaish-e-Mohammad

JIC	Joint Intelligence Committee
JS	Joint Secretary
JS-PAI	Joint Secretary (Pakistan, Afghanistan, Iran)
JuH	Jamiat-i-Ulama-i-Hind
JWG	Joint Working Group
JWG-CT	Joint Working Group on Counter Terrorism
KGB	Komitet Gosudarstvennoy Bezopasnosti
KhAD	Khadamat-e Aetla'at-e Dawlati
LeT	Lashkar-e-Taiba
LoC	Line of Control
LTTE	Liberation of Tamil Tigers Eelam
MEA	Ministry of External Affairs
MI	Military Intelligence
MoD	Ministry of Defence
MoU	Memorandum of Understanding
MoS	Minister of State
MP	Member of Parliament
MRRD	Ministry of Rural Rehabilitation and Development
NA	Northern Alliance
NAM	Non-Aligned Movement
NAP	National Awami Party
NATO	North Atlantic Treaty Organisation
NDA	National Democratic Alliance
NDS	National Directorate of Security
NSA	National Security Advisor
NSAB	National Security Advisory Board
NSCN	National Socialist Council of Nagaland
NSCS	National Security Council Secretariat
NUG	National Unity Government
NWFP	Northwestern Frontier Provinces
ORF	Observer Research Foundation
PDPA	People's Democratic Party of Afghanistan
PLO	Palestinian Liberation Organisation
PM	Prime Minister
PMO	Prime Minister's Office
POTO	Prevention of Terrorism Ordinance
PPP	People's Party of Pakistan
PRT	Provincial Reconstruction Team

ACRONYMS

R&AW	Research and Analysis Wing
RECCA	Regional Economic Cooperation Conference on Afghanistan
RIC	Russia-India-China
RSS	Rashtriya Swayamsevak Sangh
SAARC	South Asian Association for Regional Cooperation
SEATO	Southeast Asia Treaty Organization
SDP	Small Developmental Projects
SEWA	Self-Employed Women's Organisation
SIS	Secret Intelligence Service
SP	Samajwadi Party
SPA	Strategic Partnership Agreement
TAPI	Turkmenistan-Afghanistan-Pakistan-India
ToI	Times of India
TTP	Tehrik-e-Taliban Pakistan
UAE	United Arab Emirates
UF	United Front
UK	United Kingdom
UN	United Nations
UNGA	United Nations General Assembly
UNHCR	United Nations High Commissioner for Refugees
UNSC	United Nations Security Council
UNSG	United Nations Secretary General
UPA	United Progressive Alliance
USAID	United States Agency for International Development
US PACOM	United States Pacific Command
USA-PATRIOT	Uniting and Strengthening of America by Providing Appropriate Tools to Intercept and Obstruct Terrorism
WAPCOS	Water and Power Consultancy Services Ltd.

PROLOGUE

A CURSE

'Severe punishment—that is, death', declared the judge on a cold February morning in Kabul. The courtroom, inhabited by a motley crowd of two hundred spectators keenly watching the proceedings of the war tribunal, erupted in joyful chants of 'Allah-u-Akbar'.[1] The year was 2006 and the Afghan judiciary had proved, in true Kafkaesque fashion, that it functioned just well enough to sentence a war criminal after nearly thirteen years of imprisonment and more than two decades after the crimes. Assadullah Sarwari became the first and only war criminal to be tried in Afghanistan. But death was not the worst that could happen to a man who had been in Afghan prisons for all these years. The most brutal twist of his life, in fact, had occurred in a friendly neighbouring country, but more on India later. Former spymaster, deputy prime minister (PM) of Afghanistan, vice president of the revolutionary council, and politburo member of the Khalq (people) faction of the left-wing *Hezb-e-Demokratik-e-Khalq-e-Afghanistan* or the People's Democratic Party of Afghanistan (PDPA), Sarwari had the blood of many Afghans on his hands. Thousands of people had disappeared, or were killed during his one-year tenure as Afghanistan's intelligence chief in 1978–79.[2] For instance, 4,785 Afghans were killed in the Pul-e-Charkhi prison on various charges of conspiring against the party.[3] Ambitious and cunning, Sarwari was at the forefront of a truly Byzantine political struggle. On one hand, he was fighting with a rival Marxist group within the PDPA, the Parcham (flag) faction. On the other hand, as part of the so-called 'gang of four' (all Khalqi stalwarts) Sarwari had planned and executed the assassination of another fellow Khalqi—former Afghan president Hafizullah Amin.[4]

Making way for a jittery Soviet Union to send troops to Afghanistan in 1979, Sarwari also paved the way for the rise of his Parchami adversary, Babrak Karmal, as the president. In a move to reconcile the two factions, Moscow arbitrated a deal in which Karmal accepted Sarwari as his second in command for a brief period.[5] Counting on an early Soviet exit, which he expected would leave Karmal weak and susceptible, Sarwari continued his internal struggle against his Parchami comrades, and cracked down on Islamist dissidents and their families, shooting some dead and burying others alive.[6] In an attempt to deal with Sarwari without further bloodshed, Karmal eased him out within months of coming to power by appointing him as Afghanistan's ambassador to Mongolia in 1980, a position he held for six years, and removing him from politburo in 1981. In 1986, Sarwari's membership of the PDPA Central Committee was annulled and he was ordered to go to Germany, followed by an ambassadorial position in South Yemen.

By 1987, Sarwari's hopes of coming to power had been crushed by Parcham's Mohammad Najibullah, another communist spymaster who became president. Not shy to use force whenever the need arose (his preferred technique to execute prisoners was to beat them to the ground and then kick them to death), Najibullah was a tough match for Sarwari and his allies.[7] Najibullah got along well with the Soviet Union and consummately practiced the craft of inter-tribal manipulation and rivalry. However, politically and structurally, his government was far weaker than its predecessor. With the Soviets crawling out of Afghanistan and the Mujahideen offensive in full swing (via Pakistan), Najibullah's political situation was becoming increasingly precarious by early 1990. That is when Sarwari decided to end his diplomatic exile in South Yemen and join Najibullah's disgruntled chief of army staff and a fellow Khalqi, Lt. Gen. Shahnawaz Tanai. Angry at Najibullah's pro-Parcham bias, Tanai had secretly made plans with help from the Mujahideen based in Pakistan, to overthrow Najibullah.[8] But then, Sarwari's life took an unexpected, ugly turn.

Sarwari decided to have a stopover in India on his way back to Afghanistan from South Yemen. A friendly neighbouring country, India was undergoing its own economic and political crises, and was wary of interfering in the domestic affairs of another country. New Delhi had recently burnt its fingers in Sri Lanka where it had been fighting a bloody war with the Liberation Tigers of Tamil Eelam (LTTE), the most militarily potent Tamil separatist organisation. If the planned coup were to fail, Sarwari hoped to remain safe in a fragile, democratic, and friendly India. Despite Najibullah's close links with

New Delhi, Sarwari expected decent treatment from the Indians who, crucially for him, did not have an extradition treaty with Afghanistan. Either way, he planned to stay in India for a month and then fly back to Kabul, just before the coup.

On January 16, 1990, Sarwari landed in Bombay, and was cordially received by officials from the Afghan Embassy.[9] He traveled to Delhi and stayed at a plush hotel in the South Western part of the city. Little over a month later, on 20 February 1990 (sixteen years before he was sentenced to death), Sarwari was ready to fly back to Afghanistan. He was minutes away from boarding the Indian Airlines flight 451 to Kabul when, allegedly, an Afghan embassy official turned up at the immigration counter of the Indira Gandhi International (IGI) Airport, and under murky circumstances, seized Sarwari's passport that contained a valid six-month-long Indian visa.[10] A scared and exasperated Sarwari was stuck in India. Having been put out of play by Najibullah's proactive measures (without, apparently, India disapproving such moves), Sarwari's fate was now tied to the success or failure of Tanai's coup. Unfortunately for him, the attempted coup of March 1990 failed miserably. Tanai somehow managed to escape to Pakistan, while a furious Najibullah (who believed that it was Sarwari who had masterminded the coup) ordered a massive crackdown within the military and government institutions to rid them of Tanai and Sarwari's sympathisers.

Sarwari, thus, was a condemned man much before the court sentenced him to death in 2006. If he were to return to Najibullah's Afghanistan, the gallows, or maybe worse, torture, awaited him. Sarwari tried a host of methods to seek help from Indian authorities. He wrote a beseeching letter to the foreign secretary (FS) of India on 12 April 1990, drawing the latter's attention to his case and requesting security, as he feared for his life.[11] He also reached out to the then Indian PM Vishwanath Pratap Singh, and other top but uninterested politicians such as Rajiv Gandhi. No response was forthcoming. Instead, Sarwari found himself in a 'C' grade cell (meant for petty criminals and smugglers) in Delhi's Tihar Jail under the Foreigner's Registration Act on 11 June 1990. His six-month Indian visa, which he had lost with his passport, had expired and his presence on Indian soil was deemed illegal. As there were no provisions to extradite him, a request for the same from Kabul was summarily rejected by New Delhi.

He languished in jail and was dragged unceremoniously, with his hands and feet tightly chained, more than thirty-nine times, for hearings at the Tis Hazari Court in Delhi. According to reports, Sarwari was not even allowed to meet officials from the United Nations while in prison.[12] Though he was provided a legal counsel who fought his case relentlessly, not much came out of it. After thirteen months in jail, a fine of Rs. 5,000 (approx. 77 USD), tremendous humiliation, and active intervention by Amnesty International, Sarwari was secretly put on a plane in July 1991 and deported to where he had come from—Yemen.[13] A disappointed Sarwari made his frustration with India amply clear. Calling his detention 'illegal' and out of 'political vendetta', Sarwari castigated New Delhi's behavior as a 'shame for Indian democracy', something he had not expected from a 'friendly country' like India.[14]

Arguably, this is an obscure and strategically inconsequential case. Sarwari was little known internationally, hardly remembered historically, stood against Najibullah who was India's strategic ally, was responsible for murder and torture, and gravitated towards Pakistan for political support. But, as this book shows, at the heart of this ostensibly unimportant case lays the contradiction of India's policy approach towards Afghanistan. The idea of political neutrality, if one ever existed, despite India's passionate advocacy of the same, stood belied. This was the first time India facilitated a politically motivated arrest of a senior Afghan politician to ensure the political survival of an equally violent ally: an ally, one should say, of whom India was growing wary even before his actual ouster from power in 1992. Clamour for a more accommodative approach towards Najibullah's opponents had been growing steadily in New Delhi since the mid-1980s. The choice that Indian policymakers faced, thus, was real. They could have let Sarwari go and adjusted their Afghanistan policy if the coup had succeeded. Or they could continue supporting Najibullah, who presided over a highly repressive and unstable regime that was making enemies at a faster rate than building allies.

India chose the latter. Sarwari's arrest came eerily close to Najibullah's official visit to New Delhi in mid-1990. It was not hard to fathom that India was keen on keeping Najibullah in good humour even though his authority was being challenged both from inside and out. If the coup of March 1990 had succeeded, Sarwari could have been a potential asset, but with the coup having failed, he was simply an irritant between India and Najibullah. Still, New Delhi had no reason to either love or hate Sarwari. He was a serious political actor in Kabul, had been close to Moscow where many considered him a better presidential candidate than Najibullah, and he was young enough to revive his political career. He had even welcomed Indian ministers to Kabul during the late-1970s and 1980, and advocated closer relations between the two countries. In essence, he represented that breed of Afghan politician who had nothing against India, were politically ruthless, but who fell out of favour with the government of the day in Kabul, and as a result, had lost their voice in, and value for, New Delhi. In April 1992, the eventuality that worried many in India actually occurred. Within nine months of deporting Sarwari, and despite India and the UN's clandestine efforts to protect the embattled president, Najibullah's regime collapsed.

In retrospect, both Sarwari and Najibullah were the first political casualties of India's policy flux vis-à-vis Afghanistan as the Cold War came to an end. Unlike previous decades, including the years when the Soviet Union was in charge of Kabul, India was awakening to the new reality of a broken Afghanistan wrought by civil war. It was a curse, especially in India's relations with Pakistan. From now on, Indian policymakers would face situations when their chosen Afghan friends would make demands to neutralise domestic political rivals (and/or Pakistan's proxies) in Afghanistan. Fulfilling these demands could jeopardise India's political standing in the region (and the world) and endanger the lives of Indians working on the ground in Afghanistan. But if India did not help, then it would lose political ground in a neighbouring country of high strategic value. Effectively, India would be doomed if it decided to go the full way in supporting its chosen Afghan friends, and would be equally doomed if it shied away. This book shows how even three decades later, Sarwari and Najibullah's ghosts still haunt Indian policymakers as they try, with limited success, to reconcile this recurring Afghan dilemma.

1

IN PURSUIT OF FRIENDSHIP

INDIA'S QUEST IN AFGHANISTAN

'The enemy, however strong he may be, becomes vulnerable to harassment and destruction when he is squeezed between the conqueror and his allies'.

Kautilya in the *Arthashastra*, Verse 6.2.40[1]

'As Pakistan increasingly became our problem, Afghanistan emerged as kind of a counter-balance. To keep Pakistan on its toes, friendly relations with Afghanistan, which always created a kind of anxiety in Pakistan, were kept up'.

Lalit Mansingh, Foreign Secretary of India (1999–2001)[2]

The question

Already being termed an 'Asian century', rising powers such as India have a greater say in international politics today. India's arrival on the international stage, however, has raised more questions than it has provided answers. Culturally heterogeneous but socially conservative; democratic but also housing various forms of extremism; territorially united but wrought with separatism; economically strong(er) but highly unequal; constitutionally secular but divided by religion, caste, and gender; rising peacefully but making its neighbours anxious; aspiring to be a global power yet shy (or unclear) of taking the lead—how do Indian policymakers debate and implement policies on issues of material and ideational, as well as regional and global importance, in the light of these contradictions? Even though India's rise, combined with that of China, is altering the vocabulary of international politics, the answer to this question is still being explored. This book intends to decode India's foreign policy-making processes and add to a growing body of literature on this topic, by examining the widely discussed and strategically important, but grossly understudied and routinely misunderstood subject of India's approach towards Afghanistan since the Soviet invasion to the ongoing US withdrawal. The central question that concerns this book is: is containing Pakistan a key factor driving India's Afghanistan policy?

A fulcrum of global power play for decades, and a theatre of conflict, competition, as well as aspiration, Afghanistan is of critical strategic interest for India, and captures the magnitude and multitude of changes in India's foreign and security policy over the years. Situated in the heart of Asia, Afghanistan marked, if not caused, the sudden dramatic dissolution of the Soviet Union and an end to the Cold War. Then, instead of being sidelined to the margins of history, it emerged as the first frontier of the tragically termed, poorly understood, and ruthlessly executed, global war on terror. Witnessing war for more than thirty-five years including various military interventions, first by the Soviet Union, then by Pakistan (or Pakistan-supported elements), and the latest by the US-led NATO forces, Afghanistan has also seen the rise and fall of at least three ideologies (communism, radical Islam, and liberal democracy), within a short span of fifty years. Given its unfortunate history, Afghanistan came to be understood more as a buffer space where external powers play 'great games'—a term coined for the benefit of the British Raj, but which stubbornly persists to date.[3]

In 2011, then US Secretary of State and later presidential candidate Hillary Clinton espoused a regional solution to the unending conflict in Afghanistan.[4] Aiming to develop Afghanistan as a 'neutral' territory, Clinton equated today's Afghanistan with early nineteenth-century Europe. She hoped that South Asian countries would reach an agreement similar to the 1814–15 Congress of Vienna after the French defeat in the Napoleonic wars. Leading to the creation of a neutral zone in the Benelux countries, the Congress of Vienna model marked a shift in Europe's balance of power. After almost a century of war and peace, the 1907 Hague Convention further delineated the concept of neutrality famously applied in the case of Switzerland.[5] Clinton stated: 'If we [US] could get to that point with the regional powers in South Asia, that (they) would not recommence with the great game in Afghanistan, that would be a very worthy outcome'.[6] Nothing came out of it. Far from being stable or neutral (as the Afghan Taliban, even though fragmented, staged a comeback), Afghanistan today faces multiple security, political, and financial crises. Topping this is the fact that India and Pakistan continue to remain at odds with each other while the latter's alleged interference in Afghan domestic affairs has not ceased.

Although there are explanations for Pakistan's behavior towards Afghanistan, India's Afghanistan policy has elicited analogies of 'great game' and 'proxy warfare', or simply, strategic desire for access to material resources in that region, as causal explanations.[7] If anything, India's role in Afghanistan's international history (particularly from the mid-1960s onwards) has been overlooked. More generally, the voice of great powers tends to dominate the study of Afghanistan's wars, to the exclusion of a more regional perspective. This matters first, because it obscures the role of regional powers that may have had a far more enduring, and at times, critical influence on the situation. And it matters secondly because whilst commentators regularly call for a 'regional' solution to conflict in Afghanistan, there are fewer historical works that can contribute to understanding the role that regional actors have played in Afghanistan in the first place. A detailed interrogation of Indian policy debates and approaches towards Afghanistan will contribute towards filling this gap.

Despite having a vision of a strong, stable, sovereign, and territorially united Afghanistan, India's policy course has witnessed changes big and small over the past three and a half decades. In fact, similar to Clinton, former diplomat and current Indian vice president Mohammad Hamid Ansari stated in 2003 that a 'neutral status' is the best option for Afghanistan's persistent problems.[8] However, in contrast to this alleged aim of neutrality, between 1996 and 2001, India was staunchly against the Taliban regime and provided political, financial, and military support to the anti-Taliban United Front (UF), popularly known as the Northern Alliance. Marking a policy change with the entry of the coalition military machine in 2001, India voluntarily stopped such partisan support and attempted to engage most Afghan political factions. It also shifted gears from providing military support to investing in soft sectors such as post-war reconstruction and infrastructural development. Ranging from building roads, hospitals and schools, India provided a range of small development projects for different parts of the war-torn country. Nonetheless, many Afghans criticise India for lacking a coherent policy towards their country and being an unreliable regional partner, Western capitals have been unsure about the extent to which expanded Indian presence in Afghanistan (however attractive it may sound from a Western exchequer's perspective) helps the cause of peace in the region, and Islamabad blames India for destabilising Pakistan's fragile provinces of Khyber Pakhtunkhwa, Federally Administered Tribal Areas (FATA), and Baluchistan, via Afghanistan—all at the same time.

In October 2011, India signed a comprehensive Strategic Partnership Agreement (SPA) with the Afghan government. Representing another shift, the SPA indicated New Delhi's willingness to depart from its traditional policy of boycotting the Afghan Taliban. Critically, the SPA expressed India's decision to support an Afghan-led reconciliation process instead of getting embroiled in factional politics. Why did New Delhi agree to sign an agreement that challenged its declared anti-Taliban stand? Despite continuity in its traditional policy of engaging Kabul on friendly terms, New Delhi's Afghanistan policy underwent conspicuous shifts during the 1979–2015 period. These shifts have been critical in shaping South Asia's regional security and political dynamics. In fact, given the precarious security situation in and around Afghanistan today, India's choice of friends and enemies in that country, as well as the ways in which New Delhi decides to deal with them, will have far reaching consequences. A good way to ascertain India's prospective behavior on these questions, then, is to deconstruct its recent past. This book explains the sources of change in India's Afghanistan policy since the Soviet intervention, what this shows about India's Afghanistan policy specifically (a rising India in general), and, based on this examination, what can one expect from India in the future.

Partisans and conciliators

Relative to works on other aspects of South Asian history and politics, India's relations with and approach towards Afghanistan have largely evaded scholarly attention. This gap in the literature is surprising not simply because of the strategic relevance of India-Afghanistan relations, but also because of the contradictory narratives it elicits. For some observers, India's role in Afghanistan is marked by intense strategic lethargy, policy incoherence, and indecision.[9] Despite having invested nearly US$2.3 billion in aid and development after 9/11, India remains politically marginalised, if not inconsequential, in Kabul.[10] Pakistan, on the other hand, despite its unhealthy interference in domestic Afghan affairs, has nearly convinced the world of its indispensability for bringing peace in that country. To other observers however, India is waging a well-calibrated, low-level proxy war against Pakistan through Afghanistan. Allegedly, Indian intelligence agencies run training camps for militant Baloch separatists on Afghan soil in order to foment insurgencies in Pakistan.[11] Given the deep historical antipathy between Kabul and Islamabad, India's presence in Afghanistan typifies the quintessential case of the Machiavellian perfidy.[12] Archetypical of 'my enemy's enemy is my friend,' not just India's four consulates (in Jalalabad, Kandahar, Mazar-e-Sharif, and Herat) but also its humanitarian aid and developmental assistance to Afghanistan is viewed with suspicion by Pakistan.[13]

Those who subscribe to the latter view are convinced that hostility between India and Pakistan lies at the heart of the current war in Afghanistan.[14] After all, the friendships that India cultivated in Afghanistan are indicative of its anti-Pakistan bias. For starters, India's political, moral, and military support to the erstwhile anti-Taliban and anti-Pakistan United Front during the 1990s is an open secret. Yet, it is also true that India scaled back its military support to anti-Pakistan elements in Afghanistan after 9/11. In fact, for the most part, modern South Asian history is replete with instances when India refused to engage with Afghanistan (even when asked by its friends in Kabul) in a manner that would undermine, or be seen to be undermining, Pakistan's security, sovereignty, and territorial integrity. For instance, despite the animosity, India maintains a studious silence on Pakistan's claims over the legitimacy of the Durand Line, and has not given in on Afghan desires for diplomatic support on the border dispute. Why did India adopt an aggressive approach at some points in time while it remained conciliatory and accommodating of pro-Pakistan groups in Afghanistan at others? What drives India's policy towards Afghanistan and what does this reflect about its rise as a power of regional and global importance?

Based on a host of primary and secondary sources (detailed in the following sections), this book analyses these questions and brings to life India's internal debates on Afghanistan and the various themes it embodies. Starting with the Soviet military invasion of Afghanistan in 1979, to the fall of the communist-turned-nationalist government of Mohammad Najibullah in 1992, to the rise of the Taliban in 1996, and the events that ensued following the 9/11 attacks until the withdrawal of NATO forces, and the failing reconciliation process under Afghan president Ashraf Ghani, the book chronicles shifts in India's Afghanistan policy, and examines the reasons for the same. It shows that there has been a consensus in New Delhi's power circles that an independent, genuinely sovereign, territorially united, and economically strong Afghanistan is in the best interests of India and the world. Nonetheless, political rivalries within Afghanistan have exposed the fissures within India's policy-making circuits regarding what India should or should not do to help build a united and stable Afghanistan. Most of these differences are essentially over matters of operational and tactical relevance. Some Indian officials advocate a non-military, mostly economic, and politically neutral approach, whereas others argue in favour of a militarily robust, economically aggressive, and, politically partisan approach.

Conciliators: For the first group of policymakers, termed 'conciliators' in this book, India should focus on whoever comes to power in Kabul without fear or favour. For this to happen, India should build goodwill among the people of Afghanistan and politically engage with almost every entity, including the Afghan Taliban and its various factions. An approach marked by political pragmatism, not engaging with pro-Pakistan Afghan factions is not a viable option according to the conciliators. Indian policymakers with such beliefs gravitate towards the 'engage-with-all' axiom, however difficult it may be to open and sustain dialogue with pro-Pakistan factions in Afghanistan.

Partisans: For the second group, termed 'partisans', the mantra of making friends in Afghanistan is different. All factions that stand at odds with Pakistan and/or are not under the influence of, or dependent upon, Islamabad, should be India's natural allies. India should adopt an 'anti-engagement' approach, or even a 'containment' policy, vis-à-vis pro-Pakistan factions. If India's natural partners hold power in Kabul, then brilliant, but if not, then India should do whatever it can to help them become powerful. One way to empower India's anti-Pakistan Afghan friends is to buttress their material capacities and mobilise international support in their favour. However, the other way to empower them is also by making pro-Pakistan factions relatively weak, or by actively containing their rise, using (covertly or otherwise) military means if required.

Partisans and conciliators cut across the bureaucratic, diplomatic, and political spectrum of India. Pakistan and its role in Afghanistan, then, form the spirit of the debate between these two foreign policy advocacies. However, instead of being a binary, the conciliators versus partisans debate occurs on a spectrum of ideas and has tremendous nuance on different themes related to Afghanistan. There are, nonetheless, operational indicators (as detailed throughout the book) that highlight the existence of these advocacies. Constantly vying for influence, the conciliators and the partisans have shaped policy outcome at different points in history. The conciliators, for instance, were able to implement an accommodative approach vis-à-vis the Mujahideen government in Kabul in the early 1990s, while they lost out to the partisans in 1996 when the Taliban rose to power. As global attitudes towards radical Islam hardened by the end of the twentieth century and witnessed an emotional explosion after 9/11, the partisans got support internationally and dominated India's diplomatic and security landscape.

The painful realisation that India's vision of terrorism in general and Afghanistan in particular was very different from that of the US, slowly paved the way for the rise of conciliators within India's power corridors. Not surprisingly, by 2015, India warily came to respect (or, one can say, toed the line on) Kabul's decision to reconcile its bilateral differences with Pakistan peacefully, for however long the process lasted. Lastly, far from being mutually exclusive, the approaches advocated by both the conciliators and the partisans have often also worked in tandem. Simultaneous activism of these seemingly disparate advocacies generates dynamics that imparts nuance (but also confusion) to the way India behaves in Afghanistan. Most of all, the interplay between these two advocacies strengthens India's capacity to practice restraint at certain times, and be proactive at other opportune moments, and therefore, hones a strategic balance in its policy conduct, a quality that has rescued India from taking rash and immature decisions in Afghanistan.

The argument

Three core intertwined factors drive India's Afghanistan policy debates between the partisans and the conciliators. Conditioned by India's changing economic capacities and geographical disconnect with Afghanistan that gets exaggerated by Pakistan's unfriendly and sometimes hostile presence, these three drivers are:

(1) Striking a balance between Afghanistan and Pakistan. The first, and most important, factor shaping India's approach towards Afghanistan is New Delhi's desire to strike a balance between Afghanistan and Pakistan. An Afghanistan that is highly dependent on Pakistan, such as during the late-1990s Taliban regime, is not in India's strategic interest. This is because strong Pakistani presence in Afghanistan may hinder India's connectivity to the gas rich Central Asian Republics on one hand, but also allow Pakistani security agencies to use Afghan soil to undermine India's domestic security, especially in Kashmir. In this context, Afghanistan is both a curse and blessing for India and Pakistan. It is as much a theatre of conflict between these South Asian rivals as much it is an arena for coop-

eration. Whether India competes or cooperates with Pakistan in Afghanistan depends on the following two factors.

(2) International political environment. The second source of India's Afghanistan policy is the constantly evolving international political postures towards Afghanistan. Keen on being viewed as a positive and constructive team player, India's approach towards Kabul is often determined by external pressures and can be reactive in nature. This aspect is critical in the light of New Delhi's desire of having multi-stakeholder presence in Afghanistan lest Kabul becomes dependent on Pakistan's support. But then (given India does not have the capacities to support the Afghan state all by itself), whichever international actor plays the biggest role in that sphere will have the greatest leverage on domestic Afghan politics. If the Taliban regime was structurally dependent on Pakistan, the post-9/11 Afghan state is dependent on US support. This fact has profoundly shaped India's approach towards Kabul. For instance, Hamid Karzai, who rose to power with US support at the 2001 Bonn Conference, was a fait accompli for India (and also other countries) that was wary of Karzai's links with Pakistan. Indian officials wanted a candidate from the anti-Taliban United Front to gain power, but relented to American desires, embracing Karzai eventually.

(3) Domestic politics of Afghanistan. The third source that drives India's Afghanistan policy is the fluctuating degrees to which various political factions in Afghanistan want to engage with India. Despite the tremendous goodwill that India enjoys among Afghans, different political factions prioritise India differently. If New Delhi enjoyed Karzai's hospitality, it (briefly) felt cold-shouldered by the Ghani government. The deep schisms within Afghanistan's body politic makes it difficult to simultaneously maintain cordial ties with different political actors in that country. If during Najibullah's tenure India found it tricky to independently develop links with the Khalq or even the Mujahideen (which was done covertly), the same was the case (though to a lesser extent) during Karzai's presidency when India's relations with non-Pashtun leaders came under political strain (though they never broke down).

Underlining the role of the international political environment, the United Nations' (UN) legitimisation of the Mujahideen government in 1992 allowed the conciliators to chart an accommodative approach. This happened despite the fact that it was Pakistan and Saudi Arabia that brokered truce between various Mujahideen factions in Peshawar. However, the UN's failure to sustain peace subsequently and Pakistan's support to the Taliban after 1994 paved the way for the rise of the partisans (who initially collaborated with Iran and Russia to oppose the Taliban militarily, but afterwards, got active support from the US as well). Institutionalisation of the reconciliation process with the Afghan Taliban at the 2010 London conference on Afghanistan jolted the partisans, who remained vehemently opposed to the idea. Almost automatically, the influence of the conciliators rose in the power corridors of New Delhi. However, Ghani's outreach to Pakistan in 2015, contributed to strengthening the partisan narrative for a brief period under the government of PM Narendra Modi. Given the tumultuous course of India's engagement with Afghanistan, it can be safely argued that there is no single policy that New Delhi practices towards Kabul. Instead, India's foreign policy approach towards Afghanistan has a kaleidoscopic quality wherein the interplay of multiple ideas advocated by different actors—partisans and conciliators—over time and in evolving scenarios, produces changing policy patterns.

The fact that the rise and fall of partisans and conciliators, more often than not, mirrors the changing situation on the ground in Afghanistan and the international political environment, corroborates the popular criticism that India's Afghanistan policy is reactive in nature. But, at the same time, it disproves the charge that India lacks clarity of thought, the power of will, and strategic decisiveness in Afghanistan. For, being reactive does not necessarily mean lacking political judgment and a clear sense of national interests, or devising ways to secure them. And being proactive does not automatically imply strategic policy coherence. Partisanship and conciliation may not be intellectual choices that Indian officials imbibe and implement at a time of their choosing. But their robust existence highlights a preference for different tools of diplomacy and statecraft to attain the larger strategic goal of a stable, sovereign, friendly, and territorially united Afghanistan.

The one strategic constant within this mosaic of divergent policies approaches, then, has been India's insatiable search for 'friends' in Afghanistan. These friends are people or groups, preferably official but also unofficial, who are expected to be sensitive to India's national interests in and around Afghanistan. These friends are expected to appreciate India's diversity and may count upon New Delhi to occasionally support and advocate their cause internationally. Just like India's ever-changing notions of national interest, however, the Afghan cause could also be anything. It could be a request to develop infrastructure, offer financial assistance, support Afghanistan on international forums, or help these Afghan friends fight their political and military battles both inside and outside that country. Whatever the time period may be, and whoever the ruler, India has always sought such friendly relationships in Afghanistan (as it has, quite unsurprisingly, with most of the world). Whilst the nature of such relationships was hierarchical or marked by dependency during the British Raj, the partition of the subcontinent in 1947 changed the dynamic.[15] The new state of Pakistan (which allegedly carried forward the legacy of the British Raj vis-à-vis Afghanistan) stood as a geographical wedge between India and Afghanistan. This geographical wedge, arguably, unshackled India from its need and/or desires to exert influence on, or solve bilateral disputes with Afghanistan (a strategic aspect reserved for other smaller neighbours, with whom India has territorial boundaries). As an Indian analyst noted, India's geographical disconnect became its primary weakness but also its cardinal strength in Afghanistan.[16] Conversely, the 2,250-odd kilometers long open border became Pakistan's biggest strength as well as its principal weakness with Afghanistan.

Seeking such friends, at first, was easy for New Delhi and politically uncomplicated for Kabul. The 1950 Treaty of Friendship between the two countries marked the first official step in this direction.[17] A stable, sovereign, and united Afghanistan that was attracted to the vision of non-alignment globally, and wanted to balance Pakistan regionally (Afghanistan had opposed the creation of Pakistan at the UN in 1947) was, by definition, friendly. For the first three decades, till late 1970s, this bilateral dynamic remained largely intact despite its highs and lows. But then came Assadullah Sarwari and his comrades (see prologue), and things began to change. To India's dismay, developing and sustaining friendships in a polarised polity and a fractured state was not just difficult but also counterproductive. Because, under tough circumstances, Afghan friends, often desperate and wanting, would seek support that New Delhi may or may not be able, or willing, to offer.

While most requests may be legitimate, others may not be acceptable to the international community, and may also undermine ideals of democracy, secularism, equality, sovereignty, and, at times, even basic human rights (for example, in the case of Sarwari where India adopted unduly strong measures in favour of Najibullah). If India fails to provide such unconditional support, then not only its identity as a regional power, but even as a friend, comes under critical scrutiny in Kabul. Experts, thus, argue that Afghanistan is a 'litmus test for India's rise as a South Asian power with global potential'.[18] New Delhi's success or failure in managing its relations with and protecting its interests in Afghanistan provides an indication of its national strength. By highlighting the interplay of the three causal factors—balancing between Afghanistan and Pakistan, international political environment, and domestic Afghan politics—and its influence on India's Afghanistan policy, this book shows that India's presence in Afghanistan since the Soviet invasion is not just a test of national strength but also an indicator of how the world's largest democracy views itself and its place in a changing world order.

Note on theory

Though scant in its use of theory, this book uses the Advocacy Coalition Framework (ACF) to conceptualise the terms 'partisans' and 'conciliators'. A leading theory of public policy processes, the ACF's emphasis on policy change, learning, and coalition behavior helps in doing this. At the macro-level the framework assumes that specialists within a particular 'policy subsystem' play an important role in most of the policy-making.[19] The behavior of these specialists is affected by the broader socioeconomic and political system. The framework further assumes that the individual is heavily impacted by social psychology and that multiple actors in a subsystem should be aggregated into advocacy coalitions. These assumptions are determined by the relationship between the dependent variables i.e. 'belief systems' and 'policy change' and the independent variables i.e. 'policy-oriented learning' and 'external shocks', as well as 'negotiated agreements'.[20] The belief system, here, is a three-tier system that includes core beliefs, policy core beliefs, and secondary beliefs.

Core beliefs refer to ontological and normative assumptions about human behavior and the weight given to basic values such as equality and welfare of people. An outcome of social conditioning that a person undergoes from childhood, core beliefs are considered as difficult to change. Policy core beliefs, on the other hand, are the application of deep core beliefs by policy participants within a policy subsystem. While there is no direct relation or one-to-one correspondence between deep core beliefs and policy core beliefs, policies are often an outcome of deep-rooted beliefs. India's investment in economic projects in different African, South Asian, and Latin American countries, for instance, is based on the core belief of many policy participants that economic investment across the world by private and public firms is a positive thing to do. The core belief that investment is good, then determines policy core beliefs that determine how to go about formulating investment strategies and locating areas for potential investment.

Different sets of policy core beliefs help in identifying different advocacy coalitions within a given policy subsystem. While looking at US foreign policy in Iraq, for example, different advocacy coalitions could be identified based on which actor is advocating what—while some actors would have advocated the use of force, others would have advocated diplomacy or economic sanctions. However, it is possible that in some policy subsystems hugely divergent preferences—which are called 'policy core policy preferences'—lead to intransigent debates.[21] These preferences can be subsystem-wide in scope, very salient, and create long-term fissures within a policy subsystem. Secondary beliefs, in turn, are ideas over the nitty-gritty of specific policy related programmes. Policy change occurs when advocacy coalitions (like the partisans and the conciliators) with different belief systems and resources interact with each other.[22]

The ACF has much strength for the purpose of this book. Not only does it help in explaining policy change, but it also helps in identifying policy narratives and coalitions. Policy narratives are constructs, strategically crafted using words, images, and symbols to influence policy output.[23] They are ways to structure and communicate one's understanding of the world, and can be applied both in domestic and international policy domains. Any policy narrative, effectively, would 'have a setting, a plot, characters (hero, villain, and victim), and will be disseminated towards a preferred policy outcome (the moral of the story)'.[24] Different advocacy coalitions—such as the partisans and the conciliators—formed by different stakeholders within the policy subsystem, generate different policy narratives. While a 'winners' tale seeks status quo, a 'losers' tale demands policy change. Moreover, while a winning advocate would focus on costs associated with change than its accruing benefits, a losing advocate would concentrate on gains over loses. However, regardless of groups portraying themselves as either 'winning' or 'losing', there are some stable policy core beliefs 'shaped by [the] cultural context (social and economic history and view of the role of the government) in which the policy issue occurs'. Resultantly, analysing 'narrative elements of characters can reveal an advocacy coalition's policy beliefs'.[25] These ACF tools help form the analytical bedrock of this book and its argument.

In addition to helping delineate policy advocacy conceptually (not just based on political rhetoric), the ACF provides the 'middle-level' theoretical backbone that explains operational-level policy-making. Neither does it challenge global systemic theories such as realism and liberalism (or constructivism), nor does it go into the minutiae of tactical policy decisions related to a specific incident in India-Afghanistan relations. It allows for providing an operational understanding of how India's foreign policy towards Afghanistan was formulated. Partisans and conciliators, from this perspective, are not card-holding members of any policy organisation. They are not even officials representing the interests of specific institutions. These are individuals or groups who have policy beliefs on a particular foreign policy problem and they cut across India's political, institutional, and bureaucratic spectrum. While some of them advocate broad-based engagement with different Afghan factions, others advocate partisan engagement. It is possible that the same official adopts different approaches—conciliatory or partisan—at different times depending on context. So it would be incorrect to use these conceptual policy denominators as a measure of 'political identity'. Nonetheless, it is possible to identify officials who actively or passively advocated one of the two approaches towards Afghanistan. In this book, which is chronologically sequenced, the ACF allows to identify the partisans and the conciliators and how they influenced India's Afghanistan policy.

Note on definitions

Terms such as partisans, conciliators, engagement, and anti-engagement, may mean different things to different readers and policy practitioners. In this book they have been used liberally throughout, but with very specific intent. The Oxford English Dictionary, for instance, defines conciliator as 'a person who acts as a mediator between two disputing people or groups'.[26] A partisan, however, is someone who is 'a strong supporter of a party, cause, or person'.[27] Both these terms have been used with similar intent. However, a conciliator in this book may not always necessarily mean someone who is actively 'conciliating' between two fighting parties (even though many Indian diplomats have done that on numerous occasions in Afghanistan). Someone who adopts a conciliatory tone towards Afghanistan is also a conciliator, regardless of whether she or he is actually able to implement such an approach in practice. Similarly, a partisan may not always mean a person who has party-political or ideological affiliations. Any Indian policymaker advocating policies towards Afghanistan by necessarily treating Pakistan as an enemy, or is not accommodative of Pakistani interests in Afghanistan, is a partisan.

Apart from partisans and conciliators, the term 'engagement' is understood as a process whereby two political entities are involved in non-coercive diplomacy and have existing channels of interaction, either covert or overt.

Engagement here does not necessarily imply diplomatic recognition of the entity being engaged with. Nor does it imply imparting legitimacy to the ideas propounded and practices undertaken by this entity. It definitely does not mean engaging in military combat with an adversary. What it implies, simply, is dealing with a political faction without necessarily aiming at containing its rise, or even if so, then not doing that militarily or by using selective (or partisan) engagement tactics. India's debate on whether or not to engage with the Taliban, from this perspective, was that of opening a political channel with the hope of securing its interests in Taliban dominated territories, but without giving the militant group diplomatic recognition.

The idea of anti-engagement, on the other hand, implies partisan political support to one group over the other. Within the framework of such partisan support, use of coercive (military) means to communicate political intent is acceptable. The term also implies cutting diplomatic contact with the perceived adversary. However, what anti-engagement does not mean is an absence of contact with the country in question. Given the geographical proximity of Afghanistan and India, this has never been a viable strategic option for New Delhi. Even during the Taliban years, India chose to be deeply engaged with the anti-Taliban United Front (UF) rather than steering clear of the Afghan quagmire altogether. Also, anti-engagement, as seen vis-à-vis the Taliban, has not been India's traditional foreign policy approach. Even in Myanmar, a country where India officially supported the National League for Democracy, the pro-democracy political party led by Aung San Suu Kyi, New Delhi was engaging with the military *junta*. There are two reasons why the term anti-engagement is emphasised instead of 'containment'. Firstly, specific to this case, India did not have the means to effectively contain any political and military force in Afghanistan on its own. Even great powers like the imperial Britain, the Soviet Union, and the US-led NATO coalition forces, have contained Afghan militias with mixed results at best. Secondly, the most India has done to stop any group's rise to power in Afghanistan is to support its adversaries. During the 1990s civil war this was most visible. Thus, partisans may have a containment axiom to their political intent, but limited capability to carry it out militarily.

Note on sources

Contemporary politics, more often than not, is highly contested in both the academic and public domain. As Ramachandra Guha, historian of contemporary India, put it, 'those who write contemporary history know that the reader is not a passive vessel to receive the text placed before him or her. The reader is also a citizen, a *critical citizen*, with individual political and ideological preferences'.[28] Guha's dictum forms the basis of this book. Not just the reader, in the case of this book, even the protagonists that constitute this history, are not doll-like figures whose personalities and roles can be constructed or deconstructed at the author's whim or by chance discoveries of sources. Many of these actors are alive (such as many of the interviewees for this book) and have dynamic ideas and opinions. Thus, writing a book about the contemporary foreign affairs of India, specifically towards Afghanistan, is fraught with dangers. For one, there is little archival material coming to the rescue. Hidden under vast debris of classified files, a lot of admirable and appalling details about India's role in Afghanistan are out of sight, and will remain so for years to come. Hence, this book is by no means a 'complete' portrayal of India's role in Afghanistan. It does, however, exhaust most available sources to offer an analytical narrative and an explanation of why India did what it did. To this effect, the book uses a host of published and unpublished, as well as primary and secondary, sources of information.

The National Security Archives (NSA) at the George Washington University (GWU), for instance, offer declassified US intelligence dossiers and diplomatic correspondence from the 1990s. Part of the electronic briefing books of the NSA that include the 'September 11th Sourcebooks', and files on 'Middle East and South Asia', these documents highlight how Washington saw India's role in the Afghan civil war.[29] Apart from the breathtaking array of US-related documents, these electronic briefing books also include English translations of top-secret meetings of the Communist Party of the Soviet Union (CPSU) from the 1980s. These documents offer priceless knowledge on the Soviet experience in Afghanistan and how Moscow viewed India's role in Afghanistan in the 1980s. Papers of John Gunther Dean, former US Ambassador to India (1985–88), supplement these documents and show how India attempted at bringing the two big powers, i.e. the US and the Soviet Union, to the talking table for resolving the Afghan imbroglio. The National Security Decision Directives, 1981–89, available in the online archives of the Ronald Reagan Presidential Library and Museum, declassified reports and dossiers of the Central Intelligence Agency (CIA), as well as UK Foreign Office Files for India, Pakistan and Afghanistan, 1947–80, offer insights into Anglo-American decision-making on India-Pakistan-Afghanistan relations. From the Indian side, the P. N. Haksar papers, Selected Works of Jawaharlal

Nehru (SWJN), and documents related to the Transfer of Power to India (all available at the Nehru Memorial Museum and Library in New Delhi) help recounting the history of India-Afghanistan relations before 1979.

Diplomatic memos leaked by Wikileaks, though selective in their coverage, offer rich behind-the-scenes insights into US diplomacy with India, Afghanistan, and Pakistan. While the Kissinger Cables do this for the early 1970s, the Carter cables and the Carter cables 2 offer such insights for the late-1970s and early 1980s. The *Afghan War Diary* as well as the Cablegate documents shed light on Indian engagement with the US between 2002 and 2011 on wide-ranging geopolitical issues. Official Indian documents such as the foreign affairs records (FAR), the annual reports of the Ministry of External Affairs (MEA), and the debates (and questions) in the Lok Sabha and the Rajya Sabha, provide priceless details that often go unnoticed in popular analyses. Critically, the parliamentary debates indicate where and how Afghanistan figured in the discussions of India's political elite. India's interventions on the situation in Afghanistan at the UN show how India's position evolved at multilateral forums on the issue of reconciling with the Taliban. Autobiographies and diaries of senior Indian, Pakistani, Afghan, British, and American officials, on the other hand, throw light on how these figures viewed, and acted upon, relevant political developments. Reports published by the *Times of India* (ToI), *The Hindu*, the *Indian Express*, the *New York Times*, the *Guardian*, the BBC, Frontline, Outlook, and *Afghan Islamic Press* (a Taliban mouthpiece), help outline key trends of South Asian geopolitics.

A series of interviews conducted by the author further inform this book. Interviewees include middle- and top-level political, military, intelligence, and diplomatic officials in India, Afghanistan, UK, and the US, as well as some Afghan Taliban leaders and combatants.[30] For a variety of reasons, the author was unable to visit Pakistan for fieldwork, even though the Pakistani perspective on India's role in Afghanistan is well accounted for and appreciated in the book. Altogether 110 interviews were conducted. Though not all of them have been quoted, every interview was critical in guiding the analysis and argument of this book. A subset of the larger pool of policy participants involved in Afghanistan, these interviews and interviewees are diverse enough to allow appreciation for different facets of India's Afghanistan policy, and to accommodate a variety of diverging opinions on this issue. Despite the imperfection of interviewing as a research methodology that often eludes objectivity, interviews are often the only way to know more about contemporary issues. Getting to the bottom of a topic and crosschecking facts, then, is the researcher's responsibility. On South Asia, such primary material remains relatively scarce. As most of these interviews were conducted as part of the author's doctoral project, a series of ethical clearances were required before setting off to the field, and were strictly adhered to. This means, in some cases, the identity of the interviewee has not been disclosed. Instead, rather unimaginatively, letters are used to denote them. In other cases, with consent of the interviewee, his/her identity has been disclosed. Information collected in all these different interviews was triangulated to ensure authenticity of data.

Structure of the book

This book is divided into three parts: debating neutrality, debating containment, and debating engagement. Each part deals with three different phases of India's role in Afghanistan. The first part, debating neutrality, consists of two chapters that examine the history of India's relations with Afghanistan and how the latter figures in the former's popular imagination. Elucidated in the second chapter, 'Kabuliwallah', this historical context helps in grounding the survey and argument of the book. By highlighting the cultural bonds between the two countries and its people, their relations across empires, and the state of bilateral relations between 1947 and 1979 (when the Soviet Union militarily invaded Afghanistan), the chapter teases out the evolution of the three drivers of India's foreign policy towards Afghanistan. The third chapter, 'Leaning Tower of Delhi', then details the impact that Moscow's military intervention in and withdrawal from Afghanistan had on India's Afghanistan policy debates. This was the first test for Indian foreign policy-makers to decide whether to accept occupation of its neighboring country by a friendly force or not. The debate between partisans and conciliators, the chapter shows, had begun to brew long before the Soviet Union's retreat from Afghanistan in 1989 and its subsequent disintegration in 1991.

The second part of the book, debating containment, delves into events that led India to more or less embrace the proxy-war format vis-à-vis Pakistan in Afghanistan during the 1990s and early years of the twenty-first century. The fourth chapter, 'The Taliban Dilemma', specifically details how the partisans and conciliators collided head-on in early 1990s when Najibullah was ousted in a coup. The chapter also highlights debates that took place in India when Kabul fell to the Taliban in September 1996, and how India's policy evolved in accordance with regional and international developments. The newly created Central Asian Republics (CARs) in the early 1990s had unleashed a scramble for power by many regional stakeholders, of which India was one. These changing geopolitical realities, and the role of the UN in calibrating a peace process in Afghanistan played an important role in impacting India's operational logic towards Afghanistan during the Taliban era. By late 1990s events such as the hijacking of the Indian Airlines flight IC-814 by Pakistan-based militants (and its landing in Taliban-controlled Kandahar), and the destruction of the Bamiyan Buddhas in 2001 crystalised India's aversion of the Taliban. Complementing these debates on how to deal with the Taliban were India's relations with the anti-Taliban United Front (UF). The fifth chapter, 'Friends from North, Foes from South', analyses the nature and extent of New Delhi's links with the UF. This relationship, despite being an open secret, has not been delved into. This chapter argues that unlike popular perception of the UF's dependence on support from New Delhi to continue its fight against the Taliban, it was India that was strategically dependent on the UF to secure its interests in Afghanistan. The sixth chapter, 'War and Terror', then shows how the strength of India's relations with the UF got tested at the 2001 Bonn conference that pushed Hamid Karzai to power in Kabul.

The third part of the book, debating engagement, consists of three chapters and analyses India's approach towards Afghanistan after 9/11. The seventh chapter, 'Maximum Leader', details how India reluctantly accepted Karzai's presidency. Moving away from the so-called 'proxy format' of the 1990s, to the dismay of its UF allies, New Delhi threw its weight behind Karzai. The eighth chapter, 'No Good Taliban?', shows how India's security calculus was disturbed when the Taliban made a decisive comeback and the political will of the coalition forces went into a collective decline in Afghanistan. The debate between the partisans and the conciliators became acute in New Delhi when the realisation dawned that the Taliban was to stay, and its sponsor, Pakistan, would not relent under international pressure. The ninth chapter, 'First as Tragedy, Then as Farce', shows how India dealt with the US withdrawal and the continuously failing reconciliation process with the Afghan Taliban. With regional and international postures evolving, India's Afghanistan policy came to be dominated by the conciliators after 2010, but remained fierce in its determination to steer the course of reconciliation in Kabul's favour.

PART I

DEBATING NEUTRALITY

2

KABULIWALLAH

A BRIEF HISTORY OF INDIA-AFGHANISTAN RELATIONS

'Kabuliwala has done more to give us [Afghanistan] a brand which we could not buy with a billion dollars of advertisements.'

Mohammad Ashraf Ghani, President of the Islamic Republic of Afghanistan, 2015.[1]

An emotional bond

Rahmud, the great Kabuliwallah, or 'fruit-seller from Kabul', became good friends with little Mini. Love and longing for home and his daughter, who was Mini's age, sparked a fascinating bond between the tall, bearded 'Pathan' and the little Bengali child. His patient listening, quick wit, and loving gifts quickly overcame Mini's fears that the Kabuliwallah would bundle her up in his large bag, which could easily fit two or three children.[2] The developing friendship met an abrupt end one day when Rahmud was arrested over charges of assault. Unwilling to tolerate an insult, he had stabbed one of his customers. Years later, when Rahmud got out of prison, he would return to meet his little friend. But whom he will meet is not the talkative, carefree child but a shy and beautiful young woman on her wedding day. As Rabindranath Tagore put it, 'the Cabuliwallah looked a bit staggered by the apparition'.[3] It dawned on Rahmud how time had distanced him not only from Mini, but also from his daughter in Afghanistan, who must now be of marriageable age, and with whom he would have to make friends afresh.

Reflecting the depth of India's emotional connect with and imagination of Afghanistan and its people, Tagore's short story, the Kabuliwallah, has decisively influenced the way many in India view Afghans, i.e. aggressive but righteous, united against foreign occupation but wrought with familial and tribal differences, martial and possessive but also softhearted. This cultural connect is highlighted at the end of Tagore's classic when Rahmud meets him on Mini's wedding day and shows the imprint of his daughter's small palm on a piece of cloth that he took as a memory when leaving Kabul for Calcutta eight years ago. 'Tears came to my eyes. I forgot that he was a poor Cabuli fruit-seller, while I was—but no, what was I more than he? He also was a father', wrote Tagore. Afghanistan itself is pictured as a romantic place with its 'mountains, the glens, and the forests of his distant home, with his cottage in its setting, and the free and independent life of distant wilds'.[4] Despite its social and political plurality, it is these romantic notions of faraway vistas inhabited by the fiercely independent 'Pathans' that marks India's imagination of Afghanistan.

Such cultural links have influenced India's political discourse towards Afghanistan for decades. Indian President Fakhruddin Ali Ahmed stated in 1975: 'generations ago, large numbers of Afghans made India their home and have become part of its people. They have enriched our own culture. Our great poet Rabindranath Tagore in his famous story of the "Kabuliwala" painted an unforgettable image of the robust character and the affection and love of an Afghan living in India.'[5] More recently, M. K. Narayanan, a 1955 batch Indian Police Services (IPS) officer hailing from the southern state of Kerala who first became the Director of Intelligence Bureau (1987–90), Chairman of Joint Intelligence Committee (1987–92), and went on to shaping India's foreign and security policy as a powerful National Security Advisor (NSA) from 2005 to 2010, asserts that the Kabuliwallah connection was 'fundamental' in shaping India's approach towards Afghanistan in the post-2001 scenario:

> The India-Afghanistan relationship is basically an India-Pashtun relationship ... we are all part of that generation when the Afghans used to come in the old Kabuliwallah style ... it's a living memory for most of us ... they are Pashtuns and not people from the north or Tajiks and so on.[6]

When the US-led NATO forces entered Afghanistan in 2001, a retired Indian army officer privy to policymaking claims, 'there [was] an emotional bond, the Kabuliwallah bond with the Afghans ... [in 2001] there was a romantic perception about Afghanistan [in India]. As the Americans settled down and started waging their global war on terrorism, in the light of public opinion and our historical relations with Afghanistan, we [India] decided that it was not in our interest to join [the war]. So we started doing developmental work.'[7] India's search for 'friends' may be linked both to New Delhi's rivalry with Islamabad, and its historic bonds with Afghanistan. The following sections show how this bilateral connect got tested at various moments, by offering a historical overview of India-Afghanistan relations till the Soviet invasion in 1979. By doing so, it sets the historical context whereby Indian policymakers debate their policy approach towards Afghanistan.

A historical bond

Imagining India without Afghanistan, and Afghanistan without India, is impossible. Despite the phrase having become an overused diplomatic trope in contemporary South Asia, India-Afghanistan relations are truly civilisational. Historians have traced them back, at least, to the Indus Valley civilisation.[8] Having seen an invasion by 'Alexander the Great', modern day Afghanistan came under the Seleucid Empire and was ceded to Chandragupta Maurya in 305 BCE.[9] Eventually Emperor Ashoka came to rule parts of Afghanistan, introducing Buddhism to the region. The Mauryan Empire declined half a century after Ashoka's death. Leading to decades of instability, Afghanistan saw the rise of the Greco-Bactrians, then the Indo-Greek kingdoms (the Kushan Empire), and then the Indo-Scythians.[10] Islam began its advent in Afghanistan from the seventh century and spread across India between the tenth and the nineteenth century. Often taking form of violent invasions, India was conquered by a series of invaders who were based in what today has become Afghanistan. The most successful of all these conquests was of the Mughal Empire that lasted from 1528 till 1858. Beginning with the rule of emperor Babur (whose grave, *Bagh-e-Babur*, is in Kabul), the Mughal Empire included great rulers such as Akbar, Shahjahan, and the controversial Aurangzeb, all of who play an important role in contemporary India's historical imagination.[11]

No other entity underlines the depth of India and Afghanistan's historical and geographical proximity more than the Grand Trunk Road (GTR). One of Asia's oldest and longest roads connecting Chittagong with Kabul via Delhi and Lahore, the origins of the GTR date back to the Mauryan era, even though its modern version was built in the sixteenth century by Sher Shah

Suri, an ethnic Pashtun, who took over control of the Mughal Empire in 1540, with its capital in Delhi.[12] Of tremendous commercial and military value, the road knit together the countries and cultures of this region. Mughal rule, however, came to an end after the failed Indian rebellion of 1857 (Delhi, the seat of the Mughal Empire was under Bahadur Shah Zafar's rule) that led to the formal institution of the British Monarchy, or the British Raj, in 1858. The East India Company (EIC), that developed influence in South Asian politics decades before the 1857 uprising, gave Britain authority over parts of South Asia. British colonial policies towards Afghanistan over the next two centuries formed a critical historical and structural basis for contemporary South Asian and Afghan politics.

A quest for logical territorial limits of the Indian empire steered British diplomatic, political and military activity towards Afghanistan.[13] Reasons for this were as much related to defence from external threats as to exercising sovereignty over a defined territory and people. Leading up to the three Anglo-Afghan wars (1839–42, 1878–80, 1919), such an interventionist approach developed Afghanistan as something of a 'buffer zone' between colonial India and Russia.[14] The Durand Line Agreement of 1893, signed between Britain and Amir Abdur Rahman Khan, was aimed at defining these territorial limits.[15] Where to draw the line and how to define the nature of British India's relationship with Afghanistan were hotly debated subjects. Resultantly, the so-called 'ring fence' concept of a dual-layered defence system for India, i.e. an inner ring and an outer ring, came to typify imperial security imagination in the subcontinent.[16] The idea was to develop an administered frontier, a non-administered frontier, and an external frontier. Forming British India's centre was the administered frontier with defined bureaucratic mechanisms and linear boundaries; the 'inner ring' that included the NWFP, Balochistan, Kashmir, Nepal, and the Naga Hills; and the 'outer ring' that constituted Afghanistan, Persia (now Iran), Tibet, Burma (now Myanmar), Sinkiang (now Xinjiang), and Siam (now Thailand).[17] This dual-layered territorial defence system formed the backbone of colonial (and independent) India's regional strategic outlook. Management of this defence system elicited vibrant policy debates between what historians term the 'forward school' and the 'closed border school'. Though emerging in the 1820s and 1830s following disagreements between the administrations in Bombay and Ludhiana over the East India Company's approach towards the frontier regions, proponents of closed border school advocated non-interference in domestic Afghan affairs, preconditioned on Russia's non-interference in Afghanistan. Forward school proponents, however, derided this approach as 'masterly inactivity' and argued that only building military outworks in Kabul and Kandahar could stem a Russian advance. This required British India to get involved in domestic Afghan affairs. Independent India and Pakistan, to varying degrees, not only inherited this territorial construct but also the problems of governance associated with it (from Balochistan to Kashmir), as well as colonial strategic outlook embodied in these strategy-making debates. Though the impact of British bureaucratic and strategic culture on modern Indian thought is debatable, it has been difficult for Indian planners to move past South Asia's geopolitical history.

Partition of India in 1947 challenged the dual-layered defence strategy. Cutting right through the middle of what was considered India's 'center', the partition ruptured the innermost administrative frontier of the erstwhile Raj. Pakistan, and not Afghanistan, now dominated the minds of Indian strategists. Not surprisingly, the Treaty of Peace and Friendship between Afghanistan and India (1950) marked an initiation of mutually accepted diplomatic exchange and a pledge to strengthen trade and cultural links. Neither did India seek influence over Kabul's foreign policy as previously sought by the British, nor did it continue the supply of arms to the Afghan Army, as was planned according to a 1945 bilateral agreement. Though training of Afghan officers on Indian soil was permitted, weapons or salaries to these officers were not to be offered.[18] For India's first PM Jawaharlal Nehru, an ardent proponent of non-alignment as a foreign policy principle, Afghanistan's military demands could potentially become an irritant in India's quest for peace with Pakistan.[19] Yet, Nehru the realist worried that Afghanistan's goodwill for India could not to be taken for granted, and directed intelligence chief B. N. Mullik to remain vigilant lest Kabul gravitate towards Pakistan (by joining the World Muslim Federation that Islamabad championed).[20] Economic tools were to be used to this effect, with the caveat that Afghanistan did not become dependent on Indian aid. For 'generosity' as Nehru noted, 'is a risky business in the long run'.[21] Peaceful resolution of Afghanistan-Pakistan bilateral disputes was advocated.

In this context, the 1955 Asian-African Conference for International Order, or the Bandung Conference, offered an international framework within which India and Afghanistan developed their bilateral ties.[22] Envisioned as a platform for Asian and African resurgence against colonialism, the conference articulated an alternative world order and demonstrated 'neutrality' in a bipolar world. Concerned about the fallout of an arms race in the subcontinent, both India and Afghanistan used the non-alignment plank to criticise Cold War binaries. It was also meant to challenge Pakistan's siding with the US after Islamabad signed the Mutual Defence Agreement with Washington in May 1954, joined the Southeast Treaty Organisation (SEATO) in September 1954, and the Central Treaty Organisation (CENTO) in 1955.[23] An internationalist strategy of criticising countries that entered into military pacts with big powers sought to isolate Pakistan in Asia and Africa. The strategy failed, and more so for Afghanistan where the sentiment for an independent Pashtunistan broiled: a sentiment that had kept Kabul from voting in favour of recognising Pakistan as an independent country in 1947. It is not surprising then that throughout the 1950s Pakistani media charged Afghanistan and India of working together to 'capture' Pakistan in a pincer attack.[24] India categorically denied such claims as 'false' and 'insulting both to India and Afghanistan'.[25] Regardless, the theme of Indo-Afghan collaboration to undermine Pakistan's security and sovereignty became entrenched in Pakistan's national security discourse.

Indian 'Anschluss'

The 1965 India-Pakistan war tested India's relations with Afghanistan. In the light of freshly acquired US weaponry, perceived support among the people of Kashmir, and an expected command crisis in New Delhi after Nehru's death, Pakistan launched a covert campaign, *Operation Gibraltar* in August 1965, followed by *Operation Grand Slam*.[26] The aim was to insurrect an anti-India rebellion in Kashmir and then send the Pakistan army to support it. Detecting the incursion belatedly, India responded by opening a separate war front in Punjab and nearly captured Lahore in September. The war did not result in outright military victory for either side. However, Pakistan's aggression unshackled India, temporarily, of its requirement to exercise restraint. Challenged at the UN by Pakistan's foreign minister Zulfiqar Ali Bhutto for ill-treating its Muslim minority and not allowing the people of Kashmir and Nagaland to exercise their right of self-determination, India unleashed a systematic counter-offensive on Pashtunistan, Balochistan, East Pakistan, and Pakistan-administered Kashmir. 'If Pakistan wants self-determination in Kashmir or Nagaland, constituent states of India, why does it not agree to grant self-determination to East Pakistan, Baluchistan, or the disputed territory of Pakhtoonistan?', countered Indian officials.[27] It was a point of principle. If the policy of self-determination were to be applied to parts of constitutionally created states, argued New Delhi, then most of them would break up. Pakistan's plea for self-determination in plural societies, as was the case with most states of Asia and Africa, was dismissed as political adventurism that would lead to the disintegration of postcolonial states. On 20 September 1965, weeks after the Indian forces had crossed the international border and closed in on Lahore, the UN passed a resolution seeking immediate ceasefire. Indian officials had calculated that Bhutto 'will bark and bark there [at the UN] and ultimately agree to the ceasefire'.[28] Indeed, Bhutto agreed to the ceasefire, but not without giving India a dressing-down on its 'colonial' attitude in Kashmir.

India's emphasis on territorial integrity over self-determination, alongside highlighting Pakistan's domestic problems had historical precedent. Lying to the south-west of Pakistan, despite its predominantly Muslim population, Balochistan did not automatically become part of Pakistan. When offered a referendum by the British to choose between India and Pakistan, the most powerful Baloch party, the Anjuman-e-Watan, rejected the idea and sought a separate state.[29] This was similar to the NWFP, where the Khidmatgars demanded a separate Pashtunistan. Both these issues continued to simmer making them appealing 'pressure points' against Pakistan, and the 1965 war gave India a reason to exploit them. Senior Congress leaders began asking the government to move beyond moral and diplomatic sectors to provide 'concrete' support to the Pashtuns. Though it is unclear what exactly 'concrete' meant, there is little room for disambiguation about what India and Pakistan's leadership would have imagined it to be, which was armed and financial support. A serving member of parliament, Retired Colonel Bashir Hussain Zaidi, was dispatched to Afghanistan to meet Ghaffar Khan in late-September and explore the possibility of reigniting the Pashtunistan issue. The 85-year-old leader was 'full of vigour and enthusiastic about waging his struggle for emancipation from Pakistan's rule'.[30] Within India, the Pakhtoon Jirga-e-Hind, an outfit advocating for independent Pashtunistan, also pressured the government to move beyond the war of words. In November 1965, addressing a fully packed Lok Sabha, EAM Swaran Singh invited Ghaffar Khan to resume his struggle for Pashtun independence from Indian soil and promised all support that he would require in that pursuit.[31] Soon the All India Radio (AIR) broadcasted that Pashtun nationalists were setting up administrative centres in Pakistan's tribal areas and NWFP, to advance the Pashtunistan campaign.[32] Such proactive advocacy on the Baloch and Pashtun issues had an impact on how India came to be viewed in Kabul.

Afghanistan's reaction to the war, from an Indian perspective, was muted and ambiguous. Though it supported the UN's ceasefire initiatives throughout the war, Kabul did not criticise Pakistan's aggression. Instead, when the fighting was at its peak and Indian planes were bombing Pakistani cities, Kabul officially protested India's targeting of Peshawar and Kohat. Considering them part of Pashtunistan and not Pakistan, Kabul asked keep them out of an India-Pakistan war.[33] As ironic, logical and shrewd as it was, Kabul's complaint seemed equally bizarre to India. Afghanistan was undermining Indian military counteractions without being wanting to be seen as doing it at Pakistan's behest. Adding fuel to fire, Bhutto mentioned in his UN speech that Afghan King Zahir Shah had assured Pakistan's president Ayub Khan that: 'I as a king give you assurance, I as a Muslim give you assurance, I as an Afghan give you assurance, that we are with you and we will never betray you'.[34] When quizzed by India, Kabul backtracked, but the diplomatic damage was done. Perceptions about Afghanistan's lack of support to India, or a 'rupture' in India-Afghanistan relations during the 1965 war, persist.[35] According to retired Indian diplomat Chinmaya Gharekhan, who became the PM's special representative to the Middle East (2005–09), 'Afghanistan never sided with India in India's disputes with Pakistan. Afghanistan voted against Pakistan's membership in the UN ... but on issues like Kashmir, especially Kashmir, we [India] have not had any support from Afghanistan'.[36] J. N. Dixit, a powerful Indian diplomat who enjoyed Indira, Rajiv, as well as Sonia Gandhi's confidence and went on to become NSA in 2005, held similar views, i.e. Zahir Shah, 'was ambiguous about Indo-Pakistan relations [and] was not supportive of India in its conflicts with Pakistan in 1947–49, 1965, and 1971', and 'equivocated' on Kashmir.[37]

Though Zahir Shah did not support India over Pakistan directly, he did not oppose India either. Walking a tightrope in highly tense situations, Kabul saw it in its best interests to be, or be seen as being, neutral. India's military assault on Lahore raised concerns in Kabul about a potential unraveling of Pakistan. In this context, as India's advocacy on Pashtunistan gained momentum, Kabul began down-playing the issue in bilateral exchanges with Pakistan. On 30 September 1965, few days after hostilities between India and Pakistan ended, Rawan Farhadi, director-general for political affairs and the senior most official in Afghanistan's ministry of foreign affairs, informed the US diplomat in Kabul, William F. Spengler, that Kabul's strategic restraint on Pashtunistan during the war had developed enough goodwill in Pakistan to start talks on the bilateral dispute.[38] Instead of pressing for territorial revision,

Kabul would endorse more autonomy to Pashtuns within Pakistan, Farhadi asserted. While the specifics of such a dialogue were not outlined (given Pakistan's refusal to entertain Afghan gestures), Kabul tried using the war to resolve the Pashtunistan issue by dialogue rather than force.

Concerned about the AIR broadcasts of increased Pashtun activism against Pakistan, Farhadi maintained the Afghan media had been nearly 'silent' on the issue, and denied that the AIR had picked up such information from Afghan sources. If anything, Farhadi told Spengler, the Afghans were apprehensive of potential 'Indian expansionism' and did not want to see Pakistan disintegrate as that would only increase the 'danger' to Afghanistan.[39] When pressed by Spengler as to explain the exact nature of this 'danger', Farhadi retorted that an Indian 'Anschluss' against Pakistan at some point in the future could not be disregarded.[40] A coup against Ayub Khan, initiated by select Punjabi leaders and Sindhi nationalists, Farhadi reasoned, could lead to the creation of a South Asian 'federation' jeopardising Afghan claims on Pashtunistan. However unlikely this was, the conversation highlighted Kabul's concerns on Pashtunistan and Kashmir. Whether this was a calculated ploy to get Islamabad to the negotiating table on a bilateral dispute when it was under stress and seek concessions remains unclear, but Kabul did not view a powerful and assertive India as a preferred neighbour over Pakistan. If Islamabad, the relatively weaker of the two states, had not budged on the issue of Pashtunistan, then why would India? When asked about his views on potential disintegration of Pakistan, Farhadi had rhetorically replied: 'do you think we would want India at the Khyber Pass?'.[41] In this context, it is difficult to assess who was bluffing on the statement of the Afghan king's sympathy towards Pakistan—Bhutto or Zahir Shah? Though India officially blamed Bhutto, it is entirely possible that Zahir Shah did make such a statement in private, and then seeing that Pakistan's military momentum was ebbing, and India's desire for a bilateral ceasefire, denied it. The complexity (and evolution) of Afghan political opinion on the 1965 war is best reflected in Farhadi personally assuring the Indian ambassador in Kabul that Zahir Shah had not issued a statement of support to Ayub Khan, either verbally or in writing, just a few days after criticising India's 'expansionist' tendencies to Spengler.[42] Indeed, in October 1965, when Pakistan's military gambit failed to reap strategic benefits, Afghanistan, in a diplomatic U-turn, joined India's advocacy on the right to self-determination for Pashtuns and Baloch.[43] Friendship between India and Afghanistan survived the upheaval of 1965. To mend differences, Indian Prime Minister Lal Bahadur Shastri was to visit Kabul two days after signing the Tashkent Declaration (but could not due to his untimely death).[44] Nonetheless, in July 1966, India's Vice President Dr. Zakir Hussain visited Kabul to set the stage for mutually beneficial economic cooperation.[45]

A tilt and a coup

India had introduced various developmental projects in Afghanistan by the 1970s. These included the Chardeghorband Microhydel Scheme, the Indira Gandhi Hospital in Kabul, series of technical assistance schemes in the field of planning, industry, mining, irrigation, and power. Agricultural research stations were also established in Bamiyan, Kandahar, and Kabul for rice, wheat and potatoes.[46] Though reflecting political warmth, these projects had their basis laid in a geopolitical rationale that was shaped more by pressures of the global Cold War, than by the principle of non-alignment. The situation developed along four axes. Firstly, creation of Bangladesh in 1971, and then India's nuclear test in May 1974, emboldened Baloch and Pashtun separatists in Pakistan. The National Awami Party (NAP), which was then the principal political adversary of the Zulfiqar Ali Bhutto-led Pakistan People's Party (PPP), had swept across Balochistan and the NWFP in the 1970 general elections. Led by Ghaffar Khan's son, Khan Wali Khan, the NAP had strong sociopolitical links with Afghanistan and symbolised the nationalistic aspirations of both the Baloch and Pashtun people, similar to the Awami League in East Pakistan.[47] Though the NAP formed the provincial government in May 1972 (Ataullah Mengal, a leading feudal chief, became Balochistan's chief minister), it remained marred by a series of internal crises as well as political turbulence with Islamabad.[48]

Such secessionist tendencies in Pakistan and Islamabad's violent response, unnerved Kabul, which worried about the perverse impact on its polity, society, and economy (if West Pakistan's stability was disturbed).[49] Kabul's concern about Pakistan's disintegration was not new. The situation in East Pakistan in 1971 had made Zahir Shah equally 'anxious' about the perverse impact of Pakistan's heavy-handedness in dealing with ethnic and linguistic minorities in Afghanistan. He admitted to the US ambassador that while his government had been tight-lipped about the East Pakistan affair, public opinion across Afghanistan heavily favoured the Bengalis.[50] Disconnect between Kabul's concerns about the situation in East Pakistan and popular support for armed Indian intervention among Afghans was not lost upon the Indian leadership. Gandhi's confidante and Indian ambassador to Moscow, D P Dhar, had asked foreign secretary Triloki Nath Kaul to suggest Kabul to 'help the oppressed East Bengalis materially by reviving their vocal interest in the Pakhtoon movement'.[51] Karachi, however, was the trade lifeline for a land-locked Afghanistan, and instability within Pakistan could destabilise Afghanistan. Such concerns among the Afghan leadership persisted even after Bangladesh's creation, as Bhutto cracked down on Baloch and Pashtun separatists. By 1974, Kabul and New Delhi became increasingly alarmed by Bhutto's propaganda on India and Afghanistan's continuous collusion in fomenting separatism in Pakistan.[52]

Fearful of losing power domestically and further territorial disintegration, Bhutto dismissed the NAP government in February 1973 and imposed martial law. Whereas disturbances in the NWFP were common occurrences since 1947, imposition of martial law exploded the dormant Balochistan movement into a full-fledged insurgency by early 1974. The Balochistan People's Liberation Front (BPLF), which emerged as the key resistance group led by Mir Hazar Ramkhani, launched a series of attacks on Pakistani military installations. In 1975, the BPLF shifted its base from Balochistan to Afghanistan.[53] Despite underlying tensions between Pashtun and Baloch nationalisms (wherein Baluchistan was viewed as 'southern Pashtunistan'), Kabul threw its weight behind the separatists. Recruiting fighters from the Baloch and Pashtun refugee camps that were setup all across the border areas, it launched attacks from its new headquarters in Kandahar, and the fort of Kalat-i-Ghilzai, just outside Kandahar. Three forward operating bases were also setup along the border near Chaman, Dohmandi, and Gulistan areas.[54] As the number of refugees pouring into Afghanistan rose, anti-Pakistan sentiment in Kabul rose proportionately, and so did international condemnation of Islamabad's crackdown.[55] In April 1975, Pakistan received a 'rude surprise', by the then UN Secretary-General Kurt Waldheim's 'positive response' to Kabul's official complaint of a bulging refugee crises on it soil and Pakistan's 'acts of suppression in Baluchistan'.[56]

Secondly, departing from their declared objective of non-alignment, both India and Afghanistan undertook a strong tilt towards the Soviet Union in the early 1970s. For Kabul especially, by the mid-1970s, India became the second 'most important' country to cultivate good relations with, after the Soviet Union, in order to exert pressure on Pakistan over Pashtunistan.[57] Just as the importance of the Soviet factor increased in India (after the signing of the 1971 Indo-Soviet Treaty of Friendship and Cooperation), Kabul too became dependent on military and economic support from Moscow as the two factions of the PDPA came under Soviet protection.[58] Ever since its inception in 1968, India's external intelligence agency, the Research and Analysis Wing (R&AW) run by R N Kao, developed close links with the Afghan secret services, the Khadamat-e Aetla'at-e Dawlati (KhAD) and the Soviet intelligence agency, the Komitet Gosudarstvennoy Bezopasnosti (KGB).[59] Supplementing New Delhi and Kabul's tilt towards Moscow was Iraq's interest in this security complex in the mid-1970s.

Like India and Pakistan, Iraq and Iran were bitter rivals. And similar to Pakistan and Iran's cooperation, India and Iraq developed a close economic, political, and military relationship that was personified by the excellent rapport between Saddam Hussein and Indira Gandhi (especially after 1979).[60] Arming Baloch separatists on the Iranian side was in Iraq's interest, and on Pakistan's side in India's strategic interest. Kabul for its part, to avoide a standoff with Iran, communicated to Tehran that it supported Baloch separatism only in 'former colonial areas, not those living in "legally constituted territories"'.[61] As a junior level Indian intelligence official actively involved in these operations, says, 'we gave the Baloch everything, from money to guns, during the 1970s, everything'.[62] In fact, the watershed moment that led to the NAP government's dismissal in 1973 was the discovery of an arms cache in the Iraqi Embassy in Islamabad that convinced Bhutto of an armed revolt by the Baloch and Pashtun separatists with support from Iraq and India.[63] The Wali- Khan-led NAP had formed a secret militant wing called the *Pashtun Zalmay* (it included Baloch militants too) that was in active contact with Kabul, as well as the Indian and Iraqi missions in Afghanistan.[64] It was responsible for a series of bomb blasts and subversive activities inside Pakistan. Iraq had allowed the BPLF to openly run its operations from an office in Baghdad.[65] In return, the Shah of Iran, Mohammad Reza Pahlavi, provided military support to Pakistan in order to crush the Baloch insurgency.[66] The intensity of these political fissures is reflected in a secret letter sent by Ram D. Sathe (then a senior Indian diplomat who would go on to become foreign secretary) to India's ambassador in Tehran in March 1975, that 'it will be a few more days before the Iranians stridently back the Pakistanis [on Kashmir] ... Personally, I do not think we should be under any illusion about this matter. I think Iranians will definitely support the Pakistanis'.[67]

Thirdly, the 1970s saw major political upheaval within Kabul. In 1973, much to India's surprise, Zahir Shah was ousted in a bloodless coup by his cousin and former PM Mohammad Daud Khan. Ambitious, virulently anti-Pakistan, and close to the Soviet Union, Daud saw the monarchy as an ancient political system unsuitable for twentieth-century Afghanistan.[68] He wanted to usher in socialist reforms, and take a stronger line against Pakistan (and Iran), unlike the politically mild king. With Moscow backing the plan, Daud struck on 17 July 1973, while Zahir Shah was vacationing in Italy. Rejected by the Khalq (which had become an important political force by the early 1970s), Daud entered into an alliance with Parcham in order to orchestrate the coup. Daud's post-coup modernisation drive in conservative Afghanistan helped the Khalq become widely popular at his expense. Despite being viewed as a secular-socialist politician internationally, Daud's radical domestic reforms, anti-Pakistan rhetoric, and increasing emphasis on the Pashtunistan issue only made things worse. In April 1974, US diplomats in Kabul began raising concerns about Daud's activism on Pashtunistan and intensive efforts to cultivate closer 'military' ties with India as an alternative to Kabul's then 'total reliance on Soviet training and supply'.[69] By November 1974, Kabul had begun a massive military build-up along the Pakistan border with a promise of more Soviet military support including 1,170 tanks (including the T-62, T-54, and T-55, and bridge-laying tanks), over 6,000 pieces of artillery (including 500 each of SAM-7 and SAM-2 missiles), transport vehicles, infantry equipment, radars, forty Mig-21s and forty Mig-27 aircraft, and combat helicopters.[70]

India's response to this change of guard in Kabul was mixed. The Indian embassy in Kabul gave conflicting reports about the coup and its sustainability. S. K. Singh, India's ambassador to Afghanistan in 1973 (who later became foreign secretary and ignored Assadullah Sarwari's pleas in 1990), was of the opinion that Daud's regime would be stable and, with popular support, sustainable.[71] Given Daud's unambiguous stand on Pakistan and Kashmir, Singh viewed him as a welcome change in India's favour. However, for J. Daulet Singh, India's political counselor in Kabul, the coup reeked of a brewing turmoil. Given Daud's forceful personality, inclination towards violence, differences with the Afghan Army, and rivalry with the Khalq, Afghanistan's future looked bleak to Daulet Singh.[72] While S. K. Singh's judgment prevailed, Daulet Singh's words left their mark. Officially, India welcomed Daud and called him a 'great' leader who would strengthen the 'sovereignty' and 'independence' of the Afghan people (clearly a reference towards Pakistan's interference in domestic Afghan affairs).[73] Unofficially, however, India worried of the potential balkanisation of the subcontinent were Pakistan to break-up further.[74]

There were concerns that Daud's provocation on Pashtunistan and Balochistan—both due to his own anti-Pakistan rhetoric and under pressure from his PDPA partners and rivals alike—would exacerbate the situation. EAM Swaran Singh, in his address to the Lok Sabha, euphemistically termed Daud's initiatives towards Pakistan, 'courageous'. It was a polite way of saying that Kabul was on a dangerous collision course with Islamabad.[75] Lalit Mansingh, then India's deputy high commissioner to Kabul (1971–75), who later became foreign secretary, agrees that 'Daud was very anti-Pakistan and wanted us [India] to be actively involved in containing Pakistan'.[76] Daud's proposal to New Delhi was that it should militarily engage Pakistan in the east, and Afghanistan would fight in the west, and together they will 'fix' Pakistan (even though he ridiculed allegations of an India-Afghanistan nexus in public).[77] In a highly publicised visit to New Delhi in March 1975, Daud made his position amply clear:

> The one and only political difference between Afghanistan and Pakistan concerns the restoration of the legitimate rights of our Pakhtoon and Baloochis brothers. We have always expressed our willingness to settle this only difference with that country, but we see that Pakistan is not ready to give a positive response to our desire in this regard. Various governments in Pakistan have consistently employed fear from other countries in the region as an instrument for internal stability and procuring arms, while it is Pakistan itself, which by joining various military pacts, stockpiling various kinds of arms has aroused the concern of the countries in the region and disturbed the tranquility and stability in the area.[78]

Having failed to secure Pakistan's territorial integrity in 1971, the US had lifted an arms embargo on Islamabad in light of its struggles in Balochistan and the NWFP. Though this was a matter of concern for India (it became a major discussion point in the parliament), the arms consignments were not big enough to alter the strategic balance that was in India's favour after the 1971 war. New Delhi refused to join Daud in his criticism of the US and Pakistan (to Washington's amazement).[79] Such arming, however, created considerable concern in Kabul, which was fighting a covert war with Pakistan. Daud complained to the Indian leadership that 'the recent lifting of an arms embargo to Pakistan by the US government [at a] time that Pakistan is engaged in shedding blood in Balochistan and Pashtunistan, has caused grave concern to the people and Government of Afghanistan. It will lead to imbalance in the region and promote an armaments race and would create an additional threat to peace in the region'.[80] For all practical reasons, Afghanistan needed the Soviet Union and India's proactive military support. Even though, arguably, India's military aid potential was highly limited in 1970s and could have made little strategic (though symbolically potent) impact, worries about Pakistan's balkanisation and India's domestic political situation did not permit adventurism. In 1976, Indira Gandhi visited Kabul to consolidate ties and offered more economic assistance, but Daud's request for military support was politely refused.[81]

India's concern about Daud's covert military campaign and its regional repercussions were not entirely unfounded. Bhutto responded to Daud's sponsoring of the BPLF and the Pashtun separatists by offering anti-Kabul Afghan Islamists sanctuary in Pakistan through Pakistan's secret services, the Directorate of Inter-Service Intelligence (ISI). Just like the evolution of the left-wing groups such as the *Parcham* (flag), the *Khalq* (people), the Maoist *Shola-e-Javed* (eternal flame), and other minor groups such as the *Setam-e-Milli* (Oppressed Nation), the *Sada-e-Awam* (Voice of the Masses), the *Tolan-Pal Moleswak* (Afghan Social Democratic Party), the *Afghan Mellat*, and the *Mossawat* (Equality), Afghanistan also witnessed the rise of the Islamic right (both Shia and Sunni) in the mid-1960s and early 1970s.[82] Inspired by the Muslim Brotherhood or the *Ikhwanin-ul-Muslimin*, the Sunni Islamist groups were led by Kabul university professors who had completed their education at the al-Azhar in Cairo. From these circles emerged the 'Muslim Youth' or the *Sazman-e-Jawanan-e-Muslimin* in 1969 that became the *Jami'at-e-Islami* (Islamic Society) in 1973—of which Ahmad Shah Massoud, Burhanuddin Rabbani, and Gulbuddin Hekmatyar were part.[83] At the same time, the *Khuddam-ul-Forqan* (Servants of Providence) emerged from within the Afghan Ulema under the watch of Ibrahim Mojaddedi. In addition to the Sunni right-wing resistance groups were Shia groups such as Maulana Muhammad Attaullah Faizani's *Islam Maktab-e-Tauhid* (Islam School of Monotheism) and the *Sazman-e-Mujahedin-e Mustaza'fin* (Holy Warriors of the Disadvantaged), who were under Iranian influence.

Powerless when compared to the PDPA in the 1970s, members of these Islamist parties were brutally repressed by the left-leaning Daud as well as the PDPA and the Afghan Maoists, pushing them towards armed resistance. Given Daud's anti-Pakistan rhetoric, supporting these Islamist groups proved an effective deterrent for Islamabad. On 22 July 1975, the *Jami'at-e-Islami*, with Pakistan's support, attempted an armed uprising against the Daud regime. It failed. With internal fissures running high, Hekmatyar along with Qazi Muhammad Amin Waqad split from the *Jami'at-e-Islami* and created the *Hizb-e-Islami-ye-Afghanistan* (Islamic Party of Afghanistan). Though the uprising failed, the Islamists succeeded in polarising Afghan politics further, and gave Pakistan a tool to undermine Daud. Pakistan's worries about Afghan and Indian collaboration, with blessings from Moscow, after the 1971 war were credible. If India had used the issues of Balochistan, Pashtunistan, and East Pakistan mostly as diplomatic tools at UN debates till 1965, the 1971 war had made the threat from New Delhi horrifically real. Indeed, success in the eastern theatre had increased political clamour in India to launch an offensive in Pakistan-administered Kashmir, and to activate covert military support to the Baloch and Pashtun separatists in order to solve the Kashmir problem for good.[84] According to the Pakistan's security establishment, in turn, the Afghan Islamists could not just help in fomenting trouble in Afghanistan, but could also be used in Kashmir if required. It seemed like a win-win situation.

'Afghanistan is not Czechoslovakia'

The Saur Revolution of 1978 was the final shock before the Soviet military intervention in Afghanistan the following year. On 27–28 April 1978, armored military units of the Afghan Army, close to the Khalq, attacked the Afghan Presidential Palace (the Arg) followed by aerial bombing. Daud and his family was assassinated and buried in mass graves in the Pul-e-Charkhi area near Kabul. Soon after, Nur Mohammad Taraki became the first Khalqi PM of Afghanistan with support from his inner circle, or the 'Gang of Four'—Sarwari, Mohammad Aslam Watanjar, Sherjan Mazdooryar, Sayed Mohammad Gulabzoi (see prologue)—and the Soviet Union. Hafizullah Amin, another ambitious Khalqi who was at odds with Taraki and his confidants, became the deputy PM and foreign minister. Though Leonid Brezhnev, the then general secretary of the Communist Party of the Soviet Union (CPSU), denied any Soviet role in the events leading up to the revolution, the PDPA's bloody rise had shorn Afghanistan of its non-alignment rhetoric completely. The Soviet Union became the first country to recognise the new Kabul government. On 5 December 1978, much like what India did in 1971, Afghanistan signed a treaty of friendship with Moscow, which allowed Moscow to develop a robust civilian and military presence in the country.[85] Afghanistan was firmly in the Soviet orbit, and was soon recognised by New Delhi.

India's decision to recognise the PDPA regime (or the Democratic Republic of Afghanistan, DRA) in 1978 was influenced by New Delhi's dependence on the Soviet Union on one hand and aversion to rising Islamist radicalism in Pakistan, Afghanistan, and Iran, on the other (and not just its rivalry with Pakistan). In 1977, Bhutto had been ousted (and later assassinated) in a coup by Pakistan's army chief Zia-ul-Haq, who had strong Islamist inclinations. Accepting the new 'secular' regime in Kabul was a way for India's Janata Party government, which had promised 'genuine non-alignment' as a foreign policy goal, to signal to Moscow that it had not strayed off from Nehru's regional policy framework.[86] Though Indian diplomats, by August 1978, started pressing their American counterparts to diversify Afghanistan's source of developmental funding to wean off Kabul from becoming completely dependent on the Soviets (a view shared by the Americans), Moscow continued to play a preponderant strategic role in the region.[87] Then EAM Atal Bihari Vajpayee undertook his second visit to Kabul in September 1978 (the previous one having been in September 1977 soon after the change of government in India) and iterated continuity in India's friendship with Afghanistan. Offering assistance to Kabul in 'any manner' Afghanistan chose, Vajpayee articulated the consensus in India for friendly ties with Afghanistan regardless of political change in either country.[88]

However, the way Taraki was dealing with dissent and land reforms was raising concerns in New Delhi. Taraki's chief of intelligence, Sarwari, who would find himself in an Indian jail in 1990, had unleashed violent crackdowns on both inner party dissidents and the Islamists (particularly due to the backlash that the new regime faced after introducing the land reforms). Various Parchami members were being 'exiled' to foreign countries as diplomats in order to keep 'trouble' away from home. Taraki had 'exiled' Pacha Gul, a Parcham member and former Minister of Frontier Affairs under Daoud Khan, as Afghanistan's ambassador to India.[89] In an Orwellian manner, the Khalq also started denying the existence of the Parcham faction. When asked about opposition from Parcham in November 1978, Amin said, 'there has not been and is not any group in the name of Parcham. In Afghanistan there has existed only one party [the PDPA]'.[90] Senior Parcham leaders such as Babrak Karmal, were sent abroad on ambassadorial positions, and then unceremoniously removed on charges of taking 'active part in the treacherous conspiracy against the great Saur Revolution'.[91]

Apart from concerns over the Khalq's heavy-handed ways, tactical differences emerged between New Delhi and Kabul during this phase. In September 1978, India accepted Pakistan's participation in a meeting of the NAM countries, which eventually led to the latter becoming a full member in 1979. In a vote on the matter, Kabul had voted against allowing countries that are members of military pacts to join NAM, whereas India voted in favour. Outraged, Kabul strongly objected to India's stand on this matter during Vajpayee's 1978 visit. Taraki publicly complained that Afghanistan considered 'socialist countries as natural allies and friends of the non-aligned countries [but] India may not hold that view. Perhaps at some stage, India may come to the same view'.[92] Vajpayee had communicated to Taraki his discomfort with the PDPA's pro-Soviet tilt (to little avail). However, soon after Vajpayee's visit, the political situation in New Delhi became precarious. In July 1979 the Janata Party lost power due to internal political turbulence. The new caretaker government under the premiership of Charan Singh of the Bharatiya Lok Dal, a major constituent of the Janata coalition, took over and fresh general elections were announced for early 1980.

Throughout the Janata Party's rule, US ambassador to India Robert Goheen wanted Foreign Secretary Jagat Mehta to inform the Khalqi and Soviet leadership what Mehta had been telling Goheen behind closed doors, i.e. active Soviet intervention in Afghanistan would only destabilise the region, and was not in Indian interests.[93] In the wake of Taraki's coup, Goheen, with orders from then US President Jimmy Carter, began pushing India to reassure Pakistan on the Afghanistan situation by accepting Islamabad's proposal for a pact to ban nuclear weapons, and explicitly commit to the 'principle of national integrity and the inviolability of established national borders', namely the Durand Line.[94] According to the US, there was evidence that Taraki would revive the Pashtunistan and Baluchistan issues once he had a better grip over his government.[95] Mehta appreciated the US and Pakistan's concerns about the Afghan coup, but was unconvinced by Goheen's argument that Taraki would reignite the Pashtun and Baloch issues given Afghanistan's economic woes.[96] Instead, he was more worried about such anxieties developing into self-fulfilling prophecies.[97] Mehta countered that reaching any precipitous conclusions was inadvisable, and that India recognised governments in Kabul without any regards to ideology. Since the PDPA's revolutionary council seemed to be in total control, there was no reason for New Delhi to delay recognition to the new government.[98] If anything, India's engagement with Taraki would only have a moderating influence on Kabul. Mehta's rebuttal to Goheen (this specific conversation occurred in May 1978) contrasted with those of I. P. Singh, the then joint secretary on the Pakistan-Afghanistan-Iran desk, in September 1978. Singh had been warning Goheen of China's support for a communist insurrection in the northern Badakhshan province (in the wake of Sino-Soviet tensions),[99] and increasing Soviet intervention in Kabul's internal affairs, which could only lead to a Pakistani counteraction. 'Afghanistan was not Czechoslovakia' where Moscow could intervene without a strong reaction, Singh warned the US.[100] Goheen was surprised by Singh's candid views, and construed them as a marked 'switch' in the MEA's perception about Soviet intentions in Afghanistan.

Despite apprehensions, there was no real switch in India's policy approach either towards the Soviet Union, or towards Afghanistan. India's reliance on the Soviet Union on issues relating to Afghanistan, in fact, was nearly total. Thus, when a coup by Amin brought Taraki's political career to an abrupt end on 14 September 1979 (and forced Sarwari to escape Kabul in a sealed container with a six-hour oxygen supply organised by the KGB's Directorate 'S'),[101] the Lok Dal government didn't bother to discuss the situation even once in its official meetings.[102] Domestically oriented, Charan Singh did not take much note even of Amin's fresh round of political crackdowns against his adversaries when he realised that he had lost Moscow's support. Little did Amin know that Sarwari, along with his other three comrades, and Parcham leader Babrak Karmal, in response, would guide a column of Soviet tanks across the Hindu Kush on Christmas Day that same year. Not just Amin, even India's premier intelligence agency, the R&AW, was 'caught napping' when the Soviet troops entered Afghanistan.[103]

Conclusion

The three causal drivers of India's Afghanistan policy, i.e. desire to strike a balance between Afghanistan and Pakistan, international political postures, and Afghanistan's domestic politics (the origins of which lie in the pre- and post-independence political history) are mostly in confluence but can also be at odds with each other. The 1950s, for instance, allowed New Delhi to bond with Kabul using Asian and African resurgence as an international platform. This internationalist approach had the support of most domestic political actors in both India and Afghanistan, and did little to create an imbalance in Afghanistan's (or India's) relations with Pakistan. The 1960s, however, were dominated by heightening Cold War tensions and India's wars with Pakistan and China that challenged the utility of India's non-alignment posture. Nonetheless, consensus in Kabul and New Delhi did not allow regional and domestic instability to undermine bilateral relations and imparted continuity to the relationship. The 1970s, however, fundamentally altered the domestic, regional, and international dynamics of both India and Afghanistan.

Both these countries tilted towards the Soviet Union in light of their rivalry with Pakistan (and also China, for India) during the 1970s. This tilt explains India's uncritical acceptance of Daud's coup, the subsequent Saur Revolution, and the excesses of both these regimes. With domestic Afghan and Indian politics becoming increasingly fractured, siding with Moscow on the Afghan question also became a way for India to strike a balance with Pakistan. Despite 'genuine non-alignment' being a major political issue in the 1977 general elections that saw the fall of Indira Gandhi and rise of the Janata Party, New Delhi was highly dependent on the Soviet Union after 1971. Though New Delhi's concerns about the US-China-Pakistan-Iran axis were valid, its stand on the Afghan question reflected India's incapacity to question Soviet policies. What remained constant throughout this period was the Kabuliwallah connection i.e. the 'consensus'—or political will—in New Delhi to retain close bilateral ties with Kabul regardless of latter's political and economic woes. The Soviet military intervention, however, challenged even this foundational cultural tenet of India-Afghanistan bilateral relations. From now on, instead of being viewed as a 'friend of Afghanistan', India came to be seen as friend of one or the other political or ethnic faction, or simply a reluctant neighbour. And this was just the beginning of a long war.

3

LEANING TOWER OF DELHI

MANAGING THE SOVIET INVASION AND WITHDRAWAL

'We [India] have been assured that Soviet troops will be withdrawn when requested to do so by the Afghan government ... we have no reason to doubt the assurances particularly from a friendly country like the Soviet Union with whom we have close ties'.

Brajesh Mishra, India's Permanent Representative at the UN, January 1980[1]

'India's non-alignment should be genuine, [not] tilted like the leaning tower of Pisa'.

Madhu Dandavate, Janata Party leader at a debate in the Lok Sabha, February 1980[2]

'We [Afghans] are unhappy with the Government of India for not supporting the Afghan people and for supporting the Soviet troops. But that has not lessened our admiration and affection for Indians, who were close to us and who had helped us before the Soviet invasion and occupation'.

An Afghan exile from Zahir Shah's group to an R&AW officer in Geneva, 1986.[3]

U-Turn

Ram D. Sathe, a senior diplomat and then India's foreign secretary for just over a month, was asleep when his phone rang at 11.15 PM on 27 December 1979.[4] The joint secretary (JS) at the Eastern Europe desk of the MEA was on the line.[5] Yuli Vorontsov, the Soviet ambassador to India, had requested an urgent meeting with the PM or the external affairs minister (EAM) to pass a message from Soviet president, Leonid Brezhnev. Neither of the two was available at that hour. Could Sathe please meet Vorontsov, asked the JS? The meeting was fixed for just before midnight. Moscow had agreed to an Afghan request for support to stop external (US, Chinese, and Pakistani) interference and aggression, Vorontsov explained to Sathe. It was done on the basis of the 1978 Soviet-Afghan Treaty of Friendship and Article 51 of the UN Charter. Sathe noted without making any official comment. India by this point had intelligence that a Soviet armored column had closed-in on Kabul in the wee hours of Christmas Day. What bothered Sathe, at least as much if not more than the Soviet action itself, was the fact that Moscow had not bothered consulting the Indian leadership before taking the decision. PM Charan Singh and EAM Shyam Nandan Mishra were briefed about the late-night drama next morning. India's ambassador to Moscow, I K Gujral, also had no idea of the invasion till it actually occurred.[6] After four days, on 31 December 1979, the Soviet ambassador was summoned to the PMO.[7]

Having brushed the Afghan question aside (like many other foreign policy issues) throughout his 'caretaking' premiership, Charan Singh now faced an unenviable dilemma. Should India support Soviet actions in Afghanistan or not? Extending support would undermine the principle of non-alignment and marginalise New Delhi among its Asian and African partners at the NAM. Relations with the people of Afghanistan and the larger Islamic world would also suffer. There were also concerns that the Soviet juggernaut, instead of stopping in Afghanistan, may venture into Balochistan—which already had separatist tendencies—in order to access South Asian warm water ports.[8] If such an eventuality ever occurred, India's own sovereignty would be under threat. But if India decided to criticise Soviet actions, it would jeopardise support on Kashmir and a constant supply of Soviet defence equipment and oil. A hike in global oil prices in 1979 and a severe drought that reduced agricultural production by 12.5 per cent had plummeted India's growth rate by a sharp 5.2 per cent within a year.[9] With its economy structured around the socialistic five-year planning cycles and deeply linked to the Soviet Union, Moscow's economic support was necessary. Moreover, in light of Soviet support during the 1971 India-Pakistan war, criticising Moscow would amount to backstabbing a friendly power without earning practical support from the West. Washington, Beijing, and Islamabad, Charan Singh knew, would resist Soviet forces in Afghanistan regardless of India's stand.

The Soviet intervention, however, had occurred during an interregnum in Indian politics, with polls scheduled for early January 1980 and Charan

Singh's bête noire Indira Gandhi's victory almost certain. Not only did this reduce the political costs of criticising the Soviet Union, it gave Charan Singh a golden opportunity to chastise Moscow, with whom he never really got along. Without hesitation, Charan Singh castigated Vorontsov and unequivocally rejected the Soviet intervention. Any development that would change the qualitative nature of the polity of a neighbouring country concerned India considerably, and Moscow was asked to remove its troops as soon as possible.[10] As far as Charan Singh was concerned, India would criticise the Soviet Union both in Moscow and at the UN. Brajesh Mishra, India's representative at the UN, communicated Charan Singh's stand to other UN delegations.[11] He also protested American and Chinese arms supplies to Pakistan while the MEA communicated the same to Robert Goheen, the US ambassador to India, and Clark Clifford, US President Jimmy Carter's special envoy.[12] In the meantime, as it was expected, Indira Gandhi swept the polls. A pro-Soviet leader, she began exerting control over foreign policy even before her institution as the PM on 20 January 1980. Within a mere fortnight, Gandhi undid Charan Singh's stance.

Aware of the irreconcilable dilemma facing India in the wake of Soviet actions, Gandhi adopted a complicated three-pronged balancing strategy. India would say one thing at the UN, another to Kabul and Moscow, and launch an entirely different initiative with the West and Pakistan. Firstly, on 12 January 1980, Gandhi instructed Mishra to retract his previous statement criticising the Soviet Union at the UN. Instead, he was to inform the UNGA, at the 'Uniting for Peace' initiative launched by Western capitals, that Moscow had sent troops on Afghan request and would not stay there a day longer than required.[13] While India was averse to the presence of foreign troops and bases in any country, it had no reason to doubt assurances 'particularly by a friendly country such as the Soviet Union'.[14] Mishra then charged the US, China, and Pakistan for colluding in arming Afghan rebels in order to subvert Afghan politics. Pakistan had already moved seven army divisions to the Afghan border by mid-January 1980.[15] According to media reports, about 900 Chinese agents had also infiltrated Afghanistan near the 85-km-long border in Wakhan to arm and support the Maoist *Shola-e-Javed* group for fighting the Soviets.[16] Such activities, supplemented by America's active supply of 'arms to small and medium sized countries, and dividing the non-aligned countries' were seen as a threat by Indian policymakers.[17] The U-turn sent a shock wave both within and outside India. In one stroke, Gandhi had alienated substantial parts of the world, including many Afghans, as well as Indians.

Secondly, to contain the damage of her somersault, Gandhi made a public statement calling the Soviet invasion 'inadmissible'.[18] Even privately, she shifted gears with the Soviet foreign minister Andrei Gromyko on 12 February 1980. 'We don't approve of the presence of Soviet troops in Afghanistan though we have viewed it in historical perspective. This new situation has brought the Cold War very close to our area', she informed a baffled Gromyko.[19] She allegedly passed a similar message to Brezhnev in a state visit to Moscow, two years later in September 1982, and curtly told him (when asked by the Soviet general secretary) that the 'way out' of Afghanistan was the 'same as the way in' (much to the confusion of Brezhnev and then Indian foreign secretary M K Rasgotra, who witnessed the exchange).[20] There was hardly any meeting ground between Moscow and New Delhi on Afghanistan. The Indian media, reflecting the popular mood in New Delhi, reported 'a wide gap' between the Indian and the Soviet stand on Afghanistan in its editorial on 15 February 1980.[21] More than the intervention itself, Gandhi's problem was with the fact that it happened in India's neighbourhood. Having refrained from criticising the Soviet role in the 1956 Hungarian crisis and the 1968 Soviet invasion of Czechoslovakia, India was a trusted ally whose support was deemed important in Moscow. In May 1980, Sathe visited Kabul to probe the Afghan leadership's willingness for a political solution and found a regime eager to resolve the dispute and hold talks with Iran and Pakistan (even though their public utterances were markedly different).[22]

In June 1980, however, EAM Narasimha Rao conveyed Gandhi's unhappiness to Brezhnev during his visit to Moscow (India, by now, realised that Zia-ul-Haq had opened a direct channel with Brezhnev on Afghanistan).[23] Simultaneously, India's ambassador to Afghanistan, Jaskaran Teja, and special envoy (and then also an assistant secretary in the MEA) S. K. Singh informed the new Afghan leadership that India's main interest was to maintain people-to-people relations with Afghanistan and to continue supporting Afghanistan in sectors such as health, education, and hydel-power.[24] New Delhi had no desire to interfere in domestic Afghan affairs, and would 'deal with whichever government was de facto in power'.[25] Despite Gandhi's sympathy with the Afghan revolution of 1978, India 'was opposed to violence' and to 'Soviet military intervention in Afghanistan'.[26] New Delhi did not indulge in diplomatic polemics of an anti-Soviet nature, but Moscow was aware of India's 'serious reservations' regarding the implications of the Soviet military. And surely, India was equally wary of Afghanistan being dominated by radical Islamists and/or by the US.

Thirdly, Gandhi launched a diplomatic initiative with Pakistan and the West (US and UK primarily) to bridge differences. The only country missing in this diplomatic exercise was China, with whom both India and the USSR's relations were frosty.[27] To begin with, India abstained (along with sixteen other countries) from voting on the UNGA Resolution ES-6/2 against Soviet actions in January 1980, though the resolution passed with a resounding majority of 104 against 18.[28] Having shocked the world after her u-turn, Gandhi hoped that this abstention would signal to the West and Islamabad that India was not necessarily siding with the Soviets. In fact, some in India genuinely hoped that the Soviet intervention would force Pakistan to 'bury the hatchet' on Kashmir and shape a regional South Asian solution to the problem with Indian support.[29] Soon afterwards in February 1980, Swaran Singh was dispatched to Islamabad for initiating a dialogue as special envoy, and to inform Pakistani military chief and President, Zia-ul-Haq, that the latter 'could remove as many divisions as he wished from the Indian border without fear of any advantage being taken by India', and to suggest talks on reduction of force levels.[30] Gandhi knew that Russia had violated the strategic 'buffer', as the British Raj imagined Afghanistan to be, and Pakistan would surely retaliate. As a senior Indian journalist put it:

> Many of us [Indians] have also bought lock, stock, and barrel, the 19th century British view that the sub-continent's natural frontier was the Hindu Kush, that it would be dangerous for India if Soviet power consolidated in Afghanistan and that in the event it will be vital for us to ensure Pakistan's survival as a buffer between us and the Soviet power.[31]

Many in India understood, if not sympathised with, Pakistan's covert campaign against Soviet forces in Afghanistan. Opening a dialogue with Pakistan, from this perspective, was as much an exercise in signaling India's willingness to cooperate with Zia, as it was to contain change in South Asia's balance of power using diplomatic means. Sathe, and his Pakistani counterpart, Agha Shahi, undertook repeated visits during this period to discuss modalities of such cooperation. Parallel to India's outreach to Pakistan, New Delhi was getting feelers from Moscow and Pakistani separatists to exploit the situation and finish 1971's 'unfinished business'. In 1982, Fikryat Tabeev, the then Soviet ambassador to Afghanistan told J. N. Dixit, India's new ambassador to Kabul, to seriously mull a full-scale war against Pakistan in order to 'take back' the whole of Kashmir, as Rawalpindi focused on Afghanistan. Unaffected by Baloch and Pashtun requests for support to reignite insurgencies across Pakistan, Gandhi put a firm veto on Tabeev's 'adventurous' proposal citing concerns of global condemnation and an undesirable Chinese military intervention in Kashmir.[32] She even refused to organise a meeting between Ghaffar Khan and Brezhnev to discuss Pashtunistan, forcing Ghaffar Khan, in protest, to cancel his visit to Delhi for medical treatment in March 1982.[33] Khan bitterly blamed Gandhi for betraying the Pashtuns, just like Nehru had done, and for having no *raham* (mercy or in this context, can also imply sympathy) for the Pashtunistan issue.

Apart from engaging with Pakistan, India sought better relations with the US and UK, and tried building an international consensus to reach a 'political solution' (something that Afghan leader Babrak Karmal also recommended) to end the Afghan imbroglio and ensure an early Soviet exit. Soon after abstaining at the UNGA vote, Gandhi, along with British Foreign Secretary Lord Carrington, publicly stated that 'no country is justified in entering another country'.[34] London had been working behind the scenes with a cautious (about relations with Moscow) New Delhi to pursue a plan to create a 'neutral' Afghanistan,[35] involving declaration of permanent neutrality, but to limited effect (even though Pakistan was also in agreement with the idea of a neutral Afghanistan).[36]

Instead, India's idea of a political solution, without emphasising neutrality, was taken up by Austria and West Germany on London's request (eventually categorised as the 'Austrian Model').[37] Additionally, K. R. Narayanan, a career diplomat who became India's tenth president in 1997, was sent to Washington to mend fences. Narayanan's mandate was simple: control the damage. India did not want to make the US its enemy because of Soviet misadventures. There was a need to sensitise the US about Indian concerns, and urgency to resolve the conflict. Using back channel diplomacy, India began mobilising countries at the UN to work together to influence Washington and Moscow to work out a political solution.[38] The initiative failed. By June 1980, it became clear to the Indian leadership that the Soviet presence in Afghanistan would be long-term in nature.[39] New Delhi's 'quiet diplomacy', nonetheless, began reaping tactical results. In October 1981, Gandhi met with US President Ronald Reagan in Cancun at the North-South Summit, which led to a diplomatic breakthrough.[40] Indian diplomats toned down their anti-US rhetoric and Washington stopped pressurising global institutions from cutting financial support to India. On 27 July 1982, Gandhi visited Washington after a gap of eleven years to iron out differences on Afghanistan and US arms sales to Pakistan.

Strategic failure

The three-pronged strategy, despite its tactical successes, failed to reconcile the contradictions of India's Afghanistan policy at a strategic level. Driven primarily by dependency on Moscow, Gandhi's pro-Soviet tilt put New Delhi firmly at odds with the rest of the world. For many supporters of Gandhi, aligning with the Soviet Union was a practical, if not perfect, way of respecting both India's non-aligned principle and its national security interests vis-à-vis Pakistan.[41] Such dependence on Moscow, however, became both a means and an end in itself for the Indian leadership. Even though Gandhi's relations with Moscow in the 1980s were not as warm as in the 1970s, the Soviet Union became Gandhi's political shield from adversaries both within and outside India. Domestically, Moscow supported Gandhi against the Janata Party and also neutralised radical left-wing groups such as the Communist Party of India (CPI).[42] Regionally, Soviet military and political support allowed India to counter Pakistan and China. Globally, partnering with Moscow seemed an apt response to challenge the Americans too. Gandhi held the Central Intelligence Agency (CIA, the US external intelligence agency) responsible for her loss in the 1977 general elections.[43] Often feeding her incorrect information about America's anti-Indira stance, the KGB ensured Gandhi's dependence on Moscow.[44] The US, for its part, saw Gandhi's pro-Soviet tilt as R&AW-KhAD-KGB nexus against American interests.[45] Convincing adversaries of India's conciliatory and non-aligned intentions, in such a scenario, was impossible, and if not, then highly improbable.

Still, in June 1981, Rao visited Pakistan and went on to declare that India was 'unequivocally committed to respect Pakistan's national unity, territorial integrity, and sovereign equality' and its right to obtain arms for self-defense.[46] Speaking at the Pakistan Institute of International Affairs in Karachi on 11 June 1981, he added that 'we [India] have an abiding interest, even a vested interest, in the stability of Pakistan ... Our attitudes towards each other should freely evolve on the basis of our direct and clear perception of each other's interests and motivations, based on direct contacts and direct exchange of views. We should develop an individual and, if necessary, a joint capacity to resist the negative impact on us by external trends, external elements and extraneous factors'.[47] Even such outreach did not yield results. A shrewd politician, Zia offered a 'no war' pact instead and sought the withdrawal of 'at least two Indian divisions from its eastern borders' to make Pakistan feel 'sure' about Rao's (and previously Swaran Singh's) proposal.[48] Having already transformed the Afghan crisis into a strategic windfall, Zia's 'no-war' pact was aimed at blunting Gandhi's overtures. It would allow polishing Pakistan's image as a peace-loving country on one hand, but continue to build its arsenal on the other. Pakistan had already been offered a six-year US$ 3.2 billion aid package by Washington in 1981 that included forty F-16 fighter-bombers, and close to US$ 3 billion were funneled as military and economic assistance to the Mujahideen via the ISI.[49] India rebuffed the proposal. Only a comprehensive peace treaty made sense to New Delhi.

As hopes for a South Asian solution faded, Pakistan hosted the 11th Islamic Foreign Ministers Conference to develop a collective security plan for Muslim countries.[50] It was clear that neither would Pakistan give up the arms it was receiving from the Americans, nor would it look eastward for a South Asian solution. In fact, by hosting an Islamic conference, Islamabad also intended to reduce any possibility of an India-Iran strategic rapprochement, the possibility of which had increased after the 1979 Iranian revolution.[51] Agha Shahi, Pakistan's foreign minister, informed Rao of this Iranian angle over a lunch meeting in New York a few weeks after Rao's visit to Pakistan. The only success of Rao's 1981 Pakistan tour was the institution of the Indo-Pakistan Joint Commission in 1982 to facilitate trade and commerce. Zia paid a return visit to Delhi on 1 November 1982, and talks to establish the South Asian Association for Regional Cooperation (SAARC) were initiated. Nonetheless, differences between the two countries were far from resolved. Pakistan's refusal to cut support for the Mujahideen paved the way for Gandhi to credibly defend her pro-Soviet stand on Afghanistan.

Gandhi's outreach to Pakistan was driven by contradictions that betrayed the impracticability of a peace process under geopolitical duress. Expecting not just an aggressive Pakistani response to the Soviet intervention, New Delhi was also worried about Pakistan building a nuclear bomb with Libyan help.[52] To counter these moves on the ground, Gandhi ordered then R&AW chief, G. C. 'Gary' Saxena (with former chief R. N. Kao as Gandhi's security advisor) to reactivate contacts with the Sindhi, Pashtun, and Baloch nationalists in Pakistan with whom India had contacts during the 1970s. They were not to be armed just yet, but the ground was to be prepared for such an eventuality. Many separatist leaders from Pakistan started visiting India covertly soon after the Soviet intervention (a fact that was probably known to Zia).[53] This was not the case for the brief period of non-Congress rule. Both Morarji Desai and Charan Singh had toned down R&AW's capabilities and operations, mostly out of spite (they viewed R&AW as a vanguard organisation that Gandhi misused during the Emergency in mid-1970s).

Gandhi reversed this policy and wanted the R&AW-KhAD-KGB relationship to deepen. In addition to clandestine visits by low-level separatists, prominent Pasthun leaders such as Wali Khan and Abdul Ghaffar Khan visited India openly. It was in context of this momentum of Gandhi's 'covert policy' towards Afghanistan and Pakistan in early 1980s that Abdul Ghaffar Khan was supposed to meet Gandhi in 1983 (in wake of him visiting India for medical treatment), from which he eventually backed out. Gandhi's refusal to connect Ghaffar Khan with Brezhnev was symbolic of India's restraint vis-à-vis Pakistan, even if its brief experiment of initiating a dialogue with Islamabad had failed.[54] Coupling this failing rapprochement with Islamabad was Moscow's generous credit line of US$ 1.63 billion payable after fifteen years (after a two year grace period) on a 2.5 per cent interest rate to an economically strained India,[55] and an arms-transfer package that included 100 T-72 tanks (with another 600 to be license-produced in India), five MiG 'Foxbat' aircrafts, and a huge number of fast-attack boats loaded with missiles, in May 1980.[56] In return, India was to remain silent on the Afghan question. The trick worked.[57] Former Joint Director of the Intelligence Bureau, Maloy Krishna Dhar, who had recently taken charge of the counter-intelligence desk aimed at Soviet activities inside India was discouraged by the political leadership from 'penetrating' the KGB network.[58] Soviet intelligence agencies had been targeting Delhi-based Afghan refugees from diverse political backgrounds. Undermining such Soviet covert operations, he was told, 'was not compatible with the diplomatic initiative of India in Afghanistan'.[59] Concerned about New Delhi's 'lop-sided' Afghanistan policy of supporting the PDPA against the 'aspirations of the people of Afghanistan', Dhar advocated policy realignment in favour of the Mujahideen for two reasons. One, supporting the PDPA would anger Indian Muslims, and two, it would give the CIA and ISI a reason to 'incite troubles' in Kashmir and 'other strong Muslim pockets'. India, he argued to little effect, should not be seen 'as an enemy of the Islamist resistance in Afghanistan'.

Death of consensus

There is consensus among contemporary historians and policymakers that the coup in Afghanistan and the opportunity seen there by the Soviets, which led to the invasion, precipitated the larger US intervention. Though true in retrospect, at that time, at least among Indian policymaking corridors, it was seen as a 'chicken-and-egg' problem, which led to a policy compromise. Did increasing US and Pakistani interference in domestic Afghan affairs lead to the Soviet intervention, or did the Soviet intervention lead to an increase in US and Pakistani intervention? This dilemma, Indira Gandhi's pro-Soviet tilt as a response, and the ensuing debate around this response split India's political and diplomatic circles. Having already lost its reputation of being a leader of the NAM, Gandhi's Afghanistan policy came under intense criticism domestically. According to the advocacy coalition framework (that guides the analysis and arguments of this book), India's policymaking establishment had been divided into divergent advocacies that competed for influence on policy output. Existing literature on this issue argues that the 'Afghanistan imbroglio revealed the paradox of Mrs. Gandhi: international rejection coinciding with domestic approval of her policy'.[60] It is true that Gandhi had support for her policies, but only partly. Having won a solid 353 seats (out of 542) in the 1980 general election, the Congress (I) had the mandate to follow through on its foreign policy.[61] In contrast, the Janata Party had gathered a mere 31 seats whereas Janata Party (Secular) received 41 seats. Undoubtedly, the supporters of intervention won influence on policy output, however, unlike what the existing literature claims, fell far short of winning the debate. The Afghanistan question had broken the sacred foreign policy consensus that existed in India. Occurring on the plank of non-alignment and within the structural confines of Cold War politics, i.e. US and Chinese arms supply to Pakistan in the wake of Soviet intervention, debates in the Parliament of India (and outside), in early 1980s laid the foundation for the rise of partisans and conciliators in the Indian foreign policy establishment on the Afghanistan question (as detailed in the next chapter).

Gandhi's u-turn was intensely criticised by the Janata Party, the Janata Party (Secular), the Bharatiya Janata Party (BJP), the Lok Dal, and from within the Congress. Top bureaucrats such as diplomat Brajesh Mishra and foreign secretary Jagat S. Mehta (before Ram Sathe) were also staunchly opposed to the decision. Mishra, who had announced the change in India's decision at the UN, was so embarrassed that after his speech he left the UN office from the backdoor to avoid uneasy questions, and later quit his job in protest. Jagat Mehta, who was appointed FS during the 'Emergency years' in April 1976, frantically lobbied with Gandhi and Sathe in January 1980 (though he was out of office by then) to condemn Soviet actions unequivocally.[62] He worried that pro-Soviet partisanship would isolate India internationally, and indifference towards the Mujahideen would distance India from the Afghan people. Having worked closely with the Janata Party on its foreign policy agenda of 'genuine non-alignment' (despite being close to Gandhi during the Emergency), Mehta firmly believed that only a conciliatory and non-aligned policy (one that would allow India and Pakistan to rationalise bilateral relations) could prevent a negative spillover of the Soviet actions in the region.[63]

Not surprisingly, Gandhi's domestic opponents severely criticised her decision on various counts such as, (a) India had not stood by its principle of non-alignment and alienated itself among the Third World, (b) India did not show any respect for the sovereignty of a smaller friendly neighbour such as Afghanistan, (c) India did not criticise Moscow effectively in the light of these concerns, and, (d) the ambiguity around the idea of a 'political solution'—as Gandhi actively advocated—gave Moscow breathing space to continue with its military presence in Afghanistan, which would not end anytime soon. Rao and Congress (I) MP Devendra Nath Dwivedi, a renowned lawyer who hailed from Varanasi, tried defending their policy in security terms, i.e. the threat from Pakistan, China and the US.[64] The counter-attack, led by Dinesh Goswami from Assam and BJP leader Jagdish Prasad Mathur from Uttar Pradesh (UP), however, was fearsome. By emphasising national security, and believing the false claim that the Soviet Union would not remain in Afghanistan a day longer than required, the ruling government was fooling itself, argued Mathur. Indeed, Soviet ambassador to Afghanistan, Tabeev, had communicated Moscow's intentions 'to stay' in Afghanistan to Dixit in 1982.[65] According to Goswami, the government's approach was 'ambivalent' at best, and had compromised upon the key issue of Afghan sovereignty.[66] A major part of the Afghan people's opinion, which was allegedly against the intervention, was also not respected.

Manubhai Patel, a veteran Congress leader and Gandhian hailing from Gujarat, in a statement filled with irony, lauded the government for openly criticising Moscow's intervention in Afghanistan after its initial 'confused' reaction, but wondered if the government had

> compromised its attitude on the sovereignty of a country, whatever policy it might have, that an outside country could just go into such a country and threaten the sovereignty of a particular small country with condition that unless a political agreement comes about, they are not going to go out?[67]

Other Congress members such as V. B. Raju and Dinesh Singh (who was also a former EAM in 1969–70, and took the same office again during 1993–95) joined the growing criticism against Gandhi's pro-Soviet tilt.[68] Top Janata Party leaders such as Morarji Desai and Jagjivan Ram had made their anti-Congress stance clear from the outset.[69] Syed Shahabuddin, a Janata Party MP, said that 'the Russian action and our reaction thereto cannot but revive the memories of Hungary and Czechoslovakia and the ambitious and ambivalent attitude adopted then.'[70] Advocating caution in dealing with the situation, another opposition leader, Madhu Dandavate, wittily argued that India's nonalignment had to be 'genuine' and not 'tilted like the leaning tower of Pisa.'[71] For all these parties, the government should have known better than to buy Soviet theories of entering Afghanistan on Kabul's request, so as to contain 'counter-revolutionary' forces.

In September 1980, Vajpayee, who had previously (as EAM) welcomed the change of guard in Kabul in 1978, asked if the bonds of Indo-Soviet friendship are so fragile as to be shattered merely by calling a spade a spade.'[72] It was 'highly regrettable that instead of raising a powerful protest against the Soviet interference in the affairs of Afghanistan, our traditional friend and non-aligned neighbour, the attitude adopted by Mrs. Gandhi's Government on this issue right from the beginning has resulted in lowering of our prestige in the eyes of the world, reducing our credibility among non-aligned nations and isolating us from our neighbours', countered Vajpayee.[73]

BJP General Secretary, Sikander Bakht, who started his political career with the Congress then shifted to the Janata Party and finally ended up with the BJP, added that the Soviet Union was a 'modern colonial power' whose 'next victim could be Baluchistan', in which case India's borders would be threatened directly.[74] Some opposition politicians even demanded the revocation of the 1971 Indo-Soviet friendship treaty on the grounds that Moscow displayed a tendency to use friendship treaties in order to interfere in the domestic politics of other countries.[75] In April 1981, during a visit to the US, Subramanian Swamy, a Janata Party leader (who later became a staunch Hindu nationalist), argued that the Gandhi government's 'needlessly close relations' with Moscow alienated India in South Asia and elsewhere. He wondered why India should 'pay such a heavy price' when the Soviet Union 'needs us more than we need the USSR [Union of Soviet Socialist Republics]'.[76] The Lok Dal also issued multiple statements criticising the Congress (I) on its Afghanistan policy, and the Swatantra Party leadership was 'absolutely appalled' in the way Gandhi had dealt with the Soviet invasion of Afghanistan.[77]

Supporting Gandhi's alignment with the Soviet Union, however, were the various Indian communist parties, who had close to fifty seats in the Lok Sabha.[78] The communists, in fact, were resentful with the government's attempts at ameliorating its stand in light of domestic and international pressure and seeking an early Soviet withdrawal.[79] Within a week of the Soviet invasion, on 1 January 1980, the politburo of the Communist Party of India (Marxist), CPI (M) or just CPM, declared that 'to come in opposition to this Soviet help to Afghanistan is to give an alibi to the US imperialists and the Pakistani military dictatorship'.[80] Senior CPM leaders such as Samar Mukherjee and Harkishen Singh Surjeet offered die-hard support to Moscow, and by corollary, to Gandhi, on Afghanistan. Deriding anyone who put blame on the Soviet Union for repeating American, British, and Pakistani propaganda, Surjeet blamed the 'US imperialists and their policies' for 'the present state of affairs and for all that is happening in the region'.[81] He also criticised British foreign secretary, Lord Carrington, who was proposing a 'neutral' Afghanistan, for 'arguing the case of insurgents and in favour of Pakistan.'[82] As for Afghan opinion, the communists took support of Abdul Ghaffar Khan's ambiguous press statement (which Khan later retracted) that he supported the Soviet intervention.

Backing Surjeet was the CPI MP from West Bengal, Bhupesh Gupta, who dug into the Janata Party and the BJP for digressing from the heart of the matter, i.e. American imperialism and Pakistani dictatorship. 'My friends [Janata Party and the BJP] seem to be very much exercised over Afghanistan. The situation in Kabul is causing them, some of them, sleepless nights, it seems. But you should know that arms to Pakistan are coming in huge number and quantity. Modern weapons. Side by side, they would get nuclear capability to mount vicious, monstrous, pervasive threat to our country and to all the countries in the region in the interest of American imperialism' Gupta said.[83] The US Secretary of Defence, Harold Brown's visit to Beijing in 1980, according to Indian communists, was to ask China to supply arms to Pakistan as Brown found it difficult to convince the US Congress to remove the embargo on arms supplies to Rawalpindi. In this context, Afghanistan was in safe hands according to the CPI, and it was time for India to look after itself. Some communist leaders even went ahead to equate, erroneously, the Soviet intervention in Afghanistan with the Indian intervention in erstwhile East Pakistan in 1971. Other left-wing politicians such as Chitta Basu of the Forward Bloc, which was in an alliance with the CPM in West Bengal, urged the Indian government to train its guns towards the US, China, and Pakistan.

Gandhi's complicated balancing act was a 'policy compromise' in light of fiercely contesting advocacies of the supporters and detractors of the Soviet intervention. The trajectory of her policy response was both a cause and consequence of competing policy advocacies within India and abroad. It was a 'yes, but' approach in which New Delhi supported Moscow's Afghan endeavors, but only reluctantly. In praxis, India was never able to, and arguably could never have, effectively resolved the contradictions generated by the Soviet intervention. Whatever policy Gandhi would have adopted, it would have had its critics and supporters. Moreover, India's official stand to deal with whichever government was de facto in power in Kabul in 1980, was as much a sign of commitment to Afghanistan as it was a symbol of Kabul's inconsequence in New Delhi. Driven by Cold War politics, the real debate was around India's relationship with the Soviet Union and not Afghanistan. Kabul was simply a sideshow as India's Afghanistan policy became aligned with that of the Communist Party of the Soviet Union (CPSU). Moscow's Afghan friends would be India's friends, and Moscow's enemies in Afghanistan, if not enemies shall neither be India's friends.

The CPSU's pro-Parcham tilt allowed New Delhi to widen engagement with Karmal and later with Najibullah, but alienated it from other bodies of political opinion on the Afghan landscape. Not surprisingly, neither the people of Afghanistan, nor the Parcham-dominated Kabul government was completely satisfied with India's response (a theme that would dominate India's engagement with Afghanistan in the following decades). For Afghan president Karmal and PM Shah Mohammad Dost, who had welcomed Brajesh Mishra's UN speech and Jaskaran Teja's private reassurances, India's abstention in the subsequent UN resolution that criticised Soviet actions was a bad omen. Kabul was expecting undisputed support from New Delhi. On the other hand, many Afghan people—and not just the Mujahideen—who were unhappy with the Soviet intervention, grew critical of India's support.[84] Even senior Khalq leaders such as interior minister Sayed Mohammad Gulabzoi, minister of communications Mohammad Aslam Watanjar, and former spy chief Assadullah Sarwari, with whom India had developed good working relations before the events of December 1979, grew wary of India's pro-Parcham bias.[85] 'For the first time in three decades, anti-Indian sentiments have swelled up in Afghan hearts', the Indian media reported in February 1980.[86]

The Soviet withdrawal from Afghanistan in 1989 and the end of the Cold War in 1991 shifted India's position on Afghanistan from partisanship towards Pakistan to a more conciliatory approach. Receding global pressure and interest in Afghanistan shifted the strategic fulcrum of India's Afghanistan dilemma to regional and domestic politics. Though Pakistan had always been a potent factor, its emergence as the most powerful external actor in Kabul by the early 1990s augmented its relevance in India's Afghanistan policy proportionately. The only difference between the 1980s and 1990s was that these debates were not couched in ideological terms in the latter decade. They were, essentially, conceptual in nature. As detailed in the next chapter, the partisans were staunchly anti-Pakistan in their operational outlook and wanted to deal only with those Afghan political and military factions who shared this view. The conciliators were open to engaging with all Afghan factions regardless of their relations with and attitude towards Pakistan. India's debates on these lines evolved, slowly, during the 1980s. The sources of this change were same as before, i.e. India's desire to strike a balance between Afghanistan and Pakistan, evolving international political environment, and Afghanistan's domestic political scenario. The following two sections detail the evolution of these policy debates by delving into India's diplomatic initiatives with Moscow and Washington on one hand, and with Afghanistan on the other.

Leaning tower of Delhi

More than its frustration over the Soviet entry in Afghanistan, India feared the implications of the impending withdrawal. A botched departure could leave India out in the cold, while Pakistan and its Islamist proxies, who had Washington and Beijing's support, victorious in Afghanistan. Part of the aim of Indira Gandhi's visit to the US and the USSR in 1982 was to ensure a sustained dialogue between the two world powers and to seek a moderate political dispensation in Kabul after the Soviet retreat.[87] However, it was her younger son Rajiv Gandhi, who became PM on 31 October 1984 after his mother's assassination, whose 'balancing act' between Washington and Moscow in the latter half of 1980s brought India, somewhat, to the forefront in Afghanistan. Desperate to cut its losses, Moscow was looking for exit strategies from Afghanistan, and bent on making the invasion costly, Washington was looking for ways to undercut Soviet influence in South Asia. Reduction in Soviet influence in the region, however, meant the normalisation of India-Pakistan relations (and reducing India's military dependence on the Soviets). About three weeks before Gandhi was assassinated, on 11 October 1984, in a national security decision directive on 'U.S. policy towards India and Pakistan', Reagan pushed towards normalisation of ties between India and Pakistan.[88] Worried that a preemptive Indian strike on Pakistan's nuclear facilities in Kahuta may lead to an all-out war (those were the years when the Pakistan's nuclear facilities were still developing), the US was determined to engage with New Delhi regardless of Indian apprehensions about Washington's intentions.

In this context, Rajiv Gandhi's unexpected arrival as PM was a good omen for Washington and Moscow. To be clear, much like his mother, Rajiv's operational policy towards Afghanistan also had a covert edge with active involvement of the R&AW. Bent on undercutting Pakistan's influence, or as Zia called it, strategic depth, the R&AW with the KGB's support, continued to cultivate links with different Afghan groups (including the Mujahideen) as well as Pashtuns in Pakistan. The R&AW opened two separate desks, Counter Intelligence Team-X and Counter Intelligence Team-J, both of which were to wreak havoc in Pakistan and make its activities in Punjab 'prohibitively costly'.[89] The first team planted bombs across Pakistani cities, whereas the second team was focused on Khalistani groups. It was a 'tit-for-tat' model of covert warfare that India hoped would lead to a peaceful equilibrium. Rajiv had knowledge of the intricacies of these operations.[90] Nonetheless, overtly he launched a grand diplomatic enterprise with the US and the Soviet Union.

To begin with, in January 1985, India hosted a meeting of the 'Delhi Six'—India, Argentina, Greece, Sweden, Mexico, and Tanzania—who issued the Delhi Declaration condemning an arms race emerging from Reagan's Strategic Defence Initiative.[91] Soon after, in May 1985, he visited Moscow, and, as put by a senior Congress party member, 'got practically everything from the USSR that it [India] had asked for'.[92] In November 1986, reformist Soviet leader Mikhail Gorbachev, who initiated Perestroika, visited India (the first of any Soviet president to a 'third world' country) to buttress bilateral relations, but more so, to check on Rajiv's progress on the Afghan question with Reagan. In early 1985 India's foreign secretary Romesh Bhandari had iterated to US Under Secretary of State William Schneider that while India would not get into 'the game of mediation', it will be willing to play a 'more active role' if Moscow did not object.[93] Though in CIA's confidential assessment New Delhi's private efforts to influence Moscow's decisions on Afghanistan had 'irritated' the Soviets, Gorbachev did not oppose India's diplomatic activism. Rajiv developed an active channel with both Reagan and Gorbachev between 1985 and 1988. It was meant to ensure a timely Soviet withdrawal and a moderate, non-aligned, political dispensation in Kabul. Rajiv's visit to Moscow and Washington in 1985 set the ball rolling. 'We want to try so that something starts moving [on Afghanistan]', Rajiv told a roomful of journalists before flying to the US.[94] With the UN process (under Diego Cordovez) stalemated for more than three years now, Reagan agreed that Rajiv's 'intervention with Secretary General Gorbachev was so much more timely'.[95]

Rajiv wanted to convince the US that a genuinely 'non-aligned' Afghanistan was in the best interest of both the US and India, and that the new Soviet president, Gorbachev, was serious about a timely exit.[96] On the other hand, he wanted Moscow to believe that the US was not bent on bleeding Moscow in Afghanistan with Pakistani support. Rajiv was the right candidate to execute this role. A young former pilot interested in modernisation and married to an Italian woman—Sonia Gandhi (née Maino)—he got along well with the Americans (especially then Vice President George H. W. Bush).[97] He was also the chairman of the NAM, and Gorbachev 'found it easier to talk with [Rajiv] Gandhi than with Reagan and some other leaders'. Gorbachev and Rajiv's rapport, allegedly, 'was total, and their discussions were genuinely frank'.[98] US ambassador to India, John Gunther Dean (1985–88), played a critical role in facilitating this channel. In December 1985, shortly after Dean's posting to Delhi, Reagan wrote to Rajiv of the 'deep American desire to see a negotiated settlement of the tragic conflict in Afghanistan'.[99] It was a bluff, but Gandhi took up the issue and, in a public statement made during his trip to Zimbabwe in 1986, sought an end to intervention 'by all parties'.[100] Moscow responded by proposing a four-year phased withdrawal. For Reagan, however, such a long time-frame was unacceptable. Writing to Rajiv in November 1986 (after Gorbachev's visit to India), he rejected Moscow's proposals as 'untenable' and designed to 'legitimise' a 'prolonged occupation and to achieve a thinly cloaked military solution'.[101] This back-and-forth diplomacy between Moscow and Washington via New Delhi reaped no results.[102]

If anything, Moscow lost patience with India and began viewing direct talks with Pakistan as an attractive option. After a damning report of Soviet military performance by Marshal Sergey F. Akhromeyev, chief of the Soviet military, at a CPSU politburo meeting on 13 November 1986, Gorbachev made withdrawal a priority issue (within one or maximum two years).[103] Soon after the meeting, C. V. Ranganathan, India's chargé d'affaires in Moscow was informed about the politburo's decision and sought India's support to ensure stability in Afghanistan after the Soviet pullout. India's response to Gorbachev was 'to hasten slowly' with the withdrawal.[104] An active Indian intervention in Afghanistan, Ranganathan argued, held the potential to further complicate relations with Pakistan.[105] A cautious Soviet withdrawal, thus, was necessary to secure Indian interests in the region. However, instead of having the desired impact, India's persistence to elongate the withdrawal only increased Pakistan's value and convinced Moscow that all India wanted was to freeride on Soviet military presence in Afghanistan to ensure its regional hegemony. In the next politburo meeting between 23–26 February 1987, Gorbachev rubbished Gromyko's warning of India's displeasure with the former's decision to withdraw and, instead, argued that the USSR needed to establish 'direct contact' with Pakistan. 'Maybe we [USSR] should even invite Zia-ul-Haq for a meeting with me. Maybe we should even "pay" him with something. In short, we need flexibility and quick reaction, otherwise, there will be bloodshed and civil war, and Najibullah will be removed quickly', ordered Gorbachev.[106] The US had detailed intelligence of Soviet decision-making, and so did the PDPA, which was getting increasingly nervous about Soviet courting of Pakistan.[107] Nearly two decades later, when the US began planning its withdrawal from Afghanistan, India again counseled caution in the light of Taliban's resurgence, but had little impact.

Differences between the Indian and US positions also became acute overtime. Rajiv's response to Reagan in January 1987 made it apparent:

> Our [India's] position in Afghanistan is, as you know, that the country should be allowed to chart an independent, non-aligned course, free from intervention and interference. I reiterated this to General Secretary Gorbachev. I also conveyed to him the gist of what you had written to me. The General Secretary left me with the impression that the Soviet Union would like to withdraw its forces in a realistic time-frame from an Afghanistan which would be non-aligned and not unfriendly to the Soviet Union. I hope that a peaceful resolution will not elude us for long. Quite apart from other factors, an early settlement would be in India's interest.[108]

Rajiv went further to denounce Pakistan's continuing exploitation of the Afghan situation, its demand for American AWACS and the Hawkeye Naval Aircraft, and a robust nuclear arms programme that would trigger a qualitative new phase in the arms race in South Asia and enhance tensions to dangerous levels. Reagan's response to Rajiv in March 1987 was cut and dried—a non-aligned coalition government including communist leader Najibullah, as favoured by India, was not acceptable. As put by Dean himself, differences between official US and Indian policies persisted on Afghanistan and nuclear issues. 'Covertly, we [US] supported the Islamic fundamentalist Gulbuddin Hekmatyar who received the lion share of the arms and funds provided to the Afghan resistance. He was at that time "America's man"', claimed Dean.[109] In a secret national security directive on Afghanistan prepared by the White House on 1 May 1987, the Reagan administration was categorical that Moscow's decision to reduce its withdrawal timeline to eighteen months instead of four years was 'designed to persuade the world that Moscow is serious in searching for a solution in Afghanistan, yet clearly aimed to allow Soviet military operations against resistance with decreased external support'.[110] There was more convergence between Reagan and Zia than Rajiv and Reagan, despite the latter duo's excellent personal rapport. Moscow's growing frustration with the Afghan war and Gorbachev's willingness to negotiate with the US fell on deaf ears.

In November 1987, Soviet PM Nicolai Ryzhkov visited New Delhi to discuss Afghanistan among other issues such as Sri Lanka, where Rajiv had dispatched an Indian military contingent to disarm and demobilise various militant Tamil separatist groups and to facilitate provincial elections—only to get caught in a disastrous war with the LTTE. Ryzhkov made it clear to Rajiv that the US demand for a rushed Soviet withdrawal without guarantee of a representative coalition government was impossible. Rajiv agreed with Ryzhkov, and so did Afghan officials, who by now had begun worrying for their lives. In a response to 'Ronald' (and not Mr President) on 24 December 1987, Rajiv stuck to his position and informed the US president that Gorbachev and Najibullah were showing 'greater flexibility' than Reagan himself. In May–June 1988, Reagan and Gorbachev met at the Moscow Summit and signed the Intermediate Range Nuclear Force Treaty (INF) but made little progress on Afghanistan.[111] Rajiv's initiative with the two super powers had come to a naught.

Much to Reagan and Zia's consternation, India, by now, had activated a direct channel with former Afghan King Zahir Shah, who was still in Rome, to build a broad-based coalition government in case Najibullah did not last.[112] B Raman, an R&AW officer posted in Geneva from 1985 onwards—with Jaskaran Teja, India's former ambassador to Kabul and now the permanent representative in Geneva—had begun building links with Afghan exiles.[113] He facilitated high-profile meetings of these Afghans with Indian ministers, including then Minister of State for External Affairs Natwar Singh. Raman's groundwork paved the way for New Delhi to play the Zahir Shah card before the Geneva Accord that was signed between Afghanistan and Pakistan on 14 October 1988 with the Soviet Union and the US as guarantors. His links with India cost Zahir Shah dearly at Geneva, as he became a political untouchable in Islamabad.[114] A theoretical exercise at best, the accord failed to halt the Mujahideen offensives. Moreover, India's royalist gambit failed given Najibullah's disinclination to vacate the presidency. Adding insult to injury, India was not invited to attend the signing of the accord even as an observer, at Pakistan's insistence. As scholar Sergey Radchenko argues, Rajiv had 'overplayed his hand ... and India punched above its weight ... in the end neither the Soviet Union nor, especially, the US, valued its relationship with India above their respective regional and global priorities'.[115] Rajiv's failure to ensure India's role in Afghanistan—and presence at Geneva—unleashed a storm in the Indian parliament. By late 1987, Rajiv's conciliatory approach had evolved into a highly aggressive policy stance, most visible in Sri Lanka and Pakistan, but also, in theory if not in practice, towards Afghanistan.

Could Kabul be genuinely non-aligned, as India wanted, in light of India's own tilt towards Moscow and Pakistan's alliance with Washington? Not according to the Pentagon, and neither according to the Kremlin. New Delhi's pro-Soviet leanings had made India's grand strategy obsolete. As a *Times of India* editorial argued in March 1988, 'since India has had close relations with the Kabul regime and none at all with the rebel groups throughout the Soviet-occupation of that country, any last-minute attempt to project itself as a mediator could only be counter-productive'.[116] Most US officials, including Reagan, remained unconvinced (and unimpressed) by Indian's platitudes on non-alignment. Rajiv's advocacy of a coalition government in Kabul effectively meant a compromise between the Soviet Union and the US on one hand, India and Pakistan on the other, and the Kabul government and its adversaries on top of it. Such a solution went against the grain of the global Cold War politics. Despite the wisdom of India's stance, Washington was more concerned about defeating the Soviets than worrying about the potentially negative impact of supporting Afghan Islamists. In 1988, the US Congress agreed to offer another six-year aid package to Pakistan, similar to the US$ 3.2 billion deal it had offered to Rawalpindi in 1981. The amount was increased to US$ 4 billion this time.[117]

Kabul durbar

Even if one assumes that the two world powers would have reached an agreement on Afghanistan, would the situation on the ground in Afghanistan have allowed for a negotiated settlement? Not really. With the presidential palace at its center and communists at helm, Kabul was a city of intrigue in the 1980s. A space of political arbitration; its political leaders were known to be astute and ruthless. Given strained center-periphery relations, ruling Kabul was often an end in itself. Such was the case during Amanullah Khan's reign in the 1920s, Zahir Shah's reign afterwards, that of Daud Khan in the 1970s, the communists in 1980, the Taliban in 1990s, as well as Hamid Karzai and Ashraf Ghani in the 2000s. What kept Karmal and Najibullah in power, apart from Soviet support, was their capacity to run a well-oiled patronage network.[118] Soviet rubles ensured that the Parchamis bought allegiance of different Afghan factions when, in reality, no such support existed on ideological, ethnic, or tribal lines. Karmal, in his initial years did exactly that and expanded his government with representatives from outside the PDPA.[119] Surrounded by a sundry group of loyalists, however, the Parchami core had multiple layers of enemies as well. The Khalqis were the first in line, especially Gulabzoi, Watanjar, and Sarwari. Other prominent Khalqi opponents included Nazar Mohammad and Shahnawaz Tanai, both senior generals in the Afghan army with loyalty to the Khalq. Representing a threat from within the government, and having some support in Moscow, these enemies were the most dangerous. They could be co-opted financially or appointed to faraway embassies. They could also be put behind bars. The Mujahideen formed the second layer of enemies.

Given the nature of both domestic Afghan and global Cold War politics, India had to choose how to deal with the Kabul government. Pakistan, for instance, despite having diplomatic relations with Afghanistan, fought the Kabul government. India had the option to deal solely with the Parcham leadership, or develop a genuinely non-aligned (or multi-aligned) approach in which it would engage with all Afghan political outfits and accept whomsoever came to power in Kabul. By siding with Moscow, however, the Indian leadership had severely limited the scope of its Afghanistan policy. If it engaged with the Mujahideen it would undermine its relations not just with the PDPA but also with the Soviet Union. Unlike the pre-1979 Afghanistan where Indian diplomats were welcomed by everyone and welcomed everyone in return, the post-1979 Afghanistan was a much more complicated place. Two cases of India's engagement with Afghanistan in the 1980s, however, highlight its pro-Parcham bias. The first case was Gandhi's close links with Karmal. Politically moderate (relative to other communist leaders) and representing an urban intellectual Marxist elite, Karmal was not viewed as burdensome by Gandhi. Conversely, the Khalq was predominantly rural and heavily Pashtun in its demographic composition, making it susceptible to tribal politicking. Observers at the time believed that neither of the two factions were 'good communists', but dealing with an urban leader who commanded authority in Kabul was easier for Gandhi than dealing with the Khalqis.[120]

Still, Gandhi was in for a surprise on 19 July 1980, the inaugural day of the 1980 Summer Olympics being held in Moscow (boycotted by the West). In the wake of the Soviet Union's Olympics distraction, Afghan interior minister Gulabzoi and deputy PM Sarwari, allegedly, planned a coup against Karmal. In a top-secret operation, which, ironically was reported in the media, they planned to assassinate Karmal and pass it as a plane crash (similar to Zia's mysterious death in 1988) with help from Khalqi sympathisers at the Kabul airport and in the national Ariana Airlines.[121] Rifts within the PDPA were becoming acute. On 25 June 1980 Sarwari, allegedly wounded in a shooting inside the Ministry of Foreign Affairs building, had flown to Moscow ostensibly for medical treatment.[122] On his return, allegedly, the above-mentioned events unfolded. As a step towards executing the plan, the president of Ariana Airlines (a Parcham supporter) was put out of play (in order to reduce any chances of Karmal escaping Kabul?). A few days before the Olympic games, the man went missing. Well versed with the ways of the Kabul durbar, it did not take Karmal long to sense foul play. He ordered the arrest of twelve Kabul airport employees on 21 July 1980, marginalised Gulabzoi (but did not sack him given his weight within the PDPA), dispatched Sarwari to Mongolia as ambassador, and appointed his loyalist Sultan Ali Keshtmand as chairman of the Council of Ministers and Minister of Planning.[123]

Having vowed not to interfere in domestic Afghan politics and to accept whoever was de facto in power, Gandhi did not make a fuss about the issue. However, Indian ambassador Jaskaran Teja's days in Kabul became numbered. Though it remains unclear how exactly Teja handled this crisis, the MEA was not impressed by his performance. New Delhi had been getting conflicting information about events in Kabul from its embassy for the previous six months. Senior diplomats, including I. K. Gujral, who would later become PM, were finding it hard to chart a coherent policy in light of these differences. Soon after Amin's coup against Taraki in 1979, for example, Teja's political counselor opened a parallel line with the MEA in New Delhi and began contradicting Teja's assessments on Amin's longevity. Teja was confident that Amin was there to stay and had a friendly attitude towards India, whereas his counselor remained wary of Amin's crackdown.[124] According to the counselor, Amin was making enemies at a faster rate than building allies. This was unsustainable. The Soviet invasion proved the counselor right, much to Teja's embarrassment.

In December 1981, J. N. Dixit, Gandhi's confidante (who would become foreign secretary in the early 1990s and then national security advisor in 2005), was appointed ambassador to Kabul. Dixit unleashed a charm offensive with Karmal and Tabeev. An antithesis of Teja, Dixit gave the final push that operationalised India's pro-Parcham tilt. Dixit's close rapport with Babrak Karmal and Fikryat Tabeev made the Khalq doubtful of India's neutrality. In their meetings with Dixit, Khalqi leaders would be polite but non-committal towards India. They would seek to maintain friendly ties with New Delhi, but not expand them. Striking a balance between different political factions in

Kabul became an enduring theme in India's Afghanistan policy debates since the 1980s. The rise of Hamid Karzai in the wake of US-led NATO intervention in 2001, for instance, created a similar dilemma for India, i.e. whether to throw its weight behind Karzai or to support the increasingly marginal (and disunited) politicians from the erstwhile anti-Taliban United Front?

Rajiv-Najib affair

The second case underlining India's pro-Parcham tilt was Rajiv Gandhi's staunch support for Najibullah against all odds in the late 1980s. The Rajiv-Najibullah relationship evolved on political and personal levels, both of which reinforced each other. The first causal driver pushing Najibullah's case in New Delhi was his excellent relationship with Dixit between 1982 and 1985. Having met most potential candidates who were in line to replace Karmal, Dixit favoured Najibullah the most, despite knowing he represented the radical wing of Parcham that criticised Karmal's 'soft' approach toward Gulabzoi after the July 1980 incident.[125] Given his closeness with both Indira and Rajiv, Dixit's words carried weight. Dixit had convinced the Indian leadership of Najibullah's political prowess in general and pro-India attitude in particular as early as 1983, almost at the same time Moscow started debating Karmal's potential successor. Najibullah's key Khalqi competitor in the mid-1980s was none other than Sarwari. Curiously, both were former spy chiefs, both were proactive and ruthless, and both had links with (rival) Soviet intelligence agencies. Sarwari had the *Glavnoye razvedyvatel'noye upravleniye* (GRU) or the Main Intelligence Directorate's backing, whereas Najibullah had the KGB's (and resultantly Indian R&AW's) support.[126]

The GRU's argument against Najibullah was that his apparent Pasthun nationalism would (and did) become a hindrance to the Soviet withdrawal. They feared that Najibullah would not be able to undertake a genuine reconciliation with the Mujahideen. Sarwari, a Tajik from Ghazni, on the other hand, a GRU report argued, had support of many PDPA leaders, could be a moderating force, and also reconcile both domestic ethnic groups and the Mujahideen.[127] The GRU was correct about Najibullah's anti-Pakistan and pro-Pashtunistan tendencies but its assessment of Sarwari as moderate was mythical at best. Having persecuted hundreds of dissidents, Sarwari was anything but moderate. His unique selling point for some in the GRU was his contacts with the Mujahideen (especially Hekmatyar) and by corollary, Pakistan. The KGB, however, had more influence in the CPSU politburo than the GRU on Afghanistan. It was able to convince the CPSU that Najibullah, known as the 'Ox' for his powerful build, was best suited to lead the reconciliation process on terms that would secure Soviet interests in the country even after the withdrawal, and who would remain in power for a considerable time with the requisite support. Both Gorbachev and Rajiv liked the sound of it.[128]

By the late 1980s, however, more than India's dependence on Moscow, the second causal driver of Rajiv's political closeness with Najibullah was the deterioration of both India and Afghanistan's relations with Pakistan. Zia had replicated the 'Afghan model' of subversion in both Indian-administered Kashmir and Punjab. With his conciliatory diplomacy with Reagan and Gorbachev failing miserably, Rajiv's regional policy took an unduly muscular turn in light of these developments. India's chief of army staff General K. Sundarji, with support from the Minister of State for Defence, Arun Singh, launched a mock war drill called Operation Brasstacks in the desert planes of Rajasthan, in November 1986, and mobilised close to 150,000 soldiers to 'test' India's military effectiveness.[129] The move elicited a full military mobilisation by Pakistan in the Punjab sector. Though some Indian officials argue that Rajiv was unaware of the well-planned operation till January 1986, by November the same year he had a good idea that Operation Brasstacks was underway.[130] In January 1986, for instance, on his way to the airport to receive Najibullah—an odd thing for a serving PM to do given Najibullah was months away from becoming president—Rajiv allegedly asked his Minister of State (MoS) for External Affairs, Natwar Singh, whether India 'was on its way to war with Pakistan'?[131] Natwar Singh had no clue, and was appalled by MoS Defence Arun Singh's audacity to go behind the PM's back to initiate the operation. Occurring in context of Pakistan's audacious advance in Afghanistan, covert war with India, a successful nuclear weapons programme, and India's military dash at the Siachen glacier in April 1984, Brasstacks brought India and Pakistan on the verge of war. The worst, however, was still to come. In July 1987, marking the death of Rajiv's conciliatory approach in the region, the Indian army was ordered into Sri Lanka.[132]

Close links with Najibullah offered Rajiv practical measures to undercut Pakistan's growing influence and adventurism. Rajiv and Najibullah's increasingly staunch anti-Pakistan partisanship, and Moscow's shaky support to Kabul in the wake of its impending withdrawal made them partners out of necessity more than choice. The R&AW received KhAD's active support in keeping an eye on Khalistani and Kashmiri militants being trained by the ISI in the tribal areas of Pakistan. KhAD had excellent contacts among Pashtun communities in Pakistan-administered Kashmir who, among other issues, supplied intelligence on anti-India outfits operating from that region. Close collaboration with KhAD also allowed India to stir turbulence in Balochistan and ramp up covert support to the Pashtuns in Pakistan.[133] Even the IB (without informing R&AW) had infiltrated secret agents in ISI-sponsored training camp for Hizb-e-Islami fighters located near the Spin Khwar lake in NWFP in early 1980s, in order to track India-centric militants.[134] The KGB, for its part, encouraged covert collaboration between New Delhi and Kabul, and even helped in its growth.[135] The depth of R&AW's links with the KhAD became increasingly public when in April 1988 an alert security guard at the Palam Airport in Delhi saw some stray bullets fall from a crate when the cargo of Indian Airlines flight IC-452 from Kabul to New Delhi was being unloaded. An x-ray examination revealed a full cache of weapons including rocket launchers of the type that the Mujahideen were using in Afghanistan.

Curiously, before the head of security at the airport could check the contents in detail an R&AW operative whisked all crates away saying that they were government property. Within a month, the rocket launchers were found with Khalistani militants near Kalanur in the Gurdaspur district of Punjab. The news sent a shock wave across the country and rocked the parliament.[136] Was this an R&AW conspiracy or had the ISI infiltrated the Indian system so deeply that it could use an Indian passenger airliner to send weapons to arm Khalistani militants? General (Retd) Jagjit Singh Aurora of the 1971 India-Pakistan war fame, now a Rajya Sabha MP from Punjab, led the charge against Rajiv and the R&AW's mysterious activities, and successfully mobilised a wide array of opposition parties including the Janata Party and the BJP to push the government to come clean on its failures in Punjab. If the Afghan and Indian intelligence agencies were indeed collaborating to undertake such operations, it would undermine India's credibility on Punjab and Pakistan's involvement in the same.

The mystery of India's covert involvement in Afghanistan reached a new level when media reports started pouring in of Indian pilots fighting in the 1989 Battle of Jalalabad (between Najibullah's forces and the Mujahideen).[137] The reports raised questions in the parliament, which otherwise had no supervision over India's intelligence agencies.[138] Though the government denied (and still continues to deny) such allegations, a former R&AW officer deeply involved in Afghan affairs, stated that 'Jalalabad was an Indian city' in 1989 and, unlike in 2014, Kabul was somewhat dependent on Indian support to fight its battles.[139] This does not mean (nor does this intelligence officer confirm it as such) that Indian pilots were fighting in Jalalabad, or even were actively involved in supporting the Afghan air force, but it does underline India's intimate security relationship with Afghanistan at that time. By the late 1980s, however, despite the signing of the Geneva Accord and Indian and Soviet support, Najibullah's position became so tenuous that many in India, including Dixit, began to wonder whether he had become a liability.

India kept reiterating the strict implementation of the accord to little effect.[140] Rajiv himself was desperate to keep the situation under control. His 'bizarre' (and failed) invitation to Zia in February 1988 via the then foreign secretary K. P. S. Menon, two months before the accord to discuss the situation in Afghanistan, was one of the many signs that Rajiv was clutching at straws.[141] In May 1988 he dispatched Principal Secretary Gopi Arora to invite Najibullah to India.[142] It was a daring act in light of Najibullah's political fragility and the growing criticism of Rajiv's 'closeness' with Kabul, especially in the context of the IC-452 incident, and only served to widen India and Pakistan's rift over Afghanistan.[143] There were many indicators, as the Indian media reported, that the Najibullah government may be swept away in the coming months, or Najibullah's 'rivals in the PDPA may replace him with someone more acceptable to the leaders of at least some Mujahideen groups, or, indeed that even the Soviets may drop him as being inconvenient'.[144] Even India's ambassador to Kabul, I. P. Khosla, who had taken over the mantle from Dixit in 1985 (and remained there till 1989), thought that Rajiv was not being strategic. Making his reservations clear to the MEA, Khosla asked:

> Why we were [sic] inviting Najib, when his government was clearly not going to last. I suggested [to the MEA] that in the long run it might be better to cultivate relations with the other groups instead of boosting him [Najibullah]. But it was probably too late to get into strategic mode after half a century of something else.[145]

By early 1989, most Western countries, fearing violence in Kabul, had reduced their embassy staff in Kabul, and were recommending the same to New Delhi. Khosla, who had been pressing New Delhi to reconsider its policy towards Najibullah, had also sent his family back to New Delhi from Kabul.[146] In this context, in February 1989, Rajiv ordered the then chief of R&AW, Anand Kumar Verma, to secretly visit Kabul and form an assessment of Najibullah's political longevity. Accompanied by fellow intelligence officer Vappala Balachandran, Verma met with a host of contacts in Afghanistan during his two-three day visit and returned upbeat. He pressed Rajiv to continue aligning with Najibullah. In Verma's assessment, granted continuous Soviet financial and military support, Najibullah could survive 'indefinitely' if only he withstood the Mujahideen onslaught for the next six months.[147] The fact that Soviet capacities were dwindling (even though the Soviet Union's disintegration was not expected at this stage), and so did Najibullah's appeal among the people of Afghanistan (a strategic aspect when assessing any leader's political longevity), went underappreciated. While Verma's assessment proved correct in the short term as Najibullah lasted in power for three more years, Khosla's assessment stood vindicated in the longer term.

Facing policy inertia, and despite the many warning bells, instead of engaging with the Mujahideen, India had decided to continue its relationship with Najibullah. After Khosla, in 1990, India dispatched senior diplomat Hamid Ansari, who later became vice president of India in 2007, as ambassador to Kabul. But due to some disciplinary problems with his number two, Ansari was recalled to New Delhi. In his place, the diplomatic mantle went to Vijay K. Nambiar in October 1990. A 1968-batch foreign service officer (who spoke fluent mandarin), Nambiar had played a critical role in Rajiv Gandhi's momentous visit to Beijing in 1988 (and would later become deputy national security advisor in 2005). India's Afghanistan policy at this juncture was being managed by the foreign secretary, but was being crafted in detail by the relevant joint secretary and the ambassadors (Ronen Sen, a senior diplomat who represented India in Washington from 2004 to 2009, was the joint secretary on the MEA's Pakistan-Afghanistan-Iran desk at that time). PM V. P. Singh, embroiled in domestic political and economic problems, held a perfunctory meeting with Nambiar before dispatching him to Kabul without a clear political direction. In these circumstances, after consulting with Ronen Sen, Nambiar says, his job was to maintain whatever equities that India could have held in a rather complicated situation of the post-Soviet withdrawal in Afghanistan, where 'we [India] did have a fair amount of vested interest in keeping and advancing the support to the Najib regime ... [this was so because] we wanted to have influence on the Kabul people to the extent that we could'.[148] It was classic foreign policy conservatism, compounded by domestic political turmoil and Rajiv's overarching influence (despite being out of power) on the MEA's regional political outlook in general and attitude towards Najibullah in particular. The question that if India could deal with Najibullah, who had a questionable human rights record and was a political hardliner (or was perceived to be one), then why could it not deal with the Mujahideen, was often asked. Worried that opening a channel with the Mujahideen might cost India its carefully calibrated and proven relationship with Najibullah, New Delhi had never seriously mulled a post-Najibullah scenario in Kabul. Treasuring foreign policy continuity, even if such a continuum was becoming politically costly and strategically unsound, New Delhi was averse to come across as swapping sides, and giving up on friends (in this case even a personal friendship between Najibullah and Rajiv) in a war-ridden Afghanistan.

But Najibullah himself was getting increasingly paranoid of a Khalqi coup. Despite having elevated senior Khalqi leaders such as Tanai to the chief of army staff, he only became more worried about an impending coup by late 1989 and the early 1990s. At some point the situation was so difficult that Najibullah invited Tanai for a dinner at his house and made Tanai reassure his wife that the Khalq was not planning a coup.[149] Rajiv, on his part, also began fretting about the situation by 1989 when he confidentially, but impotently, expressed his rage to Mongolian president Jambyn Batmönkh and told him that India would launch a joint war on Pakistan with Afghanistan, if Rawalpindi persisted in toppling Najibullah.[150] The misadventure in Sri Lanka, increasing separatist violence in Punjab and Kashmir, and the infamous Bofors corruption scandal, cost Rajiv his premiership in the 1989 national elections. In March 1990, with Rajiv out of the picture and Moscow in its own turmoil, Tanai and Sarwari indeed attempted a coup that failed (see prologue). Sarwari's arrest in 1990, despite Rajiv being out of power, was a tipping point that reflected New Delhi and Kabul's desperation in the face of Soviet disintegration. On 15 February 1989, the last Soviet soldier returned to Russia. In April 1992, when the Mujahideen finally did oust Najibullah, Rajiv was not alive to declare a war. His successor, P. V. Narasimha Rao, had learnt how not to repeat the same mistakes that Rajiv had made.

Conclusion

Of the three causal drivers of India's Afghanistan policy—striking a balance between Afghanistan and Pakistan, evolving international political environment, and the changing nature of Afghan domestic politics—the second became paramount in the 1980s. India's notion of a non-aligned foreign policy became void as relations with the Soviet Union were given primacy during the 1980s. As a frustrated Congress (I) MP, P. N. Sukul, stated in a parliamentary debate, despite leading the non-aligned movement, India could not be equidistant from both the US and the USSR. 'How can we have equidistance? We have our own perceptions, which differ from country to country. There are countries that have helped us, who help us. In spite of this policy of non-alignment, how can we keep ourselves equidistant from the friends and foes, both? That is why, on the basis of our own experience, we have developed our friendship with certain nations, certain countries who do not want to destabilise us, who do not create problems for us but rather help and have helped us' he said.[151] The problem in Afghanistan, however, was different. India had ended up on the losing side.

In February 1989, the Peshawar-based Islamic Unity of the Afghan Mujahideen was recognised as Afghanistan's government-in-exile by Pakistan and Saudi Arabia. India maintained that it had no relations with this interim government. But a new international consensus was emerging under the leadership of the US that legitimised the Mujahideen.[152] Opposing Washington's support to the Mujahideen, in May 1990, EAM I. K. Gujral categorically informed Indian parliamentarians that 'India and USA have different views regarding political settlement of Afghanistan'.[153] Such a stance came under severe strain as Najibullah's grip on Kabul eroded further (as reflected in the March 1990 coup attempt by Tanai). Regardless of active diplomacy with the US and the USSR and the exploration of different diplomatic and coercive options vis-à-vis Pakistan, India was unable to carve out a strategically sound policy towards Afghanistan as the Soviet Union withdrew its forces in 1989. According to some scholars, India's continuing support to Najibullah even after 1989 was a natural policy because he was vehemently anti-Pakistan.[154] As this chapter shows, India's obsession with Najibullah was not as much about effective strategy formation as much it was about clinging to a failing but friendly regime with the false hope that things would change for the better. What is interesting, however, is the persistence of the idea of Najibullah—known as the 'Najibullah Model'—in New Delhi's power circles as recently as 2013 (at least), as the US-led NATO troops began withdrawing from Afghanistan. This essentially meant developing a similar relationship with Karzai (or any other Afghan leader in Kabul) after the US withdrawal, as India had done with Najibullah. That the model failed without external financial support, and just about existed with such support, seemed lost on Indian policymakers.

In contrast to the widely believed notion of India's proxy war with Pakistan in Afghanistan, the 1980s reflect that India's Afghanistan policy was not necessarily, entirely, or consistently anti-Pakistan in its political outlook. Both Indira and Rajiv Gandhi wanted to work together with Pakistan. However, the contradictory systemic pressures generated by the Soviet invasion (that pushed India into adopting an anti-Pakistan posture), and Pakistan's rigid response to India's overtures, diminished the possibility of a rapprochement on the Afghan question. Moreover, the argument that India and Afghanistan collaborated overtly and covertly against Pakistan's interests during the 1980s, despite its credibility, cannot be stretched (as it often is) to say that India's Afghanistan policy is all about undermining Pakistan. Gandhi's lukewarm response to the 1982 Soviet proposal of wresting the rest of Kashmir back was one of the many instances when India refused to undermine Pakistan's security, sovereignty, and territorial integrity. New Delhi's approach towards Afghanistan, in fact, was nuanced in its motivation and careful in its intent throughout the 1980s, and as the following chapters show, remained as such over the decades. Pakistan's hardline stance in Afghanistan, much like the 1980s, also remained the same in the following decades.

Finally, the Soviet withdrawal shifted the framework in which Afghanistan was debated in India. Instead of debating on the lines of Cold War alignments or non-alignment, India's Afghanistan policy debate became increasingly focused on Pakistan and gave birth to the partisans and the conciliators. Should India engage with pro-Pakistan Mujahideen factions in Afghanistan? Should it limit contact only to those factions that are wary of, or openly at odds with, Pakistan? Should it maintain a presence in Afghanistan given the turbulence that country was witnessing or should it move out lock, stock, and barrel? These are question that were actively debated in the Indian parliament, its ministries, and in the popular media in late 1980s and early 1990s. As the next chapter shows, the sobering reality of Najibullah's fall made even anti-Pakistan partisans in India reconsider their approach towards Afghanistan. What India also realised in the wake of Najibullah's fall, was the worth of the Kabuliwallah connection and the Afghan people's fondness for India. Contrary to what many in New Delhi had expected, there were only few Afghans who wanted to have absolutely no relations with India. As an Afghan exile explained to an R&AW officer in Geneva in 1986, 'we are unhappy with the GoI for not supporting the Afghan people and for supporting the Soviet troops. But that has not lessened our admiration and affection for Indians, who were close to us and who had helped us before the Soviet invasion and occupation'.[155] In 1992, India would recognise the Mujahideen government after having stood against them since the 1970s, and would be embraced by (some) Mujahideen in return, given the sheer weight of goodwill for India among Afghans.

PART II

DEBATING CONTAINMENT

4

THE TALIBAN DILEMMA

PARTISANS VERSUS CONCILIATORS

'For most Americans, the Soviet withdrawal is the victory. For our South Asian friends, it is only the first act in a much larger drama'.

Arnold L. Raphel, US Ambassador to Pakistan (1987–88)[1]

'Najib was an albatross around our necks, but we could not abandon him'.

Phillip Corwin, UN Information Officer in Kabul in April 1992[2]

'It seems the Indian Government has been formulating its Afghan policy without taking cognisance of the ground situation in Afghanistan. India needs to know a lot more about Afghanistan's present realities in order to be able to formulate a more realistic Afghan policy'.

Wakil Ahmed Muttawakil, member of the central shura of the Taliban, June 1996[3]

A failed escape

Najibullah was a lonely man on the morning of 17 April 1992. His one chance to escape from Kabul, at around 3 AM, had failed miserably.[4] Looking forward to joining his wife and daughters, who had left two weeks before for New Delhi,[5] he had planned a secret flight to India along with Benon Sevan, head of the UN's humanitarian aid division to Afghanistan. To prevent India-Pakistan bilateral relations from worsening further over Najibullah, Sevan had already taken Pakistani PM Nawaz Sharif into confidence before requesting India to give the embattled Afghan president political asylum.[6] It had taken India's PM Narasimha Rao less than an hour to communicate that India would host Najibullah as state guest in New Delhi. On that fateful morning, however, driving with his armed bodyguard and a team of UN officers, Najibullah's convoy was refused entry into the Kabul airport. The password he used throughout the journey from home to the airport did not work at the penultimate checkpoint.[7] The airport was under the control of Abdul Rashid Dostum, an Afghan of Uzbek heritage, who led a local militia against the Mujahideen in the northern province of Jowzjan, and had been receiving political, financial, and military patronage from Najibullah. In a total 'wild card', as the then Indian ambassador to Kabul Vijay K. Nambiar terms it, Dostum turned hostile towards his patron, and shutdown the airport for the next 24 hours.[8]

On the airport's runway stood a plane, and in the plane awaited Sevan. Dostum's men had decided not to storm the plane, and Sevan had decided not to disembark. After a furious exchange of abuses with and impotent threats to Dostum's men, Najibullah turned his convoy around. But he would not return home. He feared that the people who sabotaged his escape would not let him live. His minister of state security, General Ghulam Faruq Yaqubi, was found dead in his house. While some allege that he committed suicide, Nambiar, who was in touch with Najibullah and his UN handlers, does not rule out assassination.[9] Either way, Najibullah was escorted to the UN compound instead of the presidential palace. Not just Dostum, most of his party men had also abandoned Najibullah. Foreign Minister Abdul Wakil and army chief General Mohammad Nabi Azimi, keen on their own political and physical survival, wanted to offer Najibullah as a prisoner to the advancing Mujahideen forces.[10] They had rushed to the airport on getting news of Najibullah's escape attempt, and asked Sevan to disembark the plane to avoid further embarrassment and potential violence (they wanted Sevan alive and safe given his UN connection). Wakil, accompanied by many other members of the Watan party, castigated Sevan for trying to get Najibullah out of Afghanistan secretly. In his next step, an angry Wakil sent out a national broadcast via Radio Kabul stating that 'Najibullah tried to escape but had been stopped by the armed forces ... He must be held to answer certain questions to the Afghan people. The government had no intention of killing him. The soldiers at the checkpoint could have killed him, but did not'.[11] In a matter of hours, Najibullah had become a 'hated dictator' for Wakil, and Massoud, who was leading the Mujahideen into Kabul, had become his 'esteemed brother'.[12]

Sevan had wanted to save Najibullah from exactly such a fate. The plan was worked out with the Indian leadership's political approval. At about 3.20 AM Najibullah's UN handlers informed Nambiar about Dostum's sudden intransigence, and at 4.35 AM Nambiar promptly reported to the UN compound. He was the first ambassador to meet with Najibullah that morning. Such were the UN and Indian expectations (or miscalculation in hindsight) that they had not thought of a 'plan B', in case the exfiltration plan failed.[13] Still, on being pressed by the UN officers, Nambiar agreed to look into giving Najibullah asylum at the Indian embassy complex on the condition that the UN would make an official request for the same. Using a 'ham radio' that was available to him at the time (only the UN had an INMARSAT phone), Nambiar contacted New Delhi to report the developments and sought official clearance for hosting Najibullah in his residential compound. However, protecting Najibullah and his family in Delhi was one thing, but giving him protection in the Indian embassy compound in Kabul, quite another. At 5.15 AM, India refused to grant Najibullah asylum in its embassy. Nambiar argues that 'he [Najibullah] was far safer in the UN compound ... [by sheltering him in the] Indian mission, we would have suddenly walked into all kinds of subcontinental rivalries, and problems would have then visited on us ... and there was no way in which we could reasonably expect security and safety for Najib in the Indian compound'.[14] New Delhi was worried about potential reprisals against the Indian community in Kabul if people found out that Najibullah was hiding in its embassy. There were few hundred Indian citizens including embassy staff in Afghanistan at that point.[15] In a conversation with Najibullah later that morning Nambiar communicated India's concerns about hosting him in the embassy. Najibullah allegedly understood Indian concerns, and, as per Nambiar, 'was quite adamant that this [his safety] was the responsibility of the United Nations'.[16]

J. N. Dixit, who was India's foreign secretary (1991–94), and who championed Najibullah in early 1980s, was concerned that offering him protection in the embassy would further complicate the situation politically. India may never be able to build strong relations with the Mujahideen on a fresh note. Dixit could not voice this dilemma openly.[17] There were many in India who wanted to give Najibullah asylum on the grounds that he was just 44 years old with political constituencies among Pashtun communities, and argued that giving up on him would imply capitulating to the Mujahideen. Najibullah himself had ealier confided to Nambiar that he might be able to influence Afghan politics, however limitedly, from outside Afghanistan more than from the inside, in face of the Soviet disintegration.[18] The remaining secular and nationalist elements of the *Hizb-e-Watan*, it was calculated, would remain in Afghanistan and be represented in a coalition government that the UN was trying to cobble together. However, there were others in India who argued that giving Najibullah asylum would further antagonise the Mujahideen leadership, something that India should avoid. The assumption was that once the anger settled, the Mujahideen would not throw away a beneficial relationship with India.

Caught in an awkward situation, India remained non-committal till the UN Secretary General Boutros Boutros-Ghali paid an unscheduled visit to New Delhi on 22 April 1992. Boutros-Ghali's sole aim was to push Rao into taking initiative and exfiltrating Najibullah from Kabul (despite the UN's abortive attempt) and give him asylum in India. After six days of deliberation on Boutros-Ghali's request, which included detailed talks about possible options between Najibullah and Nambiar, home minister S. B. Chavan publicly announced that India would be willing to shelter Najibullah 'if he so desires'.[19] Playing upon a situation where Najibullah's 'desire' was the last element that would have helped his cause either politically or personally, the statement reeked of political caution.

Adding insult to injury, on 4 May 1992, when Indian parliamentarians asked about India's talks with Boutros-Ghali and its decision to host Najibullah, minister-of-state for external affairs, Eduardo Faleiro, informed that despite the general feelers for asylum from Najibullah, 'the government are not aware of any decision taken by the United Nations in this regard, and the question [of Najibullah] is hypothetical as no such request has so far been received'.[20] When pushed as to what exactly would the government's stand be if such a formal request were to come, Rao and Faleiro balked. 'As and when we get some specific request first we will try to pin down, concretise this general past request into some specific situation and request through the United Nations office, that is where he [Najibullah] is, at the moment', said Faleiro.[21] Rao added that despite being in 'almost hourly touch' with the situation in Afghanistan he 'would not venture to make any statement'.[22] In the light of changed circumstances, India had calculated that giving asylum to Najibullah might turn out to be prohibitively costly in political terms. If Najibullah would have escaped successfully, then India could have offered it as a fait accompli to the Mujahideen. Not anymore.

India refused to undertake a follow-up covert operation, by air or otherwise, to exfiltrate Najibullah from Kabul. With the Mujahideen having formed an internationally recognised though practically dysfunctional government, undertaking such an operation would amount to undermining Afghan sovereignty. Boutros-Ghali was informed that India was prepared to send a plane to Kabul only if the UN officially asked for it, and only after the UN reached a political agreement with Pakistan and the Mujahideen on the issue. But, as was being encouraged by the UN, India would not 'spirit out' Najibullah surreptitiously.[23] 'We had discussions of various possibilities with Najib [who] himself knew that he couldn't push India to take any kind of quasi-military action like this. It was not possible unless it was already discussed and negotiated [with the Mujahideen and Pakistan]', says Nambiar.[24] And at that time, India knew that negotiations with the Mujahideen would not work out, especially after the failed escape attempt. Either way, with a conservative Rao as PM of a minority government, and India's ongoing economic woes, such a covert operation was not a feasible option. As Nambiar put it, 'we didn't want to do something flamboyant and then get caught with our pants down'.[25] After years of partisanship towards the Mujahideen, in the wake of Najibullah's unceremonious ouster, the logic of conciliation began resonating in India's corridors of power.

Apart from keeping its promise of supporting Najibullah's family in Delhi, India did nothing more. Adjusting to the harsh realities of the end of the Cold War era, what Rao, Dixit, and Faleiro hoped for instead was the evolution of a definable political structure in Kabul, i.e. the Mujahideen government, with which India could make contact and move forward in its bilateral relationship.[26] The ignominious end to the Najibullah affair underlined the limits of influence and capacity of both India and the UN in shaping events on the ground. The end of Soviet influence in Afghanistan, and India's economic strains in the early 1990s severely limited New Delhi's policy options in Kabul. As an R&AW officer recollected years later, 'Dixit and gang had the guilt of not saving Najibullah. We sent the plane [in which Sevan was waiting for Najibullah, but which was not actually an Indian plane] to Kabul thinking that the Mujahideen would let him go. We told the world that we are taking Najib out, but had no understanding with Dostum. We should not have waited that long to take him out.'[27] Nambiar concurs that Najibullah could have left Kabul a little earlier, but he blames the UN, especially Sevan, for political and operational overreach:

> Let's not forget that this [exfiltrating Najibullah] is really something that has to be done under national ownership. If you think you can carry such stuff and move around, then you must have the physical capacity to do it. You must have boots on

> the ground. That's why even Najibullah had said, "we want boots on the ground", UN boots on the ground. Obviously they couldn't do that. It takes time to do that. The fact is, I don't think that Benon [Sevan] thought that it would come to this. He didn't expect that anybody, certainly from inside the country, would stop Najibullah from going to the airport.[28]

Dostum, many years later, told an Indian intelligence officer that had New Delhi paid adequate bribes, Najibullah might have been a free man.[29] Even if one agrees that the Indian leadership felt guilty for giving up on Najibullah, Dostum's argument that India had the capacity to bribe Dostum's men into letting Najibullah escape in those circumstances, fails to convince. Neither did India have the required capacities, nor Dostum (who had cut a deal with Massoud) the political will to let Najibullah go. 'That criminal Najibullah who we trusted, he was selling us for his own interest', Dostum had bellowed in May 1992 when Indian journalists sought clarification of his stance.[30] Najibullah had made the mistake of first creating an independent militia led by Dostum, and then trying controlling it by cutting supplies to keep the strength of his militia at a maximum of 10,000 men—both out of necessity as funds from Moscow were drying up, but also out of want, in order to keep Dostum's political ambitions in check. The plan boomeranged. Najibullah's ghost, much like his bête noir Sarwari, would haunt India. Indeed, in 1994 India dispatched senior diplomat, M. K. Bhadrakumar (who was director, 1989–91, and joint secretary, 1992–95, of the Pakistan, Afghanistan, and Iran desk at the MEA), to meet with Massoud in Kabul. Then-Indian foreign secretary Krishnan Srinivasan—an Oxford-educated diplomat hailing from the south Indian state of Tamil Nadu—had asked Bhadrakumar to consolidate India's relations with the authorities in Kabul, reopen India's mission there, and request Massoud to let Najibullah fly to India (though this was an ancillary issue).[31] Massoud refused, claiming that letting Najibullah go would not be agreeable to other Mujahideen leaders.

Bhadrakumar retrospectively thinks that Massoud viewed Najibullah as a potential political asset given his ethnic and political background. But it is highly possible that the Panjshiri leader wanted to ensure that Najibullah did not become New Delhi's 'trump card' in Afghanistan, and wanted to reserve that spot for himself.[32] Srinivasan concurs: 'We would have been very happy to have Najib[ullah] in Delhi ... and not that it was a consideration of ours but he would have had some political traction in Afghanistan [even afterwards], and that was why the Tajiks refused to let him go ... because they felt that if he enjoyed some residual traction and if was supported by India, he could have a political future in Afghanistan which would be to their detriment'.[33] While the real reasons why Massoud took this decision remain unknown, it is true that Najibullah's wife, Fatana, resented New Delhi's tilt towards Massoud. Nambiar says, it was a '*dharam-sankat*' (moral dilemma) for her to support India's seemingly anti-Pashtun, and in this case even anti-Najibullah, tilt toward the United Front in order to counter-balance Pakistan and the Taliban (despite the fact that the Taliban assassinated her husband).[34] She never forgave Massoud (and Dostum) for stopping Najibullah from leaving Kabul, the UN for failing in its responsibility to secure Najibullah's release, and then for New Delhi to work closely with these men.[35] These assessments, however, still don't explain why Massoud left Najibullah in the UN compound in 1996 while retreating to the safety of Panjshir under attack from the Taliban. Perhaps he genuinely believed that keeping Najibullah hostage was an article of faith and releasing him would undermine his authority among his Mujahideen associates? Either way, while some Afghan officials still thank India for hosting Najibullah's wife and daughters,[36] others complain that India did not stand up for its friend when he needed New Delhi's support the most.[37] India's pro-Najibullah Afghanistan policy, as reflected in those highly tense but crystal clear moments, ended in failure. New Delhi's inability to protect Najibullah, furthermore, earned it the label of being a reluctant and opportunistic neighbour who abandoned its sole ally in Kabul for new partnerships.

'Plane-load of Mujahideen'

Most factors that drove India into a tight embrace with Najibullah—i.e. dependency on Moscow, failed attempts to curb differences with Islamabad, near total disconnect with Washington (on the Afghan question) and the Mujahideen, and Najibullah's anti-Pakistan predilections—had vanished by the end of April 1992. The end of the Cold War, and collapse of the Soviet Union had put India on survival mode. Domestically, the failure of the socialist economic model steered India into its worst debt crisis ever. Excessive borrowings had pushed the government's internal debt from 35 per cent of GDP in 1980–81 to 53 per cent of GDP by the end of 1990–91.[38] With its foreign exchange reserves drying up, India could hardly finance three weeks worth of imports. Insurgencies were raging in Kashmir, Assam, and Punjab, and a failed military venture in Sri Lanka stared India in its face. It had not only cost the exchequer a lot of money but even Rajiv Gandhi's life. Internationally, alignment with the Soviet Union caught New Delhi on the wrong foot strategically. If in 1980 Indira Gandhi counted on Soviet economic and military support to rescue the Indian economy from collapsing under the weight of bulging oil prices and a severe drought, there was no such support forthcoming in 1991. In contrast, Pakistan had played a key role in fighting the Soviets in Afghanistan with US support and despite its heavy dependence on foreign aid; it had a real rate of growth of 5–6 per cent in 1991.[39] Having brokered the Peshawar Accord on 24 April 1992 that installed the Mujahideen government, Pakistan deeply influenced politics in Kabul while India was bundled up with a territorially and economically broken Russia and a revisionist Iran.

These harsh economic and political realities of 1991 set the stage for change. Narasimha Rao, senior Congress leader and former EAM, led the transition. A pragmatist, Rao realised the need for an overhaul in both India's domestic economic structures and foreign policy approach. As detailed in a recent political biography, Rao brought these changes despite running a minority government that enjoyed little confidence from within and outside the Congress party.[40] After initiating the New Economic Policy that shelved the socialist model and liberalised the economy, Rao went ahead and changed the template of Indian foreign policy. On Afghanistan, in particular, India took another u-turn. Willing to move beyond the confines of anti-Pakistan partisanship despite strained India-Pakistan relations, Rao put India's Afghanistan policy on a firmly conciliatory track in 1992.[41] Enunciated in what is known as the Rao Doctrine, India was to (a) 'deal with all Mujahideen groups without fear or favour and contact should be established with anyone and everyone willing to meet us despite the militancy of their Islamism'; (b) India should 'deal with whosoever was in power in Kabul and focus would be on cultivating a friendly government that was sensitive to India's vital interests and core concerns (sic)'; (c) India should 'deal strictly with the government in Kabul, no matter its proximity with Pakistan or its security agencies'; (d) India 'would neither arm any Afghan group nor ostracise any group—not even the Wahhabi group of Ittehad headed by Rasul Sayyaf'; and (e) India will 'focus on P-2-P [people-to-people] relations', build goodwill among all Afghans and 'meaningfully contribute towards Afghanistan's economic welfare,' within its limited scope.[42] And finally, unlike other countries that had shut their Kabul embassies in 1989, India was to retain its diplomatic mission as long as possible despite the anarchy.[43] Unlike what is seen today, India and Pakistan, despite the violence in Kashmir, discussed the Afghan situation regularly throughout this phase.

On 30 April 1992, two weeks after Najibullah's fall, India officially recognised the Mujahideen government. The very next day, Nambiar, on Rao's orders, met with the acting Afghan president Sibghatullah Mojadeddi (April–June 1992) and opened contact with all senior Mujahideen leaders and conveyed to them India's abiding interest in sustaining and nurturing friendship and cooperation with Afghanistan.[44] Soon after, on 15 May 1992, the government announced humanitarian relief and medical supplies worth Rs 160 lakhs and airlifted them to Kabul in July 1992. Additionally, 44,000 tonnes of wheat was also dispatched to Afghanistan on a grant basis. With air transit not being an option (for so much wheat), the shipment was sent to Bombay, from where it went to Orissa, and then all the way up to Russia. It was supposed to come down to Mazar-e-Sharif and then Kabul, but by the time it reached the troubled Soviet Central Asian republics, the whole shipment was looted. 'It was the saga of the most incredible measure', recalls Nambiar, who was responsible for tracking the progress of the shipment.[45]

On 30 August 1992, Burhanuddin Rabbani, the new president of Afghanistan, sought a re-fuelling stopover in New Delhi on his way to the NAM Summit in Jakarta. While the MEA officers dealing with the issue (especially Bhadrakumar and then 'acting' foreign secretary Srinivasan) many in New Delhi's power corridors were against the idea of hosting 'Wahhabis' in Delhi as state guests.[46] Rao, however, accepted the request. India hosted Rabbani and a 'plane-load of Mujahideen' commanders including, as Bhadrakumar notes, 'some frightening names vowed to eternal enmity toward India'.[47] Srinivasan received the delegation at the Palam airport, and held talks with them. Srinivasan describes them as confidence-building measures to assure Rabbani that the Mujahideen in Kabul and the Indian government were comfortable working with each other.[48]

Calling it a huge step forward, Srinivasan describes Rabbani's visit that summer as a bonus for India. He says:

> It showed that the Rabbani government was inclined on having some dealings with us [India], and that they were not entirely in the pockets of the Pakistanis—which is very helpful ... It suited us very well ... maybe we didn't make more of it, but I think at that time it was a great bonus as far as we were concerned.[49]

To reciprocate the visit, in September, then diplomat and now-vice president Hamid Ansari flew in an Indian air force plane to Mazar-e-Sharif from Delhi with caches full of medical supplies (Nambiar had joined Ansari from Kabul), and met with Dostum and gave him the supplies.50 While in Kabul, Nambiar, who till now had been actively engaging with Najibullah and his officials, began building a strong rapport with Mojaddedi's deputy foreign minister, a tall Popalzai Pashtun from Kandahar, named Hamid Karzai, who would later become Afghanistan's president in 2001, and form a powerful bond with India.[51] In mid-July 1993, the foreign ministers of India and Afghanistan (Dinesh Singh and Hedayat Amin Arsala respectively) met in New York to consolidate ties further.[52]

Rise of the conciliators

The conciliators, led by Rao, determined India's Afghanistan policy output in 1992. Despite the previous Congress party government, under Rajiv, having supported Najibullah, the Congress under Rao took a radical departure from the past. Reasons for such a conciliatory policy shift were many, and not just because India was facing multiple crises. Firstly, in 1991, Najibullah had accepted to reconcile with the Mujahideen under Sevan's five-point plan, denounced the remaining Soviet forces in Afghanistan, and converted the PDPA to the *Hezb-e-Watan Party* with strong Islamic symbolism. With Najibullah changing tone and the international community supporting the change, New Delhi had little choice but to accept engagement with the Mujahideen both in principle and practice. In a déjà vu of sorts, New Delhi conceded to politically engage the Taliban in 2011 at the request of the then-president Hamid Karzai and the changing beliefs among coalition forces that such a dialogue was necessary given the ineffectuality of the military option in containing the insurgency. Through 1991–96, India delivered medical aid and food supplies to Afghanistan under the UN Assistance Mission, similar to its aid policy after 2001.[53] Notwithstanding Najibullah's evolving approach, pressure had been building within India to change its Afghanistan policy ever since Gorbachev announced his intention to withdraw Soviet troops.

As mentioned in the previous chapter, the news of Soviet withdrawal shifted India's policy debate from the 'non-alignment versus pro-Soviet' framework to survival mode. Indian parliamentarians' concerns about the safety of Indian citizens and the Hindu and Sikh minority communities across Afghanistan, was a critical factor that shifted India towards a conciliatory, or even a defensive, approach. New Delhi was essentially debating ways to exist in an Afghanistan where a dominant Pakistan was vigorously pushing India out.[54] In this light, speaking in March 1989, Subramanian Swamy, a Janata Party leader, called for urgent reformulation of India's Afghanistan policy, which 'had been one of failure'.[55] With the Soviet Union having withdrawn from Afghanistan, India needed to 'undertake initiatives so that they don't become as isolated as they have been in the recent past' argued Swamy. Saudi

Arabia and Pakistan had recognised the Mujahideen government in 1989, and it was time for India to show the Mujahideen that they were not only dependent on Pakistan, and that 'their brother nation India could be there for them too'.[56] Given his political evolution into a radical Hindu nationalist today, Swamy seems an unlikely conciliator vis-à-vis the Mujahideen (but such are the quirks of Indian politics).

Swamy's use of the term 'brother nation', however, had a strong cultural context, that being the Kabuliwallah connection. Despite New Delhi's political choices, India was adored among Afghans, including the Mujahideen. In 1991, when Bollywood superstar Amitabh Bachchan visited Afghanistan to shoot for his film *Khuda Gawah* (God is Witness), he was welcomed with open arms by Afghans from all walks of life, despite the precarious security situation.[57] The goodwill quotient among Afghans not only made it easy for the conciliators to pursue a friendly relationship with the Mujahideen, but also made it senseless to not have such relations. When some MPs objected to Swamy's conciliatory advocacy, citing concerns of what Moscow would make of it, Swamy wittily replied:

> Don't worry. Moscow knows that you [India] are a loyal servant of theirs. Pakistan is fully supporting the Mujahideens and our continued hostility towards the Mujahideens would mean that ultimately Pakistan and Afghanistan would get together at the cost of our national interest. Therefore, I suggest that we immediately take diplomatic initiatives to see that India's image in Afghanistan—and particularly amongst the freedom-loving people of Afghanistan—is restored, that by taking suitable initiatives we are able to once again play a role.[58]

India's conciliatory u-turn was not just driven by its desire to survive, but also, if not equally, by its economic interests and ambitions. The Soviet Union's disintegration had created five new resource-rich states in Central Asia: Kazakhstan, Kyrgyzstan, Turkmenistan, Tajikistan, and Uzbekistan. India was in a race to access these resources. New Delhi was viewing Afghanistan not just in a South Asian context, but also in a Central Asian context. According to a senior Indian diplomat, posted in Iran in the late 1980s, 'Central Asian states were becoming independent and had a lot of natural resources that we [India] wanted to access. Our concern was that if we don't do this, the Chinese or other countries would take over. So we knew that we needed to be active'.[59] Indeed, India signed a list of MoUs with the Central Asian states in 1993 and tried to cultivate strong and friendly relations with all. The BJP, for instance, kept pushing Rao to detail how exactly he was expanding India's presence in Central Asia.[60] Apart from economic interests, India also wanted to ensure Central Asian support at the UN on Kashmir.[61]

Swamy, the big conciliator, visited Afghanistan on 31 December 1990 and 1 January 1991, in his capacity as minister of commerce with additional charge of the ministry of law and justice, and met the top brass of the Afghan government, ranging from Najibullah to Wakil. Their discussions ranged from regional politics, to trade and commerce. Unlike before, Swamy found a surprisingly high amount of interest among his parliamentary colleagues on the exact nature and extent of India-Afghanistan trade and its future prospects.[62] With the economy at its lowest ebb, India's foreign policy was being strongly dictated by economics, and Afghanistan was not to be left behind. Trade between the two countries stood at Rs. 56 crores (approx. 0.86 USD) in 1988–89 and rose to Rs. 105.18 crores (approx. 1.6 USD) in 1989–90. The figure, it was expected, was to rise to Rs. 120 crore by the end of 1991, signifying a sharp rise (even if it was little relative to other countries).[63] However, at the heart of the debate, was the issue of land routes. India wanted to export more to Afghanistan (even though this made the Afghan leadership uncomfortable for fear of developing high levels of trade deficit), and connect to the resource-rich Central Asian Republics. But how? The problem in 1992 was not related to Pakistan which was ready to allow India to use its territory for exporting goods to Afghanistan. It had to do directly with India's relations with the Mujahideen. As Swamy explained, 'it is possible to go through Pakistan, but then we have to pass through Mujahideen territory and we have not really done anything concrete'.[64] Other options included opening an air link to Kabul or to use Iran's Bandar Abbas port to connect at the Islam Qala border in West Afghanistan's Herat province. Both options were prohibitively expensive in 1991. The need to constructively engage with the Mujahideen, thus, had never been more pressing.

In this context, though the communists challenged the government's acceptance of fundamentalists in Kabul, the conciliators received multi-party support when the Rao doctrine was implemented in 1992.[65] E. Ahamed, leader of the Indian Union Muslim League (IUML) from Kerala who later became minister-of-state for external affairs (2011–14), eagerly supported Rao's initiative. Publicly averse to giving Najibullah asylum in India, Ahamed's conciliatory advocacy had little to do with his Islamic credentials. 'It is proved beyond any shadow of doubt that those who ruled Afghanistan were puppets in the hands of the Soviet Union Government ... there are writings on the wall when we deal with Afghanistan. We must strive hard to maintain the best friendship with Afghanistan', implored Ahamed.[66] Similarly, B. Vijaykumar Raju of the Telugu Desam Party from Andhra Pradesh, despite being wary of

Pakistan's dominance in Afghanistan, concurred with Rao. On 3 May 1992, the BJP National Council passed a resolution endorsing Rao's decision on Afghanistan. BJP MP Jaswant Singh, a foreign affairs expert who would become India's powerful external affairs and defence minister in 1998, argued that the government should cautiously, but surely, move ahead with its opening up to the Mujahideen.[67] Despite the rise of violent Hindu nationalism in early 1990s (the Babri Masjid Demolition took place in December 1992), Jaswant Singh was able to lobby the BJP along conciliatory lines.[68]

This was an achievement given the fact that just two days before such a statement, various members of the BJP National Council had raised apprehensions about the Mujahideen's Islamist credentials, influence of Pakistan on the latter, and how such Pakistani influence might lead to the Mujahideen supporting Kashmiri and Khalistani separatists.[69] The BJP, however, gave Afghanistan the benefit of the doubt politically as it was unclear whether it would adopt the Iranian, Iraqi, or Turkish model of dealing with religion and matters of state. Najibullah's fall, nonetheless, was greeted as good news. The BJP declared that Najibullah's fall brought an end to the suffering of Afghan people for the previous fourteen tortuous years, and in light of this news India should ensure friendly relations with whosoever came to power in Kabul.[70] Other MPs from the Bihar Congress, such as Chandresh P Thakur, also actively advocated that the government should work with other 'middle powers' to build a concrete international consensus against big-power intervention and open dialogue with all entities on the ground.[71]

The *Times of India*, which had been partly critical of India's heavy tilt towards Najibullah, had also become harsher in its criticism by 1989. One of its columns carried a blunt piece titled 'India cannot gain by ignoring the Mujahideen', in June 1989.[72] India's pro-Najibullah policy had no moral sanction in the light of the Soviet Union's brazen invasion of Afghanistan. 'The stridently aggressive attitude towards the neighbours is digested by pseudo-nationalists alone. The common man fails to understand the fire-and-brimstone diplomacy' whereas India's 'national allergy to "Muslim fundamentalism"' seemed misplaced.[73] Citing India's recognition of the Palestinian Liberation Organisation (PLO), the article sought a rectification of India's initial wrong (Gandhi's pro-Soviet U-turn in 1980) and recognition of the Mujahideen government. All indicators favoured the rise of the conciliators in 1992.

The MEA's annual reports indicate how dominant the conciliators were till 1996, when Kabul fell to the Taliban. Post-1996 India breached almost all tenets of the Rao doctrine. In 1991–92, the MEA, apart from detailing bilateral visits and Indian aid figures to Afghanistan under the Indian Technical and Economic Cooperation programme, stated that:

> India continued to extend full support to the political settlement of the Afghan crisis based on her conviction that any such settlement should recognise the legitimate interests of all concerned and be arrived at by the Afghans themselves without any external interference.[74]

Of particular importance here is India's recognition of legitimate interests of all concerned, which included the Mujahideen. Coming at a time when Najibullah was still in power and Kashmir was burning, the statement reflected a mood of broad-based political reconciliation. In 1992 and 1993, India's primary position remained the same on 'all concerned entering a dialogue', and New Delhi 'urgently' called for a 'renewed international peace initiative, possibly under UN auspices'. Throughout this period, the MEA assessed India-Pakistan relations as showing a 'downward trend', much like the situation on the ground in Kashmir.[75] Regardless of this downward trend in its relations with Pakistan, and the worsening Afghan civil war with the different Mujahideen factions fighting each other to grab power in Kabul, India remained on a conciliatory path. On 7 March 1993, Pakistan brokered what is known as the 'March accord' in its attempt to stabilise the situation and form an effective interim government in Kabul. Instead of undermining the accord, India welcomed it with the hope that it would bring peace to Afghanistan.[76] In 1994, while India was still coming to terms with the capabilities of the newly formed Taliban, the MEA reported that 'India supports a peaceful political settlement which is acceptable to all sections of the people of Afghanistan.'[77] The parallel anti-Pakistan partisan narrative of collaboration between the Afghan Mujahideen and the Kashmiri separatists, with active support from the ISI, had failed to stem the rise of the conciliators.[78]

Kashmir connection

Most detractors of dialogue with the Mujahideen in the early 1990s (and the Taliban afterwards) argued that the Mujahideen would embolden separatism, Islamist radicalism, and militancy in Kashmir. Narayanan, who was director of the intelligence bureau until December 1989, confirms, that he was 'deeply worried' about what was going on in Afghanistan and its impact on Kashmir.[79] Indeed, Hamid Gul, former DG-ISI, had testified that the Soviet departure from Afghanistan encouraged the ISI to couple-up its wars in Afghanistan and Kashmir. Years later, Gul admitted: 'we [Pakistan] wanted to mirror the success in Kashmir by sending them into Indian-administered Kashmir to manipulate the Kashmiri people's anger at India's refusal to grant them autonomy. We would train the freedom fighters. We would arm them'.[80] Connection between Afghan Islamists and Kashmir became an enduring theme in India's approach towards Afghanistan over the decades. Even if the existence of this connection is not in doubt, the success of replicating the Afghan model in Kashmir, despite Gul's assertion and Indian conviction about the same, remains questionable. In May 1990, for instance, after tremendous media pressure, the government clarified that it was closely monitoring the activities of Kashmiri separatists and trying to assess if they had been in touch with the Mujahideen to obtain weapons and training, or even to join them to fight in Afghanistan.[81] However, no corroborative evidence emerged to confirm the presence of Afghan Mujahideen in Kashmir.[82] Though there were indications that Hekmatyar's *Hizb-e-Islami* had been training some Kashmiris, most other Mujahideen groups (especially Massoud and Rabbani's *Jamiat-e-Islami*) despite their sympathy for the cause, refused to support Kashmiri militants.[83] On 27 September 1992, Rabbani articulated his stand on Kashmir very clearly. 'We condemn oppression against Muslims wherever they may be. We hope the Kashmir issue is resolved on the basis of UN resolutions and talks and negotiations,' he said.[84] The Mujahideen were wary of getting caught in the India-Pakistan rivalry. Moreover, given the internal rifts within the Mujahideen, good relations with India were seen as an insurance against Pakistan's micromanagement of their internal affairs.

Thus, New Delhi's opening up to the Mujahideen, was not simply about optics and signaling good-faith to a rising political dispensation in a neighbouring country. It was loaded with strategic intent. India did not want Rawalpindi to dictate the terms of peace in a post-Najibullah Afghanistan. More than direct links between the Mujahideen and Kashmiri militants, India fretted over the boost that the Mujahideen's rise would give to Pakistan in fomenting militancy in Kashmir. Dialogue with different Mujahideen factions was necessary to strike such a strategic balance. Rabbani, Massoud, and Mojadeddi proved to be perfect candidates to open such channels. They had worked closely with Pakistan but reflected independent agency. Hekmatyar's case was more complicated. A Pashtun from Kunduz, Hekmatyar represented urban Islamists that were radicalised at the Kabul University in the late-1960s. Without any geographical base like Massoud and Rabbani (who were rooted in the Panjshir Valley) Hekmatyar thrived on external support. Though Hekmatyar's relationship with Pakistan was mainly transactional in nature, he was dependent on Rawalpindi and amenable to accepting Pakistan's demands for training Kashmiri militants. Pakistan's inability to manage these intra-Mujahideen differences became evident in the fact that the Peshawar accord of 24 April 1992, facilitated by Pakistan's PM Nawaz Sharif with Saudi blessing, blew up in its face in less than a week, as Afghanistan descended into civil war. In May 1992 Mojaddedi raked up the Durand Line issue and, much like Najibullah and most previous Afghan leaders, rejected it as an international border.[85]

Internal rifts within the Mujahideen had been evident since the beginning of the Soviet intervention. Aware of these differences, and despite Rajiv's official policy of dealing only with Najibullah, the R&AW and the MEA had developed covert contacts with the Mujahideen by late 1980s. These links were not just limited to the perceived anti-Pakistan elements. India opened covert channels with Mojadeddi, Rabbani, Sayyaf, Massoud, Dostum, as well as Hekmatyar. A currently serving top MEA official, 'L', who was posted in Iran from 1988 to 1991, met with all Shia Mujahideen factions in Tehran to see if there was any convergence of interests. This meeting took place before Najibullah's fall and, to the diplomat's surprise, 'a lot was common in their and our thinking about Afghanistan and its politics and security ... we shared a lot of perceptions and built upon them after that'.[86] Given that overt governmental contacts with such figures could have posed political problems or embarrassment to both India and Najibullah, these links were kept secret. Some such links were also facilitated by Indian academics and journalists—a practice that India followed well into the post-2001 phase when engaging with the Afghan Taliban.

An emerging conciliator, it was clear to Dixit that Islamabad was unable to secure control either over Rabbani, Massoud, or even Hekmatyar. This assessment was critical in shaping the conciliator's policy approach and advocating engagement. While the conciliators agreed that the Mujahideen (and later the Taliban) were sponsored by the ISI, they did not see these groups as being remotely controlled by Pakistan. Moreover, opening channels with the Mujahideen was also an imperative to revive the inflow of critical intelligence related to the Punjab and Kashmir insurgencies that R&AW received from the erstwhile KhAD, which had dried up after Najibullah's fall.[87] According to B. Raman, a senior R&AW officer who had helped open a channel with the royalists in 1985, the Mujahideen were hurt and disappointed by India's pro-Najibullah tilt and New Delhi's reluctance to support the Mujahideen's struggle against the Soviet occupation. But such feelings did not turn the Mujahideen 'hostile to India'.[88] Many Afghan Mujahideen leaders 'maintained secret contacts with the R&AW even while cooperating with the ISI and the

CIA against the Soviet troops in Afghanistan', claimed Raman. Rajiv had supported this covert angle to his Afghanistan policy, but only to a limited extent. All the three R&AW chiefs from Indira Gandhi's time to that of Rajiv, that is G. C. Saxena, S. E. Joshi, and A. K. Verma, had followed a triangular strategy towards Pakistan that is 'co-operative relations where possible, hard-hitting covert actions where necessary, and close networking with Afghanistan'.[89] Rao, allegedly, altered this strategy.

Even though Pakistani sources dispute Rao's mild approach given R&AW's continued links with the Mujahideen, Rao did reduce, if not abandon, the lethal angle to India's covert action in Afghanistan and Pakistan.[90] Vikram Sood, former chief of R&AW (December 2000 to March 2003), confirms Rao's conciliatory approach, but in critical terms. Apparently Sood, who in 1994 was years away from becoming India's spymaster, had formulated a plan to develop Indian's offensive covert infrastructure in Afghanistan. While the then chief of R&AW supported his plan, Rao refused to give it political clearance.[91] Sood terms Rao's decision-making as 'policy drift ... out of indecision' (even though there is emerging literature that credits Rao for taking some of the most audacious and contentious policy decisions that transformed India).[92] Fear of escalating a covert war with Pakistan and balancing domestic civil-military relations are two possible reasons for Rao's aversion to using covert tools of coercion. But there were historical considerations as well. Rao had come to power after an LTTE suicide bomber assassinated his predecessor Rajiv Gandhi, a proponent of coercive diplomacy. Indian intelligence agencies had played a critical role in the Sri Lankan conflict, first to train and equip the LTTE against the Sinhalese-dominated Colombo government, and then to overtly fight against them.[93] Indira Gandhi had also been assassinated by her Sikh bodyguards as a revenge for her decision to deploy the army to flush out Sikh militants from the revered Golden Temple in Amritsar in 1984. Having learnt from the after-effects of employing coercive techniques for political purposes, subsequent Indian PMs, but especially Rao, became wary of resorting to them liberally. Rao's aversion to the use of force was visible in December 1992, when he refused to deploy the army to protect the Babri Masjid despite credible reports that the Hindu *kar-sevaks* would most definitely demolish it.[94] Rao and his successors didn't want to escalate conflict with Pakistan over Kashmir, or in Afghanistan, given India's precarious economic and political situation. Often derogatorily termed as 'lacking political will' (much like the closed border school during the British Raj, which was derided as 'masterly inactivity'), aversion to coercive diplomacy was an important tenet of the conciliators in the 1990s.

Such an approach, however, came under increasing strain as the situation in Kashmir deteriorated, and the Taliban came to power in Kabul. A critical challenge came in mid-May 1995. Haroon Khan, mostly known as 'Major' Mast Gul, who was a Pakistani militant from Khyber Pakhtunkhwa and a senior commander of the Hizb-ul-Mujahideen (HM), entered into a major standoff with the India army in Charar-e-Sharif, a small town in Kashmir's Budgam district. The standoff resulted in total devastation of the town and the burning of the sacred Sufi shrine of Charar-e-Sharif. Worst of all, Mast Gul escaped the scene and reappeared in Rawalpindi a few days later, where he received a hero's welcome.[95] Apart from unleashing a storm in the parliament (mostly on how Rao had proven incompetent on Kashmir as well as Pakistan, among his other failures) the Charar-e-Sharif incident concretised the notion of the Afghan Mujahideen's involvement in Kashmir. C D Sahay, former chief of R&AW (2003–05), and an expert on Kashmir and Pakistan, acknowledges: 'Around 1995, there was a view in Kashmir that the ISI had started inducting Taliban and Afghan Jihadis into Kashmir, particularly in Doda/Kishtawar area. Local verification however, revealed that the new group of militants were battle-hardened Pakistani mercenaries relieved of Jihadi duties in Afghanistan'.[96] Because Mast Gul was a Pashtun, the fact that he was a Pakistani national and not Afghan, had been overlooked during those tense moments. Targeting Rao's conciliatory approach, CPI leader Biplab Dasgupta wanted New Delhi to put pressure on both Pakistan and Afghanistan's Mujahideen government and ask why their militants were infiltrating Kashmir and what efforts they were making to curb these activities.[97] Jagmohan Malhotra, former governor of Kashmir (1990), known mostly by his mononym Jagmohan, also criticised the government for not being able to stop Hizb-ul-Mujahideen's visibly 'Afghan' looking men from infiltrating the shrine and planting explosives in there.[98]

The fact was, that most of these 'Afghan looking men', like Mast Gul, came from Pakistan's tribal regions while feeding into Indian officials' cultural generalisation that Pashtuns were Afghans. Despite knowing that it was the ISI that had built training camps for the HM under its covert K-2 programme (run by Brig. (Retd.) Imtiaz and supported by Brig. 'Badam'), where it was training fighters for Kashmir and Punjab, many (though not all) Indian officials began viewing the Afghan Mujahideen through a Kashmir-centric lens.[99] Reports had been pouring from early 1993 that some Afghan nationals had crossed the LoC to join HM militants in Kashmir. This number, however, was a meager twenty-five to thirty over a period of seven to eight months beginning November 1992.[100] Most of these were private individuals who had been recruited to join the Kashmir 'struggle' rather than being sponsored by either the *Hizb-e-Islami* or the *Jamiat-e-Islami*. As the then EAM Dinesh Singh, defending the government's conciliatory approach towards Afghanistan, explained to his parliamentary colleagues, New Delhi was aware that Pakistan has arranged training facilities for Kashmiri militants in locations within Afghanistan. However, it firmly believed in Kabul's assurances that the Afghan government was not involved in any assistance being provided to Kashmiri militants.[101] In reality, the bigger worry from Afghanistan was not the intrusions in Kashmir, but the influx of Afghan refugees in light of the ongoing civil war. Starting with approximately 15,860 in April–May 1992, the number rose to 18,139 by February 1993, and 24,662 by May 1995 (and eventually reached 60,000 by 2011).[102] Either the Indian government would need to provide for them, or ensure their safe return with help from the Mujahideen government. Though most of such Afghans stayed back in India, the Rao government was keen on the latter option.

Taliban dilemma

On 16 May 1996, Narasimha Rao stepped down as PM of India, and on 25 September 1996, Kabul fell to the Taliban. The two events, though unrelated, changed the course of India's Afghanistan policy once again. Rao's departure meant a key conciliator was out of office, and the Taliban's ascendance meant that Pakistan's influence in Afghanistan had increased manifold. That New Delhi had taken few operational measures to counter the Taliban's rise at the outset, underlined India's post-Cold War foreign policy flux. Despite knowing that the strategic border post of Spin Boldak in Kandahar had fallen to a new militia called the Taliban in October 1994, that the Pakistani army had provided heavy artillery cover fire for the same, India did little to safeguard its interests.[103] Both the MEA and R&AW wrote the Taliban off as another Pakistan-supported fringe militia.[104] The Taliban's existence only corroborated Indian advocacy of Pakistan's interference in Afghan domestic affairs. In fact, whatever intelligence India received about the intricacies of the Taliban in 1994–95, ironically, came from Massoud, who had opened a channel with the Taliban (to defeat Hekmatyar). Bhadrakumar had undertaken a mission to Kabul in the winter of 1994 to engage with Massoud and Rabbani (on Srinivasan's orders). Just like his R&AW counterparts, he received detailed insights into the newly emerged militia from Massoud.[105] On his return to Delhi, Bhadrakumar advised the leadership to not offer military support to any side given the fluidity of alliances on the ground.

Within two days of coming to power in Kabul, the Taliban (which was no longer small) lynched India's former ally Najibullah and hung his body (with that of his brother) in central Kabul.[106] Najibullah was shot in the head and his beaten and bloated body was hung from a crane. Kabul's fall and Najibullah's gruesome murder came as a shock to New Delhi (and the world). In keeping with international reaction, India's official policy was unambiguously opposed to the Taliban's political and social conduct. This opposition had four key aspects. Firstly, New Delhi closed its embassy in Kabul and evacuated its personnel citing safety concerns. As with most other countries, India had no diplomatic presence in Kabul throughout the period of Taliban rule from 1996 until 2001. Based on this absence, Indian officials and analysts conclude that India had 'no contacts with the Pashtuns' during these six years.[107] Secondly, it endorsed the UNSC Resolution 1076 which criticised the Taliban for violating human and women's rights, and decided not to recognise the regime as Afghanistan's legitimate government.[108] Existing literature treats this phase of India-Afghanistan relations as a diplomatic black hole without much substance to the relationship. Moreover, India's anti-Taliban stance has been assessed as strategically sound and politically correct by former Indian officials.[109] This is because of the Taliban's ideological make-up and perceived anti-India stance. Thirdly, India maintained diplomatic links with the internationally recognised Rabbani government and hosted Massoud Khalili, Rabbani's political aide, as its ambassador to New Delhi. Khalili was constantly in touch with the Indian government and lobbied for the latter's support against the Taliban.[110] Finally, India provided covert military, financial, and medical support to the anti-Taliban United Front (UF) in coalition with Russia, Iran, and the Central Asian Republics (CARs).

India's material support to the UF is an open secret. Based on interviews with India's intelligence and diplomatic officials, declassified US intelligence dossiers, as well as existing media reports, it can be confirmed that India clandestinely gave the UF material (and not just moral and diplomatic) support.[111] This was done considerably, if not entirely, from the Farkhor air base in South Tajikistan (among other places). These facts form credible bedrock for the emphasis of existing studies that India was averse to the pro-Pakistan Taliban. But, why change policy in 1996 when India was open to engaging with pro-Pakistan Afghan factions in 1992? Existing studies emphasise a geostrategic and human rights rationale to this approach. The Taliban was understood, and justly so, as a movement of misogynistic Islamists with a highly questionable approach to human rights. Monotheistic practices as understood by these students of Islam, and often imposed with brute force in practice, gave India space to construe it as an entity with little understanding of matters of statecraft and international diplomacy. This was coupled with a peculiarly strong belief that the Taliban was Islamabad's proxy force.[112] Pakistan's use of militant non-state actors like the Harkat-ul-Ansar (HuA) and the Hizbul Mujahideen (HM) to foment violence in Kashmir buttressed this belief. Fears that the Taliban would support separatism in Kashmir took root, and much more strongly than during the late 1980s and early 1990s. Though credible, this argument does not capture the inherent contradictions in India's policymaking process on Afghanistan.

Firstly, if the anti-Pakistan 'proxy thesis', framed by the idea of realpolitik, were true, then engaging with Taliban would have been within reason. Having gained effective control of more than 60 per cent of Afghan territory by 1997, the Taliban had emerged as a coherent military force dominated by ethnic Pashtuns. Plus, keen on international recognition, the Taliban was cautious before taking an openly anti-India stance. According to declassified intelligence reports used by the US government, HuA militants were being trained in Paktia and Khost by the ISI since mid-1990s.[113] The HuA received between US$ 30,000 to US$ 60,000 per month as aid from the ISI and were also being financed by Al Qaeda.[114] With their fighters sharing camps, ideological affinities between AQ and the HuA grew and HuA leader Fazlul Rahman Khalil started endorsing fatwas that Al Qaeda issued, even to the ISI's consternation.[115] It can be argued that these were the groups that were pivotal in maintaining the momentum of the Kashmir insurgency, and thus, their unchallenged presence in Afghanistan linked the Taliban to Kashmir.

But did the Taliban have control over these training camps given Al Qaeda and the ISI's role in sustaining them? Sahay, India's former spymaster says that in R&AW's assessment, the Taliban did have the capacities to clamp down on these camps.[116] However, it was unwilling to do so given its links with the ISI, and ideological affinities with HuA. MoD analysts, examining Pakistan-Taliban relations in 2000, however, offered a nuanced reading, i.e. these camps were 'not vital to Taliban policy' even if they were central to Pakistan's policy in Kashmir and Afghanistan.[117] The few Afghans who fought in Kashmir in the 1990s cannot be directly linked to the Taliban.[118] If anything, the Taliban had consistently denied their active presence (or any such intention) in Kashmir, even if they had sympathy for Kashmiri separatists. Confidential conversations between US officials at that time confirm that the Taliban had no intention to halt training of HuA cadres, which had begun as part of a deal with the ISI.[119] The Taliban's lack of resistance to HuA's presence on its territory seems like a pragmatic decision that ensured continuous material and diplomatic support from Pakistan.

Secondly, how was New Delhi so clear about not engaging with a 'Pashtun dominated' force? The certainty portrayed around the 'Islamic fundamentalist' argument is counterintuitive given India's historical and cultural engagement with radical Islam. Some antecedents such as the Indian National Congress' support to the Khilafat Movement between 1919 and 1924, and New Delhi's unhindered diplomacy with post-1979 Shiite Iran and the Wahhabi Gulf states are cases in point. Interestingly, India also accepted the presence of the radical Islamist and pro-Pakistan Hekmatyar in the Afghan government in 1992 (even though Hekmatyar never really joined the government in Kabul). Thirdly, given India's active dealings with the UF after 1996, it was clear that New Delhi was not shy of engaging with Afghans regardless of their ideological bent and human rights record. Neither were the UF commanders less Islamic nor did they have clean human and women's rights records. India's foreign and security establishment, effectively, faced a dilemma over who to support in Afghanistan and how. Compounding this dilemma was the fluidity of events on the ground in Afghanistan and India's domestic security and political challenges throughout the 1990s. If in 1992 the conciliators dominated policy formulation, the worsening situation in Kashmir, Rao's departure, the Taliban's rise, and Najibullah's murder proved major setbacks to their advocacy.

Conciliators respond to the Taliban

There was little ideological parity between mainstream Indian political parties and the Taliban. One of the few Indian politico-religious figures that supported the Taliban regime in Kabul was Syed Ahmed Bukhari, the Shahi Imam of Delhi's Jama Masjid (he would later also support the 9/11 attacks). What the conciliators wanted was simply to engage with the Taliban, at least politically and covertly even if diplomatic recognition was out of the question.[120] The goal of such engagement was to understand the internal dynamics of the regime better and assess whether a workable (short of granting them official recognition) relationship could be established. They saw reason in Pakistan's Afghanistan policy and concurred that a non-combative stance in Afghanistan would allow constructive engagement with Islamabad. However, such conciliation required India's continuous diplomatic presence in Kabul despite the civil war. Shutting its embassy in September 1996 reduced India's scope to explore and understand the Taliban movement on its own merit. Curiously, India's decision to close its Kabul embassy in 1996 is often treated as a definitive marker of its aversion towards the Taliban. Such was not the case. Still working on a conciliatory principle, New Delhi had ordered its diplomats to keep working in Kabul till it became impossible to continue working. India was the last country to shut its embassy as the Taliban approached the capital and remaining Indian diplomats escaped with bags full of cash (to bribe warlords on the way) using a circuitous route to reach the Bagram airport from where they took a flight to India. Moreover, this was not the first time New Delhi shut its mission in Kabul. Every time fighting broke out in and around Kabul (after Najibullah's fall), most countries including India would close their embassies and remove diplomatic representatives. In fact, this was the fourth closure of India's Kabul mission between 1992 and 1996.

The Indian embassy was first targeted in June 1992 (and remained shut until September 1992) by some Mujahideen elements after the Peshawar Accord was signed.[121] At the same time, about 1,800 Hindu and Sikh Afghan nationals crossed over to India within a month 'unable to bear the reported hostility of the new Mujahideen rulers in Afghanistan'.[122] The second closure happened between February and September 1993, when fighting broke out between Hekmatyar and other Mujahideen factions including Mohaqiq's Hazara dominated *Hizb-e-Wahdat*, the *Jamiat-e-Islami*, and Dostum's newly created *Jumbish-e-Milli*. Pakistan and Saudi Arabia brokered what was called the March accord in 1993 between the fighting factions as they agreed to a ceasefire until the next elections at the end of 1994.[123] The third, and penultimate time India packed up its mission was between January 1994 and 3 May 1995, when Dostum and Hekmatyar joined hands briefly to oust Rabbani and Mohaqiq, and the Taliban emerged as a player on the Afghan stage.[124] Regardless, under the conciliators' influence, India maintained robust links with the Rabbani government, hosted Afghan leaders, continued distributing aid throughout this period via the UN, and reopened its embassy as soon as it could. What was different with the Taliban was India's decision to keep its embassy shut (and this had to do with the rise of the partisans).

Though the conciliators were in agreement with their detractors that the Taliban was being sponsored by the ISI, they did not see the Taliban through an Islamist lens or as necessarily being a proxy force for Pakistani agencies despite the former's dependence on the latter. For Dixit, writing in 1996, the Taliban was a student movement primarily reflecting Pashtun interests with most of its recruits coming from the tribal areas of Pakistan.[125] While Dixit was aware of the problems associated with opening channels with the Taliban, he stated,

> to think that India can play a direct mediatory or intervening role in this violence-ridden situation is impracticable and unfeasible ... In the coming three to five years, it would be sufficient if India managed to maintain contact with all groups in Afghanistan and joined hands with other neighbouring countries which are genuinely interested in pacifying and normalising the situation in that country.[126]

India did not maintain contact with all Afghan factions, and instead demonised the Taliban.

Did Najibullah's murder by the Taliban make conciliation an unattractive option in 1996? Though it is true that the event tipped the balance against the conciliators, their fundamental beliefs remained robust and continued to sow doubt about India's anti-Taliban, anti-Pakistan partisanship. In October 1996, many Indian diplomats remained unconvinced that Pakistan could control the Taliban remotely in the long haul.[127] These officials asserted that the Taliban have an 'ethno-nationalist' identity, disputing the consensus that the Taliban was simply an Islamist force without much regard for nationalism (like Al Qaeda).[128] Such ethnic understanding of the Taliban was a view that dominated the US foreign bureaucracy too, which was advocating a policy of 'limited engagement to try to "moderate and modernise" the Taliban', despite the repugnance of the Taliban's world-view.[129] Analysts within India's MoD had reached a similar conclusion by highlighting strains between Pakistan and the Taliban, and the limits of influence that the ISI enjoyed over the Taliban on core issues such as the Durand Line.[130]

There were divisions within the Taliban. While the moderates were inclined towards cooperating with the UN and the international community in February 1996, hardliners such as Mullah Omar gained influence due to Pakistan's support.[131] The flexibility of this assessment and the conciliators' thriving existence is reflected in debates during the temporary fall of Mazar-e-Sharif on 25 May 1997. As the Taliban moved west and north from Kandahar, most factional leaders including Hekmatyar and Herat's Ismail Khan fled Afghanistan. Mazar-e-Sharif's fall initiated Dostum's exile as well. The only faction actively resisting the Taliban was the *Jamiat*, confined to the Panjshir valley north of Kabul. India, like many other countries, momentarily faced a fait accompli, that is either it engaged with the Taliban or remained out of Afghanistan for the foreseeable future. The situation became acute when the US received a Taliban delegation in Washington in February 1997 while Pakistan, Saudi Arabia, and the United Arab Emirates (UAE) recognised it as Afghanistan's legitimate government.[132]

On 26 May 1997 the MEA came out with a cautious statement saying that the 'new situation is entirely within the domestic sphere of Afghanistan,' and Afghans have a right to decide their future 'free from outside influence and interference'.[133] On 28 May 1997, three days after Mazar's fall, Indian media reported: 'India seeks to open channel with Taliban.'[134] According to the report, a fast-emerging 'dominant' view in the MEA was that India will 'have to deal with the reality in Afghanistan' for its 'long term national interest'.[135] Officials had privately started admitting that India's Afghanistan policy over the last year had 'met with a setback'. Interestingly, the Taliban (similar to Rabbani in 1992) had sent 'feelers' to engage with India. Mullah Muttawakil sent the first feeler on 23 October 1996 in his interview to the Pakistani journalist Rahimullah Yusufzai, which was published by the *Outlook Magazine* in India. A key member of the ruling central Shura of the Taliban, Muttawakil stated:

> We [Taliban] certainly can have better ties with New Delhi if India stops interfering in Afghanistan and assures us that Afghanistan's embassy in New Delhi will not be allowed to be used against the Taliban by Rabbani's appointees there.[136]

Muttawakil wondered 'what has the Taliban done to attract Indian ire?' Frustrated over India's unrealistic Afghanistan policy, Muttawakil argued that New Delhi must be required to know 'a lot more about Afghanistan' so as to formulate a successful policy. Critically, when asked about the Taliban's views on Kashmir and the conditions of Muslims in India, Muttawakil responded (again, similarly to Rabbani in 1992): 'For the moment, we won't say anything ... We want friendly ties with neighbours and have no intention of either interfering in affairs of other countries or allowing them to interfere in our affairs.'[137] Though wanting to engage, the Taliban's proposal came with conditions attached. It wanted New Delhi to cut all ties with Rabbani and throw its weight behind the Taliban.

The second signal came on 11 June 1997, before the Taliban's retreat from Mazar-e-Sharif. This time it was Mullah Abdul Jalil, deputy foreign minister of the Taliban, who wanted India to stop treating the Taliban as an enemy. Phrases used by both Muttawakil and Jalil were similar in their criticism of India's Afghanistan policy. Talking from a position of strength, Jalil said:

> We can consider forging mutually beneficial ties with India if it brings positive changes in its Afghanistan policy ... The Taliban wants friendly ties with all countries, both Islamic and non-Islamic. With our neighbours, including India, we would like to have normal relations based on the policy of non-interference. Until now, India has been interfering in Afghanistan's affairs. We want this interference to end. In fact, we will be waiting for signs that indicate a change of heart in New Delhi.[138]

Former Indian Foreign Secretary K. Raghunath (July 1997 to November 1999), a staunch anti-Taliban partisan, confirms that India did not entertain the two feelers. The question was often put that if the Taliban makes overtures, which they did, should India talk to them? 'And the answer is no, because we don't get anything by talking to them', says Raghunath.[139] A 1962-batch diplomat, Raghunath was tremendously influential in foreign policy-making (given the political turmoil of the mid-1990s when no single party formed a stable government). He played a key role in undercutting the conciliatory approach in 1997 to influence policy change by mobilising opinion in wake of the Taliban's ascendance, which had come as a surprise to India. Nonetheless, according to the media reports, multiple sources within the MEA (barring Raghunath) gave two reasons why the Taliban should be engaged. Firstly, the Taliban wanted international recognition and was not sure for how long non-Pashtuns would accept their domination. Secondly, 'an influential section within the Taliban is said to be deeply suspicious of Pakistan'.[140] Reflecting India's understanding of political nuances within the Taliban early in the civil war, a strong constituency within the MEA sought political recognition for the Taliban, if not diplomatic recognition. Allegedly, this was India's 'uniform recognition behavior' towards governments of 'disputed legitimacy' until the 1971 India-Pakistan War or the Bangladesh Liberation War.[141] Raghunath disagreed with the notion that in international affairs one must engage with all. However, while the merits of engagement or lack thereof can be debated, Raghunath's claim that there was 'no disagreement' over the question of engagement with the Taliban does not stand up to rigorous examination of multiple sources.[142]

An intense dialogue between the conciliators and their detractors in early 1997 was reflective in EAM (soon to be PM) Gujral's shifting gears on the Taliban question. Having called it 'obscurantist' at the Lok Sabha in September 1996, Gujral's response to a media question on whether the Taliban should be resisted in March 1997, was: 'It is not for me to say so. We are neither a party in the war in Afghanistan, nor would we like to be.'[143] Not only this, Gujral was actively portraying India as a non-player in Afghanistan:

> Let us keep in mind that India is not involved in Afghanistan. But we are concerned about what's happening there. Our policy is in conformity with the UN policy. We believe it's their own problem and there should be no outside intervention. And the Taliban are an outside intervention—the support to the Taliban, I mean.[144]

The statement reflects the dominant Indian view of the Taliban as Pakistan's creation, but there was more to it. In the same interview Gujral stated that India 'will go more than half-way to make its neighbours feel secure', including Pakistan—without expecting quid pro quo.[145] Dixit's June 1997 statement that India should have a 'flexible approach towards the Taliban' supported this stand.[146] However, regardless of Gujral and Dixit's advocacy, India took sides. The R&AW provided active support to Rabbani and Massoud, as alleged by Muttawakil in October 1996 and proven in retrospect. The fact was that India's activities in Afghanistan (particularly military support to Rabbani's forces) did not have political clearance (just yet). Politically, India had nothing to do with the internal situation of Afghanistan. Therefore, while the conciliatory advocacy dominated policy output between 1992 and 1996 and later gained some momentum in light of the Taliban's territorial gains in North Afghanistan in 1997, it remained unsuccessful in shaping the practical course of actions after the fall of Kabul.

Rise of the partisans

Running parallel to the conciliators' advocacy were proponents of containment of the Taliban. Here termed partisans, these officials advocated containing the Taliban by bolstering anti-Taliban elements in Afghanistan. To be clear, the conciliators and the partisans were in agreement over facts such as Pakistan's support to the Taliban. With the same resource and information available to advocates of both these coalitions, the difference lay in approach. There were three key aspects to the partisans' belief system. Firstly, that the Taliban was a 'Pakistan-raised, Pakistan-trained and equipped, new Islamist fundamentalist force' in Afghanistan.[147] Secondly, that the Taliban would advance Pakistan's strategic interests instead of uniting Afghanistan. Thirdly, not only should the Taliban not be recognised but also active counter-measures should be taken to stop its ascent. There was consensus in India's political circles that the Taliban was a 'creation' of the ISI.[148] K. Subrahmanyam, a top Indian strategist, reported on the Taliban's links with Pakistan and Saudi Arabia in December 1994, and noted the West's (primarily the US) 'tacit' support to the student movement.[149]

Indeed, foreign secretary Srinivasan gave multiple warnings to Frank Wisner, the then US ambassador to India, but received no response (and viewed that as US complicity in the rise of the Taliban).[150]

The views of the Indian media reflected official Indian thinking on these foreign policy issues. On 21 October 1994, for instance, the *Times of India* sought a 'reassessment' of India's 'hands-off approach' and advocated an active policy of India providing a 'neutral' platform to the warring factions.[151] Throughout 1995, the *Times of India* gave a blanket assessment of ISI-Taliban nexus and claimed that 'working under the guise of bringing peace to a war-ravaged countryside through the strict implementation of the Shariat, the ISI has sought to further its own agenda.'[152] They also called Hekmatyar a 'Frankenstein's monster' created and nourished by Pakistan and overlooked by the US. The US was bashed as a destabilising actor in Afghanistan (an allegation that disturbed the US given its concerns over the Taliban's rise, which it considered just as unrepresentative a Pashtun entity as the Tajik-dominated Rabbani regime).[153] In contrast, Iran's former President Akbar Hashemi Rafsanjani was viewed as a 'harbinger of hope' and Russia a 'close friend.'[154]

Partisans emerged winners in 1996–97. Unlike 1992 when the Congress party, under Rao's leadership, had adjusted its Afghanistan policy to accommodate the Mujahideen, in 1996, most Congress leaders such as Pranab Mukherjee were openly advocating that to 'contain the Taliban is our only objective.'[155] The CPI, the CPI (M), and the BJP supported this stand.[156] In a plot dominated by oil politics, terrorism, strategic depth, ethnic tensions, and territorial disputes (Durand Line and Kashmir), the Taliban, Pakistan, and the US were the 'villains', and the Afghan government factions and other anti-Pakistan Afghan factions coupled with Iran and Russia were the 'heroes'. 'There was nobody who was doubting this policy [containing the Taliban]. Nothing was to be gained, in fact, everything was to be lost by showing the slightest signs of wanting to engage.'[157] Raghunath conveyed a similar message to Lakhdar Brahimi, the then Special Envoy to the UN Secretary General on Afghan Affairs, during the latter's visit to India on 12 September 1997.[158] The foreign secretary was categorical that 'all bastions of freedom in Afghanistan were demolished and [that] the Taliban was running riot, and they ran a kind of regime of atrocity.'[159] He argues that the Taliban would have treated recognition from India as a certificate to their 'Jihad ideology', which was much in contrast with secular Indian sensibilities. Strongly supporting Raghunath's line within the MEA was Vivek Katju, who later became the joint secretary on the Pakistan, Afghanistan, Iran desk (JS PAI), and India's first ambassador to Afghanistan after 9/11.[160] A 1974-batch diplomat, Katju was considered a hardliner on Pakistan, had developed close links with the UF, and was staunchly anti-Taliban.

Salman Haidar, Raghunath's predecessor as foreign secretary (March 1995 to June 1997) gives a similar assessment of the situation. 'Our relationship with Afghanistan, as I understand, has a lot to do with Indo-Pak relations ... The Afghan civil war was a time when this was very visible. Pakistan was backing the Taliban, we hated the Taliban, and the Taliban was seen as a group damaging Indian interests'.[161] The key reason given for this emotion of 'hate' was the 'unstable situation in Kashmir' where 'there was plenty of tinder'. When asked why India did not engage the Taliban knowing well that this could raise the Taliban's stake in supporting Kashmir insurgency, Haidar says that while 'the logic of what you [author] are saying is absolutely correct, but the time was not right ... I don't think the situation had developed to the point where some exploration of differentiating between different types of Taliban and different types of groups within Afghanistan was possible ... Terror meant Taliban'.[162]

According to Shyam Saran, foreign secretary from August 2004 to September 2006 (but who played an important role even in the 1990s), the Taliban was 'seen as trying to exclude India from Afghanistan and prove[d] to be very hostile to India. That is one of the reasons why India withdrew its diplomatic representation from Afghanistan. And during that period also saw its interests in supporting the Northern Alliance (United Front).'[163] Haidar, Raghunath, Katju, and Saran, all concur that not only did India view the Taliban as a hostile entity but also wanted to work towards containing its rise. Lalit Mansingh, foreign secretary between December 1999 and March 2001, adds that India 'lost all contact with Afghanistan during those six years'.[164] This was despite Saran's assertion that India's outlook towards Pashtun communities was not altered by the rise of the Taliban, and that 'not all Pashtuns are Taliban or not all Pashtuns are fundamentalists'.[165]

These statements reflect India's historical links with Pashtun elites. Most interviewees within and outside India's state establishment corroborate this viewpoint. However, most Pashtun leaders that officials recall as being close to India were from the NWFP. These include Ghaffar Khan and his brother Khan Sahib, from the Pashtun-dominated Awami National Party (ANP).[166] In Afghanistan, apart from former King Zahir Shah, Indian officials continue to idealise Najibullah and Daud Khan.[167] The common thread connecting all these leaders is their tough stand on Durand Line. India, thus, mostly engaged with leaders who had anti-Pakistan predilections. This aspect played an important role in India's decision to not engage with the Taliban. Though Pakistan was aware of the Taliban's aversion to the Durand Line, New Delhi could never accurately assess the extent to which the Taliban would be interested in challenging Islamabad. In addition to a lack of understanding of fragile Taliban-Pakistan relations, Najibullah's killing strengthened the partisans. This is reflected in India's 'strong condemnation' of the act, and hosting of Najibullah's family in India ever since.[168]

Vijay Nambiar, who had been in Kabul as ambassador in 1992, acted *in loco parentis* to Najibullah's daughters, and managed India's policy transition after the Mujahideen's rise to power, encouraged a partisan stand against the Taliban. He rejected conciliatory voices in the MEA as a crisis-induced reaction wherein some policymakers wanted to salvage the most out of the Afghan situation, and saw non-engagement with the Taliban as a 'missed opportunity' to consolidate India's presence in Afghanistan.[169] He argued that India could have tried reaching out to the Taliban, but such a contact would not have translated into a working relationship. This was because Pakistan would not have allowed the Taliban to undertake any politically, economically, or strategically consequential transaction with India.[170] This policy aspect got highlighted in a Lok Sabha debate regarding the situation in Afghanistan on 27 November 1996. Gujral, despite being a proponent of good neighbourly relations, bluntly criticised the Taliban and Pakistan:

> The pursuit of obscurantist doctrine by the Taliban leadership and the consequent denial of human rights, especially the rights of women, have been extensively condemned. The implications of these events have been assessed, especially the risk of an adverse impact on India's security.[171]

On the security aspect, Gujral highlighted India's worst fears over a Taliban-led Afghanistan.

> We have recently seen credible reports in the international media on the Taliban handing over terrorist training facilities to the Harkat-ul-Ansar. It is reported that at these training camps Pakistani and other youth are being trained for terrorist activities in Kashmir.[172]

Just before this debate, the then PM H. D. Deve Gowda met Rabbani at the World Food Summit in Rome, following which India sent a delegation to Mazar-e-Sharif led by the MEA's Secretary (East) on 10 November 1996 to meet Dostum and discuss the modalities of cooperation. Iran and Russia were informed that India would continue to maintain contact with the 'legitimate' Afghan government. While stating that 'there could be no military solution',

New Delhi made no bones about signaling where its heart lay when Gujral said that 'a complete cessation of foreign interference' was a 'prerequisite for the resolution of the situation'.[173] Soon after, India activated aid and arms supplies to the UF in concert with Russia and Iran.[174]

Spy talk

Partisan narratives emerging from the MEA and the Prime Minister's Office (PMO) in 1996–97 had support from India's military and intelligence agencies as well. Consideration of this community's advocacy is critical given its involvement in the Baloch and Pashtun separatist movements in Pakistan (even though some Indian intelligence analysts note, inaccurately, that Rao and Gujral systematically scrapped India's covert coercive capabilities in the 1990s).[175] Even David Sedney, former US Deputy Assistant Secretary of Defence for Afghanistan, Pakistan and Central Asia says that 'India may not have done all the things Pakistan says it does till now [2014], but they may start doing that in future'.[176] What then did Indian spymasters and military officials think? According to a top Indian military intelligence officer closely following Afghanistan: 'Indians had nothing to do with the Taliban ... and Pakistan made sure that we have no connections with the Pashtuns.'[177] This was, at a minimum, one reason why India could not properly assess the possibility of collaborating, if need be, with the Taliban on the Durand Line issue. The official adds somewhat caustically:

> We're fascinated by the Pashtuns but they have done nothing for us. When they have a choice to make between Pakistan and India then they may not side with us. Any intelligence agency [read R&AW] that says that they have contacts and leeway among Pashtuns—they are cheating themselves.[178]

Reconfirming India's links with Afghan elites, the official stated that the only reason Pashtuns would choose India over Pakistan is because they want their 'elite status' back in Afghanistan. 'Pakistan has made them Jihadis'. Confirming that the R&AW maintains links with the Taliban, the official claims that such covert contacts don't last long. Finding the Taliban's philosophy 'repugnant', the official said that engaging with the Taliban openly 'was a very difficult choice' in 1996.[179] Another former top officer of India's military intelligence said that when in office, while he viewed the Taliban as Pakistan's proxy, he was open to building contacts with them and gave adequate instructions in that order to his junior officers posted in Afghanistan.[180] Most of such contacts, however, were made after 2001 and not before. According to Sood, former R&AW chief, India didn't really have a 'game-plan' on Afghanistan pre-2001. 'We didn't make any concerted attempt, it was sporadic effort. If Rabbani said something then we would sit together and chat about it,' and see what could be done.[181] Not expecting the Taliban to reach Kabul, Sood considers its rise as 'a shock' to the R&AW, which left the latter 'numb for a while'.[182] On the question of engaging with the other non-Taliban Pashtuns, Sood hinted that though the R&AW tried to build networks, the killing of Najibullah was a massive blow:

> [The] rest of the Pashtuns were not willing to talk, they were too scared. And we didn't want to upset them because at that time we were also not very sure how it was going to play out. And remember, the Taliban was Pakistan-based so the proper assessment whether all Taliban were Pashtun or Pashtuns are Taliban was not made fully.[183]

For the same reason, R&AW had refused to engage with Hekmatyar who sent secret signals to India in October 1994 when he lost Pakistan's support in the wake of the Taliban's rise, and by when New Delhi for its part had begun consolidating its relations with Rabbani and Massoud. While it is unclear whether the ISI knew about Hekmatyar's contacts with R&AW, a faction within the covert agency was nervous that abandoning Hekmatyar for the Taliban might wreck ISI's efforts in Kashmir as a lot of Kashmiri insurgents had received training in Hekmatyar's camps.[184] Sood confirms that India's non-engagement with the Taliban or Hekmatyar (whom they accepted as part of the Rabbani government until the time it lasted in 1992) was not as much about ideology as it is often portrayed. It was primarily because of little capability to understand the situation in depth on the ground. Haidar reiterates this point:

> There are two elements. One, lack of capacity, and two, more important, lack of desire ... India has always been the last of the people around to accept that there can be different types of Taliban.[185]

X, a former Indian intelligence official active in/on Afghanistan during the 1990s and 2000s, says: 'we had no contacts with the Taliban in the 1990s ... we knew that the Pakistanis were supporting the Taliban, and in turn, we were looking for any and all anti-Pakistan outfits in Afghanistan to support.'[186] Having provided financial support to the UF, X had built very strong covert links with various anti-Taliban outfits. Viewing the Taliban as a 'monolith' that could not be engaged with, X played a pivotal role, with support from Vivek Katju and K. Raghunath in the MEA, to keep the political leadership in New Delhi away from opening channels with the Taliban. Even though X nurtured the view among the Indian leadership that more than Islam, it was the tribal loyalties that formed the glue for the Taliban, he saw the movement as a monolith under Pakistan's firm grip. Therefore, it was not just the Pakistan factor or the insurgency in Kashmir that helped the partisans' rise in 1996. A serious gap in knowledge and capacity compounded by India's economic and political resource crunch during the 1990s added weight to their force. The arrival of the BJP government in 1998 and its increasingly aggressive stance on Kashmir further strengthened the partisans. Critically, though for different reasons, Moscow, Tehran and the CAR's staunch anti-Taliban stance, coupled with the UN's condemnation of the Taliban strengthened the partisans tremendously and sealed the conciliators' defeat. Constituting a negative social construct of the Taliban (and in some cases even the Pashtuns), and a sense of realpolitik to engage with anti-Pakistan elements on the Afghan landscape, the partisans were able to influence policy in their favour.

Conclusion

Theoretical constructs such as the ACF can help conceptualise policy advocacies and unpack under-appreciated policy currents of India effectively. India's Afghanistan policy in the 1990s was more than just a negative-correlate of Pakistani actions. This was despite Pakistan's use of asymmetric warfare in Kashmir and Punjab. The strategic importance of friendly relations with Afghanistan and their impact on Pakistan was not overlooked, but India's final policy approach had at least two angles to it. The existence of the partisans and the conciliators vis-à-vis the Taliban proves this point. Both the coalitions saw the center of gravity for most Afghan and Indian security problems in Pakistan. As scholar Chris Ogden argues, 'Pakistan's support of various insurgencies and terrorism against India has ... entrenched the contemporary Pakistan-terrorism nexus within India's (foreign and domestic) security perspectives'.[187] However, different coalitions advocated different approaches to the problem. The conciliators advocated engagement with the Taliban and all those warring factions deemed unfriendly to India and close to Pakistan. The partisans advocated selective engagement with only those factions that had a positive predilection towards India (or a negative predilection towards Pakistan).

The late-1990s phase of partisan domination in Indian foreign policy experience paved way for the narrative that the Afghanistan conflict was a byproduct of the India-Pakistan rivalry. Though partially true, this argument conflates political interpretation and beliefs with policy outputs. It misses the rise of the conciliators in the late 1980s and early 1990s, and is based on a stringent assumption that India-Pakistan rivalry is cast in stone. Even if it is true that most Indian officials view Afghanistan through a security-dominated Pakistani lens, and most Pakistani officials view it through a security-dominated Indian lens, the policy outputs over time indicate nuance and political sophistication. Based on this credible but partial understanding of the policy narratives that influence India's approach towards Afghanistan, most contemporary studies foresee an imminent proxy war between India and Pakistan in Afghanistan. India, as this chapter shows, did indeed engage with and accommodate pro-Pakistan factions after the Soviet withdrawal in 1989 until 1996. The Taliban's rise to power in Kabul in September 1996 challenged India's conciliatory approach. Nonetheless, the decision to sever ties with the Taliban and to bolster anti-Taliban factions was highly debated in New Delhi. Many in India saw the Taliban as a militant Islamist force sponsored by Pakistan. For others, however, it was an ethno-nationalist movement representing Pashtun interests, and not necessarily under Islamabad's control.

The three drivers of India's Afghanistan policy—striking a balance between Afghanistan and Pakistan, evolving international political environment, and the changing nature of Afghan domestic politics—determined which of the two policy advocacies won the day to influence policy output. In the early 1990s, the Mujahideen government was an internationally recognised entity that was open to engaging with India despite New Delhi's excessive focus on Najibullah. Moreover, recognising the Mujahideen was also the only possible option that could allow India to strike a balance with Pakistan. Non-engagement would have isolated India further on the Afghan landscape. That its economy had crashed and its international partnerships had unraveled in the face of Soviet disintegration, added weight to the conciliators' advocacy over that of the partisans, regardless of a searing insurgency in Kashmir. Such was, however, not the case in 1996 when the Taliban rose to power. Not only did the Taliban have no international support, it was considered a pariah regime. Despite bringing some degree of stability to the prevalent warlordism, it did little to earn world sympathy.

The key policy coup led by the partisans in 1996, however, was India's alignment with Russia, Iran, and the Central Asian Republics to support the United Front morally, financially, and militarily. This was a radical departure from the 1992 Rao doctrine and was squarely aimed against the Pakistan-supported Taliban. Supporting the United Front, which was still the recognised government of Afghanistan at the UN, was viewed as the only viable option to strike a balance between Afghanistan and Pakistan, even if it meant undermining the powerful Kabuliwallah connection with the Pashtun communities. As Narayanan (who was then out of office) observes, this desire to prevent Afghanistan from being 'taken over' by Pakistan put India in an awkward position where it found itself opposing its 'natural allies', i.e. the Pashtuns (who dominated the Taliban movement). Nambiar, who had been in Kabul till 1992 and later worked as Narayanan's deputy NSA in 2005, concurs that the changing situation on the ground in Afghanistan pushed India into developing relations with the non-Pashtuns as a balancing measure against Pakistan's overbearing influence in Afghanistan and increasing pressure against India in that country.[188] In effect, India was trying to run with the hare, and hunt with the hound, by supporting the United Front against the Taliban and trying to portray itself as politically neutral and non-interventionist at the same time. This was markedly different from India's dealing with the rise of the Mujahideen in 1992. What stayed the same in 1996 (with the situation in 1992) was the Taliban's desire, like the Mujahideen, to engage with India. The partisans dominated the policy scene throughout the late 1990s. Though the temporary fall of Mazar-e-Sharif in 1997 put pressure on the partisans to engage with the Taliban and view the Afghan landscape realistically, this did not happen. The next two chapters explain why.

5

FRIENDS FROM NORTH, FOES FROM SOUTH

INDIA, UNITED FRONT, AND THE HIJACKING OF FLIGHT IC-814

'India played a very important role in getting Dostum and Massoud together [in the 1990s]. Massoud was very unhappy with Dostum. We [India] got the Shias and Dostum and Massoud together and gave money. We were looking for all anti-Taliban groups and trying to get them to work together.'

X, R&AW official who worked closely with the United Front in the 1990s[1]

'If we see the negative dimension of the [IC-814] hijack, we also need to see the positive dimension ... all the people were rescued ... it was great and positive work that the Taliban did ... [also] the Taliban has an independent viewpoint, regardless of what Pakistan says'.

Syed Akbar Agha, close to the Taliban in 1990s and former chief of the Jaish-ul-Muslimeen, 2013[2]

Friends from north

The emergence of the anti-Taliban *Jabha-yi Muttahid-i Islāmi-yi Millī barā-yi Nijāt-i Afghānistān* (United Islamic Front for the Salvation of Afghanistan) umbrella, mostly known as the Northern Alliance, or just the United Front (UF) in 1996, was a necessary condition for the rise of partisans in India. Support from regional allies such as Iran, Russia, and the Central Asian

Republics, however, offered strategic sufficiency.[3] It had nothing to do with India's fondness for the Tajik, Uzbek or Hazara communities over the Pashtuns. New Delhi, as put by popular Indian media in 1996, had 'no option but to help Rabbani' at that point in time, for which there were strong moral and legal grounds.[4] Shaped in the context of the Taliban's stupendous rise and South Asian geopolitics, India's siding with the UF is often seen as a natural progression of New Delhi's Afghanistan policy in the 1990s, especially in light of strained relations with Pakistan.[5] In accordance with the UN's position, there was allegedly little disagreement in India over providing political, diplomatic and moral support to Rabbani and Massoud. The military component of this relationship, however, was covert. Officially, India was actively advocating non-interference by external players in Afghanistan, but unofficially, it was providing military and financial support to the UF.[6] This was similar to Pakistan's support to the Taliban, but small in comparison. Such popular discourse on India's links with the UF miss the many contradictions of this policy approach.

India's links with the UF, despite their endurance, were highly complex and delicate. For one, India's decision not to engage with the Taliban did not automatically imply siding with the UF. The question, after all, was not just about giving diplomatic recognition to the Rabbani government, but about the nature and extent of the support that India provided. Mostly symbolic, India's material support to the UF was insufficient in helping turn the military tide against the Taliban. As the twentieth century came to a close, and the Taliban's control increased across Afghanistan, India's covert war chest was used more for counter-bribing UF fighters whom the ISI was simultaneously cultivating.[7] The blunt balance of power logic guided this activity, which contributed to alienating the Taliban and other Pashtun communities from India. Also, having practiced non-interference in Afghan affairs from at least 1992 (as Rao had promised, and somewhat delivered on) why did New Delhi change its approach in 1996? The Taliban after all, wanted to engage with India, just like the Mujahideen. Moreover, throughout the 1990s India had no capital investments (despite India's desire of having some) or human personnel to protect in Afghanistan.[8] New Delhi's relationship with Kabul was simply that of a minor aid donor with its recipient. In such a situation, arguably, a neutral role would have helped India retain its goodwill among all Afghans, allay Pakistan's anxieties (or even contain its regional ambitions), and expand its economic footprint like the Chinese, the Americans, and multinational companies such as Bridas and Unocal.[9] None of this happened.

There is, in fact, no evidence to suggest a split-opinion in India on the question of engaging with the UF, like there was vis-à-vis engagement with the Taliban. The UF commanders, especially Massoud, were treated like secular 'heroes' in Indian circles. The partisans had come to dominate both policy and discourse on the Taliban dilemma. The question on the UF simply was about how to engage with them: whether to provide military support or not. The covertness of these operations and the Taliban's unpopular dominance on the international (and Indian) news wires makes granular analysis of this relationship difficult. However, a study of MEA documents, statements by Indian officials, declassified US intelligence reports, primary interviews with Indian and Afghan officials facilitating this relationship, and media archives are revealing. Despite being on the same page politically, the UF was more important for India's Afghanistan policy than the other way round. Also, India was the least important cog in the regional wheel that ensured the survival of the UF, until the US intervened militarily after the events of 9/11. In fact, according to some Russian officials, Pakistan's support for the Taliban paled in front of what Rabbani was receiving from Iran.[10]

Three aspects highlight the complexity of this relationship. Firstly, India's relations with different UF factions began with discord before they became functional and gained momentum. Most commanders such as Massoud, Dostum, Mohaqiq, Abdul Haq, and Haji Abdul Qadir (all former Mujahideen) had been critical of India in 1992. 'India had let down the Afghans and we hope that efforts are made to rectify these mistakes', said Abdul Haq, from the *Hizb-e-Islami (Khalis)* on 30 April 1992.[11] Indian journalist Shekhar Gupta, who was in Kabul at the time, interviewed Massoud two weeks later to check whether he shared Haq's anger on India. Massoud did not pull any punches: 'we want friendly relations with all countries. But we cannot forget India's policies during our Jehad'.[12] India's failed attempt to rescue Najibullah had not impressed the Mujahideen leadership. Already angry at New Delhi's biased Afghanistan policy, Massoud threatened to review all bilateral agreements India had signed with the communists. Even on the Kashmir issue, as India's then ambassador in Kabul Nambiar put it, these Mujahideen factions 'kept their counsel' but were generally 'supportive of the Pakistani position'.[13] But this did not mean a breakdown of diplomatic ties. Adopting a conciliatory approach despite their disappointment, the Mujahideen were keen on developing a stable relationship with India, but on their own terms. Rao had surely rectified the errors of his predecessors on Afghanistan, but the Mujahideen would take a call on the nature and expanse of this relationship (such was the case, arguably, throughout the 1990s).

The Mujahideen's suspicion with India was not a one-way affair either. Even though Rao had penned a conciliatory approach and the Mujahideen had reciprocated, Massoud and Haq's disappointment offered fodder to some of India's partisans who challenged the conciliators. Underlining the fact that partisans and conciliators cut across party politics and bureaucratic lines, the then home minister Y B Chavan stated on 27 May 1992, that 'the possibility of the Afghan Mujahideen concentrating on the Jammu and Kashmir border now, with the help of the Pakistan army, to give a fresh impetus to militants in the valley cannot not be ruled out.'[14] Indian media reported that a 'Pak-Afghan nexus bodes ill for India.'[15] According to reports Najibullah's ouster was the closest Pakistan had 'ever been to realising its much publicised "strategic depth" military doctrine'. Three aspects that India needed to keep an eye out for, warned commentators, were (a) Massoud's request to Pakistan to restructure the Afghan militia, divided along ethnic lines, into a federal army; (b) Mojaddedi's swift invitation to Pakistan's officials for restoring civilian infrastructure; and (c) Pakistan's decision to 'dump' Hekmatyar in support of Massoud and elevate Rabbani as the next President after Mojaddedi. The *Times of India* criticised India's policy efforts as a 'lost opportunity' and for its rigidity on dealing only at the 'government level', whereas Pakistan grasped 'the ground situation and [backed] the winning side in time.'[16] This criticism stood vindicated as the Indian embassy in Kabul, among those of other countries, was shutdown due to vandalism by Mujahideen elements in June 1992. By July, about 1,800 Afghans who practiced Hinduism and Sikhism fled the country, 'unable to bear the treatment meted out by the Mujahideen commanders,' particularly Dostum.[17] The MEA's annual report 1992–93, not surprisingly, mentions nothing about this period and focuses only on relations after September 1992, by when India had begun consolidating relations with the *Jamiat-e-Islami* and Dostum's *Jumbish-e-Milli*.

Afghanistan's 'Che Guevara'

The second aspect of India's relations with the UF was that they were personality-driven. New Delhi associated most with Massoud and his second-tier leadership and to a limited extent with Dostum, while others like Ismael Khan, Mohaqiq, and Karim Khalili were to be engaged with because they had influence on the ground.[18] The UF was a tactical alliance, or confederation, between warlords (or commanders) of different militias across Afghanistan who had differences among themselves but accepted Massoud's mediation.

India's own links with these leaders were tactical, and based on their fallout with Pakistan. According to Sood, the R&AW developed links with the Hazaras and the Tajiks with ease, while Dostum remained 'dicey, but was to be kept.'[19] However, former Pakistani envoy to the Taliban regime, Iftikhar Murshed, claims that 'while India had, in the past, gone out of its way to advertise its good relations with the Rabbani regime, it was significant that New Delhi should have disclosed (through planted stories in the media) that it had also "established direct contact with General Dostum".'[20] The *Times of India* indeed wrote such stories. Links with anti-Taliban factions were facilitated via New Delhi and Tajikistan (as well as other places), but India did not actively send its intelligence personnel to Afghanistan.[21]

The Afghan official responsible for facilitating the link with New Delhi throughout 1996–2001 (and then from 2001–07) was *Jamiat's* Massoud Khalili, allegedly 'the right–hand person of Massoud'.[22] Alumnus of the University of Delhi, Khalili had a good grasp of Indian politics and sensibilities. On 17 October 1996, soon after Kabul's fall to the Taliban, Khalili correctly assessed that 'the fall of Kabul came as a surprise to India. It was a new situation and they took time to reassess their position ... India should raise its voice when it sees Afghanistan's neighbour, in this case Pakistan, interfering in our domestic affairs'.[23] As former Indian ambassador to Iran and current vice president, M. Hamid Ansari said: 'India's relations with the Rabbani government in the 1992–96 period were of a limited nature and lacked substance.'[24] Nonetheless, with backing from R&AW and influential MEA officials, the decision to support Rabbani and Massoud was taken.

Once the decision had been reached, the MEA started steering Massoud's image in India. According to Aunohita Mojumdar, covering external affairs since 1997: 'All along we were encouraged to support the Northern Alliance'.[25] While there are no signs of specific instructions being given to such effect by the MEA, 'it was generally understood that the Northern Alliance ... were the good guys'.[26] Pranab D. Samanta, former bureau-chief of the *Indian Express* (and currently national affairs editor at the *Economic Times*), agrees that the image of the UF was positive.[27] The focus, however, was on Massoud rather than any other UF commanders. Dostum was most problematic and not least because of his 'opportunism—his men had little tolerance towards minorities even in comparison to the Taliban.[28] However, senior MEA officials had maintained direct links with Dostum throughout, with a pronounced one being the visit of Secretary (East) to Mazar-e-Sharif in October 1996. Nandan Unnikrishnan, an Indian journalist who stayed with Massoud for three days to profile him and shoot a documentary, confirms that India was focused on Massoud. Impressed by the Tajik commander's skills and acumen, Unnikrishan considered him to be a 'visionary'.[29] New Delhi's links with the second rung leadership of the group such as Mohammed Fahim, Abdullah Abdullah, Engineer Arif, Yunus Qanooni, and Amrullah Saleh also proved crucial.

Ironically, while the Taliban or Hekmatyar's fundamentalism was medieval, Massoud's interpretation of religion and statecraft did not exactly provide succour to the women of Afghanistan, who were driven into *purdah*. One of the first statements that Massoud made in 1992, after taking control of Kabul, was his intent to follow the Shariat.[30] X, the R&AW official who was actively engaged in Afghanistan, lays bare India's deliberate but successful attempts to paint the UF as a progressive political and social force. 'Whatever one may say about the Northern Alliance as a force and the Taliban, Massoud was essentially an Islamist', he admits.[31] Though he started wearing jeans and corduroy pants with his *pakol* at some point, that's not how Massoud had started. People very close to the Panjshiri leader told X that Massoud went through an image makeover and tried to portray himself as the Che Guevara of Afghanistan. But with his wife and family, he was very conservative. Even Rabbani, whom India portrayed as the legitimate leader of Afghanistan, was 'close to Pakistan and could not have been trusted,' says X.[32] Rabbani's men may be fighting Pakistan and the Taliban, but he himself had very strong links with Pakistan and had sent his family to live in Pakistan. Critically, the UF had its own share of human rights violations that the UN and Human Rights Watch actively condemned.[33] Knowing this, India sheltered families of Abdullah and Qanooni (among various other leaders) and gave them personal and political space, all on Indian government funds.[34]

Abdullah closely facilitated India's relations with the UF and helped New Delhi build political constituencies in north and west Afghanistan. India's attempt to provide these leaders with an option other than Pakistan reaped political rewards for years to come. Critically, compatible with Indian political traditions, the UF was portrayed as a 'secular nationalist face of Afghanistan,' in contrast to the Taliban's fundamentalism.[35] Dostum and Mohaqiq's excesses, and also those of Massoud, were largely written-off as wartime politics, whereas the Taliban remained pariah. As A. S. Dulat, the R&AW's chief in 1999–2000, says, 'while I was heading R&AW, we didn't try to reach out [to the Taliban] because we were so hooked onto the Northern Alliance, but then everything changed once the top Alliance military person, Ahmed Shah Masood, was killed'.[36] India had not built any credible alternatives to play a decisive role in Afghanistan. Its approach, despite being politically partisan, had all the markers of 'dependence' on the UF. Such partisanship, argues Dulat, was in fashion at that time. 'Masood's death narrowed down our [Indian] options ... [but] the thing is that this game was similar to what we were doing in Kashmir in 1988 and 89, when we were hooked to Farooq Abdullah' but neglected other Kashmiri leaders, 'which wasn't very smart'.[37] One may think that one has the best person, but that is often not the end of matter, argues Dulat. Not surprisingly, Massoud's assassination two days before 9/11 came as a major shock to India.[38]

India had developed close links with the *Jamiat-e-Islami* and Haji Qadir, a powerful Pashtun leader from east Afghanistan, even before the UF came into being.[39] Once the UF was formed, India automatically chose to support it financially and, as put by X, 'to only the bare minimum, just to keep their noses above the water.'[40] Most of this was done with X running the show from India's side, having developed a close rapport with Engineer Arif (Muhammad Arif Sarwari, Massoud's chief of intelligence) and his interpreter, Amrullah Saleh, who later led the Afghan intelligence services, the National Directorate of Security (NDS). In fact, X concedes that there was little overt political clearance for such covert activities during the Deve Gowda and Gujral governments, even if they agreed with the R&AW's approach. It was not until the entry of Brajesh Mishra as NSA in 1998 that India openly adopted an 'interventionist approach' in Afghanistan. While X refuses to give details of how he went about doing his business in cultivating links with the UF, he accepts that India was closest to Massoud and actively dealing with Dostum, who at that time was the *Amir* of north Afghanistan and had very close links with Russia and Uzbekistan. There was, however, more to India's role in its engagement with the UF. New Delhi was working as the communication system for these anti-Taliban commanders and tried hard to keep them all together under the UF umbrella. Says X:

> More than Iran and Russia, different Afghan factions understood us [India] well. India played a very important role in getting Dostum and Massoud together. Massoud was very unhappy with Dostum. We got the Shias and Dostum and Massoud together and gave money. We were looking for all anti-Taliban groups and trying to get them to work together.[41]

Indian spies conducted shuttle diplomacy between different UF factions to iron out their differences. Often leading to Massoud and Dostum targeting each other's senior aides, these rifts were potent enough to disintegrate the resistance to the Taliban. On 28 December 1999, for instance, when

India was busy dealing with the IC-814 hijacking, Massoud's men allegedly killed Abdul Chereek, a senior aide of Dostum in Sar-e-Pul. It was big blow to Dostum.[42] Just when New Delhi's attention was diverted to the hijacking crisis, Massoud had struck. New Delhi tried limiting Massoud and Dostum's differences but was failing at doing so effectively on the ground. However, the results of this covert shuttle diplomacy were visible in the India-friendly Afghan cabinet that was instituted in 2002 after the entry of the coalition forces and ouster of the Taliban.

'Pakistan's Vietnam'

The third aspect of this relationship was that despite partnering because of a 'common enemy', India and the UF were on separate strategic wavelengths. The UF's primary motive was to defeat the Taliban, which meant countering Pakistan. India's motive was to undercut Pakistan's influence by actively supporting any group that was willing to fight the Taliban. That Pakistan provided military supplies to the Taliban was an open secret. This time, however, under the watch of the Taliban, Pakistan had placed its own soldiers on Afghan soil to defeat the UF.[43] This fact played a critical role in tipping the balance in favour of the partisans over the conciliators. Of interest here is the duality of India's approach. Despite the MEA's official line of a stable Afghanistan and non-interference from external players, there was a silent under-current in India's security establishment that viewed Afghanistan as Pakistan's Vietnam and preferred the Pakistan army to get bogged down.[44] According to Major General (Retd.) Yeshwant Deva, this was so because 'Pashtuns within the Pakistan army, who have family ties in Afghanistan, would want it to become more engaged.'[45] More so, he continued, Pakistan would like to maintain some control over the Taliban (using its Pashtun-based 'Frontier Corps').[46] Neither was this approach novel to India's Afghanistan policy, nor subdued in popular narrative. In fact, according to Pramit Pal Chaudhuri, former member of India's National Security Advisory Board (NSAB) and a strategic affairs editor at the Hindustan Times, 'ultimately the game is how do you make Afghans strong enough to fight Pakistan or to bleed Pakistan inside Afghanistan ... If Pakistan were to be bogged down, it will be fine by us. And we will get another five to ten years of relative peace on our border with Pakistan.'[47] By this logic, it was in India's interest to keep the UF afloat but not too strong. The UF on the other hand, wanted an end to the conflict and full control over Afghanistan.

To be clear, there are multiple discourses on India's covert military support to the UF even today. According to Shyam Saran, India 'saw its interest in supporting the Northern Alliance. Not only supporting in political terms but also providing material and even military support.'[48] A host of former Indian diplomatic and intelligence officers, as well as Afghan officials close to Massoud in the 1990s corroborate India's involvement in the military sphere.[49] Interestingly, Ahmad Wali Massoud (younger brother of Ahmad Shah Massoud) offers a counter-narrative. In his words, India gave

> some political and moral support and probably some humanitarian support as well. Because the support was not in any other kind or any other form at all. It was not in the form of military [supplies]. Although from time to time the Resistance forces were being accused by the Taliban or by the Pakistani circles that India was supporting the Resistance militarily or sending advisors or arms, but they are all baseless.[50]

Wali Massoud's statement, however, is a minority view even in Afghanistan. According to most interviews conducted with former Massoud supporters (most of whom are still close to the Massoud family or Abdullah Abdullah and Qanooni), India did play a role in the military sphere. Allegedly, Ahmad Shah Massoud secretly visited India in 2001 to seek military support few months before his assassination on 9 September 2001.[51]

The debate today is more over the 'nature' of military supplies India provided the UF, i.e. were they 'lethal' or 'non-lethal'? As early as 23 October 1996, the Taliban said they had 'information that the Indian Government, until the very end was providing political, economic and military assistance to Burhanuddin Rabbani's illegal and unrepresentative government in Kabul'.[52] According to the Taliban, India was the key air link for the Rabbani administration in Kabul and helped keeping Ariana Afghan Airlines afloat.[53] Used for flying military supplies when operating out of New Delhi, Indian technicians were employed at the Bagram Airbase to keep warplanes combat-ready. There is proof that as early as mid-May 1995, the Indian government did consider Rabbani's requests for training Afghan pilots in the civilian sector.[54] However, given the little civilian traffic going to Kabul because of the security situation in Afghanistan, one can question the purpose of training Afghan pilots. New Delhi also supplied military spares for the UF's Russian-made weaponry, alongside medical treatment for Rabbani's wounded soldiers.[55] Islamabad had been alleging that under the MEA's cover of humanitarian assistance, Rao was funneling material support to Rabbani. This included sending spare parts and technicians to fix Soviet weaponry to allow Rabbani and Massoud to continue their fight against Hekmatyar and later the Taliban. According to Pakistan's army and intelligence sources, groups of two or three Indian cargo planes landed on Afghan soil on 15, 16, 21, and 27 June 1995. Apparently, while Rabbani denied such support from New Delhi, Dostum reported to the UN envoy Mahmoud Mestiri that Ukraine had supplied Masoud with thirty jet fighters while India was supporting this by providing military hardware.[56]

All this had happened before the fall of Kabul to the Taliban in September 1996, i.e. mostly under Rao's watch. Such a claim is at odds with the Rao doctrine. However, given Rao's predilection for political deception, determined foreign policy decisions (he had recognised Israel soon after coming to power, despite domestic criticism), and the non-lethal nature of such covert support, it is highly likely that India did give such support throughout the 1990s.[57] Though unable to confirm the covert element of this relationship, Krishnan Srinivasan, who was foreign secretary in 1994–95, confesses that the R&AW briefed him unusually regularly on their assessment of the situation in Afghanistan despite the issue not being top priority for the political and diplomatic leadership.[58] In Srinivasan's reading, the R&AW's focus on Afghanistan was essentially because they had developed considerable expertise and contacts with the anti-Pakistan factions in the country. In fact, much before the Taliban became a force worth reckoning, powerful Mujahideen leaders including Mohammad Fahim—who would lead the United Front column into Kabul in the wake of the US military intervention in 2001—visited New Delhi multiple times in 1994–95. Srinivasan, in his capacity as foreign secretary, would be asked by R&AW to meet these leaders for lunches in Delhi hotels.

> I remember distinctly meeting with Fahim [in 1994]. Now, these people were not coming just to have a meal, and certainly not with me. So, obviously there was more going on that meets the eye. There were quite a few of them ... but nearly three to four times I had lunches, teas, etc with Afghans ... always just general chit chat, but obviously they were in Delhi for other purposes ... of course the R&AW never tells you all that they know ... but even so I was very happy with what they did say ... and I think they were giving some material support to various groups in Afghanistan.[59]

According to Indian media sources, however, such a relationship was forged after the Taliban's entry into Kabul. India began covertly flying technicians to service the UF's fleet of Russian-built helicopters, as well as advisors to train Massoud's men in anti-armour techniques.[60] Spare parts and high-altitude warfare equipment worth more than US$ 10 million were also supplied and, despite the government's denials about Indian doctors treating Rabbani's soldiers in December 1996,[61] India opened a field hospital at the Farkhor air base in south Tajikistan in early 1999, close to the Afghan border.[62] Given the limited impact of such covert Indian support to the United Front, either before or after the rise of the Taliban in Kabul, it is clear that Rao did ameliorate R&AW's operations in Afghanistan in comparison with Rajiv's interventionism, but did not abandon them. From this perspective, Pakistan's claim about India's role in Afghanistan was correct, even if exaggerated.

American journalist Steve Coll concurs that India gave US$ 10 million in cash to Massoud sometime after 1999.[63] Declassified US diplomatic cable and intelligence dossiers also confirm India's provision of weapons to the UF. However, dates of such transactions are still kept classified in these cables (erased by a black marker).[64] According to a former Massoud loyalist who facilitated this relationship, 'India's help was mostly in terms of cash and medical supplies'.[65] India chipped in to the UF's kitty, which needed between US$ 2–3 million per month to survive and fight the Taliban.[66] Strictly speaking, it can be argued that India provided 'non-lethal' military support to the UF. However, given the critical role that this support played in keeping the UF afloat, the concept of lethality is metaphysical at best. What is of import is the limited nature of this support (jointly with Iran and Russia). In comparison to India's heavy military engagement either in Bangladesh in 1971 or Sri Lanka in the late 1980s and afterwards, its assistance to the UF was miniscule. As former US Assistant Secretary of State for South Asian Affairs Karl Inderfurth stated in March 1999, most of such support was coming from Russia and Iran, and that too was uncertain. 'Iran and Russia [and by implication India too] are more likely to end diplomatic and covert support to [Massoud] than Pakistan would be to end its support to the Taliban', he wrote in a secret report to the White House.[67] There was no guarantee of India's sustained military support to Massoud if 9/11 had not happened. X, India's secret agent in Afghanistan agrees that India's support to the UF, in collaboration with Iran and Russia, was not sufficient and may not have lasted very long. 'We were a poor country, and were barely managing to provide them [UF] support. Pakistan was more committed to the Taliban, and had the advantage of geography,' he admits.[68]

India's relations with the UF, therefore, were much more complex than the simplistic 'proxy thesis'. And this is precisely because of India's tendency to view Afghanistan through a Pakistan-centric lens. India's dilemma of normalising relations with Pakistan, but also undercutting Islamabad's influence in Afghanistan provided the context to India-UF relations. According to Indian analysts, Jaswant Singh's visit to Kandahar during the IC-814 hijacking incident was a signal of India's evolving policy narrative on Afghanistan, that is that India could not do away with the Pashtuns entirely.[69] Not surprisingly, India's distance from the former UF factions only grew after the US-led NATO intervention in 2001. As X concedes, after 2002, India lost its influence in Afghanistan 'by not supporting its friends from the former Northern Alliance.'[70] The gains of the 'great game that we played so successfully in the 1990s in Afghanistan, were lost during Manmohan Singh's government, which fruitlessly went about engaging Pakistan', he argues.[71] For most Indian policymakers, if it was not in India's interest to have a strong Taliban writ in Afghanistan, neither was it in its interest to have a strong UF (or any single ethnic faction) that disturbed the sociopolitical balance of Afghanistan. The dominance of one single interest group would have meant continuous tension. The essence of this strategic outlook and the policy narratives emerging from the same is best seen in India's initiative to influence Qanooni and Abdullah, at the Bonn conference in 2001 to give-up some ministerial positions.[72] Not long after this conference, in yet another u-turn, India switched political support in favour of Karzai, and yet again, risked alienating its friends in the north.

The UN fails

In addition to domestic causes, international attitudes towards the Taliban also strengthened the partisans over the conciliators. On 22 October 1996, the UNSC passed Resolution 1076 calling for 'an end to hostilities, outside interference and supply of arms to the parties of the conflict; [and] denounc[ing] discrimination against women and girls in Afghanistan'.[73] Seen as anathema, the Taliban had failed to legitimise its rule within and outside Afghanistan. Despite being recognised by Pakistan, Saudi Arabia, and the UAE, the Taliban failed to convince the world to undermine the Rabbani government. Instead, images of rough justice including stoning women to death in football stadiums came to symbolise the Taliban. Massoud, on the other hand, emerged as a visionary commander fighting this menace. Passed unanimously within the UNSC, India embraced resolution 1076, refused to recognise the Taliban, and refused to reopen its embassy in Kabul like many other countries. It allowed the Rabbani government to retain an embassy in New Delhi with Massoud Khalili as ambassador. India's political sympathies were out in the open. As per the advocacy coalition framework, the partisans found allies in the form of world opinion on the Taliban, and a solid diplomatic tool in the form of resolution

1076 to manipulate New Delhi's policy towards not engaging with the Taliban. This was anomalous in light of the Rao doctrine and India's bitter experience of emerging on the losing side in 1992. Two questions emerge. One, how inextricably linked was India's Afghanistan policy to the UN deliberations to broker peace? And two, how did regional and global strategic alignments shape India's Afghanistan policy? While the following paragraphs examine India's role at the UN, sections after this delve into Iran, Russia, and the CAR's role in strengthening the partisans.

A traditional believer in the UN and the norms espoused by the international institution, India wanted it to play an active role in resolving the Afghan conflict.[74] In addition to stabilising the situation, from an Indian perspective, UN intervention would undercut Pakistan's influence on domestic Afghan affairs. Expecting Pakistan and its proxies to limit their ambitions in the wake of a UN brokered truce, the idea was to bring an international conflict monitoring agency that could help endorse an 'Afghan solution'.[75] New Delhi had 'welcomed the UN Secretary General's Five-Point Peace Proposals in May 1991' and wanted full settlement of the Afghan crisis, 'based on her conviction that any such settlement should recognise the legitimate interests of all concerned'.[76] Drafted by Benon Sevan, the proposal entailed a triangular dialogue between Najibullah, the Pakistan government and the Pakistan-based Mujahideen. Its key elements entailed an intra-Afghan dialogue to build 'a credible and impartial transition mechanism', that would have a broad-based mandate from the people of Afghanistan and allow them an opportunity to participate in free and fair elections, and lead to a cessation of hostilities during the transition.[77] The dialogue failed to take off. Instead, Islamabad brokered the Peshawar Accord, leaving little space for India to maneuver the situation to its benefit. Nonetheless, as the Peshawar accord failed and Rabbani reached out to New Delhi in September 1992, and amidst growing tensions with Hekmatyar, the MEA called for an urgent renewal of the peace initiative under the UN.[78] India stated that 'the absence of any political process, leading to the settlement acceptable to all sections of the Afghan people, has accentuated sectarian and ethnic tensions which could seriously undermine Afghanistan's unified character as a nation-state'.[79]

The UN's failure to broker peace, both in 1988 and 1992, raised serious doubts about its conflict resolution capacity. This was also the time when former Yugoslavia broke into five different states between 1989 and 1992; the Nagorno-Karabakh war was raging since 1988, and a civil war broke out in Tajikistan in which the *Jamiat-e-Islami* was actively involved. In December 1993, the UNGA adopted Resolution 48/208 requesting the Secretary-General to dispatch a special mission to Afghanistan that could assess the situation and find out how the UN can assist Afghanistan.[80] Resultantly, Mahmoud Mestiri became Sevan's successor as the UNSG's special representative to Afghanistan in February 1994. India's response, despite its calls for a renewed UN initiative, was lukewarm: 'A new peace initiative launched by the United Nations under the Special Envoy of the UN Secretary General Ambassador Mahmoud Mestiri is underway. But prospects for a peaceful political settlement in the near future still remain uncertain', remarked the MEA.[81]

The difference between India and the UN's thinking was underlined in an exchange between British secretary of state for foreign and commonwealth affairs, Douglas Hurd, and foreign secretary Srinivasan at the Hyderabad House in Delhi in mid-1994 (in the presence of foreign minister Dinesh Singh, who could not speak due to a stroke that left him partly paralysed). London had supported Mestiri's settlement plan on Afghanistan throughout, and was keen on seeing Rabbani step down (allowing Hekmatyar to assume power). When Hurd expressed these views to Srinivasan, the latter lashed out that Rabbani, from India's perspective, was the best possible alternative in the circumstances, and New Delhi did not see any reason why he should hand over power.[82] In what he remembers as an especially unpleasant and acrimonious exchange, Srinivasan viewed Hurd's argument (of pressuring the head of government of another country to step down) as 'preposterous'.[83] India's preference for Rabbani over Hekmatyar reflected the ongoing tension between Rao's officially conciliatory approaches and the thriving anti-Pakistan partisanship among policymakers. Having become increasingly comfortable with Massoud and his associates, Indian policymakers did not want to risk another exploratory round of dealing with and subsequently cultivating Hekmatyar in a constantly changing conflict environment. London and New Delhi's positions on Afghanistan, thus, were just as far apart in the 1990s, as they had been in the 1980s, and as they remained throughout the US-led war after the 9/11 attacks.

The Taliban's emergence in October 1994 plunged Mestiri's mission into total disarray.[84] Moving towards Kabul at a spectacular pace and having defeated *Hizb-e-Islami* and *Hizb-e-Wahdat*, the power balance in Afghanistan hung between the Taliban on one side and the Rabbani government in Kabul with Ismael Khan in Herat and Dostum in Mazar-e-Sharif on the other in 1995. Instead of changing tack, given the evolving situation, Mestiri stuck to his transition plan and sought a ceasefire followed by elections. Rabbani stalled the plan, making Mestiri's mission irrelevant. Not surprisingly, in a speech at a donor conference in Stockholm in June 1995, Mestiri denounced the 'Rabbani government as an illegitimate faction dominated by Tajiks'.[85] Mestiri was particularly wary of Moscow's efforts to build a Massoud-Dostum alliance in the face of the Taliban and thought that this could be 'quite damaging to the peace process'. In the same speech, he proposed that the UN and international community should challenge 'the legitimacy of those who claim to be in power [Massoud-Rabbani]'.[86] The UN held Rabbani responsible for undermining its peace plan at various points in time, but mostly in the latter half of 1995 just before and after the fall of Herat.[87]

Similar to then Pakistan's PM Benazir Bhutto's denunciation of the Rabbani government as 'illegitimate' in early 1995, Mestiri's statement did not cut ice with New Delhi. Having reopened its Kabul mission in May 1995 after a period of forced closure, the official Indian view became grimmer. The MEA noted:

> The situation has been further exacerbated by the interference of Pakistan directly and more so through its creation, the Taliban. The peace initiative launched by the United Nations under the Special Envoy of the UN Secretary General Ambassador Mestiri suggesting transfer of power as an interim arrangement was not found acceptable by all factions. As a result, prospects for a peaceful political settlement in the near future still remain uncertain'.[88]

In what top Afghanistan expert Amin Saikal calls an 'above the horizon' approach, UN mediators could not grasp the complexity of the Afghan problem.[89] Mestiri made the same mistakes as Sevan and could do little to pacify the situation on the ground. His overtly hostile stance towards the Rabbani government did little other than to attract strong rebuttals from the *Jamiat-e-Islami*.[90] The compelling failure of Mestiri's mission was underlined in the UNSC meeting on 9 April 1996, where it was concluded that foreign intervention in Afghanistan was thwarting international efforts to achieve a negotiated settlement to the conflict. The vice-minister for foreign affairs of Afghanistan told the council that the special mission had failed to explicitly identify foreign interference as the root cause of the conflict and to recommend effective measures to terminate it.[91] Dixit, writing in 1996 on the eve of Kabul's fall, worried that 'Afghanistan faces the prospect of not only turmoil and violence but also disintegration as a country if things are not brought under control soon'.[92] He worried that the UN and its special envoys to Afghanistan, Sevan and Mestiri, had not been able to reconcile the political, ethnic, or military contradictions in that situation.

The Taliban's takeover of Kabul in September 1996 crushed whatever little hope was left for the UN to intervene in Afghanistan. With Mestiri's mission an utter failure, the UN Resolution 1076 was little more than an exasperated sigh by the UN. Prakash Shah, India's representative to the UN in 1996, made it clear that India had been a principal victim of state-supported terrorism and its export from across its borders. 'It was essential that the main focus of United Nations' peace efforts in Afghanistan should be the cessation of hostilities and prevention of foreign interference and outside support to rebel forces', Shah noted.[93] Advocating caution and adopting an internationalist approach, Indian diplomacy was being steered by the conciliators till this point. With the Rao doctrine still somewhat influential, India was open to engaging with any faction that came to power in Kabul. Mestiri's failure to comprehend a highly fluid situation and propose adequate reconciliation mechanisms by the end of 1995 undermined India's internationalist strategy in Afghanistan. However, until this point India firmly hoped that the UN-led approach would work.

For India, the UN could have been successful in brokering peace in Afghanistan but only if Mestiri recognised Pakistan's open, and controversial, support to the Taliban. Accepting this fact would have strengthened Indian claims that Pakistan was using military coercion both in Afghanistan and Kashmir. This, however, did not happen. Remaining defensive at the UN over Pakistan's allegations of Indian military's human rights violations in Kashmir, New Delhi struggled to keep the Kashmir issue a bilateral matter with Pakistan. Wanting to bring Kashmir into the international spotlight on one hand, Pakistan wanted India to keep out of Afghanistan on the other. According to the MEA, 'India effectively countered efforts by Pakistan to get the UN and its agencies to pass resolutions against India on issues of human rights and Kashmir'.[94] Engagement with different Afghan factions and accepting the UN-led process became imperative in this context. Kabul's fall in September 1996 left India clueless as its capacity constraints had already limited its policy options in Afghanistan. In the meantime, all other regional players found their favourites. Iran threw its weight behind the Shiite and Hazara-dominated *Hizb-e-Wahdat* and Herat's Ismael Khan, while Uzbekistan with Moscow's support backed Dostum in the north and Massoud in Kabul. According to Raghunath and Saran, India did not view the situation as much in ethnic terms, but increasingly saw it in its interest to support anti-Taliban outfits.[95]

Persian connection

Iran was pivotal in tilting the balance in the favour of partisans after Kabul's fall. The rise of the Taliban, a Sunni militant group supported by Saudi Arabia and the US, went against Shia-dominated Iran's regional interests. The UN's failure to broker peace led Iran to seize the opportunity to conduct an international conference on Afghanistan on 29–30 October 1996. Coming after months of shuttle diplomacy by Iranian diplomats, the conference witnessed a confluence of interests between every regional player barring Pakistan. Islamabad's aversion to India's participation in the conference did not cut ice with Tehran. The then Iranian President Akbar Hashemi Rafsanjani's refusals to entertain Pakistan's calls to isolate India made Islamabad boycott the conference.[96] About a week earlier, Indian president K. R. Narayanan had visited Tehran to discuss Afghanistan and Kashmir and found a receptive audience.[97] Pakistan's refusal to include India on Afghanistan directly impacted India's stance on engagement with the Taliban. Salman Haidar, then India's foreign secretary, who attended the conference with Vivek Katju, says India was actively excluded on Pakistan's insistence while the US went along.[98] This meeting in Tehran, however, was the 'only meeting' in those days which was critical and was based on a common cause between India and Iran. Even then, 'we [India and Iran] had interests, but we did not have that many options'.[99] Haidar's successor, Raghunath, concurs that in his meetings with the Iranians 'there was confirmation of our common interest that the Northern Alliance [United Front] needs to be helped and this whole threat to peace, security, and stability in Afghanistan must be countered.'[100] Pakistan's decision to refrain from attending the conference in protest at India's participation, according to the MEA, 'signified closer understanding between India and Iran on a crucial regional issue.'[101]

Occurring in the context of Tehran's bitter rivalry with Washington over the former's acquisition of nuclear reactors from Moscow, and Iran's denunciation of the Taliban as a US creation abetted by Islamabad; there were strong grounds for India-Iran bonding (something that Zia had actively tried to contain during the 1980s).[102] Rafsanjani's April 1995 visit and Iranian foreign minister Ali Akbar Velayati's January 1996 visit to India proved critical in cementing ideas on a variety of strategic issues. If diplomatic signals count for anything, India's keenness to develop links with Iran was clear in Rao's personal visit to receive Rafsanjani at the airport.[103] During his meeting with Rao, Rafsanjani extended support on Kashmir and sought India's support vis-à-vis Washington and on Afghanistan.[104] Rafsanjani's visit strengthened the perception of a US-Pakistan nexus that may be detrimental to India's interests. According to K. Subrahmanyam: 'Any Pakistani involvement in the containment strategy against Iran at the behest of the U.S. will destabilise a Pakistan which will have an openly acknowledged nuclear arsenal.'[105] Challenges emanating from an unstable Pakistan will have to be dealt by India, added Subrahmanyam.[106] As India and Iran grew close, Benazir Bhutto's visit to Iran in November 1995 did little to change the negative Pakistan-Iran dynamic. The rise of the Sunni Taliban in Afghanistan and Shiite militancy within Pakistan restricted normalisation of relations between Islamabad and Tehran.[107] India's unconditional backing to Iran during the mid and late 1990s was visible in India's refusal to accept the Bill Clinton administration's efforts to link Iran with terrorism.[108]

Lalit Mansingh, former foreign secretary, states India's strategic dependence on Iran in Afghanistan during the 1990s and early 2001 as such:

> We [India] discovered that we could play a security role during the Taliban period when the Northern Alliance was formed. And since Russia and Iran were on the same page we were very comfortable in giving military assistance. But then we didn't have to worry about the routes because we had the active support of the Iranians. And therefore getting military supplies across to the Northern Alliance was not a big problem. With the help of the Russians and the Iranians we could do that. But the fact is that it also acknowledges that India can't work alone. India by itself cannot play a major role in the security situation of Afghanistan.[109]

To consolidate bilateral relations and signal strategic convergence between India and Iran, PM Vajpayee visited Tehran on 10 April 2001. A 'pathbreaking document', as external affairs and defence minister Jaswant Singh called it, the Teheran declaration emerged from the visit.[110] Emphasising the need for 'a broadbased government in Afghanistan, which reflects the aspirations of all Afghan people', the declaration firmly condemned the Sunni Taliban's extremism.[111] Despite the conciliator's endurance in 1992, changing regional alignments and particularly the Persian connection, proved fertile ground for the partisans' growth by 1996, and dominance afterwards.

Russia's bear hug

Providing muscular agency to India and Iran's strategic convergence on Afghanistan was Moscow's threat to use force against the Taliban. Blaming Washington for helping the militia, Vladimir Lukin, international advisor to Russian President Boris Yelstin, said in October 1996 that brazen US interference in Afghan affairs to counter Iran was 'primitive and short-sighted'.[112] Having lost the First Chechen War in August 1996, and gone through the Nagorno-Karabakh war, Moscow was anxious of the Taliban's emergence as a dominant force. With the Tajik civil war far from resolution and the 1991–93

Georgian Civil War fresh in memory, Moscow was clear in its anti-Taliban intent. Denouncing Pakistan's armed support to the militia, Nikolae Schevechenkova, head of Russia's diplomatic mission in Mazar-e-Sharif, said on 20 October 1996: 'If the Taliban comes to the North there will be terrible bloodshed. And if our borders are under threat we would take appropriate measures.'[113] Schevechenkova's tough message had political precedent. Moscow had already stationed a division worth of troops in Tajikistan near the Afghan border.

On 4 October 1996, Kazakhastan, the Kyrgyz Republic, Uzbekistan, Kazakhastan, and Russia had met in Almaty to discuss regional stability and security. Occurring just a week before the Tehran Conference, the Almaty meeting concluded that the Taliban was a direct threat to the domestic stability and national interests of the Commonwealth of Independent States (CIS) member countries as well as the region. Though the various Central Asian nations were concerned about a heavier Russian military presence on their soil in the wake of the Taliban's rise, and were open to a negotiated settlement, they had limited say in the final outcome of the conference.[114] Turkmenistan, at the same time, was supplying energy to the Taliban and was firm on remaining on good terms with all Afghan protagonists (a classic conciliatory approach), in order to ensure safe passage of oil pipelines for which US and Argentinian firms such as Unocal and Bridas were actively lobbying the Taliban.[115] Issuing a joint statement at the end of the meeting, the CIS countries appealed to the Taliban to cease military activities and threatened that if this did not happen, the CIS would give an 'adequate response'.[116] Supporting the meeting, the MEA was keen on Russia's support on this issue. Having signed a defence agreement in 1997, Moscow and New Delhi were increasingly converging on various geopolitical issues.

For one, India paid heavy amounts to Russia for supplying weapons to the UF from Tajikistan. In the process, not only did the UF receive what it required to fight its battles, even the Russian defence industry received a boost.[117] Russia extended support to India on Kashmir, and India agreed to legitimise Russian military actions in international forums and strengthen bilateral relations throughout the 1990s. Critically, all Central Asian countries concurred with partisan tenets towards the Taliban. As official documents note, India's interaction with countries of the (Central Asian) region underscored a common commitment to the stability, unity, independence and territorial integrity of Afghanistan as well as a shared approach that the violation of these principles would adversely affect the entire region. Developments in

Afghanistan have a direct bearing on the situation within Central Asia and their efforts to achieve political stability.[118] A forward diplomatic and military approach, entailing containment of the Taliban, became a regional norm. Regardless of internal debates between the conciliators and the partisans in context of India's own military and diplomatic capabilities, the external situation had quickly shifted in favour of the partisans.

Going against the evolving regional sentiment towards the Taliban and engaging them politically, as conciliators advocated, could have cost India diplomatic support on Kashmir from Moscow, Tehran and some, if not all, Central Asian states. This was reflected in India's active diplomacy with Kazakhstan, Turkmenistan, the Kyrgyz Republic and Tajikistan. President Narayanan visited the Kyrgyz Republic and Kazakhstan in September 1996. He was in Asthana discussing Afghanistan (among other issues) with Kazakh President Nurulsultan Nazarbaev, two days before Kabul fell to the Taliban. Nazarbaev visited India soon after in December 1996. As a result of decisions taken in these visits, India and Kazakhstan formed joint working groups on a variety of sectors including nuclear energy, hydrocarbon, and defence. Additionally, in February 1997, India, Iran and Turkmenistan signed a trilateral agreement on the international transit of goods. Similar meetings were held and agreements signed between Uzbekistan and India. The MEA stated that India maintained 'the tradition of close political understanding and mutual cooperation', and had sympathy for the efforts made to 'normalise the political situation within the country through peaceful dialogue and negotiations.'[119] Tajikistan soon allowed India to run a field hospital in Farkhor and allowed Indian journalists to cover the Afghan civil war from Tajik territory.[120] With New Delhi throwing its weight behind the UF, Tajikistan became a staging base for its covert operations.[121]

Uzbekistan was the only country whose integrity towards supporting the UF was being doubted by India. Worried about the Islamist Movement of Uzbekistan (IMU) and under Moscow's influence, the Uzbeks supported the Almaty Conference and advocated military activism against the Taliban if needed. However, by the early 2000s, when the Taliban seemed firmly rooted in Afghanistan and was also getting diplomatically involved in other regional processes like the six plus two dialogue, the Uzbeks 'started changing their mind'.[122] According to X, Pakistan and the Taliban must have given 'silent guarantees that they will keep the IMU in control if Uzbekistan stops its support to Massoud'.[123] Indeed, in mid-2000, Uzbekistan started asking most UF leaders to leave their country and seek refuge elsewhere. However, these aspects of Pakistan's links with Uzbekistan require further evidence. What was clear, nonetheless, was that the stage to isolate Pakistan in the region was set, and as Saikal put it, 'Islamabad's support for Taliban has driven the Pakistan government into a cul de sac as the entire region has ganged up on the side of the ousted Afghan government'.[124] Even China, the alleged 'all-weather' friend of Pakistan, urged Islamabad to curb the Taliban's ambitions.[125] By mid-1997, barring the three supporters, no other country agreed to diplomatically recognise the Taliban.

Regional advocacies on Afghanistan had decisively shifted in favour of the partisans in 1996. The UNSC Resolution 1076 reflected the international community's aversion to the Taliban. Nonetheless, with its hands full with various other conflicts in the region, the UN failed to broker peace in Afghanistan. This post-Cold War context of weak nation-states struggling to consolidate legitimate power lent credence to the partisans' coercive diplomacy. Despite calls for peaceful resolution of the Afghan civil war, the Taliban's entry antagonised the region barring a few countries. For India, which had till now treaded a defensive diplomatic path, any idea of political accommodation of the Taliban became problematic. Given its regional interests, rivalries, and aspirations, keeping on good terms with Iran, the CIS, and Russia became a priority for New Delhi. Realising that the ISI was running training camps for the HM in Khost and Nuristan to foment Kashmiri insurgency, New Delhi adopted an active counter-insurgency approach domestically and sought strategic (anti-Pakistan) coalition-building internationally.[126] This regional coercive strategy of which India became a part in late 1996 was key in keeping the partisans dominant over the conciliators in May 1997 when Mazar-e-Sharif fell to the Taliban temporarily.[127] India wanted to lobby Washington as well, but the US was on a different page. Not having experienced serious violence on its own territory or against its citizens, the US did not view localised Islamist insurgencies abroad as a national threat in 1996.

As detailed by Pakistani journalist Ahmed Rashid, American oil companies were busy eyeing Central Asian oil reserves and hosting Taliban delegations in the US to lobby for their support.[128] Washington's policy beliefs shifted somewhat in August 1998 after its embassies in Nairobi and Dar-es-Salaam were bombed. But they were altered decisively after the 9/11 attacks. If the international dynamic was critical in increasing the partisans' influence on India's Afghanistan policy behavior in 1996 and 1997, how did the situation on Afghanistan impact this between 1998 and 2001? Just like the Mujahideen in 1992, the Taliban wanted to engage with New Delhi. Though it was wary of India's support to the UF, the Taliban knew that the only country in the region that can really balance Pakistan's influence on Afghan affairs was India. On the morning of 25 December 1999, top Taliban leadership in Kandahar woke up to just such an opportunity. The Taliban, from their perspective would do everything right. However, eight days after Christmas, to the Taliban's perennial wonder, instead of being thankful, the Indians began hating the Taliban even more.

'A basket of worst alternatives'

At 4.53 PM, exactly twenty Christmas eves after the Soviet invasion of Afghanistan, at the dawn of the twenty-first century, India's worst nightmare vis-à-vis Afghanistan came true.[129] Five armed men belonging to Pakistan-based *Harkat-ul-Ansar* (later called *Harkat-ul-Mujahideen*) hijacked the Indian Airlines flight IC-814 en-route to Delhi from Kathmandu.[130] The plane was first taken to Amritsar where Indian authorities were unable to hold it. After Amritsar it was forced to land in Lahore, where Pakistani authorities re-fuelled it and subsequently the plane was taken to Dubai. In Dubai, after negotiations, twenty-seven hostages including women, children, and Rupin Katyal, the one passenger that had been killed, were offloaded. The plane was then taken to the Taliban's stronghold, Kandahar, on the morning of Christmas day. Lacking diplomatic relations meant that no Indian official was immediately available to engage with the Taliban and negotiate with the hijackers. But soon after, India dispatched MEA Joint Secretary (Pakistan-Afghanistan-Iran) Vivek Katju, senior Intelligence Bureau (IB) officials Ajit Doval and Nehchal Sandhu, and senior R&AW officials C. D. Sahay and some more intelligence officials to Kandahar to negotiate. While the Cabinet Committee on Security (CCS), India's highest decision-making body on security, called the final shots; EAM Jaswant Singh dealt with the crisis in real-time with R&AW chief Amarjit Singh Dulat briefing him regularly. The UN, for its part, sent Erick de Mul, the UNDP chief in Pakistan, as an observer and negotiator, who convinced the Taliban to ensure the safety of passengers in the plane.

From the Taliban's side, Mullah Omar (*Amir-ul-Momineen*), Mullah Akhtar Mansour (civil aviation minister), Mullah Wakil Ahmad Muttawakil (foreign minister), and Mullah Akhtar Mohammad Usmani (military chief of Kandahar who controlled the airport) called the shots. Allegedly, in the shadows, at the airport, were ISI officials.[131] In fact, according to Sahay, the ISI supported the operation actively throughout the incident (including in Kathmandu), and managed it from Karachi, just like the 2008 attacks in Mumbai.[132] Such was the ISI's influence on the Taliban, in Sahay's assessment, that the latter had handed over the control tower to the ISI operatives to carry out negotiations with the Indian team. Moreover, while initially the Taliban refused to allow the plane to land in Kabul, it changed its position once advised by the ISI that it was their operation to secure the release of HuA leadership.[133] The negotiations lasted eight days with India securing freedom for all passengers and crew at the cost of releasing three top militants: Masood Azhar (who created the *Jaish-e-Mohammad*, JeM, within weeks of his release and was an important go-between the AQ and the ISI),[134] Omar Saeed Sheikh (later arrested in Pakistan for the alleged kidnapping and murder of American journalist Daniel Pearl), and Mushtaq Ahmad Zargar (responsible for running militant training camps from Pakistan-administered Kashmir).[135] Having no relations with the Taliban till then, the hijacking incident left a deep imprint on India's vision of the Taliban.[136] The incident lay bare the difference between India and the Taliban's world-view. Already wary of the Taliban, India went further into an embrace with the fractured United Front.[137]

New Delhi faced two different policy dilemmas during the hijack. Firstly, having concluded that the hijacking was being clandestinely supported by Pakistan and had roots in the Kashmir problem, the question was whether to negotiate with the hijackers or not. According to L. K. Advani, senior BJP leader and then home minister, negotiating with the hijackers would make India look 'soft' on the issue of terrorism and would amount to 'appeasement of terrorists'.[138] He wanted India to exercise proactive policies similar to those of China and Israel, which was storming the plane militarily, regardless of the human and economic costs involved.[139] Other leaders, including Vajpayee, Jaswant Singh, and Brajesh Mishra (who was India's representative to the UN in 1980 when the Soviet intervention occurred), viewed the crisis from a humanitarian and political perspective.[140] More killings due to government inaction, or hyper-action, would mean political suicide for the BJP-led National Democratic Alliance (NDA) government. The policy direction, thus, was: '(a) the earliest termination of the hijacking; (b) the safe return of the passengers, crew and aircraft; and (c) safeguarding national security.'[141] Negotiations with the hijackers became imperative to achieve these objectives. Consequently, talking to the Taliban became essential. After years of no contact, when circumstances forced India to engage with the Taliban. Secondly, there was the long-term strategic dilemma of how to deal with the Taliban, particularly because the UF was close to being wiped out militarily by then, and more disturbingly, had no value for India during the hijacking crisis itself.

Though the eight-day ordeal left India convinced of the Pakistan-Taliban nexus, it also left New Delhi shocked by its own strategic failure to develop ties with all Afghan groups. As MoS for external affairs Ajit Panja told the parliament three months after the incident, the termination of the hijacking in the manner it was achieved was the 'best possible solution in a basket of worse alternatives'.[142] For then foreign secretary Mansingh, India had realised at that point, that it 'had lost out in Afghanistan'.[143] Almost every interviewee, from the MEA to the Indian security agencies, agree on this point. Could India have adopted a different approach to the hijacking episode to reconcile these two dilemmas? According to Dixit, New Delhi had the option to refuse direct negotiations with the hijackers, and let the Taliban sort the situation and take responsibility.[144] This was not feasible because India had not recognised the Taliban. Any attempt to allow the Taliban to handle the crisis would require political recognition, something that the Taliban wanted. Two, even if India recognised the Taliban politically, the latter could have simply stated the hijackers demands to New Delhi and left it at that—it was a risk at the least. Either way, India would have had to contact the Taliban. To be clear, this policy dilemma over negotiating with the hijackers, which had their own coalitions, was context-specific and had only an indirect link to the larger debate between the partisans and the conciliators. India's limited engagement with the Taliban, in this context, does not automatically imply a change in its larger policy approach vis-à-vis the Taliban. In effect, India's policy of non-engagement with the Taliban did not change.

Does this mean that there was no real debate over the Taliban question after the IC-814 incident? Though not in public given how emotive the topic was (and still is), debate between the partisans and the conciliators continued. With a strategic failure staring them in the face, the question of how to develop India's presence in the Pashtun-dominated areas of south and east Afghanistan gained salience in New Delhi's strategic circles. Focus on the UF had paid little dividends during the IC-814 crisis, while Pakistan achieved a strategic coup. The contours of the debate, however, underwent a change. While the partisans started pointing towards political and tribal nuances within Pashtuns, the conciliators grudgingly accepted the limited reach India can possibly have even if it tried to cultivate ties with the Taliban. Who were the conciliators in office at that time? Based on multiple interviews, personal memoirs, and crosschecks it can be established that Jaswant Singh, Brajesh

Mishra, Vajpayee, Dulat, and Dixit were some of the key conciliators during and after the hijacking.

These conciliators advocated direct communication channels with the Taliban, if not outright political recognition. According to some, Singh's unilateral decision to fly to Kandahar had a political purpose, which was to open that channel of communication with the Taliban.[145] Jaswant Singh concurs that he wanted to meet Mullah Omar and had extensive discussions with Muttawakil as well. Any visit of a senior political figure from India to Kandahar meant tacit political signaling to the Taliban, that New Delhi is ready to engage.[146] This was, however, not advisable according to Sood.[147] Even more ill-advised was releasing those three 'goons'.[148] Singh's decision to fly to Kandahar had outraged X as well. Considering it absolutely unnecessary, X thought that Singh's visit 'was an act of bravado put up by an ex-army man who had forgotten that he was a politician. All was done and dusted by the time Singh reached Kandahar'.[149] Singh's decision to visit Kandahar, however, was a purely political call, without any input from the foreign affairs and security bureaucracy.[150] Singh admitted that 'Vivek Katju, Ajit Doval, and C. D. Sahay were not unanimous on his decision to fly to Kandahar, but they wanted someone with the authority to make spot decisions.[151] The opposition, led by Congress, kicked up a storm in the Lok Sabha over the BJP's handling of the hijacking and Singh's decision to visit Kandahar.[152]

According to Sood, 'it was exaggerated hope that we could make a breakthrough with the Taliban, the Muttawakil and types. They were not in a good mood, they had just scored a victory over you, and they had got these goons out. And they were still under considerable Pakistani control ... So there was not going to be any possibility of the Taliban coming to talk to you [India]'.[153] Indeed, the first person to be greeted and hugged by the Taliban was Masood Azhar while Singh waited. And the man waiting to receive Azhar was none other than Mullah Akhtar Mansour, who emerged as the Taliban's top leader in 2015 (and was later killed in a US drone strike in May 2016).[154] The fact that the Taliban did not allow India to undertake military action against the hijackers in Kandahar and positioned their forces in an offensive position against the Indian planes cemented the perception of Taliban-ISI nexus in Indian minds.[155] A top security official privy to the IC-814 negotiations and a key partisan, confirms:

> There was no redefining of policy vis-à-vis Afghanistan at that point. We knew that Pakistan is controlling them [Taliban]. We had lost ground in Afghanistan and there were minority views that we should talk to the Taliban, not everyone felt like that.[156]

The hijacking crisis deepened India's perception of the Taliban being Pakistan's agents. Raghunath, who had retired as the foreign secretary less than a month before the hijacking incident, disagrees with the notion that Jaswant Singh's visit had much to do with opening a dialogue with the Taliban. In his opinion, the visit can be explained only in the immediate context of the hijacking, and not in the larger strategic context of India's approach towards the Taliban.[157] From the political side, Advani, a staunch partisan, was much opposed to any 'appeasement' of 'terrorists' or those who 'abet terrorists'.[158] Farooq Abdullah, then chief minister of Jammu and Kashmir, was also averse to the idea of releasing the prisoners, and did it only on Dulat's persistent requests.[159] What was clear, according to these partisans, was that India should actively try preventing, if it can, a similar kind of fundamentalist Sunni regime emerging in Kabul.[160]

Singh never said it in so many words that he wanted a 'strategic dialogue' with the Taliban. However, the contours of India's international diplomacy had changed drastically after Pokharan II. The NDA government was actively courting Washington to ease the pressure of sanctions imposed by the US after India's nuclear tests in May 1998. According to some Indian observers, senior individuals in the NDA government knew in the late 1990s and early 2000s (around the IC 814 incident) that non-engagement with the Taliban was not an option anymore.[161] However, this was not a systemic change and many senior bureaucrats were firmly opposed to the idea of engaging with the Taliban (as the above interviews summarily reflect). Such change thinking among India's political leadership apparently stemmed from the realisation that relations with the United Front were unlikely to be sustainable on a long term basis.

India had also tried reaching out to the Taliban through Indian Muslim clerics from the Deoband seminaries in Uttar Pradesh (UP) during the hijack.[162] Being from the same school of the Sunni sect, the Taliban viewed the Deobandis with respect. In fact, the Jamiat-e-Ulema-e-Pakistan, headed by Maulana Fazlur Rahman, the Taliban's ideologue and leader of the opposition in Pakistan (between 2002 and 2007), organised the 134th anniversary of the Deoband seminary in Peshawar just months before the 9/11 attacks which over half a million Pashtuns from Pakistan's frontier region as well as from Afghanistan attended.[163] However, soon after, India's Deobandi clerics termed the Taliban's techniques 'un-Islamic' and disassociated Deobandi Islam from the Taliban's practices. The partisans firmly influenced policy output despite doubts over India's actions from a geo-strategic perspective. Why were some officials from the bureaucracy so opposed to the idea of engaging with the Taliban even after realising that India had lost out in Afghanistan? Was it simply an 'ideological stand'? While India's interpretation of the Taliban from its domestic context played a critical role, this was not the only reason for the partisan's dominance. India's close relations with Russia and traditional suspicion of the US added weight.

Foes from south?

Within ten hours of the hijacking, all three militants were escorted to Pakistan. Adding insult to injury, India received a bill of US$ 111,324 from the Taliban reclaiming costs towards food, fuel, and other services rendered towards flight IC-814.[164] Unsurprisingly, India's anger at the Taliban, only grew. The juxtaposition of the Taliban's narratives on the hijacking incident, however, also highlight the strong biases in India's own interpretation of the situation. To be clear, despite being opposed to the Taliban, India officially thanked them for their 'correct' approach as mediators.[165] Singh was 'gratified to report that the Taliban is fully cooperating with the relief team and the negotiating team'.[166] Even Khalili, Rabbani's emissary to India and a die-hard anti-Taliban advocate said, 'the Taliban are not beasts, they are also human beings.'[167] In fact, there were many instances during the negotiations when the Taliban pressured the hijackers to alter their demands and propose a blanket deal rather than a piecemeal approach to the release of the hostages.[168] However, India also blamed the Taliban for allowing the three militants to leave Afghanistan, and for having 'sympathies' with the hijackers.[169] The Taliban's stance and involvement in the crisis underwent several stages.[170] Having never dealt with such a situation before, they were both worried about an impending foreign policy disaster on their soil but also hopeful of turning it into an opportunity to win international acclaim.

As mentioned above, the Taliban had no role in the planning or execution of the hijacking. According to Syed Akbar Agha, former head of the Jaish-ul-Muslimeen and a close aide of Mullah Omar, 'the plane was hijacked by the Pakistanis and not under the guidance of the Taliban. And if we see the negative dimension of the hijack, we also need to see the positive dimension'.[171] The safe return of the plane and all hostages was the positive in Akbar Agha's words. 'All the people were rescued ... it was great and positive work that the Taliban did'. Also, 'the Taliban has an independent viewpoint, regardless of what Pakistan says,' he added.[172] Hakim Mujahid, the Taliban's representative to the UN in 2001, corroborates this point. There was no diplomatic relationship between the Indian government and the Taliban. 'And the Indian government also made the mistake of not recognising that [Taliban] government at that time ... and I do remember that the Taliban authorities very wisely dealt with that [IC-814] case and they could release safely the Indian airplane. That was also a point of making good relations between the Indian government and the Taliban authorities. But both India and the Islamic Emirate of Afghanistan could not exploit that opportunity (sic)'.[173] Instead, on 19 December 2000, India co-sponsored (with the US and Russia) UNSC Resolution 1333,[174] that banned all military assistance to the Taliban and ordered a closure of its various training camps.[175]

When asked what the Taliban conveyed to Pakistan during the hijack, Mujahid was categorical: 'that it will be good for the Pakistani authorities to not allow the plane to come to Afghanistan. Not to use Afghanistan's soil for this kind of incidents'.[176] Reports from the *Afghan Islamic Press*, an online news bulletin used by the Taliban to advocate its views, confirm that the Taliban wanted the plane to leave Afghan soil immediately.[177] Once it was established that the plane was not in the condition to fly due to technical faults, the hijackers were asked to surrender or release the hostages. Though Indian officials remained unconvinced, this narrative does hold currency. Dulat confirms that the message India was getting from the Taliban during the hijacking was 'we [Taliban] don't know you [India] guys, you don't want to know us'.[178] This was one reason why Jaswant Singh, whatever the intent and consequences of his visit to Kandahar may have been, 'was totally out of his own when he landed in Kandahar'. For Dulat, a long-time conciliator, the IC-814 experience should have taught India a lesson, which was to talk to everyone, because once a state decides on blanket engagement, no actor gets too comfortable.[179] Expecting the Taliban to be sensitive towards India after rejecting the regime (in addition to Pakistan's preponderant presence at Kandahar), despite the former's attempts to open channels with New Delhi, was unrealistic.

Differences between the Taliban and Pakistan, though not threatening to Islamabad, had existed from the very beginning as the Taliban refused to recognise the Durand Line. Just like all other Afghan governments, the Taliban began entering Pakistan's tribal agencies like Mohmand and claimed it as Afghan territory by planting their flags.[180] Raghunath, a partisan who rebuffed the Taliban, confirms that while it was in the Taliban's interest to engage with India to seek recognition, India had nothing to gain from it.[181]

This is not to say that all Taliban leaders were unanimous in their intent to engage with India. When quizzed by India's Central Bureau of Investigation (CBI) sleuths in 2003 after being arrested by the US, Muttawakil mentioned that the Taliban's military commander in Kandahar during the hijack, Mullah Usmani, was the ISI's liaison on the airport, and the one who was in touch with the hijackers and among the first Taliban leaders to greet Masood Azhar (along with Mullah Mansour).[182] Based on the interrogation of Muttawakil, in 2004 India 'urgently' requested access to and information on Mansour, Usmani (reportedly in US custody), and Abdul Rauf (allegedly, a key conspirator), only to be rejected by Washington. In a side-story, the US wanted to tie the investigation of IC-814 hijacking with an entirely separate 1994 kidnapping incident of US citizen Bela Nuss in Indian-administered Kashmir (for which Omar Sheikh had been arrested in India) and the subsequent kidnapping and killing of American journalist Daniel Pearl (also orchestrated by Omar Sheikh).[183]

In 2009, Muttawakil stated that the final 'deal was struck between the hijackers and the [Indian] government. The fact that the hijackers disappeared into Pakistan, well, that was not within our jurisdiction.'[184] Indian authorities never accepted this claim, and continue to believe that the Taliban, which exercised jurisdiction in Kandahar, while adopting an attitude of correct facilitators, consistently sympathised with the hijackers and proactively released the militants.[185] As Sahay puts it:

> If [the] Taliban were really interested in helping India out in securing the release of the hostages, [they] would not have parked the hijacked aircraft at a VIP location at Kandahar airport and both our aircrafts (one carrying the negotiators and the other carrying Masood Azhar etc) at the far end of the airstrip. They clearly saw more danger from us than from the hijackers. The armed Talibs were constantly pointing their guns at us and not towards the hijackers.[186]

India lodged an official complaint with the International Civil Aviation Organisation that pressed the Taliban to prosecute the hijackers under the Hague Convention, and pressed the need to extradite the hijackers and the released militants to India.[187] Muttawakil still challenges this Indian view today. Moreover, in contrast to the popular Indian perception that the Taliban did not allow Indian commandos to storm the plane and position their soldiers in an offensive position, Muttawakil argues that the 'key actors [hijackers] wanted to take the plane to another destination, but we [Taliban] didn't allow that'.[188] There was tremendous mistrust between the hijackers and the Taliban as well. When Taliban sent workers inside the plane to clean the toilets, the hijackers became suspicious that the Taliban was planning to undertake a commando raid, and began to frantically search the cleaning staff.

The official Indian version of the Taliban's role in the hijacking incident is loaded with contradictions. If, as Indian policymakers argue, the Taliban indeed had sovereign jurisdiction over Kandahar and were expected to follow the rule of law and arrest the released militants and the hijackers, then why did India not open a political channel with the regime before the hijacking? If it were simply a question of sympathies, then a dialogue with the Taliban before the hijacking incident could have allowed New Delhi to ensure sensitivity towards its interests at Kandahar. Nothing of this sort was done, even if many thought it to be a prudent and pragmatic foreign policy approach. When the hijacking incident did happen, the Taliban's call for recognition came to be viewed more as blackmail than barter. In retrospect, even anti-Taliban partisans such as X concur that the Taliban did not like the hijacking. 'That [hijacking] is not *Pashtunwali*. But they [Taliban] were helpless. The pressure from the ISI was tremendous. They did have sovereign intent, but could not exercise it in practice'.[189] Sahay, for his part, though dismissing the question as hypothetical, rejects the idea that India would have gained much during the hijacking incident even if it had prior diplomatic relations with the Taliban—such was the ISI's influence on the Taliban.[190]

When asked how he expected India to react to Taliban's role in the hijacking, Muttawakil believes 'they [India] should be grateful, no doubt, but I don't think they are. After I was released from Bagram, I happened to meet some Indians. When they found I was there in Kandahar, I thought they would be grateful. But their behaviour was not proper'.[191] Finally, Muttawakil thinks that India's view of Afghanistan through a Pakistani-lens can do more harm than good to its ties with Afghanistan. He adds, 'one of India's biggest mistakes was to support the puppet Soviet regime in Kabul because the Mujahideen were based in Pakistan. India's second mistake was not to recognise the Taliban.'[192] With ruptures emerging within the Taliban and between the Taliban and the ISI, it is not unreasonable to believe that there was an authentic desire to engage with India during the 1990s. This does not mean all Taliban officials advocated good relations. There were competing advocacies within the Taliban on the India question, but interestingly, the dominant one was pro-engagement rather than anti-engagement. On the other hand, in India, anti-Taliban partisans dominated. A lack of communication between the two (due to geographical and material factors) led the partisans to feed upon the anti-India minority within the Taliban. Those Taliban that wanted to engage with India remained nonplussed by India's behaviour.

Sometime in 2000, the Taliban emissary to Pakistan, Mullah Abdul Saleem Zaeef paid a visit to India's then ambassador in Islamabad, Vijay K Nambiar—who had been in Kabul during the momentous events of April 1992 when Najibullah had tried to leave Kabul. While both had a cordial meeting, the whole exercise, according to Nambiar, lacked substance. 'I realised there was no way in which we [Taliban and India] are going to be truly connected with each other in any kind of an understanding', says Nambiar about the meeting.[193] Nambiar, a partisan, believed that the Taliban had been unable to swing itself out of the 'Pakistani circle of reasoning', making it difficult for India to seriously engage with them.[194] Even Hekmatyar, he says, could have been better than the Taliban in asserting his independence from Pakistan. In February 2001, senior Indian analyst Raja Mohan met with Zaeef during his visit to Islamabad. Coming after the IC-814 incident, and before the unraveling of the Taliban regime, Zaeef strongly urged India to change its approach towards the Taliban and not see the group as a proxy of Pakistan. Zaeef claimed that 'it is clear from our [Afghan] history that we are an independent people. We only follow the injunctions of Allah, our creator. We don't accept bondage to any other nation [read Pakistan],' and that the Taliban's links with Pakistan 'will not have an impact on Indo-Afghan ties'.[195]

Similar to the statements issued by Muttawakil and Jalil in 1996 and 1997 respectively, Zaeef noted that India's support to its adversaries counts as interference in Afghanistan's internal affairs. When expectedly asked about the Taliban's support for militants operating in Kashmir, Zaeef was categorical: 'We do not want atrocities to be committed against Kashmiri people ... We condemn any acts of violence by any party. We want to see the Kashmir issue resolved through peaceful dialogue.'[196] There were, of course, no takers of this argument in New Delhi in 2001. As Sood later exhorted 'we could have done business with the likes of Muttawakil and Zaeef.'[197] X states that 'the Taliban never fought against India. They never sent fighters to Kashmir and did not wage a Jihad against us. Whatever few Afghans were found in Kashmir came in an individual capacity and not as Taliban fighters'.[198] Even Dulat wonders why India has had such a closed mindset and why it has not tried in earnest to reach out to the Taliban.[199] Signifying a change in policy over the years, India allowed Zaeef to visit Goa in 2013 for a literary fest called 'Think'.[200] Inviting political ire from opposition parties, Indian officials defended Zaeef's visit on the grounds of opening channels with the Taliban.

If India became more inimical to the Taliban after the IC-814 incident, what was the policy output of the partisans versus conciliatory debate? The outcome was visible not so much in Afghanistan, as much as it was domestically in Kashmir. All three militants released at Kandahar were actively involved in the Kashmiri insurgency, as well as global jihad. Having lost its credibility as a security provider in the wake of IC-814, the BJP government adopted an offensive strategy in Kashmir.[201] On 17 January 2000, a fortnight after the hijack crisis, home minister Advani announced the Union Government's plan to deploy twenty-six companies of the Central Reserve Paramilitary Forces (CRPF) (more than 3,000 personnel) to 'address terrorism' in Kashmir.[202] This was in addition to the six CRPF companies that were already present there. Advani also asked the J&K state-security establishment to 'take a proactive approach against terrorists in the hinterland and establish area domination by day and by night.'[203] Apparently, the BJP's house was divided over Kashmir as well, and not just Pakistan and Afghanistan. Singh was actively trying to bring the US on board on Kashmir, while Vajpayee was simply 'unsure' of these proactive measures.[204] If anything, both Vajpayee and Advani viewed J&K principally as a source of inner-party ideological legitimacy and mass support.[205] Indian narratives emanating from South Asia's nuclearisation, to the India-Pakistan Kargil conflict, and the IC-814 hijack, were sewn together in Kashmir's security predicament and the BJP's 'offensive approach'. On Afghanistan, apart from the bitter realisation of India's limits to influence, the IC-814 incident streamlined India's thinking to develop a positive presence in Pashtun-dominated areas, first in principle and then in practice after the Bonn conference in 2001.

Conclusion

Of the three causal factors that shape India's Afghanistan policy, all three were peculiarly aligned to support the rise of the partisans. The rise of the Taliban with Pakistan's support in 1996 had steeply altered the political balance within Afghanistan in Pakistan's favour. For Indian strategists, this was a reflection of the Pakistan Army's much sought-after 'strategic depth' in Afghanistan. However, unlike its partisan approach towards the Taliban, India remained open to talks with Pakistan throughout the 1990s. Starting with the 1992 Rao doctrine that espoused dialogue with all neighbours, to the 1996 policy approach by PM Gujral that sought to fix the 'tormented relationship between India and Pakistan' through constructive engagement, successive Indian and Pakistani leaders attempted to diffuse tensions.[206] Vajpayee and his Pakistani counterpart Nawaz Sharif signed the Lahore Declaration in

February 1999, whereas Sharif's successor, Pakistan's military chief Pervez Musharraf, tried to broker a truce soon after the Kargil conflict in 1999. These moves signified the importance attached to diplomacy amidst tension with Pakistan.[207] Towards the Taliban, however, despite calls for a flexible approach, Indian policy remained staunchly averse.[208]

The Taliban's rise completely fragmented and polarised domestic Afghan politics (much more than during the 1980s) and offered little operational scope for India to strike a balance both within Afghanistan, and between Afghanistan and Pakistan. With the Taliban at the helm the latter power balance became deeply skewed in Pakistan's favour—something that India did not view to be in its strategic interest. But it was the changing international political environment towards Afghanistan that played a critical role in the rise of the partisans in 1996. Unlike what most Indian commentators argue, the shift in India's position occurred not simply because of the Taliban's militant Islamic practices or their dependence on Pakistan's security agencies (these aspects categorised the Mujahideen as well) but due to the breakdown of the international consensus on Afghanistan in the mid-1990s, as the UN failed to reconcile the warring factions. Only three countries, Pakistan, Saudi Arabia, and the United Arab Emirates, recognised the Taliban as Afghanistan's official government. Instead of accepting its rise, regional powers such as Russia and Iran felt threatened by the Taliban and decided to contain its rise (militarily if required). It was this change in regional geopolitical equations that allowed the partisans in New Delhi to ally with Moscow and Tehran, and these three countries threw their weight behind the anti-Taliban United Front. They criticised others countries such as the US and China, which had functioning back channels with the Taliban, for abetting the latter's rise.

Though the breakdown of international consensus offered an opportunity for the partisans in India to initiate a policy change in 1996, it was the risk of losing allies in Moscow and Teheran that sealed the defeat of the conciliators. By 1996, both Russia and Iran had come to support India's case on Kashmir at the UN. Reaching out to the Taliban would have cost India this support as well as the connection to the United Front within Afghanistan. The only thing New Delhi could achieve by opening such communication was the 'possibility' of winning 'some' Taliban figures over. This policy dilemma was reconciled to some extent during the presidency of Hamid Karzai after 2001. With the international community's support, Karzai expanded relations with India and launched a reconciliation drive with cerain Taliban figures that were disillusioned by Pakistan. But until the events of 9/11 took place, India's

Afghanistan policy remained in a state of flux. However, before Karzai's rise, what was the state of India's relations with US and Pakistan? The next chapter details how India's relations with the US and Pakistan, the destruction of the Bamiyan Buddhas, and the Afghan war after the 9/11 attacks, impacted India's approach towards Afghanistan.

6

WAR AND TERROR

DESTRUCTION IN BAMIYAN AND THE AFTERMATH OF 9/11

'It is the blackest day in the history of civilisation when this 2000-years old world heritage is being destroyed by the so-called people who parade as the protectors of Islam.'

Najma Heptullah, BJP MP in Rajya Sabha, March 2001 on the destruction of the Buddhas in Bamiyan.[1]

'The Taliban is a creature of Pakistan, and now Pakistan is in danger of becoming a creature of the Taliban.'

Jaswant Singh, former External Affairs and Defence Minister of India[2]

'Pakistan must understand that there is a limit to the patience of the people of India.'

Atal Bihari Vajpayee, PM of India in a letter to US President George W Bush in the wake of 9/11 and the attack on the Jammu and Kashmir Assembly that killed 38 people on 1 October 2001[3]

An overflowing 'cup of evil'

When tanks, anti-aircraft guns, and artillery shells failed to make an impact, truckloads of dynamite were drilled in to demolish the world's tallest Buddha statues.[4] Carved in the sandstone cliffs of the central Afghan province of Bamiyan, the statues were pre-Islamic cultural heritage, and were too strong to destroy with a few bombs. But such was the Taliban's determination to end idolatry that they persisted with the destruction for nearly a month.[5] The Taliban's leader, Mullah Omar, had passed a decree on 26 February 2001, ordering the elimination of all non-Islamic statues in Afghanistan. By the end of March, the Buddhas of Bamiyan had ceased to exist. Statues kept in the Afghan National Museum in Kabul were not spared either. The world erupted in rage. Countries with high numbers of Buddhists such as Sri Lanka, China, Japan, Laos, Myanmar, Bhutan, Cambodia, and Thailand protested heavily. Even Pakistan, Saudi Arabia, and the UAE, who recognised and supported the Taliban, joined the protests. As Dixit put it, for India where Buddhism was born and 0.8 per cent of whose population still practiced it,[6] the Taliban's 'cup of evil doing' had begun to overflow.[7]

This was not the first time the Bamiyan Buddhas had come up in India's policy debates. BJP MP Vijay Kumar Malhotra had raised concerns over the Taliban's intent to destroy them since May 1997. Then PM Gujral, who was under some, if not considerable, influence of the conciliators, shared the concern but could do little about it.[8] Bamiyan was untouched by the civil war in 1997 and did not occupy strategic priority. The ghastly events of 2001, however, put both the partisans and the conciliators on the same page, as India activated its diplomatic channels to further isolate the Taliban internationally. On 2 March 2001, both houses of the parliament unanimously passed a resolution condemning the destruction as 'medieval barbarism' and 'sacrilege to humanity'.[9] Parliamentarians from both national and regional political parties cutting across the ideological spectrum denounced the Taliban.[10] When placing the resolution in the house, Jaswant Singh offered to arrange for the transfer of all these artifacts to India where they would be kept safely, 'in the full knowledge and clear understanding that they are, in the first place and above all, treasures of the Afghan people themselves'.[11]

Coming from a Hindu nationalist government, Jaswant Singh's statement was loaded with irony. The BJP and its ideological parent organisation, the Rashtriya Swayamsevak Sangh (RSS), had allegedly incited a large crowd of Hindu *Kar Sevaks* (volunteers) to demolish the Babri Masjid (Mosque of Babur) in 1992 in the central Indian state of Uttar Pradesh (UP). Former Indian defence minister and Samajwadi Party leader Mulayam Singh, a senior regional politician from UP challenged the BJP saying, 'if the pro-Hindu organisations of the country themselves do not respect Buddha, assassinate Mahatma Gandhi, demolish mosques and Buddhist *stupas*, how can they expect Taliban to listen to them and stop the destruction of the two giant statues?'[12] The *Shahi Imam* of Delhi's Jama Masjid, Syed Ahmad Bukhari, took this further by publicly announcing his willingness to negotiate with the Taliban to hand over the statues on the condition that Vajpayee would accept the demolition of the Babri Masjid as a national shame. Linking the demolition of the Buddhas to Babri Masjid, Bukhari implored that 'the Taliban action should be seen in totality and not in isolation'.[13] But the advocacy of opening an informal channel with the Taliban, for whatever reason and advocated by whomsoever, had long been dead. On 9 March 2001, after consulting with various heads of states, the UNSC, and the UN Secretary General, India co-sponsored a UNGA resolution[14] calling upon the Taliban to abide by its commitments to protect Afghanistan's cultural heritage.[15] Nothing came of it.

Instead, the Taliban justified the act on grounds of Western hypocrisy and provocations. Sayed Ramatullah Hashimi, Taliban envoy in the US, along with Mullah Abdul Saleem Zaeef, Taliban envoy to Pakistan, put the blame on a delegation of European diplomats that had recently visited Kabul.[16] With a drought-like situation and a long winter staring them in the face, millions of Afghans faced the prospect of starvation that year. Instead of offering financial support for starving Afghan children, the European delegation offered money to repair and maintain the Buddhas. When the Taliban sought that money in the form of humanitarian aid the delegation balked, outraging the Taliban. 'When your children are dying in front of you, then you don't care about a piece of art', bellowed Hashimi.[17] He did not mention the Indian offer to extract these artifacts and a Japanese offer to purchase them, the financial proceeds of which could go towards feeding starving Afghans.[18] The fact was that the Taliban, with support from and under the ideological influence of Al Qaeda, had begun to clamp down heavily on Afghanistan's religious minority communities and women.

In May 2001, the Taliban issued another decree against the Hindu and Sikh communities of Afghanistan. Hindu men were debarred from wearing *salwar kameez* or a white turban, and were to wear black caps and a red *tilak* on their foreheads as an identification mark. Hindu women were directed to drape themselves fully in yellow cloth and wear an iron necklace in public. Hindus and Muslims were not allowed to live together anymore, and Hindus were ordered to display a yellow flag on their houses.[19] With a Hindu nationalist government in power in a conservative India, the decree touched a sensitive communal chord unleashing massive protests. Not only did the BJP condemn the decree, it took the matter up with the UN, the US, the EU, and other countries with common interests. Massoud Khalili, the United Front representative in India, condemned the decree. 'Hindu Afghans had been part and parcel of Afghanistan's culture. They have lived freely, worshipped freely, and wore whatever they liked and fought for Afghanistan's liberation each and every time', he stated.[20]

No common ground existed between India and the Taliban. The Taliban did not even figure heavily in parliamentary debates on terrorism, and whenever it did, it was mostly linked with Pakistan and the Kashmiri militants. For instance, in a heated joint parliamentary session on 28 August 2001, on the security scenario in the light of terrorist and other internal and external threats, the Taliban was the least discussed entity, with the popular notion being that India was doing little to secure its interests in Afghanistan.[21] The bigger concern vis-à-vis Afghanistan was that the prolonged conflict since the 1980s had prompted 12,083 Afghans to migrate to India by February 2001.[22] By November 2001, another 275 Afghan Sikh and Hindu families were stranded in Pakistan, hoping to travel to India by road.[23] Given the number of Afghan refugees in Pakistan, which ran into millions, and in different Western countries, which ran into hundreds of thousands, India was hosting a trifling number of Afghan migrants. Nonetheless, the issue was potent enough to raise a red flag.

Concerned about the plight of these migrants, India was also worried about the potential impact of growing Afghan refugees in India (however small their numbers may be in relative terms). Social hostility against Afghans, in the backdrop of the situation in Kashmir and the IC-814 hijacking incident, had gone up. Moreover, despite more than 65 per cent of these refugees being Hindu or Sikh, India refused to integrate or naturalise them.[24] Given the state of affairs in Afghanistan, it was impossible for them to return anytime soon. Not being a signatory of the 1951 UN convention relating to the Status of Refugees or the 1967 Protocol, nor having any specific legal framework and national refugee status determination system, India had little recourse to accommodate Afghan refugees. To make things worse, a monthly subsistence allowance for refugees was stopped by the government as early as 1992, earning complaints from the United Nations High Commissioner for Refugees (UNHCR).[25]

Effectively, all the three drivers of India's Afghanistan policy—New Delhi's desire to strike a balance between Afghanistan and Pakistan, international political environment, and domestic Afghan politics—favoured anti-Taliban partisanship in March 2001. Given the global outcry over the destruction of the Buddha and the IC-814 hijacking episode, India's diplomatic and military measures against the Taliban were to be expected. Domestic political factors supplemented these dynamics. Differences between a Hindu nationalist government and a militant Islamist regime coupled with deteriorating relations between India and Pakistan ensured the domination of partisans. However, apart from the IC-814 episode, a lot more had happened between 1996 and 2001 that helped partisans remain dominant within India's establishment. The demolition of the Buddhas only vindicated a growing partisan trend and fed into an aggressive political discourse against Islamist politics that had already begun to crystalise globally and later became the 'war on terror', as the twentieth century came to an end.

Six plus two

Disconnected geographically and limited in capacity, India adopted an internationalist strategy towards Afghanistan. Unilaterally, as most parliamentarians thought, it did little. Whenever the government was questioned in the parliament about its Afghanistan policy, a slew of UN resolutions that India supported (or co-sponsored) were offered. India's participation in the Group of 21 countries that was created in November 1996, as well as cooperation with Russia, Iran, and the US was also displayed as a mechanism to secure national interests in Afghanistan.[26] Such an internationalist approach was combined with vague assurances of tightened border controls, gearing up the intelligence machinery, upgrading the police forces, and better inter-state coordination.[27] That the various UN resolutions were making little impact and that most Western countries (and also China) were openly engaging with the Taliban was left unsaid. In reality, the one multilateral forum that did have limited impact on the Afghan political situation which was the six plus two (6+2), did not allow India entry. Comprising of Iran, China, Pakistan, Uzbekistan, Tajikistan, and Turkmenistan as core members, it had the US and Russia as the 'plus two'.

From the Taliban's side there was no dedicated team of negotiators at this forum, but Mullah Omar chose various officials to represent its interests. These included Mullah Mohammad Hasan (former governor of Kandahar), Mullah Mohammad Rabbani, Wakil Ahmad Muttawakil (foreign minister), Abdul Karim Zahid (deputy foreign minister), Amir Khan Muttaqi (representing the Kandahari leadership and close aide to Mullah Omar).[28] Yunus Qanooni and Abdullah were representing the UF at the six plus two. Created on Uzbek president Islam Karimov's initiative, and baptised by the UN, the process emerged from the Tashkent Declaration in 1999 and its first official meeting took place on 14 January 1999. Titled *On Fundamental Principles for a peaceful Settlement of the Conflict in Afghanistan*, the declaration had prompted a UNSC Presidential Statement SC/6743 condemning the Taliban for 'undermining international efforts to facilitate the restoration of peace in Afghanistan'.[29]

For the then UN Secretary-General, Kofi Annan, the six plus two was an essential forum to broker a peaceful resolution, especially in context of Mazar-e-Sharif's fall and the murder of eleven Iranian diplomats in August 1998.[30] In retaliation, Tehran had mobilised 70,000 troops on the Afghan border, only to be restrained by the UN.[31] That same month, as part of 'Operation Infinite Reach', US President Bill Clinton ordered cruise missile strikes in Afghanistan and Sudan in response to the bombing of US Embassies in Kenya and Tanzania by Al Qaeda.[32] Failing to assassinate its key target Osama bin Laden, the seventy-five cruise missiles ended up destroying, among much else, the Muawai militant training camp run by the ISI to train anti-India outfit Harkat-ul-Ansar's cadre.[33] The strikes came after Washington's failed attempts to extradite bin Laden from the Taliban. These developments were critical in changing US belief systems as it came to increasingly view the Taliban through a terrorism-centric lens. As for Iran and Russia, their aversion to the Taliban only rose as the latter captured Taloqan and Kunduz in North Afghanistan with Pakistan's help.[34] Barring Pakistan, the dominant advocacy within the six plus two grouping, thus, was Taliban-averse. Though Washington remained lukewarm in pressuring Pakistan, Russian PM Yevgeny Primakov assured continuous support to Jaswant Singh in July 1999 and categorically stated that 'the globe cannot live with a Talibanised Pakistan that has the bomb'.[35]

Despite, largely, being on the same page with the partisans in India, the six plus two process did not go down well in India. New Delhi's exclusion from the grouping at Pakistan's behest irritated New Delhi considerably.[36] Having lost faith in the UN's capability to resolve the conflict and seething over its marginalisation from international groupings, the MEA officially criticised the process saying that it was 'inherently flawed on account of its narrow and constricted base'.[37] India asserted that notwithstanding its lack of recognition of the Taliban, and its opposition to the manner in which the Taliban permitted itself to be manipulated by Pakistan, direct contact was established with the regime during the IC-814 hijacking. The Taliban's correct role as facilitators during this crisis was noted, but it was clear that the fundamentals of India's Afghanistan policy would not change. Though India welcomed the 1999 Tashkent declaration that vindicated its stand and supported the partisans, it remained critical of multilateral processes on Afghanistan in which it did not have a role. When the Congress-led opposition challenged the government's lack of persistence on joining the six plus two and meekly accepting Washington's exclusion of India,[38] Jaswant Singh dismissed the allegations saying, 'we did take a decision that we will have nothing to do with six plus two because the countries that were part of the six plus two were a part of the problem. How can problems [Pakistan] become solutions? And, I don't want to name the countries'.[39]

Jaswant Singh's reaction was problematic for various reasons. Firstly, regardless of India's absence, the six plus two proved somewhat effective in pressuring Pakistan to bring the Taliban to the negotiation table. It was, arguably, the only platform at that point in time that saw different Afghan factions talk with each other.[40] The Taliban representatives who attended the meetings came under pressure from Pakistan, notwithstanding Mullah Omar's declaration that the Taliban will attend the meeting only if it is recognised as the legitimate government of Afghanistan.[41] Soon after the creation of 6+2, Pakistan offered a peace deal to the UF, only to be rejected by the latter. The UF, despite being militarily hard-pressed, had few reasons to give tactical diplomatic space to the Taliban. Pakistan itself had become heavily isolated and was losing clout in wake of the 1998 Chagai nuclear tests. India, on the other hand, was actively lobbying Washington with Vajpayee calling the US a 'natural ally' soon after the Pokharan nuclear tests.[42] Secondly, regardless of Indian concerns about being actively excluded from the 6+2, the UN did engage with India on the Afghan question throughout this period. A twelve-member UN delegation visited New Delhi in May 2001 to assess the feasibility of economic sanctions against the Taliban. While India was happy with the sanctions arrangement, Pakistani President Musharraf refused to cooperate. Much like the 6+2, which failed under its own weight, no economic sanctions on the Taliban would have much impact if Pakistan did not desire them.

Thirdly, the US was getting increasingly frustrated with Pakistan's non-cooperation in the 6+2. In March 1999, US Assistant Secretary of State on South Asia, Karl Inderfurth, confided his vexation with Pakistan's obstinate support to the Taliban to Secretary of State Madeleine Albright. US efforts, he mentioned,

> will have to shift away from trying to work with Pakistan, and to a lesser extent with Iran, in the 6+2 toward bringing greater pressure on Pakistan and Iran. We will look to Russia to support this process particularly with Iran. We may have to move from a 6+2 process to a Eight Minus One process, emphasising the isolation of

Pakistan.'[43] If this eight minus one framework also failed then, 'another stick we [US] might think of using on Pakistan is the idea of expanding the Six Plus Two to include other Central Asian states and India, a move that Pakistan would oppose.[44]

As these cables demonstrate, the US had come a long way from being supportive of Pakistan, and the six plus two played a role in shaping this opinion.

As India expected, the process failed. According to a detailed, unpublished, report prepared for the British government, a close advisor of the Taliban leadership stated that the six plus two meetings were convened on false pretences. 'Uzbekistan had informed Mullah Omar that Rabbani was willing to surrender, and that he wanted to discuss this in Uzbekistan. The UF had meanwhile been informed that the Taliban were ready to make a deal'.[45] As one attendee of the meetings outlined, the first meeting was little more than a meet and greet, and the second didn't see any serious discussion. There appeared to be no common ground between the two positions. In contrast to previous contacts, there appeared to have been some room to discuss a joint government that would see a number of governorships and ministries going to the UF, but this didn't appear to be enough for the UF. Massoud refused to disarm his militia, and the Taliban refused to offer more than 50 per cent share of the government or, as one participant claimed, even 50 per cent.[46]

Regardless of the 6+2's failure, the final pre-9/11 shift in global positioning on the Afghan question happened in June 2001, as the Taliban undertook a military build-up close to the Tajikistan border. The military maneuver brought Moscow and Washington in a tighter embrace that resulted in joint military measures to contain the Taliban's advance (to the partisans' delight).[47] India was asked to facilitate US and Russian plans for limited military actions against the Taliban. Organised within the 6+2 framework, India's former foreign secretary Chokila Iyer was formally requested to support Russian action in the Second Indo-Russia Joint Working Group (JWG) meeting in Moscow in 2001.[48] Russia's Federal Security Bureau chief Nicolai Patroshev, undertook personal visits to Tehran and New Delhi to lobby for support. According to Indian officials, New Delhi and Tehran were to expedite the mission while the US and Russia, with the help of Tajikistan and Uzbekistan, were to combat from the front. The aim was to push the Taliban lines back to the 1998 position, 50 km away from Mazar-e-Sharif.[49] The probability of military action only increased when the Taliban banned UN representatives from the territory it controlled, and Russia picked up intelligence that the Taliban was aiming to create 'liberated zones' all over Central Asia and Russia.[50] Washington and Moscow's convergence on the Taliban question, by 2001, signified a key shift in global threat perceptions after the end of the Cold War. Such shifting threat perceptions and the rise of anti-terror rhetoric turned the tables for Pakistan. Starting as a legitimate and powerful actor in Afghanistan in the early 1990s, Islamabad came to be seen as a revisionist and destabilising entity. India, for its part, as the next section shows, convinced the US about the rightness of its strategic assessments on the Taliban and Pakistan.

Engaging Washington

If one is to go by popular discourse, many officials in countries such as Russia, Iran, and India, believed that Washington was tacitly supporting the rise of the Taliban. The US involvement in the region, however complex it may be in reality, was reduced to a caricature of an energy-hungry capitalist. Topping this, many Indian officials were convinced that Washington viewed Pakistan as the lynchpin of its South Asia strategy, and was going soft on the Pakistan-Taliban nexus.[51] If the US defended its South Asian policy as being balanced and pragmatic, as it often did, Indians derided it as being simplistic.[52] The fact was that US officials were concerned about the Taliban's rise within Afghanistan and its support to Kashmiri militants. The same month when Gujral had briefed the Parliament about Taliban's alleged training to HuA in November 1996, US Ambassador to Pakistan Thomas W. Simons had confronted Taliban's 'Acting Foreign Minister' Mullah Ghaus about the HuA bases in Taliban-controlled territories in Khost.[53] Noting that the US was concerned about HuA's activities, Simon threatened that the US might declare HuA a terrorist organisation. But Ghaus flatly denied the allegations.[54] Simons was neither convinced nor impressed. Nor was Walter Andersen, then Chief of the South Asia Directorate in the State Department. 'The Taliban knew that training of Kashmiri militants was under way in Afghanistan ... engaging the Taliban [in such circumstances] would have been a very difficult choice for the Indian government', Andersen argues.[55] The US continued to unofficially engage with the Taliban regardless.

The Africa bombings and the US response of launching cruise missiles in Afghanistan (and Sudan) gave India an opportunity to steer US policy closer to its own political wavelength. In his interactions with the then Deputy Secretary of State Strobe Talbott, Jaswant Singh emphasised that 'the Taliban is a creature of Pakistan, and now Pakistan is in danger of becoming a creature of the Taliban'. He wondered why the East African bombings had not 'made the scales fall from your [US] eyes' about Pakistan?[56] Afghanistan itself was not the top priority of this dialogue, but the Taliban had become an adjunct to India and Pakistan's bilateral issues. Astutely playing US anxieties over terrorism to India's advantage, Vajpayee shifted tack by asserting that the India-US dialogue had been 'altered by what happened on August 20th at 11 p.m.' when the US cruise missile slammed into their targets in Afghanistan.[57] This tactical shift meant that India would 'lie back [on the nuclear issue] and wait for the [US] administration's suddenly heightened preoccupation with Islamic terrorism to replace its upset over the Indian nuclear program'.[58]

New Delhi wanted to convince the US that a secular, democratic, and stable India was a better strategic partner in South Asia to challenge Islamist radicalism than Pakistan. But the US, Jaswant Singh argued, had to stop pressurising India to sign the Comprehensive Nuclear-Test-Ban Treaty.[59] The MEA kept its reaction to the US missile strikes equally mixed. While joining Washington in condemning international terrorism, the MEA cautioned the US against undertaking 'unilateral action'.[60] 'An effective international cooperative effort to identify and act against those responsible for international terrorism—whether individuals, terrorist groups, or states,' was advocated. The MEA's standard line was conditioned by the perception that India and the US had the same enemies, and similar friends. The UF buttressed this narrative in the Afghan context by emphasising that the US 'should target the fire, not the smoke' by attacking militant bases in Peshawar, Quetta, and Islamabad.[61] As India lobbied the US on the nuclear question, Al Qaeda's anti-West rhetoric steadily began to rise. In February 1998, the World Islamic Front led by bin Laden issued a statement castigating the US for 'occupying the lands of Islam in the holiest of places, the Arabian peninsula', and blaming the 'crusader-Zionist alliance' for conspiring against Islam.[62] Kashmir, Chechnya, Afghanistan, Africa and all regions experiencing Islamist extremism were on Al Qaeda's radar. Pakistan on the other hand, embarrassed and outraged for having lost its intelligence and military personnel in US missile strikes, condemned Washington for undertaking the strikes.

To further cement India and US cooperation on Afghanistan and terrorism, Vivek Katju (former JS of the Pakistan, Afghanistan, and Iran desk at the MEA) and Alok Prasad (deputy NSA) met Inderfurth on 2 September 1999, two months before the IC-814 hijacking. They wanted US support for Indian covert operations in Afghanistan, while Inderfurth, allegedly, wanted India to stop the Ariana flights (often loaded with ammunition and spare parts) between Afghanistan and Amritsar as a goodwill gesture. India happily complied.[63] S. Iftikhar Murshed, former Pakistani envoy to the Taliban regime, says that such meetings ensured 'greater Western sympathy for India's portrayal of Pakistan as a state sponsor [of] terrorism'.[64] India's calculation that changing US beliefs on international terrorism would bring the two countries closer was spot-on. Differences on Afghanistan between India's partisans and top US officials began to bridge the East Africa bombings. However, the US refused to publicly acknowledge Pakistan as a state-sponsor of terrorism, despite knowing the extent to which Islamabad was supporting the Taliban and other militant groups in the region.[65]

Such caution on part of the US resonated with the conciliators in India. Inderfurth, who himself was a conciliator, was convinced that the Taliban was a vehicle of Pashtun ethnic power and not just an Islamist movement. In his view, the Taliban would control most parts of Afghanistan for at least a year or even more (in 1999). The largest single ethnic group, the Pashtuns, simply would not permit non-Pashtun suzerainty over the country. But that very fact made it necessary for Pakistan to let diplomacy take over protracted military engagements, and bring the Taliban to the negotiating table. But Pakistan's rigidity in the six plus two had begun to challenge Inderfurth's patience. In a secret cable to Albright, he advocated that 'we [US] will continue our policy of trying to mitigate Taliban behavior where and when its ill-advised policies cross our path. Its policies now preclude us from offering the Taliban what it wants—recognition as the rulers of Afghanistan'.[66] The Taliban, he argued, should be recognised if, and only if, it clamps down on the terrorist networks, undertakes effective measures against the cultivation, processing, and trafficking of illicit narcotics, and improves its respect for human rights in general and treatment of women and girls in particular. For this to happen, however, the US needed to continue engaging with the Taliban and seek other levers to influence its behavior.[67] Despite his cautious conciliatory approach, Inderfurth had no doubt about the Pakistan-Taliban nexus. He had foreseen, in 1999, that if things don't change, the Taliban might just have to be treated as an enemy regime, and Afghanistan a pariah state.

Inderfurth's advocacy on the Taliban, in 1999, occurred in the context of structural shifts in South Asia's power balance. In May 1998, both India and Pakistan had tested their nuclear arsenal inviting condemnation and sanctions from the international community. Washington was particularly shocked at its failure to intercept the Indian tests and its inability to deter Pakistan from conducting retaliatory tests. Overt nuclearisation of the subcontinent had grave security implications. If the probability of a full-scale conventional war between

India and Pakistan went down, the probability of asymmetric warfare under the nuclear umbrella went up. Nuclear weapons gave Pakistan, the relatively weaker of the two states, strategic parity with India. This situation was aggravated by the Kargil conflict between May and July 1999, when Pakistani troops entered the Indian-controlled territory in the Kargil sector of Kashmir and held key strategic positions disrupting the Indian army's supply lines. Calculating that India would not respond heavily due to the nuclear factor, Musharraf ordered the operation just weeks after the signing of the Lahore declaration.[68]

New Delhi, however, responded with full military and diplomatic force, leading to an unconditional withdrawal of Pakistani troops.[69] An ally of Pakistan all these years, Washington blamed Islamabad for being the aggressor and sided with India, strengthening the hands of the partisans.[70] The Kargil conflict had strong reverberations in Afghanistan as well. As soon as the conflict started, Brajesh Mishra ordered the release of a large amount of secret funds to the R&AW to up the ante on Pakistan in Afghanistan.[71] With the Baloch and Pakhtun separatist insurgencies in a dormant state, the R&AW was ordered to do whatever it could to bring Pakistan and the Taliban under military pressure in Afghanistan. The US knew it all. Interestingly, however, the US refuses to publicise specific details about the time, quantity, and nature of India's covert armed support to the UF against the Taliban until today. The various declassified CIA dossiers and diplomatic cables that mention India's role in Afghanistan during the 1990s, have dates and specifics about Indian spies blacked out.

The shift in the US perceptions on Afghanistan had generated (misplaced) rumours that Washington was conspiring with New Delhi to oust the Taliban by force. Refuting them strongly, the Clinton administration maintained that it was looking for political alternatives based on negotiations and not military force. In this context, then US President Bill Clinton's March 2000 visit to India is considered positively transformational.[72] Clinton did a five-hour stopover in Pakistan after spending five days in India, only to inform Musharraf that he had irrefutable evidence of the 'alarming level' of support that the ISI was providing to anti-India militant outfits, including the HuA.[73] Vajpayee paid a reciprocal visit to the US in September 2000 and sought deeper collaboration on counter-terrorism. The India-US Joint Working Group on Counter-Terrorism (JWG-CT) had been in place since February 2000. And foreign secretary Chokila Iyer undertook a series of trips to Washington for discussing modalities of bilateral cooperation on terrorism.[74] By 2001, as the MEA stated, there was increased recognition by the US of the problem of terrorism in South Asia and the nature and origin of cross-border terrorism in India.[75] Going one step further, N. N. Jha (then convener of foreign affairs for the BJP) argued that the JWG-CT was a sign that the US recognised India's emerging global status.[76] Gujral noted:

> At one stage the US needed the Taliban to pursue its economic and other operations in Central Asia. But information available now is that it is evolving other options in the region to protect and advance its interests. Whether this would be sufficient to make it swing to India's side is question that would have no definite answer at the moment.[77]

A similar JWG was formed with Russia in September 2000. These platforms allowed India to share its concerns regarding non-state militant actors in Pakistan and the Taliban's proactive military offensives in North Afghanistan with Moscow. Putin had put Russian forces on high alert in case offensive action was required. The Taliban's recognition of Chechnya-Ichkeria as independent Islamic states in January 2000 had irritated Moscow tremendously.[78] The destruction of the Bamiyan Buddhas in March 2001 simply added fuel to this raging fire.

Two events in September 2001 fundamentally altered India and the US' strategy towards Afghanistan. On 9 September 2001, two Al Qaeda suicide bombers, pretending to be journalists, assassinated Ahmad Shah Massoud, India's closest ally in Afghanistan.[79] The bomb had been concealed in the video camera and the battery pack belt. Massoud was rushed to the Farkhor field hospital in Tajikistan that India was running for the UF, but died in the helicopter on the way. Another United Front official, Mohammad Aasim Suhail was also killed while former UF ambassador to India, Massoud Khalili and journalist Mohammad Fahim Dashty, who was writing a book on Massoud, were injured.[80] With its key binding force gone, Massoud's absence crippled the United Front and led to its eventual disintegration. For the partisans, India had lost its main partner on the ground in Afghanistan, raising questions of how to handle this leadership vacuum (Rabbani had developed serious differences with many by then). But the dilemma was short-lived. Subsequent attacks on the World Trade Center in New York on 11 September 2001 changed everything. The US decision to use military force to capture bin Laden and oust the Taliban was a blessing for the partisans who found allies in the world's sole superpower soon after losing Massoud.

Don't trust the Americans

The US response in the wake of the 9/11 attacks was a short-lived blessing for the partisans. The American bombing campaign in Afghanistan was accompanied by heightened tension between India and Pakistan. On 1 October 2001, four powerful bombs went off in the Jammu and Kashmir (J&K) state legislative assembly complex killing thirty-eight people.[81] J&K chief minister Farooq Abdullah was a target, and the Jaish-e-Mohammad, a jihadi group active in Kashmir and supported by Pakistan, took responsibility for the attack. In response, Vajpayee wrote an urgent letter to President Bush offering support in Afghanistan and imploring him to pressurise Musharraf to control the JeM. He had already undertaken a three-nation tour of Russia, the US and the UK after the 9/11 attacks to articulate India's stance on terrorism.[82] Though hot-pursuit of militants in Pakistan-administered Kashmir was not launched, the security apparatus in Kashmir had been tightened and put on high alert.[83] 'Pakistan must understand', wrote Vajpayee (to Bush), 'that there is a limit to the patience of the people of India.'[84] Jaswant Singh publicly offered military help to the US and argued that 'if one of the instruments of terrorism is military, and the whole point of spreading terror is through military means, how can you respond to a strike of steel by any other means than steel?'[85] Further demonstrating India's angst about cross-border terrorism, Vajpayee made a vigorous anti-terrorism pitch at the UNGA on 10 November 2001, endorsed the UNSC Resolution 1373, and piloted a Comprehensive Convention on International Terrorism (CCIT) to strengthen the legal framework for countering international terrorism.[86] Even public mood in India, as a *Bombay Times* survey in Mumbai reflected, was supportive of US actions. 80 per cent of the respondents agreed that the attack on Afghanistan was justified, while 53 per cent said that they should be limited only to Afghanistan (rumors of the US venturing into other Middle Eastern countries such as Iraq or Syria were ripe by this point in time).[87]

Despite the MEA's previous warnings to the US of not undertaking unilateral action, after the East Africa bombings, the BJP-led NDA government was pleased with the US military intervention (official UN sanction for military action in Afghanistan came in December 2001, whereas the US had begun bombing much earlier). As part of the initiative, the US Department of the Treasury designated the Jaish-e-Mohammad and the Harkat-ul-Ansar (and some other Pakistan-based militant outfits) as global terrorists on 23 September 2001. However, US Secretary of State Colin Powell, who was in India when the J&K state assembly attacks took place, despite condemning the attack as an act of terror, did not directly hold Pakistan responsible.[88] Instead, in a breathtaking tactical U-turn, Musharraf agreed to abandon the Taliban and side with the US by October 2001. In a call to Musharraf, Powell had made seven specific demands from Pakistan: one, halt Al Qeada operatives at the border; two, blanket over flight and landing rights; three, access to Pakistani air and naval bases as well as borders; four, immediate intelligence and immigration information; five, curb all domestic expression of support for terrorism against the US and its friends and allies (including India); six, cut off supplies to the Taliban; and seven, end diplomatic support to the Taliban.[89]

Musharraf, to Washington's surprise, agreed to support the US in each of the seven actions. In turn, the US would give Pakistan massive aid and ammunition packages. Instead of becoming a nuclear pariah, Pakistan, once again, became a frontline state in America's war, this time on terror, engulfing Indian parliamentarians into a similar and equally impotent debate to that witnessed in 1980, when the Soviet Union invaded Afghanistan. If in 1980 most Indian officials were averse to Soviet actions but reluctantly supported them out of necessity, in 2001 many in India supported US actions but grew skeptical because of the way the US executed the war. Viewing 9/11 as a ghastly, but also an enlightening moment for the US, India expected empathy from Washington on the issue of cross-border terrorism. America's partnering with Pakistan as a frontline state, with the hope that Islamabad would curb expressions of terrorism against the US and its allies, especially India, was a disappointment for New Delhi. Indeed, top US officials including secretary of defense Donald Rumsfeld knew that many Pakistani officials (despite Musharraf's tilt) were retaining ties with the Taliban and various other militant groups operating against India.[90]

In a joint parliamentary session on the international situation arising out of the 9/11 attacks, there was agreement on the benefits of ousting the Taliban, as well as India's proactive measures to increase engagement with Afghanistan's upcoming political dispensation. On the economic front, despite concerns of a global economic downturn, no particular negative economic fallout was expected given the minuscule levels of trade between Afghanistan and India. With its global exports growing at 1.95 per cent and imports at 1.81 per cent, the Ministries of Finance and Commerce and Industry were happy that the sluggish global energy demand had reduced oil prices.[91] A dip from US$ 28 per barrel on 11 September 2001 to US$ 20 per barrel on 20 November had relieved pressure on India's balance of payments. Even the INR per US$ appreciated 0.3 per cent in this time frame, and the Reserve Bank of India (RBI) assured the domestic Indian market that adequate foreign exchange would be provided if the supply-demand gap increased due to the war. The question of whether India should support the US or not lingered, however, as disagreements emerged in three different aspects: (a) Washington's acceptance of Pakistan as a frontline state in the war against terror and the myth of the Taliban's disintegration, (b) undermining of international institutions such as the UN (whose official sanction came in December 2001, even though it was clear from the outset that the UN would approve such military action), and (c) the need for Vajpayee's 'complaint letter' to Bush after the J&K assembly attack. The Leader of the Opposition, Dr Manmohan Singh, who became PM in 2004, with support from the communists and regional parties such as the Samajwadi Party (SP), led the charge against the NDA government's position on these issues.

The Congress party was emphatic that thc BJP's over-enthusiastic statements of support towards the US (and Washington's lukewarm response) were unwarranted. Instead, diplomatic energy should have been channeled towards convincing the world community that what was happening in 'Jammu and Kashmir is Pakistan-sponsored, aided, and abetted naked international terrorism', and Islamabad should not be made a stakeholder in this war on terror.[92] Otherwise, another round of arms race will begin in South Asia, as it happened after the Soviet military intervention. Vajpayee's letter to Bush, in this context, was perceived as a sign of weakness, or India being seen as a 'lackey' of US imperialism, as senior SP leader Janeshwar Mishra and the Left parties put it.[93] Given India's tortuous relations with the US, most Indian policymakers advised the government not to trust Washington. The dominant perception in Indian circles was that the US was a fair-weather friend unlike Russia that stood with India in its hour of need (in 1971 and at other times). Other Congress leaders such as Eduardo Faleiro and Kapil Sibal condemned the killing of 'thousands of innocents' in Afghanistan due to the US bombing,[94] and advocated a holistic approach towards dealing with the 'culture of terrorism'.[95] For Sibal, throwing missiles and cluster bombs on a 'wretched' country like Afghanistan that had a life expectancy of 43 years,[96] 23 per cent literacy rate, per capita GDP of less than US$ 700 per year, no access to safe water, sanitation, healthcare, education, and infrastructure, may help [with] catching Osama bin Laden, but was not an adequate answer to dealing with terrorism.[97]

CPM MPs such as Nilotpal Basu, in addition to voicing similar concerns, had an ideological difference with the US. For Indian Communists, the government's offer to use Indian military bases in America's war against Afghanistan would 'seriously undermine national interests'.[98] None of the US actions addressed the root cause of terrorism, which was to overhaul the amoral capitalistic system that contributed towards the growth of religious fundamentalism and sectarianism. Other regional parties such as the SP, the Telugu Desam Party, the Rashtriya Janata Dal, and the Nationalist Congress Party, also held the US partly responsible for the Taliban's growth. Shortsighted support to groups like the Taliban for economic and energy interests, these parties argued, made Afghanistan a safe haven for terrorist outfits. For Basu, it was surprising that the Congress government under Rao had celebrated the rise of the Mujahideen in 1992 as freedom fighters. Fight against terrorism of any sort could only be ideological, he asserted. Not surprisingly, left parties had organised protest rallies against both the US actions in Afghanistan and India's support for it.[99]

Fali S. Nariman, a senior lawyer and a nominated member of the Rajya Sabha, argued that America's simplistic motto of finding bin Laden dead or alive was bound to fail. Instead, India and the US should ratify the Rome Statute of the International Criminal Court of 1998, which required ratification from 60 states (only 43 had ratified it then), and the New York International Convention for the Suppression of Terrorist Bombings of 1997. Strengthening the institutional muscle of international organisations such as the International Criminal Court (ICC) and the UN, and using proper legal channels to fight terrorism was the need of the hour. The US had already introduced the USA PATRIOT Act (Uniting and Strengthening of America by Providing Appropriate Tools to Intercept and Obstruct Terrorism) in response to the 9/11 attacks, with the aim of curbing and preventing future acts of terrorism.[100] In a similar move, India introduced the controversial Prevention of Terrorism Ordinance (POTO) on 24 October 2001, which offered sweeping powers to the state for undertaking search and arrest of individuals or groups they thought were involved in terrorism-related activities.[101] Though these laws gave the US and India operational freedom to crackdown on perceived terrorists, they were essentially curative strategies rather than preventive measures.

Vajpayee countered these allegations by arguing that unconditional support to the US, and his letter to Bush, were not signs of weakness or being a US 'sidekick'. They were, instead, portents of power and reflected India's growing confidence. Having experienced cross-border terrorism all these years, India had found an ally in the US and thought it was best to engage on areas of mutual interest on an equal basis. The government argued that even if it was incorrect of the US to bypass the UN (which was incorrect, as there was tremendous support for the US invasion, and official UN approval in the form of UNSC resolution 1386 came within weeks), but India was still consulting the UN, its NAM partners, the EU, and many other countries, and not just banking on the US.[102] India's foreign policy was based neither on nostalgia, nor on prejudice, but on national interests, and the question of whether or not to trust the US never arose, and should never arise, pressed Vajpayee. India could only have secured its national interests in such circumstances, Jaswant Singh argued, by 'influencing [the situation] not through staying away, but influencing through engagement, and having engaged, influencing through persuasion'.[103] If such influence does not work, and India sees that any country is acting in a fashion that is not conducive to India's national interest, then New Delhi will have nothing to do with that country. But 'prejudice' cannot be a good foundation of India's foreign policy. As for the killing of innocents, Vajpayee conceded to that point and agreed to raise it with Washington.

In contrast to the heated debate on US actions post 9/11, and India's response to the same, all Indian policymakers were in agreement that Afghanistan should remain united and develop as a broad-based multiethnic democratic polity, which does not allow its soil to be used as a training ground for terrorists, and for infiltration into India.[104] Some opposition MPs also recommended that instead of the administrative burden being borne by any single country administration, the UN should manage Afghanistan in its transition period, just like Cambodia was after the fall of the Khmer Rouge. The UF, which had entered Kabul with US armed support, were being widely welcomed in India. Barring SP's Janeshwar Mishra, who worried that whoever comes to power in Kabul will be an American 'stooge' (Hamid Karzai was indeed called such until he fell out of favour with his Western benefactors years later), most political parties were confident that the UF leaders such as Burhanuddin Rabbani, Abdullah Abdullah, Faheem Khan, Yunus Qanooni, Ismail Khan, Dostum, or even the former king Zahir Shah, would be ideal to form the government.[105]

Underlining the dominance of anti-Pakistan partisanship in the Parliament, both the government and the opposition emphasised that no Taliban member should be given political space in the post 2001 Afghanistan.[106] Even Hekmatyar, who was dependent on Pakistan and had political currency in some pockets of Afghanistan, should be kept at arm's length. Despite the US military intervention, India was convinced that the Taliban had not been destroyed. It had only been displaced to the mountains of Afghanistan, or the tribal regions of Pakistan, from where it could easily launch an insurgency against the US forces, or be diverted towards Kashmir by the ISI. Fazlur Rehman Khalil, leader of the Harkat-ul-Mujahideen, had already crossed into Afghanistan to join the Taliban in its fight against the US. There was, however, a curious and subtle conciliatory twist to India's diplomacy on the Taliban even then. Vajpayee, though resolute in his advocacy of a Taliban-free Afghanistan, accepted incorporation of 'moderate' Taliban figures in the new Afghan political dispensation.[107] Who exactly these people were was unclear, but the catch was that they will not be part of mainstream politics as 'Taliban', but could be included in a different, more tolerant, incarnation.[108]

To ally, or not to ally

As Indian officials debated whether or not to support the US in Afghanistan, the Commander-in-Chief of the US Pacific Command Admiral Dennis Blair and US Secretary of Defence Donald Rumsfeld emphasised improved India-US defence ties. Navy-to-navy and high-tech defence cooperation, Blair stated, could form the 'most significant' component of this bilateral relationship. Indeed, while Vajpayee was in Russia soon after 9/11, the *USS O'Brien* stood silently docked in Chennai.[109] Against international maritime laws, India had even escorted the US warship through the Malacca Straits inviting objections from Malaysia.[110] In late November, just before the Bonn Conference began, Blair paid an official visit to New Delhi. Even though Vajpayee denied media reports of a Cabinet meeting in early November to discuss the possibility of entering into a military alliance with the US, Blair did meet the Cabinet Committee on Security (CCS), the highest decision-making body on matters of national security, to seek India's military support.[111] The meeting was both critical and highly sensitive, and its details remain classified.

In the meeting, chaired by Vajpayee (and attended by Jaswant Singh, Brajesh Mishra, defence minister George Fernandes, home minister L K Advani and the chiefs of the three military services of India), Blair made a formal request for access to Indian naval and air bases for International Security Assistance Force (ISAF) planes and carriers, and Indian troops on the ground in Afghanistan.[112] Blair's demand was ironic given Pakistan's active collaboration in the war by this time and Washington's growing discomfort with excessive Indian presence in Afghanistan. Nonetheless, naval bases in Goa and Mumbai for the US fleets to assemble, and 'stage-through' facilities at air force bases for the US to employ long-range bombers, were sought. The meeting ended with India refusing to put boots on the ground, but allowing over flight, landing, and refueling facilities for US air mission and port calls by naval ships as well as intelligence sharing, and helping with the investigation of the 9/11 incidents.[113]

The split between the partisans and conciliators is reflected in Indian deliberations over Blair's proposal. Though the details of this meeting remain classified, media reports and interviews with senior Indian policymakers indicate a divided house. According to a *Times of India* report, at least two members of the CCS made a 'vigorous pitch' for accepting US demands and advocated joining the war on terror unconditionally. Admiral Sushil Kumar opposed the idea, saying that the US and its allies did not, at least until then, enjoy a UN mandate on Afghanistan (which was offered on 20 December 2001), and that India had not declared war on Afghanistan. Vajpayee concurred with the conciliators' counter-argument and refused to cater to all of Blair's requests.[114] Though the identity of individuals advocating military alignment remains secret, Advani's aversion of the Taliban and Jaswant Singh's open support for military cooperation are well known. India had agreed to 'facilitate' military action in April 2001, and had been providing military and logistical support to the UF since the mid-1990s. In this context, the US demand for military support fit the partisan's vision of Afghanistan perfectly. However, India's final decision to not send troops signified that it was keen on keeping all options open instead of taking sides and developing hostilities with Afghans.

The dilemma of whether or not to ally with the US became acute on 13 December 2001, when five gunmen allegedly associated with the JeM and the LeT barged into the parliament and killed fourteen people in a shooting spree. India was shocked. In a subsequent parliamentary address, Jaswant Singh stated that the ghastly attack 'on 13th December 2001 has shocked the entire nation. The terrorist assault on the very bastion of our democracy was clearly aimed at wiping out the country's top political leadership'.[115] Between May 1990 and April 2000, Indian security forces had seized 33,763 weapons of various caliber, three million rounds of ammunition, 122,332 explosive devices, and a large volume of other war material in Kashmir, and 4,536 incidents of violence had occurred in 2001 alone.[116] The parliament attack by Kashmir-focused and Pakistan-based groups unshackled India from restraining to use force. On 14 December 2001, India launched Operation Parakram and mobilised its armed forces, all set to undertake offensive action against Pakistan. Lasting ten-months until October 2002, Operation Parakram did not end in all out war. Powell's shuttle diplomacy between New Delhi and Islamabad helped contain the situation.[117]

An India-Pakistan war would have undermined the US initiative in Afghanistan (in addition to destabilising the region). With Pakistan having changed its policy and cooperating with the US, it was important for Washington to ensure that fresh Indian pressure on Pakistan would not derail the ongoing war efforts in Afghanistan. Operation Parakram reflected India's willingness to undertake military brinkmanship with Pakistan. New Delhi hoped that Washington would support its cause given its own preoccupation with terrorism. This was made clear by Jaswant Singh to the then US ambassador to India, Robert Blackwill, and US special envoy to Afghanistan, James Dobbins, both of whom were in New Delhi five days after the parliament attack. Blackwill gave a very sympathetic ear to the Indian leadership, but was gravely concerned about the situation in private, and was planning to use his leeway with Jaswant Singh and Brajesh Mishra to deescalate the situation. Dobbins, however, politely but bluntly, began reducing India's expectations of increasing its profile in Afghanistan in light of the fresh tension with Pakistan. Though India readily accepted Karzai to stay on board with the US at Bonn, it did not mean an automatic US approval of a heavy Indian presence in Afghanistan. Instead, as Dobbins clarified, India was to be kept at a distance lest it unsettled Pakistan.[118] Satinder Lambah, Dobbins' Indian counterpart, expectedly, was disappointed.[119]

The debate over India's military engagement in Afghanistan ended in the light of Operation Parakram. Security donors to Afghanistan decided, at a conference in Geneva in April 2002, that all regional actors must be kept out of the security domain.[120] India's last-ditch effort in Geneva (made by Lambah and a senior Indian army general) to convince Dobbins about letting India raise the Afghan National Army made little impact.[121] Gharekhan, former Indian representative to the UN and special envoy to the Middle East, found this decision wise.[122] However, he suspected that it was taken primarily to assuage Pakistan's concerns vis-à-vis India. Only India, he argued (somewhat spuriously) had the capacity to play a decisive role in Afghanistan's defence sector. Iran's troubled ties with the US, the CAR's limited capacity, and Chinese and Russian reluctance, convinced Indian officials that the West aimed this decision solely at India. It fed into India's apprehensions towards Washington's tilt towards Pakistan, that only increased when the US refused to entertain Indian military involvement despite Afghan requests (despite the fact that levels of violence in Kashmir went down after 9/11, mostly due to US pressure on Musharraf).

Vikram Sood, then chief of R&AW, clarified to the political leadership that US was not going to touch India-specific militant groups, and would only target Al Qaeda and the Taliban.[123] 'So if you [political leadership] think that they will help you sort your problem, forget it. That's not going to happen', he counseled. But the partisans were euphoric about the whole affair and wanted to be friendly with the US in the hope of a high strategic yield on the security front. As Sood put it, the BJP wanted to get out of a failed marriage by building strategic links with the US, but this was not how it worked, as such collaboration on Afghanistan was not in US interests. Shyam Saran concurs that given India's policy of containing Pakistan, the idea of militarily aligning with the US in the wake of 9/11 was a potent one, but it did not happen.[124] For Arun Sahgal, who was then the Director of Net Assessment at the Integrated Defence Staff, says that India's approach began with euphoria, but 'then the opportunities started to cease ... and the realisation came that the Americans are not in it for us, they are in it for themselves'.[125] Other senior diplomats such as Rajiv Sikri, term the political leadership's enthusiasm for aligning with the US as unwarranted.[126] India's initial enthusiasm to offer naval and air bases was rooted in its rationale of showing loyalty to an outraged US. Indian bases, however, could not have helped the US pursue its war in Afghanistan. All India could do was help with air and naval supplies, but the US would still need to cross Pakistan's airspace. 'So what good were our bases in India? The bases that were more important for them were in Central Asia, and they [US] got a few,' Sikri argues.[127] Another source of the Indian bureaucracy's caution against the US was rooted in differences over US operational plans in Afghanistan. Wary of getting bogged down in a long-term counter-insurgency or nation-building, the US was aiming for a crisp military campaign to root out terrorism. From an Indian standpoint, this was impossible.

Gautam Mukhopadhaya, India's ambassador to Afghanistan (2010–13) and the liaison officer part of the team that opened India's embassy in Kabul 2001, concurs that India was given very limited space to operate in Afghanistan. 'Though we [India] came on the back of victory of the Northern Alliance and ouster of the Taliban, the US was a very powerful factor in Afghanistan', he says.[128] The US influenced the UN thinking, as there was a lot of sensitivity towards Pakistan's demands. The western diplomatic community was wary of Indian presence. Despite the fact that the UF, which was a substantial component of the Karzai government, backed strong relations with India, Karzai too was prone to thinking that Afghanistan was a victim of India-Pakistan rivalry.[129] Apparently, US views on India's security role in Afghanistan evolved between November 2001 (when Blair visited New Delhi) and April 2002, making it difficult for India to expand its security profile in Afghanistan. The gap between India and the US on the war on terror grew so much in these months that when the Kaluchak massacre in J&K happened on 14 May 2002, a livid Congress party leader Pranab Mukherjee tore into Jaswant Singh for making false promises based on exaggerated expectations about India being a beneficiary of the US war in Afghanistan.[130] Criticising Washington's double standards and the BJP's support for the same, Mukherjee asked 'how does one justify that you are fighting terrorism by co-opting a country which has accepted terrorism as a State policy?'[131]

Officials from India's National Security Council Secretariat (NSCS) underline the bureaucracy's conservatism towards the US in Afghanistan well after 2001. Benoy Khare, former Assistant Director of the Joint Intelligence Committee (JIC) at the NSCS, who analysed intelligence reports from all Indian spy agencies, says, 'all of them, the MEA, the R&AW, the IB, the MI, they came and told us, "don't trust the Americans", they will not help you do what you want to do in Afghanistan.'[132] But these were years when people like K Subrahmanyam, with support from Brajesh Mishra and later NSA M. K. Narayanan, were trying to change the bureaucracy's outlook towards the US. Indeed, Manmohan Singh had appointed Subrahmanyam to head a task force to examine the different aspects of global trends in strategic affairs in November 2005. A towering, Kissinger-like figure, Subrahmanyam could build consensus within India's policy community on strategic issues. Within six months, the task force came up with a classified document on how India should conduct diplomacy after 9/11.[133] Mostly an exercise in internal propaganda, the paper advocated deeper engagement with the various emerging power poles across the world and underlined the benefits of aligning with the US.[134] With George W. Bush, a heavily pro-Indian president in the White House, convincing the Indian bureaucracy to reduce its mistrust for the US was not a daunting task. Narayanan, who became NSA in 2005, explains this change in Indian thinking as such:

> From an Indian standpoint we felt that he [Bush] certainly was an unusual American and that he would not do anything that would hurt Indian interests ... my assessment is that change in our attitudes even in Afghanistan started with the advent of the Bush era ... the principle issue is that Bush in the White House made it easier for India to be accepted in various American quarters ... I think there was a fundamental shift in the US about India [as] they really wanted us to emerge [and] never asked us whether you want to fight terrorism. Countering China may have been a long term [US goal] but they didn't articulate it as such ... I would take Bush at his word.[135]

Slowly, but surely, the impact of Subrahmanyam, Narayanan, the larger Indian political leadership (both the Congress and the BJP) and Bush's outreach began to make an impact. India began cooperating with Washington in an unhindered fashion on most strategic issues and the bilateral relationship bloomed in the wake of the India-US nuclear deal.

Bonn compromise

Not just in the military domain, India was further marginalised by Afghanistan's post-Taliban political formation processes as well. India was, for instance, not invited to the critical Bonn Conference that occurred between 27 November and 5 December 2001.[136] Lakhdar Brahimi, the UN's special envoy to Afghanistan, who chaired the conference, had decided to not offer India a place in the guesthouse Petersberg that was meant only for delegates from the six plus two and the P-5 countries, (but not for the G-21, which India was a part of).[137] Even when India did join as an observer, along with sixteen other countries, it remained on the sidelines and accepted Hamid Karzai's rise (as part of the CIA-led Pashtun rebellion in the Taliban's stronghold in south Afghanistan).[138] Samajwadi Party leader Janeshwar Mishra's prognosis that whoever came to power in Kabul would be the American *Mahaprabhu's* (Great Lord) man came true at Bonn. Satinder Lambah, Vajpayee's special envoy to Afghanistan and Pakistan, was dispatched to Bonn (soon after he opened India's embassy in Kabul in November 2001). The Rome Group, the Cyprus Group, the Peshawar Group, and the UF, represented different Afghan stakeholders.[139]

Former King Zahir Shah, a Durrani Pashtun, headed the Rome Group. The Cyprus Group was close to Iran, and the Peshawar Group mostly represented the Gailani family known for its secular royalist credentials.[140] The UF that was led by Yunus Qanooni, had Russia, Iran, and India's support. Missing from the conference were Pashtun Islamists such as Hizb-e-Islami (Hekmatyar), Hizb-e-Islami (Khalis), the Haqqanis, Abdul Rasul Sayyaf of the Ittehad-i-Islami, the Taliban, and Afghanistan's urban elite that had not taken sides during the civil war. Islamabad sent Arif Ayub, Pakistan's former ambassador to the Taliban, and Farooq Afzai, an ISI officer.[141] Afzai's Indian counterpart, X, had also flown to Bonn and was booked into a hotel near Guesthouse Petersberg (where the conference was happening) and maintained covert communication channels with the different Afghan factions.[142] Dobbins represented the US, Zamir Kabulov represented Moscow, Robert Cooper represented the UK, and Iran sent senior diplomat and Foreign Minister Javad Zarif. Close to the UF, and actively engaging with the Rome Group, Lambah argues that India played an important role at Bonn for two reasons.[143]

Firstly, India, along with Iran and Russia was crucial in negotiating a settlement between different Afghan factions, Lambah claims.[144] The conference had run into a deadlock when Qanooni refused to give key ministerial berths and 75 per cent parliamentary representation to Karzai and other Pashtun groups.[145] Lambah, along with Kabulov and Zarif and other top diplomats, tried convincing Qanooni at a midnight meeting in Brahimi's room to make the concessions, whereas X convinced Haji Qadir and the Rome Group 'to strike the deal with Karzai and the UF for the sake of Afghanistan'.[146] In the end, eleven of twenty-nine berths in the provisional Cabinet went to Pashtun candidates.[147] Secondly, Qanooni flew with Lambah to New Delhi one hour after signing the agreement. This, according to Lambah, was a clear signal to the rest of the world on where India stood.[148] This was followed by Abdullah, Dostum, and Karzai's visit to New Delhi in 2002, and the fact that India was the first country to reach Kabul after the fall of the Taliban. The devil, however, lay in the detail.

The world knew that India stood behind the UF, and that was the problem. Instead of being an effective conciliator, India was a partisan in the conflict, and from that perspective, it compromised its partisan policy at Bonn. In the wake of Pakistan's support to the US, the partisans had been undermined, leaving Lambah with few policy options to pursue. From the very beginning, Lambah supported the idea of a Pashtun president and found Karzai an acceptable candidate whom India could work with.[149] Despite having supported Qanooni throughout the civil war, India relented under US pressure and wanted to ensure close cooperation between Lambah and Dobbins, and helped pave the way for Karzai's rise. Though an important role in its own right, even on this issue, it was Iran's Javad Zarif's short one-to-one meeting with Qanooni, after the midnight session, that made the difference, and not necessarily the advice that came from Lambah.[150] Most participants believed India was simply supporting its proxies along with Russia and Iran.[151] For any deal at Bonn, it was imperative to strike a political equilibrium not just inside Afghanistan but also outside (thus Dobbins and Brahimi's decision to bring Moscow, New Delhi and Tehran on board on Karzai's candidature before they went on to pressurise Qanooni). And to that effect, India's presence antagonised Pakistan, which was on the frontlines in the war on terror, even if it played a limited role in the conference itself.[152] As for India, despite having negotiated his way into the conference, in a candid lunch meeting with Dobbins, Lambah acknowledged the India-Pakistan competition in Afghanistan and promised that his government would move cautiously on expanding its strategic presence in order to make sure that India was on the same wavelength as the US.[153]

India's presence at the conference had run into obstacles from the outset. New Delhi had been excessively focused on the UF and to a limited extent, on the Rome Group. As a senior Afghanistan analyst working for India's Ministry of Defence put it, 'once Operation Enduring Freedom happened we got in [Afghanistan] but didn't know who to talk to. In that situation, the US pushed Karzai and gave India a legitimate face to talk to'.[154] But Rabbani's marginalisation at Bonn (he wanted to continue as president and consolidate his power base) strained India's UF-centric approach, and eventually made it redundant as the UF disintegrated under the weight of its own contradictions. Principally, thus, India viewed its support to the Rabbani government till 2001 as legitimate engagement with an internationally recognised government. In practice, however, it was anti-Pakistan proxy calculus at its extreme that only limited India's influence at Bonn.

The conference also showed that both India and the UN had lost faith in each other's capability to broker peace in Afghanistan. According to Abdullah, current Chief Executive of Afghanistan, Brahimi actively discouraged the Afghan government from getting too close to India.[155] The reason was always related to Pakistan's sensitivity towards Indian involvement. Even though Washington and many other countries eventually came to terms with the necessity of India's presence in Afghanistan, the UN remained wary. Finally, even if India had decided to boycott the conference, it would not have altered the outcome. X accepts that the US would have ensured a deal that favoured them with or without India's help. In fact, X had been reluctant to visit Bonn in the first place knowing the limits of India's influence, but was pushed by Brajesh Mishra for the R&AW had to have some presence on the ground in Bonn. As X put it, 'we eased the way for the US and the UN at Bonn. And Dobbins does not give us credit for that. But it's true that we were not the most important player in town those days'.[156]

What impact did the Bonn conference have on India's approach towards Afghanistan in the subsequent months? First, it gave fresh impetus to the debate between the partisans and the conciliators. Instead of debating whether to engage or not with the Taliban (at least not yet), the dilemma was whether to balance relations between different Afghan factions within and outside the new government, and if yes, then how. Though the 9/11 attacks and Operation Parakram helped in consolidating the partisan's coercive strategy, Washington's alliance with Pakistan and support for Karzai complicated its implementation. Dissolution of the UF added to the partisan's woes, making them miss Massoud's binding presence. As 'R', a former R&AW official specialising on Afghanistan and Pakistan, explains, Massoud's death was 'a blow to India'.[157] However, India's political dilemma was mild given Qanooni, Abdullah, and Fahim's presence in important cabinet portfolios ranging from defence to foreign affairs.

Second, India realised that selective engagement with non-Pashtun factions would not work in the post-Bonn context. Shyam Saran, who crafted India's diplomatic engagement in Afghanistan as foreign secretary, categorically says that 'yes, we had very close linkages with the Northern Alliance [United Front] people, but now [post Bonn] we had to broaden our constituency there [Afghanistan] and therefore we also started reaching out to the Pashtuns, including Karzai himself.'[158] Narayanan confirms this aspect of India's outreach to the Pashtuns.[159] With the baggage of having supported the Soviets first and non-Pashtuns afterwards, India wanted to come out of the jinx of being seen as a biased player in Afghanistan. Once again, changing dynamics on the ground as well as external pressures, brought the conciliators to the fore, ensuring that India did not lose out on Karzai.[160] New Delhi airlifted forty tonnes of medical supplies to Dushanbe in October 2001 to support the UF fighters,[161] immediately offered a US$ 100 million worth line of credit to Kabul, dispatched doctors and paramedics, pledged one million tonnes of wheat for internally and externally displaced Afghans, and promised to develop infrastructure projects.[162] What began as a humanitarian footprint eventually became a developmental footprint.[163] Such was India's determination to engage with Afghanistan (read Karzai) that it also gagged Abdullah (by putting a heavy police cordon around him when he came to Delhi after the conference) from speaking to the media, lest he made an anti-Pakistan or anti-Karzai statement from Indian soil, just like Qanooni had done soon after landing in India from Bonn, causing New Delhi considerable embarrassment.[164]

As the next chapter details, after Bonn, India adjusted to its traditional approach, which was Afghanistan is Afghanistan, and not a potpourri of ethnic fragments. 'Probably it would not be wrong to say that we [India] felt the need to compensate a little bit the Pashtuns and therefore we may have made a little extra effort to reach out to the Pashtuns, but even that I would say is easy to overstate', says Gautam Mukhopadhaya, India's ambassador to Kabul (2010–13).[165] The Afghan leadership confirms this. For Ahmad Wali Massoud, the younger brother of Ahmad Shah Massoud, India's shift in stance after the 2001 Bonn Conference was 'so immediate, so quick' that 'people in the Resistance [UF] did not take much notice of what happened.'[166] Abdullah also testifies to this shift in India's approach, and wanted India not to focus all its political energy on Karzai.[167] All the three drivers of India's Afghanistan policy—external political environment, India's desire to strike balance between Afghanistan and Pakistan, and domestic Afghan political equations—were aligned in a manner that the appeal of the conciliators went up in India after Bonn. With the US in the picture, Russia and Iran's salience had gone down (relative to the 1990s) in Afghanistan (for India). Even though Zamir Kabulov had little confidence in the West's plans for Afghanistan, Moscow did not influence the course of events after 9/11.[168] China too maintained a low profile and was blamed for free riding on the US security umbrella.

After years of disconnect, the *Kabuliwallah* bond with the Pashtuns started to form a strong undercurrent in Indian policy circles once again. A majority of India's diplomatic and security officials interviewed for this book evoked this historical bond. Having opened consulates in Kandahar, Jalalabad, Mazar-e-Sharif, and Herat, in addition to its embassy in Kabul, India began developing an independent understanding of intra-Pashtun political and tribal dynamics. Further reflecting cultural aspects to India's decision-making, G. Parthasarthy, former Indian ambassador to Pakistan, stated that given modern Afghanistan's political and social history, India could not have sent a Sikh regiment (or any other Indian regiment) to run a Provincial Reconstruction Team (PRT) in Pashtun-dominated areas of Afghanistan.[169] As conciliators advocated throughout the 1990s, India was slowly coming to terms with engaging everyone on the Afghan political landscape. Sood, who was the architect of India's covert infrastructure in Afghanistan (the most potent covert investments India made in Afghanistan were immediately after the Bonn conference), clearly states that historical bonds played an important role in the heyday of the war on terror. 'By 2002–03 we started saying that we can't keep the Pashtuns out forever. They constitute the single largest [ethnic] group, and are the closest to the [Pakistan] border. You can't deal with Balochistan unless you deal with the Pashtuns. And there are groups like the ANP and the old Wali Khan group who are our friends. So you [India] can't dump them, you've got to keep them. That's how this started'.[170] This element of increasing India's covert footprint in Balochistan was a driver of India's relations with Pashtun political figures in Afghanistan. After the 2004 Afghan presidential elections, India increased its support for Karzai (who had begun to distance himself from Pakistan), to the chagrin of its former United Front allies.

Conclusion

India's Afghanistan policymaking was neither an exercise in a vacuum nor a fixity rooted in national interests. It was a process of continuous negotiations by Indian policymakers at the domestic, regional, and international levels. The three drivers of India's Afghanistan policy were aligned in a manner that ensured the dominance of partisans at the dawn of the twenty-first century. Firstly, the Taliban's rise decisively shifted the balance of power in Pakistan's favour within Afghanistan, undermining Indian desires of a balance between Kabul and Islamabad. New Delhi's decision to ally with Russia and Iran and offer military support to the UF ensured that Pakistan remained regionally isolated, and the Taliban did not overrun the whole of Afghanistan. Even though the US, as well as many conciliators in India, doubted that Pakistan exerted absolute control over the Taliban, the regime was dependent on Pakistan's material and diplomatic support. In such a scenario, even if the Taliban differed with Islamabad on specific political issues, its sovereign agency remained limited. The IC-814 hijacking incident and the HuA and Al Qaeda militant training camps were perfect examples of the Taliban's limited sovereign authority over its domestic affairs. Even senior Taliban leaders such as the 'moderate' Mullah Rabbani, who were opposed to hosting international Islamist militants on Afghan soil, had little operational influence on these matters and were eventually purged by Mullah Omar.[171] But then, even if moderate Taliban figures had dominated the Taliban's decision-making processes, the Taliban's limited capacities would have made it impossible for them to crackdown on these training camps.[172] Non-Afghan fighters during the Taliban era, thus, were both a blessing and a curse for the regime. They supported the Taliban in its battles against the UF, but also became its Achilles Heel.[173]

Secondly, though there was a decisive regional consensus against the Taliban regime, Washington decided to pursue limited unofficial engagement with the Taliban (despite finding its ideology repugnant). This was the kind of engagement that conciliators in India had advocated throughout. However, such engagement by the US was inadequate for strengthening the hands of the conciliators in India to change policy course. Instead it was seen mostly as a suspicious American ploy to safeguard its energy interests at the detriment of regional security. It is in this context that the partisan-dominated India continued to chastise the US for abetting the rise of the Taliban. The 1998 East Africa bombings, which coincided with the nuclearisation of South Asia, changed these dynamics. India found it imperative to get the US on board on the nuclear debate (in order to lift the sanctions that came with the Pokharan tests), but also saw an opportunity to peddle US anxieties on terrorism. Instead of following Washington's half-hearted advocacy of engaging with the Taliban, India actively influenced US perceptions on cross-border militancy and the illegitimacy of the Taliban that supported global terrorism. September

11 was a watershed moment that decisively shifted US policy attitudes along partisan lines. However, after the tumult of the initial weeks after the 9/11 attacks, the Bonn Conference underlined the limits of India's partisan advocacy on Afghanistan. Having put all its eggs in the UF basket, India was disappointed when the US appointed Karzai as the interim president, allowing the conciliators a comeback. Karzai's rise, despite leaving a bad taste among Indian policymakers, was a blessing for both the partisans and conciliators. Legitimised by the international community, Karzai started talks with Pakistan to the conciliators' delight. But soon after, as these talks failed to reap results on the ground and the Taliban made a comeback, much to the partisans' pleasure, Karzai turned unimaginably hostile towards Pakistan.

PART III

DEBATING ENGAGEMENT

7

'MAXIMUM LEADER'

HAMID KARZAI, INDIA, AND THE KABUL DURBAR

'India has a critical interest in the survival of the Karzai regime.'

M. K. Narayanan, NSA of India (2005–10)[1]

'Mr. Karzai is no Massoud but he can meet the current challenge even now [in 2013] if he abandons the narrow politics he has pursued since 2001.'

Vivek Katju, Indian Ambassador to Afghanistan (2002–05)[2]

'I met [Mohammad] Mohaqiq the other day and asked him these questions that the [Karzai] government is saying that you are going off talking to the Pakistanis and so on. But I can't tell the president [Karzai] politely that please don't try to shoot them [Karzai's opponents] off from our back now.'

Gautam Mukhopadhaya, India's Ambassador to Afghanistan (2010–13)[3]

New beginnings

Two planes, one Indian and the other Pakistani, landed in Afghanistan on 21 November 2001. The massive Il-76 carrier of the Indian Air Force descended at Bagram airbase after a 17-hour flight from New Delhi (bypassing Pakistani airspace) that included two stopovers (one near Dubai and the other in Meshed, Iran). The Pakistani plane landed at the Kunduz airfield nearly 300 km north of Bagram. Kunduz was under Taliban and Pakistani control, whereas the United Front had overrun Bagram with US support. Despite American warnings against it, India had dispatched a team of intelligence officers, diplomats, and doctors (consisting of special envoy Satinder Lambah, joint secretary Arun K. Singh, chief liaison officer Gautam Mukhopadhaya, X, three army doctors, and three nurses) to restart diplomatic links with Kabul.[4] The Pakistani plane, however, undertook multiple sorties over the next few nights to evacuate hundreds of Pakistani soldiers (including, allegedly, two army generals), the Taliban leadership, ISI agents, and Al Qaeda figures.[5] Pakistan's airlift was hardly a secret given the heavy media presence around Kunduz, but the US Secretary of Defense, Donald Rumsfeld, and chairman of the Joint Chiefs of Staff General Richard Myers, bluntly denied any knowledge of it.[6]

An incensed India sent diplomatic notes to the UK and the US protesting the airlift, but no response was forthcoming. The R&AW had eavesdropped upon Musharraf's demand from the US for allowing the airlift as a quid pro quo for Pakistan's support in the Afghan war. National Security Advisor Brajesh Mishra decided against making the news public via government channels, for fear of upsetting US president George W. Bush (whose support was critical on various other issues including India's nuclear programme). Instead, he (along with R&AW officials) fed information about the airlift to investigative journalist Seymour Hersh, who reported it in the *New Yorker* on 28 January 2002.[7] But the damage had already been done. Within days, reports of thousands of militants waiting on Pakistan's side of the border began pouring in, about which Indian policymakers had full knowledge.[8] Though obliged under the UNSC resolution 1373 to desist from supporting any outfit or person involved in or linked with terrorism, Pakistan would not do it, argued India. This was mainly because Islamabad's support in Afghanistan was under US pressure, and 'not out of choice', argued Jaswant Singh.[9] Pakistan's duplicity, he emphasised, was clear when a series of failed assassination attempts were made on Afghan defence minister Mohammad Fahim and interim president Hamid Karzai.[10]

India's return to, and Pakistan's temporary exit from Afghanistan was a surreal, spectacular, and highly iconic moment that perfectly captured the strategic competition between New Delhi and Islamabad in Afghanistan. India became the first country to return to Afghanistan after being the last to leave in 1996. To ensure continuity of the partisan approach that India had adopted throughout late 1990s, Katju was recalled from his ambassadorship in Yangon to serve in Kabul.[11] Pakistan, on the other hand, was entering the first phase of a tortuous journey that involved simultaneous balancing of relations with the US, many angry jihadists, and an aggressive India. The alacrity with which the Indian team reached Bagram and subsequent visits by Abdullah, Qanooni, and Dostum to New Delhi raised the specter of Pakistan's non-cooperation in Afghanistan. To assuage the situation, Washington pushed Dostum and other Afghan leaders to undertake a similar visit to Islamabad, while Brahimi pressured Abdullah not to seek Indian support.[12] The US and the UN also agreed to focus on the six plus two and P-5 countries at Bonn, which excluded India. Despite the fact that India rejected US requests for troops on the ground (US PACOM Chief Admiral Dennis Blair was in India around the same time as the Kunduz airlift), New Delhi criticised the US for getting two-timed by Pakistan.[13] Having engaged Washington along partisan lines all these years, geography had failed India in the ultimate analysis. Despite being a preferred long-term strategic partner of the US in South Asia, India's value in the Afghan war was limited at best. The limited role of the US during Operation Parakram further underlined the limits of India's anti-Pakistan partisanship.

Nonetheless, the heyday of the Afghan war also highlighted that despite being limited, India's presence was indispensable in Afghanistan. Any attempt to exclude India would be counter-productive if the aim was to stabilise Afghanistan. And the harder Pakistan tried to marginalise India in Afghanistan, the stronger New Delhi's resolve became in maintaining (and expanding) its presence in Kabul and containing Pakistan's influence—adding to already high levels of mistrust between the two South Asian rivals. Not surprisingly, years later, in December 2015, after months of heavy firing along the Line-of-Control, the Lashkar-e-Taiba's inability to substantially infiltrate into Indian-administered Kashmir, the Afghan Taliban's failed attempts to capture Kunduz and the Kandahar airfield, and after tremendous attempts to engage with India on bilateral disputes, Pakistan invited New Delhi to moot on Afghanistan. These talks allowed the concretisation of the Comprehensive Bilateral Dialogue between the two neighbours and saw the launch of the Turkmenistan-Afghanistan-Pakistan-India (TAPI) pipeline despite a grim security situation.[14]

'(Nice) Big brother is here to stay'

Not a single pen had moved from its place in the Indian embassy complex in Kabul, which had been abandoned in a rush in September 1996.[15] While dust accumulated in the deserted embassy compound, the Taliban had been using the Indian ambassador's residence in Wazir Akbar Khan, and had not bothered clearing it of ammunition before escaping the UF military onslaught after 9/11.[16] Given the scale of Kabul's destruction during the civil war, the embassy complex was in surprisingly good shape, allowing Lambah to confidently announce that after fixing the '*pani* [water], *bijli* [electricity], and telephone connections'; the embassy would begin issuing visas within two weeks.[17] Despite the Bonn compromise, the Kunduz airlift, and exclusion from Afghanistan's security sector, New Delhi rapidly expanded its profile in the humanitarian and development sectors in Afghanistan. The aim was to reconnect with Afghanistan both at the elite and the community level by using India's growing economic capabilities. Consulates in Jalalabad, Kandahar, Mazar-e-Sharif, and Herat were opened to manage India's developmental projects and political presence across the country (and to track Pakistani activities in Afghanistan).[18]

Divided into four broad areas, India's aid to Afghanistan covered humanitarian assistance, big infrastructural projects, small development projects (SDPs), education, and capacity development.[19] Cumulatively, India committed US$ 2.3 billion as aid in the years after the US intervention. This included building the Zaranj-Delaram highway connecting west Afghanistan to Iran's Chahbahar port via the border town of Milak in Sistan-Baluchistan (US$ 150 million), the parliament building in Kabul (US$ 178 million committed and US$ 28 million spent), the 42 megawatt Salma dam on the Hari Rud river in Herat (US$ 130 million), and installing a power transmission line between Pul-e-Khumri and Kabul (US$ 120 million) in collaboration with the Asian Development Bank, among other projects.[20] The Steel Authority of India Ltd (SAIL), a public sector industrial undertaking, secured mining rights at Afghanistan's largest copper mining site in Hajigak in 2011 (though little movement occurred on the project). It was a spectacular show of support that had created a buzz in Afghan circles about India's growing developmental footprint in the country.[21]

Inspired from India's successful community engagement experiences in Sri Lanka and Nepal, hundreds of SDPs were launched in Afghanistan in conjunction with providing food assistance for primary schools, supplying 250,000 tonnes of wheat, and offering training to about 1,000 Afghan army officers every year.[22] Most of these goods reached Afghanistan via Iran. To make such linkages viable, a tripartite preferential trade agreement was signed with both Afghanistan and Iran in 2003. Fearing Indian economic domination in the region, Pakistan refused to ship Indian wheat (and other products) to Afghanistan via its territory on spurious grounds that the wheat was infested and carried diseases.[23] In response, India converted the wheat into high-protein biscuits that would not become spoiled in the four to six weeks that it took Indian goods to reach Afghanistan via Iran's Bandar Abbas port and the through the Islam Qala border in Herat.[24] The Zaranj-Delaram highway was India's strategic response to further bridge this geographical gap with Afghanistan (exaggerated by hostilities with Pakistan). Though being actively used by the Taliban and generally unsafe for travel, the highway is meant to help reduce Kabul's dependence on the Karachi port for its sea links and allow India to ship goods and material to Afghanistan at lower costs. The Indian Development Cooperation Research (IDCR) mapped India's total development cooperation with Afghanistan between 2002 and 2013 as such.

As per Graph 1, India's total aid commitment and expenditure, despite a slight slump between 2009 and 2011, grew in 2013–14. Graph 2 further highlights that 42 per cent of India's total aid to Afghanistan went into infrastructural development, 25 per cent in government administration, 24 per cent in provision of food, 3 per cent each in multi-sector engagement and health, 2 per cent in education, and 1 per cent in training and capacity

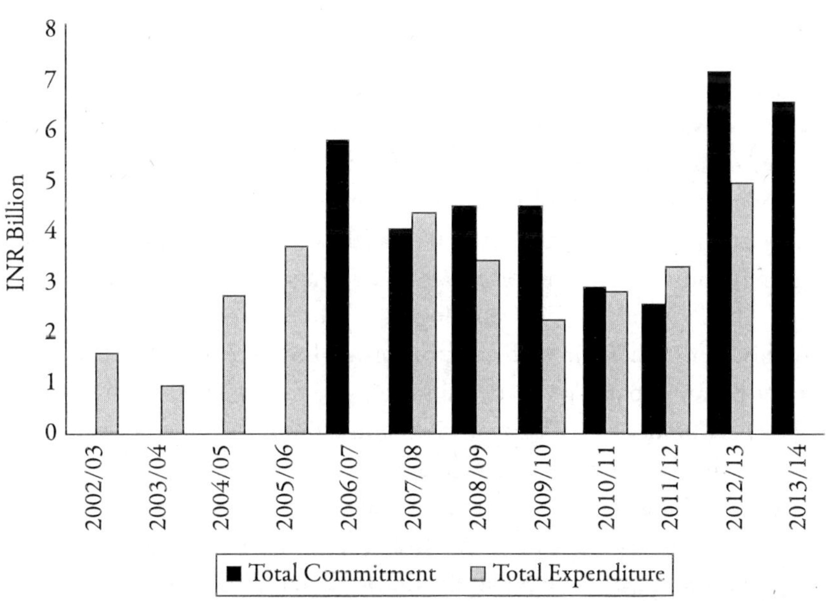

Graph 1: India's total Development Cooperation with Afghanistan 2002–2013[26]

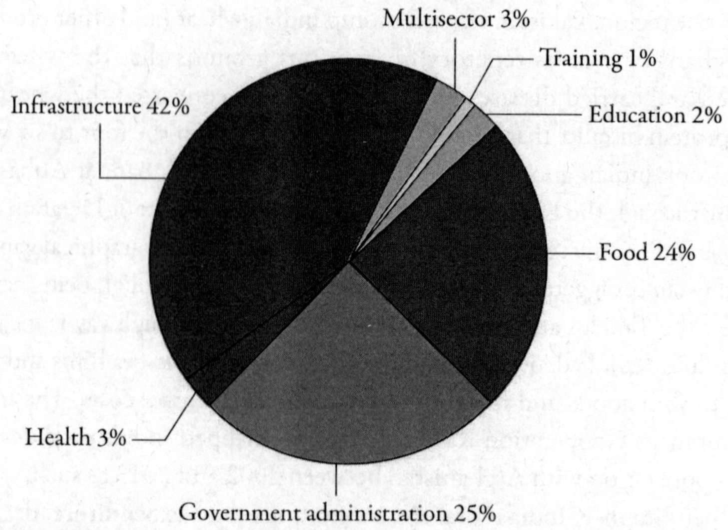

Graph 2: Sectoral breakdown of India's development cooperation with Afghanistan[27]

building. In addition to these projects, the number of Indian citizens in Afghanistan was estimated at 3,000 in 2011.[25]

The scale at which India expanded its presence across Afghanistan after the ouster of the Taliban betrayed its regional aspirations. In a confidential diplomatic cable, the US ambassador to India, David Mulford, noted that India's ever expanding strategic presence offered a terrific opportunity for the US to collaborate with New Delhi in Afghanistan. The '(nice) big brother' he told his bosses, 'was here to stay'.[28] By December 2005, seven public and nine private sector Indian companies were involved in air ticket sales, TV transmission, microwave transmission, power transmission, construction of common facility and tool room centre (Rs. 401.08 lakhs), dam construction, telecom, banking, consultancy, and offering cold storage facilities in Afghanistan, employing a total of 798 employees.[29] The Self Employed Women's Organisation (SEWA), with support from India's Ministry of Women's Affairs, began imparting vocational training to nearly 3,000 Afghan women in *Bagh-e-Zanana* (a park for women and children).[30] Media cooperation between the two countries also increased substantially, allowing India to develop the Kabul TV, the Jalalabad TV, and then to support big media conglomerates such as the Tolo TV.[31] Indian Airlines began operating direct flights between Delhi and Kabul from 31 March 2005, while Iran's Mahan Airways agreed to operate two services per week between Tehran and Delhi

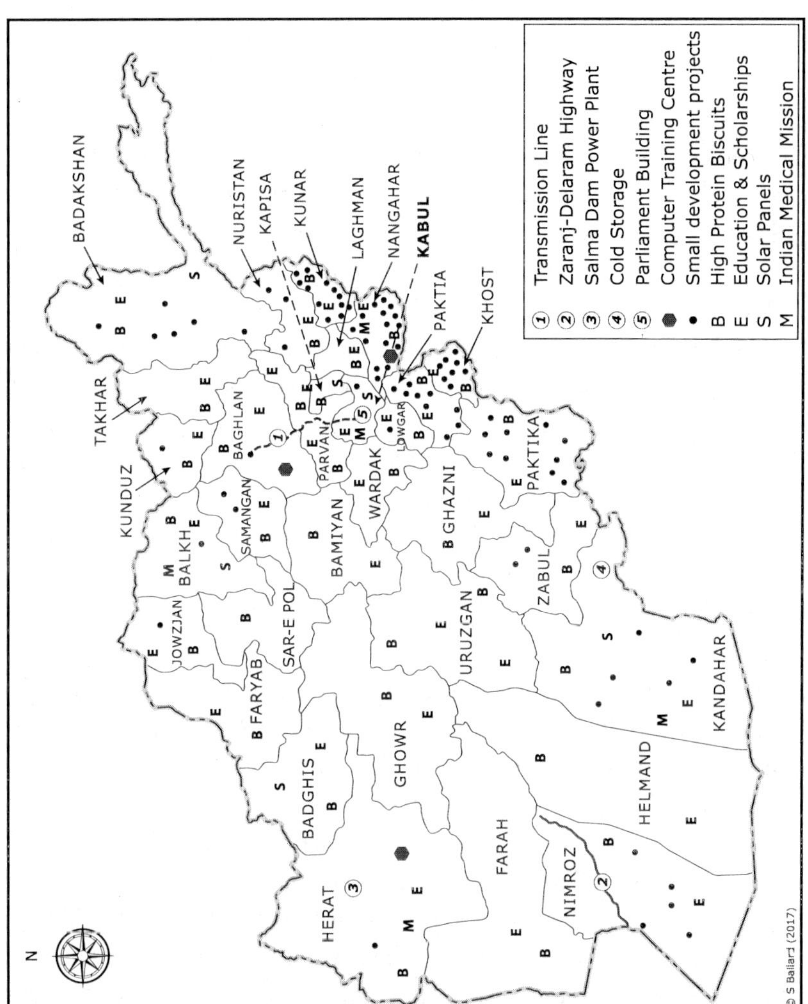

Figure 1: India's Small Development Projects in Afghanistan[33]

via Kabul till then.[32] Thousands of Afghan officials, including parliamentarians, were trained in India. New Delhi also gifted three civilian airliners, 274 buses (of which 234 were actually routed through Pakistan), renovated the Indira Gandhi Institute for Child Health in Kabul (Rs. 981.56 lakhs), and worked on the Habibia School (Rs. 2017.78 lakhs).[34] The two countries signed many more MoUs and trade agreements over the course of the war.[35] Soldiers from the Indian army's English Language Training Team were dispatched to Afghanistan (and housed in guarded guesthouses such as the Park and the Hamid in central Kabul) to give language training to officers of the Afghan forces. These Indian army officers became high value targets for Pakistan in Afghanistan. In addition to the coalition military umbrella, a carefully curated mix of 250–300 Indo-Tibetan Border Police (ITBP) soldiers and private security companies employing Afghans provided security for this robust Indian presence in Afghanistan.[36]

With higher stakes came more stakeholders. In addition to the government officials, strategic experts, and media outfits (that constituted the partisans and the conciliators throughout the 1990s), newer stakeholders emerged during the 2002–15 period. Though the PM, the NSA, the MEA and other foreign and security policy institutions were still the most powerful actors charting the policy course, private and public sector businesses and Indian chambers of commerce gained policy influence. The Federation of Indian Chambers of Commerce and Industry (FICCI) and the Confederation of Indian Industry (CII), for instance, became enablers of India's developmental footprint in Afghanistan.[37] Strategic think tanks such as the Observer Research Foundation (ORF), which is closely linked to the Reliance Industries as well as the MEA, and the MoD-sponsored Institute for Defence Studies and Analyses (IDSA), began framing policy discourse on Afghanistan. In popular Indian television and print media too Afghanistan gained salience in the wake of attacks on Indians in Afghanistan. From the intelligence community, in addition to the R&AW, the military intelligence also played a role on the ground after 2002.[38] The political compromise at Bonn, and the partisans' reluctant acceptance of Karzai as president, was a low cost to pay for what India was getting in return, which was a promise to reengage with Afghanistan and to rebuild its lost economic and cultural presence in that country. As Mukhopadhaya put it, 'there was a universal welcome to the return of the international community in Afghanistan', and India would not be left behind.[39] However, the question of how these seemingly benign projects would enhance India's political and strategic presence in Afghanistan persisted.

An interesting example of India's use of its aid for political purposes was indicated by the scholarship programme it ran in Afghanistan. Directly under the Indian Council for Cultural Relations (ICCR), these scholarships were used to coopt provincial Afghan politicians.[40] Barring the airfare, the scholarships covered full tuition fees, accommodation, and even offered a limited living allowance, making it a highly attractive deal for Afghan students.[41] The catch however was that Indian consulate officials could decide who to offer these scholarships based on independent political judgment, in consultation with the Afghan Ministry of Higher Education and local power brokers. As a result, whomever the local Afghan politician or strongman would recommend, would be offered the scholarship. It was a classic case of building micro-dependencies wherein Afghan politicians would build a reputation of 'helping' their constituents by facilitating education and stay in India. In return, the politician would develop a vested interest in securing Indian presence in the region and ensuring safety of Indian personnel. Mukhopadhaya and Saran argue that these projects had tremendous appeal among Afghans, and that building goodwill in Afghanistan was 'a great deal' in itself.[42] True, unlike Western aid projects that alluded towards developing the Afghan state and lead towards nation building, Indian projects were limited in ambition and investment, but high on visibility. Yet, Afghan responses were mixed.

Mahmood Khan, a young parliamentarian from Kandahar, for instance, asserted that India's 'heavy investment' in Afghanistan's reconstruction was highly cherished by Afghans from across the spectrum.[43] Critically, Khan concurred, these projects, big and small, buttressed India's image as a growing economic power that could support Afghanistan in the long run, and whose developmental and democratic model Afghanistan could emulate. Jawed Ludin, Janan Musazai, and Ershad Ahmadi, all senior foreign policy officials in the Afghan government also testified that the SDPs played an important role in impacting lives of the locals in rural Afghanistan.[44] However, there was no accounting for how the SDP funds were actually used once they had been handed over to the local Afghan administration on the ground. For Mohammad Tariq Ismati, Afghanistan's former deputy minister at the Ministry of Rural Rehabilitation and Development (MRRD), keeping track of every project was not possible, and calculating exactly what impact these projects had on the ground was also not possible.[45] Afghan Chief Executive Abdullah Abdullah, a close ally of India, was even more sceptical:

> Perhaps that [SDPs] was to win the hearts and minds of the population given how that was done. I don't know. The focus was mostly in eastern and southern part of

> Afghanistan. And looking at the situation there and how helpful such assistance was towards stabilising those areas is a big question mark.[46]

While there is no systematic evaluation of the Afghan Taliban's perspectives on Indian developmental projects, the few existing media reports indicate that despite being sceptical of India's political intent behind these projects, they generally welcomed the Indian presence.[47] Bitter that India never invested so heavily in Afghanistan's developmental sector in the 1990s, Taliban spokesperson Zabiullah Mujahid stated in 2010 that all these projects were meant to promote India's interests in Afghanistan. 'If India were so fond of the Afghan people, why did it not undertake development projects under Taliban rule?' he commented.[48] Nonetheless, for mid-level Indian diplomats who worked in Afghanistan, India's Afghanistan policy changed tremendously. According to one such official India 'not only focused horizontally across the country, but also vertically, in the rural areas'.[49] Such horizontal and vertical presence in Afghanistan, it can be argued, was possible only because India never sought a detailed accounting of funds that it gave for these SDPs and did not install a big bureaucracy (like other Western aid agencies including USAID and DFID) that went about monitoring these funds. Operational flexibility in the aid sector, apart from increasing goodwill, gave India some political weight in Afghanistan. All this was made possible by Karzai, who warmly welcomed India's presence in the country despite initially being wary of New Delhi's closeness with the United Front.

'Maximum Leader'

With the Taliban ousted, arguably, there was no reason for the partisans and the conciliators to compete over policy output after 2002. Supporting the new Kabul government in its developmental endeavors would have been enough. Fine in theory, exercising such neutrality was practically difficult in Afghanistan's factionalised polity. Just as former President Najibullah had the Khalq, the Mujahideen, and Pakistan as enemies, Hamid Karzai too had adversaries within and outside the government.[50] Ranging from senior members of the former UF, Rome, Cyprus, and Peshawar groups to the various Taliban factions that soon reemerged from bases in Pakistan, Karzai had many rivals. As Narayanan put it, Karzai was a 'maximum leader' in country that, despite the world's desire, did not function as a democracy.[51] Karzai had, indeed, manipulated Afghanistan's domestic politics along pro-Karzai and anti-Karzai lines. While the US supported him, Pakistan, despite recognising his presidency, openly supported the Taliban (and, ironically, even lobbied support of former UF leaders against Karzai over the years). India, however, began weighing its odds despite its big-ticket aid projects in Afghanistan.

In the early months of his rise, a militia-less Karzai was unknown to New Delhi. This was despite the fact that he had obtained a Masters in Political Science from the Shimla University from the north Indian state of Himachal Pradesh in 1984 (during the peak of the anti-Soviet jihad), understood Indian culture and sensitivities well, and had engaged with Nambiar in the early 1990s (after which India had lost touch with him). While Indian policymakers began highlighting Karzai's fondness for India based on his educational background in subsequent years, policy mandarins in New Delhi were wary of his geopolitical outlook at the beginning of the war. For instance, according to Mukhopadhaya, who was posted in Kabul in 2001, Karzai strongly nurtured the belief that Afghanistan was a victim of India-Pakistan rivalry.[52] The United Front, however, had disintegrated after Massoud's death two days before the 9/11 attacks happened, leaving Rabbani, Mohaqiq, Dostum, Abdullah, Ismael Khan, and Qanooni competing for ministerial positions, and coalescing behind or against Karzai. The question then was, who to support and how?

Partisans and conciliators debated this question just as vigorously as other issues on how to approach the Mujahideen and the Taliban. Though both saw the necessity of supporting Karzai in the changed context, the issue was whether this support will be symbolic or substantial? Unlike previous decades, conciliators such as Shyam Saran wanted to ensure that India did not commit the same mistake of adopting a partisan line and play political favourites. India should expand its political base and reach out to non-Taliban Pashtun leaders including Karzai, he argued. 'Those who were in positions to make decisions in 2004–05, and certainly I as foreign secretary was part of that, the sense was that it's extremely important that we have a broad-based constituency in Afghanistan', he states.[53] Partisans such as Vivek Katju, who was appointed ambassador to Kabul in 2002, however, advocated supporting former UF allies independent of Karzai. As the next section details, the partisans wanted India to offer limited support to Karzai, but remain politically aligned with the ostensibly tried-and-tested anti-Pakistan leaders and India's old 'friends' such as Abdullah and Qanooni (and other former UF officials).

Marking a subtle but substantial switch in India's Afghanistan policy, the conciliators won the day. Driven by changes in domestic Afghan politics, including Massoud's demise, as well as international pressure at Bonn, the policy shift almost went unnoticed in the early days of Karzai's presidency. The key conciliatory tenets remained the same after 2002, that is: (a) India should engage with whosoever is in power in Kabul and cultivate a friendly government sensitive to India's core interests; (b) deal strictly with the government in Kabul regardless of how its relations with Pakistan are; (c) don't adopt a selective engagement strategy, wherein preference is given to one group or community over others; (d) develop P-2-P relations and build public goodwill for India in Afghanistan. The various MEA annual reports after 2002 underline India's conciliatory approach. Bilateral relations between the two countries attained new levels of intensity and cooperation by 2004, based on regular political and economic interactions.[54] By 2005, the bloodiest year in Afghanistan since the ouster of the Taliban, Manmohan Singh and Congress leader Rahul Gandhi visited Kabul and stayed overnight at Karzai's request, displaying solidarity with the new government.[55] With the Afghan Taliban having launched an insurgency against the ISAF and Afghan forces, the security situation in Kabul had become increasingly precarious. Worried about repeated attacks by the Taliban and the Hizb-e-Islami (which supported the Kabul government but was opposed to Western forces) with support from Pakistan, India saw reason in strengthening ties with Karzai.[56] In November 2006 Shivshankar Menon, then India's foreign secretary, a staunch conciliator who later became national security advisor (2010–14), categorically informed the US under secretary of defence, Eric Edelman, that New Delhi was dedicated to 'empowering Karzai' and will strengthen him politically and economically.[57]

India's tilt towards Karzai was supplemented by the fragmentation of the UF. Riddled with rifts since its inception, the UF could not withstand the changes at Bonn. The UF's disintegration complicated India's relations with its various leaders. Dostum was viewed as an opportunist (by Indian policymakers) who could not be trusted with long-term partnerships, whereas the Massoud brothers (Ahmad Zia and Ahmad Wali Massoud) had lost political weight even if they were to be engaged with. Ismael Khan in Herat and the Hazara Shia groups including that of Mohaqiq and Karim Khalili engaged with India but looked for guidance from Tehran, limiting New Delhi's room for strategic maneuver. Qanooni and Abdullah on the other hand were heavyweights and had tremendous support from India, but were unable to come to power given Karzai's political value within and outside Afghanistan, and his manipulative capabilities in order to survive. As a member of the National Security Advisory Board (NSAB) put it, 'basically the game was to look for Pashtuns who would be friendly and interested in working with India.'[58]

Karzai's snubbing of former UF leaders had not gone unnoticed by top Indian leadership. PM Manmohan Singh had personally asked Karzai to 'avoid isolating' the UF leadership and to manage better relationships with all ethnic groups.[59] Such requests, however, did not translate into serious diplomatic pressure (both Russia and Iran supported Karzai and wanted to strengthen him further despite being wary of his political marginalisation of non-Pashtuns leaders). This aspect is reflected in the vast difference between what Indian security and diplomatic officials thought in private and what they said in public about Karzai. Publicly, the MEA reported in 2007 that Afghanistan under Karzai, 'had made progress towards internal stability in a democratic and pluralistic framework', despite the Taliban's audacious revival.[60] But privately, senior MEA and R&AW officials thought that Karzai was walking a delicate political line by politicking against non-Pashtun candidates and was 'not advancing the cause of peace and stability that much'.[61] Even top retired Indian officials such as Brajesh Mishra and M. K. Rasgotra, were critical of Karzai for being unable to 'stabilize Afghanistan' in private conversations with serving US officials.[62] Nonetheless, India only increased its support for Karzai and signed the Strategic Partnership Agreement (SPA) with Kabul in October 2011. For Rakesh Sood, India's ambassador to Afghanistan (2005–08), India was engaging with the legitimate Afghan government recognised by the international community. Sood firmly believed that playing favourites along partisan lines was not in the character of India's foreign policy (a contestable claim).[63] Mukhopadhaya also asserts that despite enlarging its humanitarian and developmental footprint, India steered clear from Afghanistan's internal politics.[64] In November 2009, in the fog of debate about reconciliation with the Taliban, joint secretary Yash K. Sinha told his US counterpart that India was not interested in 'micromanaging' Karzai.[65] Sensitive about Afghanistan's sovereignty, India refused to take decisions that could be perceived as being biased in the domestic Afghan context. New Delhi was not interested in Afghanistan's political processes, it just wanted unambiguous outcomes, which were to ensure that no political leaders that were dependent on Pakistan for sustenance, entered the government with ease.

Such balancing between Afghanistan's contradictory desires of deeper and decisive Indian engagement (often on partisan lines) on one hand, and not being seen as intrusive and undermining Afghan sovereignty on the other hand, was a diplomatic tightrope. Different Afghan factions secretly wanted India to adopt a partisan stand (like Pakistan), instead of engaging with all factions and convincing none. Ironically, even Karzai's advisors and spokespersons such as Waheed Omar, who engaged with India regularly, thought that New Delhi was either not committed towards Afghanistan (given its reluctance to support Karzai militarily) or was just confused.[66] Shivshankar Menon agrees about the limitations of the conciliatory approach.[67] Unlike the 1990s, when India was seen as supporting non-Pashtun interest groups over those from the Pashtun communities, the opposite perception of India being too pro-Pashtun developed after 2002. What conciliators thought as being state-to-state relations, were being viewed as a pro-Pashtun approach by Karzai's opponents. Such accusations of taking sides even if India just talked to different factions, Menon argued, were bound to occur in an ethnically divided country. 'We [India] used to be accused of this [taking sides] even in the 1940s and the 1950s. When we supported Badshah Khan and the Khudai Khidmatgars, we were told, "what is this, you rely on Pashtuns". And this is because of Congress Party's old links [but] how can it be that we don't do anything there [in Pashtun areas]', he asks rhetorically.[68]

India's initial SDPs, which were focused in south and east Afghanistan, had nurtured the perception that the Pashtuns were being favoured over other communities. The fact was that first round of SDPs were offered to communities who needed them most and were first off the block to ask for them. And all of them were from southern and eastern regions that were worst affected by the conflict. Handled by Afghans themselves (and not Indian personnel), each SDP cost a maximum of US$ 3 million, and was implemented without heavy bureaucratic clearances by central Afghan ministries where corrupt officials would ask for bribes. Given the popularity of these SDPs, not only did the Taliban never attack them, but they also came to appreciate India's people-friendly approach—further cementing the notion that India was pro-Pashtun.[69] India's attempts at spreading these SDPs across the country in central, north, and west Afghanistan did little to assuage such concerns, and were mostly seen as token projects. When quizzed about the political intent behind these SDPs, and their focus in Pashtun-dominated areas, Mukhopadhaya accepted that probably it is not wrong to say that India felt the need to compensate the Pashtuns more than other communities after 2002, and therefore it made extra effort to reach out to south and east Afghanistan.[70] Developing presence in all major urban centres of Afghanistan was given priority. Mukhopadhaya's predecessor in Kabul, Jayant Prasad, however, categorically states that he went to Kabul with a clear mandate of reconnecting with the Pashtuns in Afghanistan's countryside (a mandate strongly backed by NSA Narayanan).[71] The SDPs, and social contacts via the government and the various NGOs helped in achieving this aim.

India's conciliatory approach had two key adjuncts. Firstly, it was accompanied by a disconnect between the Indian embassy in Kabul and the MEA in New Delhi. Not only did New Delhi do little about this growing image of India's pro-Pashtun tilt and political indecisiveness in Afghanistan, but it also did not adequately understand the political strengths the developmental projects had imparted it politically. For Mukhopadhaya, 'sometimes in Delhi we don't realise that our biggest weakness [in Afghanistan] is not knowing our strengths', that is that India has not been very good at using its political capital for political outcomes.[72] Secondly, this disconnect exacerbated the growing disillusionment with India among Afghans from across the sociopolitical spectrum. Without a clear direction either from the PMO and the NSA (especially after 2010, according to some officers), Indian diplomats and intelligence officers working in and on Afghanistan were often left wondering how to execute policies on the ground.[73] In such an instance, when Afghanistan's security situation did get worse over the years, instead of holding to a firmly conciliatory approach, engagement with Karzai took a partisan turn. In fact, soon after the 2004 national elections in Afghanistan, India began to bet most of its political capital on Karzai, and dealing with different factions only via the palace.[74]

A partisan angle to India's support for Karzai developed as the latter settled into the presidency. In his first visit to New Delhi in January 2002, along with foreign minister and rival Abdullah, the first thing Karzai told Jaswant Singh was that Afghanistan's relations with India should be 'tactical' because of Pakistan. It was a clear signal of Karzai's limited enthusiasm for India, regardless of his university education in Shimla. Abdullah, who witnessed the exchange in disbelief (but also, to an extent, relief, for such statements increased his political value in New Delhi) claims that Jaswant Singh was 'shocked' by what he heard, but was too polite to make an issue of it.[75] Strongly holding the view that Afghanistan was a victim of India-Pakistan rivalry, Karzai also offered to mediate between the two South Asian rivals if they would agree. The partisans were disappointed and worried about what course Afghanistan would take if Karzai continued to harbor doubts about India's stance on Afghanistan. Eventually these differences were smoothened as Karzai's initial outreach to Pakistan failed in light of the Taliban's resurgence. Converting him into a fierce critic of the Pakistan army, the Taliban's revival pushed Karzai into an embrace with India. So much so that he admitted at a 2012 press meet in New Delhi that India had supported Afghanistan 'a lot in the security sector'.[76] When pushed by a senior Indian journalist to explicate how, Karzai bluntly and wittily replied, 'if I tell that, then it will not remain a secret'.[77] Concerned that he might get assassinated, India, in collaboration with the NDS, had contributed in providing him a covert security cover (the extent and nature of which is unknown). Karzai's political dexterity and mistrust in Pakistan had transformed him, somewhat, into the twenty-first-century avatar of Najibullah.

Top US officials had noted this aspect of India's partisan tilt towards Karzai. US Vice President Joe Biden, in a briefing about the Afghan war to president Obama, underlined: 'what Pakistan doesn't want, as a matter of faith, is a unified Afghan government that is led by a Pashtun sympathetic to India', whereas Karzai was just that kind of Pashtun.[78] Such partisan support for Karzai and his supporters came to be known unofficially in Indian policy circles as the 'Najibullah Model'. The MEA's basic line in Afghanistan, according to Pramit Pal Chaudhuri, former member of the NSAB, was—'can we have another Najibullah in Kabul?'[79] Though not a formal policy announcement, this was allegedly, the driving force behind supporting Karzai to the hilt when his relations soured with the West. Given the influence of partisans in India's establishment and the fondness with which Najibullah was looked upon in the 1980s, it was reasonable to expect New Delhi to desire for the 'Najibullah Model' as the US started planning a withdrawal. Unlike the early 1990s when India played a defensive game in the wake of the Soviet withdrawal, in 2014, India worked very well with the Pasthuns, especially Karzai. As an Indian analyst observed, 'India today [in 2013], more than ever in the history of Independent India, has a degree of influence in the Pashtun lands', he asserted.[80] Karzai and the villages in south and east Afghanistan, where he commands authority, are areas where India has invested heavily, both overtly using the SDPs and other projects, and covertly in the security sector.

This is indicative in India's strong links with the current chief of Kandahar Police and a big power broker in the southern province, General Abdul Razzik. A close ally of Karzai, Razzik received tremendous support from the US, and has been on the Taliban's hit list for many years.[81] However, he is a controversial figure, involvement in drug trafficking, and accused of mass murder. In February 2010 (soon after the London conference where reconciliation with the Taliban was given primacy), US officials challenged Razzik to disclose the source of such staggeringly high levels of wealth that he had accumulated over the years. Smiling wryly, Razzik informed said officials that part of his wealth came from his two brothers who worked in Dubai and India. Though he had visited Dubai, he had never set foot in India.[82] Though impressed by Razzik's confidence, the US ambassador to Kabul, Karl Eikenberry, had 'no illusions about his [Razzik] corrupt activities'. Eikenberry was certain that Razzik's brothers were laundering his illicit wealth via Dubai and India, without New Delhi doing much about it. Many such relationships (including with Gul Agha Sherzai in Nangarhar, whom Razzik knew well) would ensure India's presence in Afghanistan's southern and eastern provinces.

Karzai's political dexterity appealed both to India's sense of regional ambitions and India's insecurities. Shyam Saran agrees that India developed 'fairly strong constituencies among the Pashtuns ... and one of the reasons is that we have very good relations with Karzai [who] is a Pashtun, and ten years ago when this whole exercise began, he was regarded as pro-Pakistan. He was put there because the Pakistanis were comfortable with having him as the head of the government [but] the situation changed over time.'[83] The curious aspect about the 'Najibullah Model' was that it failed when support from Moscow dried up in 1992. And so did India's partisan approach towards Afghanistan (when it failed to secure Najibullah's escape). Karzai's reluctance to sign the BSA with the US then put a big question mark on the efficacy of another Najibullah type ally in Afghanistan. Shashank, India's foreign secretary in 2003–04, argued that the slow shift in India's position towards Karzai, was mostly a signal to different Afghan factions that they are free to do what they liked, but should 'not hurt India' in any which ways.[84] Indian diplomats continued to cultivate Karzai, and encouraged his opponents to accept his authority. Such political balancing was a daunting task for those diplomats who did it, and New Delhi cared little about the fallout if the balancing failed.

Afghan reactions

Unlike the popular goodwill that India enjoys across Afghanistan, narratives about India's political role among Afghanistan's political elite are complex (especially among the Afghan clergy that resents the spread of Indian culture in the country). India's tilt towards Karzai, expectedly, generated two opposite reactions: one critical and other supportive. Karzai's political opponents criticised that India was relying too heavily on one man in a country wrought by political factionalism and instability. By doing so, New Delhi was being biased against its former UF allies. This perception sharply contrasted India's strategic intent towards, and positive self-perception in, Afghanistan. Indian officials, for instance, were convinced about their neutrality in Afghan politics. But the gulf between what India thought it was doing and how Afghans perceived Indian actions grew. Was this a communications failure or was India really biased? To some extent, it was both, and to a large extent, India simply did not mind cold-shouldering any group or personality till they developed an overtly hostile posture towards India.

The perceived zero-sum nature of Afghanistan's politics became a hurdle for the conciliators. Karzai made it difficult for India to engage with his adversaries, while his adversaries blamed India for not paying adequate attention to their grievances against Karzai. Even when Indian diplomats agreed with the opposition that Karzai was manipulating them to remain in power, it could do little to change that. The deep aversion and mistrust between different Afghan political factions throughout 2002–15 only compounded these pressures. Mohammad Halim Fidai, former governor of Wardak, stated that his biggest worry was the possibility of another round of Afghan civil war due to fallout between different factions in active Afghan politics, and not due to the resurgence of the Taliban. In this context, he argued, it was imperative that India engages with all political factions and not just the government or the Panjsheri leadership.[85] Managing this tightrope, however, was getting increasingly complicated, if not worrisome, for New Delhi. Ahmad Wali Massoud, Karzai's bitter rival, notes India's shift as follows:

> During the Resistance [UF] they [India] were supporting, like Iran and like Russia, the Resistance against terrorism and Taliban ... but since 2001 when the new government came, they completely shifted towards the new government. Now, the support that the Resistance forces enjoyed before this government, after 2001 they [India] gave none of this support.[86]

Corroborating this sense of alienation with India were four different interviews with Afghan media personnel and political analysts (all sympathetic towards the UF and its various leaders) who claimed that former UF leaders felt 'abandoned' by India's thrust towards Karzai in particular and Pashtuns in general.[87] Their indication was mostly towards Mohaqiq and the Massoud brothers. Haji Mohammad Mohaqiq, head of the Hazara dominated Hizb-e-Wahdat was cautious of India's infamous reluctance of helping its friends but was not as bitter as Wali Massoud. India did put a lot of weight behind Karzai, said Mohaqiq, but then it 'supports whosoever is in power and not just the Pasthtuns'.[88] Abdullah says that the sense of alienation voiced by various UF leaders is incorrect and the 'scope of their thoughts should have been much more than just a narrow line'.[89] Nonetheless, he adds, 'as far as India is concerned, we didn't have any particular expectations on a personal or factional level. But at the same time it has been our advice to all the countries involved that only listening to the government will not do the job. That's the official line. Yes of course they have to deal with the government of Afghanistan and the relations have to be based on that, but at the same time there is goodwill among the people of Afghanistan and there is the voices of the people of Afghanistan also have to be heard'.[90]

The message was clear: India's Karzai-centric approach had its shortcomings. What Menon discarded as a bound-to-happen phenomenon in a factionalised polity (or as a mandatory political cost India pays in engaging with Afghanistan on a state-to-state basis), was taking a toll on India's political capital in the country. And Islamabad had begun capitalising on the trend. Pakistan lobbied 'enormously' to strengthen relations with former UF leaders who had fallen out of favour with Karzai, and were getting increasingly disillusioned by India.[91] The Massoud family, Mohaqiq, Dostum, and other second-tier Afghan politicians from north, west, and central Afghanistan, all began engaging with Pakistan.[92] Wali Massoud admitted that a Pakistan's delegation visited him in April 2013 and wanted him to 'meet the head of the ISI in whichever part of the world' he liked. They asked him why are they were fighting each other when they could be friends. 'They [Pakistan] come with logic', noted Wali Massoud.[93] Similar to India that used its higher-education scholarships as a tool of coopting the Afghan political elite (by offering their children or relatives opportunities to study in Indian universities), Pakistan offered scholarships to former UF leaders (classic tit-for-tat).[94]

In May 2013, Ahmad Zia Massoud, former Afghan vice president and leader of the National Front Party, openly criticised Karzai's focus on the Durand Line and ramping up the Pashtun rhetoric with Pakistan:

> By benefiting from such national issues, the President wants to stir people's support in favour of his favourable candidate in the forthcoming polls ... This, in no way, will be the solution to solve our complicated border issue with the neighbouring countries through the media and stimulation of public emotions and sentiments. It could be solved through logical diplomatic dialogues.[95]

Not just non-Pashtun leaders, even Hanif Atmar, a senior Pashtun leader and current national security advisor of Afghanistan, believed, at least in 2013, that 'one big mistake that Afghanistan did was the signing of the SPA first with India rather than with Pakistan. Islamabad had offered us an SPA before India did but we refused to sign it.' Being a bigger power in the region, New Delhi would have understood Kabul's logic of engaging with Pakistan, Atmar argued.[96] Atmar launched a spectacular diplomatic initiative to reconcile differences with Pakistan with support from current Afghan president

Ashraf Ghani in 2014. The consistency with which Pakistan intervened in Afghan affairs had made it a loathed, dreaded, hated, but also, ironically, an awe-inspiring neighbour in Afghanistan. In contrast, India's image of a reluctant and indecisive regional power bode ill for New Delhi's quest for broad-basing political relationships in Afghanistan.

Prasad and Mukhopadhaya concede that India failed to convince the non-Pashtun political elite of its conciliatory intent. According to Mukhaopadhaya, 'it has been an issue of communication ... but then they [opposition groups] have legitimate grievances against president Karzai. They feel betrayed and so on. This is not against Pakistan, they want us [India] to fight their battle ... I met Mohaqiq the other day and asked him these questions that the government [Karzai] is saying that you guys are going off talking to the Pakistanis and so on. But I can't tell the president politely that please don't try to shoot them [the opposition] off from our [Indian] back'.[97] The only other former UF leader with whom India got along well was Atta Muhammad Noor, the governor of Balkh and Abdullah's staunch ally. An extremely powerful figure, Atta Noor wanted to make Mazar-e-Sharif, the capital of Balkh province, into Afghanistan's Dubai (economically), and did not nurture presidential ambitions unlike other non-Pashtun leaders.

India was unable to help Karzai's opponents in ways they had asked for (supporting them politically and/or financially against Karzai). Instead, Indian diplomats tried convincing Karzai's opponents to accept his presidential authority. This was done right from the 2001 Bonn conference (where Lambah tried convincing Qanooni to give up ministerial berths to Pashtun candidates), till the 2004, 2009, and the 2014 national elections.[98] 'But then president Karzai started marginalising them slowly, and in odd ways. For example, Abdullah was released of his duties [as foreign minister] when he was on a visit to Washington. So there were genuine issues there', says Prasad. India's unfazed support to Karzai regardless of these concerns was simply a measure of New Delhi's focus on strategic outcomes in Afghanistan instead of processes. Karzai's wrongdoings were reconciled with the long-term interest of maintaining India's long-term presence in Afghanistan (tied to Karzai's political fortunes), to ensure that Kabul was a counter-balance to Islamabad, and to secure an internal political balance within Afghanistan. Prasad had many long discussions with Karzai, most of which were never mentioned even in diplomatic cables given how sensitive and unguarded these talks were. He argues that 'in the long term we know that a non-Pashtun candidate may be politically problematic, and that it is important to have a Pashtun as the head of the state'.[99] Narayanan concurred.

Even R&AW officials found it difficult to assuage concerns of the different political factions and manage the 'peculiar' zero-sum political landscape of Afghanistan.[100] Interviews with Indian intelligence practitioners and policymakers show that the partisans versus conciliators debate about the post-Bonn political dispensation was not just influenced by the three core drivers of India's foreign policy towards Afghanistan, but also by the disconnect between policymakers in New Delhi and those enabling and implementing policy on the ground in Afghanistan. India developed tremendous goodwill and political capital in Afghanistan that New Delhi could channel in a politically favourable direction, but India often fell short of using this capital for political gains. Trapped in rhetoric to broaden constituencies among Pashtun communities, the conciliators' engage-with-all approach yielded limited results at best, and confused many and alienated some Afghans at worst.

But there was another, highly appreciative, viewpoint on India's conciliatory approach. This came from Karzai's political team. Former deputy foreign minister of Afghanistan, Jawed Ludin, categorically states that 'the shift that we [Afghanistan] saw in India from a faction-based approach to a state-to-state relationship was very crucial'.[101] India was the first country to shed the 1990s civil war inhibitions and focus on the central Afghan government as the main interlocutor. He argues that the other good thing about India's conciliatory approach was that it 'understood our [Afghan] imperatives for engaging with Pakistan. In trying to work with them [Pakistan], and they [Indians] were very careful about that concern of working with Pakistan'.[102] Topping up this political shift with tangible 'gifts' such as big and small aid projects, scholarship program, and electricity, only won more accolades for the conciliators from the Afghan government. Ludin's successor, Ershad Ahmadi, and Afghanistan's former ambassador to Pakistan, Janan Musazai, also appreciated India's conciliatory approach.

For Ahmadi, India did try to have a holistic approach in its dealing with Afghanistan's different political groupings. 'I think there was the fact that India tried to embrace the new Afghanistan, the new leadership, and engage on all aspects of Afghan reconstruction on the national level. And itself tried to correct that sort of partisan perception of moral and traditional support', he says.[103] However, whether such conciliatory approach has been effective or not is a question worth exploring more. Musazai found India's conciliatory approach of treating Afghanistan as an independent, sovereign state as 'smart, right, and good'.[104] Partisan engagement, he argued, will be seen as a 'clear interference in our [Afghan] domestic affairs'.[105] Mahmoud Saikal, deputy foreign minister for economic affairs in 2005–06, also testified that an open-minded approach was remarkable.[106] Karzai often praised India's Afghanistan policy throughout his presidency. With the Afghan government supporting a conciliatory line, New Delhi did not change policy course eventually by deepening engagement with factions outside the government.

'Karzai is no Massoud'

The partisans, throughout Karzai's presidency, wanted to deepen engagement with his opponents to show that India had not given up on them. Pessimistic about Pakistan's role in Afghanistan and Kabul's capacity to effectively counter the Afghan Taliban, partisans viewed Karzai's opponents as India's natural partners. By not supporting them, according to this advocacy, India was burning a bridge, as was evident from Wali Massoud's criticism of India's pro-Karzai tilt. If the conciliators treated Afghanistan as a weak but sovereign state, the partisans advocated independent and stronger relations with extra-governmental actors (in this case, ironically, most of Karzai's opponents were part of the government). If the conciliators drew conceptual strength from the principle of sovereignty and the need for stability, the partisans delved into breathtaking anti-Pakistan realpolitik. The Pakistan army's determination for strategic depth in Afghanistan, partisans argued, would never allow Afghanistan to develop as a strong and stable country. For instance, Narayanan told the US ambassador to India in a private conversation that 'Pakistan is outsourcing its problems to Afghanistan ... and that democracy could prevail against terrorism rather than for the reasons Pakistan thinks.'[107] Unlike the conciliators who viewed Afghanistan on its own merits, the partisans nurtured an unhealthy obsession with Pakistan. Afghanistan for them was not neutral territory.

Averse to Afghan groups with links to Islamabad, the partisans' logic of engagement, even with the post-2001 Afghan political dispensation, was rooted in containing Pakistan's influence. Clear about their aversion to the Afghan Taliban, the partisans were less clear on the extent to which India should support Karzai. Concerned that Islamabad would play favourites. Partisans wanted to cobble strong links with the former UF leadership and their contemporaries including the Massoud brothers, Abdullah, Mohaqiq, former Afghan intelligence chief Amrullah Saleh, Qanooni, and Dostum. If anything, they argued, just like during the 1990s, India should try to ameliorate differences between various former United Front leaders who had drifted apart after Massoud's assassination. Though open to the idea of engaging with Pashtun leaders, they did not want to make such engagement the cornerstone of India's Afghanistan policy. This had to do with both a generic lack of trust in Pashtun leaders among some Indian officials (as highlighted in chapter 4), and Pakistan's influence in south and east Afghanistan. Implementing such partisanship in practice, however, was impossible due to international pressure. The only time when partisan advocacy gained potency was during crises like attacks on Indian citizens and assets in Afghanistan, and briefly after the 2010 London conference where reconciliation with the Taliban was internationally institutionalised.

Katju, X, and R, another senior R&AW officer, were among some officials who advocated anti-Karzai partisanship. Influential in India's strategic and foreign policy circles, despite having retired, Katju did not mince words when expressing his reservations about Karzai's capability to handle the Afghan Taliban's resurgence:

> In the 1990s, the Taliban and Pakistan could not fully achieve their objectives largely because of Ahmed Shah Massoud. Mr. Karzai is no Massoud but he can meet the current challenge even now if he abandons the narrow politics he has pursued since 2001. More than ever, he needs the skills of the Panjsheri leaders, Abdullah and Qanooni, the analytical capacities of the former Intelligence Chief, Amrullah Saleh, the courage of the Hazara leader, Mohaqiq, and the tenacity of the Uzbek leader, Dostum. Along with them he needs to travel, with all its risks, especially to Pashtun areas to warn against the long-term dangers the Taliban represent to Afghanistan's future. Perhaps this is too much to ask of Mr. Karzai.[108]

R categorically added that immediately after the Bonn conference, and before Karzai's political sustainability was assured in the 2004 elections, 'we [India] had a very close relationship with the Northern Alliance, and we naturally wanted to build on that'.[109] He even denies that there was any disagreement in the bureaucratic and security echelons regarding an UF-centric approach after the Bonn conference. This was because India 'should have an interest in supporting such groups who are only taking on the Taliban and the Pakistani ISI'.[110] X, who was part of the government until relatively recently was 'disappointed' by the Manmohan Singh government for not cultivating strong links with 'our friends from the North and focusing simply on the Kabul government, or, more so, with the Pashtuns.'[111] He blames that as the key reason for India's lack of influence in Afghanistan today. 'We are unable to keep the north together politically, leave militarily. There is infighting among former United Front guys. That's bad. Also, we don't have the capital or ability to help the Pashtuns in south as much. Kandahar is important, but Pakistan has more reach there. Despite what Shivshankar Menon says, we have lost both north and south', argues X.[112] Finally, as previously highlighted, according to a senior Indian miliatary intelligence officer, 'we're [Indians] fascinated by the Pashtuns but they have not done anything for us. When they have a choice to make between Pakistan and India then they may not side with us'.[113]

NSA M. K. Narayanan was arguably the most influential, and nuanced, partisan. He adjusted to the realities of post-2001 Afghanistan unlike Katju, R, and to a limited extent X. Instead of limiting support to Karzai, Narayanan invested heavily in the former and the fervently anti-Pakistan intelligence chief from Panjsher, Amrullah Saleh, with whom Narayanan shared an excellent rapport (and whom he rated to be among the top three or four intelligence chiefs in the world).[114] In 2008, after the bombing of the Indian embassy complex in Kabul, for instance, Narayanan reached out to Saleh to assess possibilities of jointly targeting militant infrastructure in Pakistan.[115] 'Talk-talk is better than fight-fight, but it hasn't worked. I think we need to pay [Pakistan] back in the same coin', he advocated (this line had support among many conciliators such as Menon, but who decided not to make public proclamations about their intent).[116] The statement was not bereft of context. Saleh, under Karzai's watch, had developed links with a host of anti-Pakistan elements operating across the Durand Line, including Baloch separatists. As a later section in this book details, Karzai knew of, and didn't obstruct, the presence of Baloch separatist leaders (such as Brahamdagh Bugti, who had a vast network of militant supporters in Balochistan) on Afghan soil. Pakistan had been protesting against Kabul's support to such elements ever since an insurrection broke out in Balochistan in 2004. This aspect of Karzai's covert approach towards Pakistan was potent enough to address any concerns that partisans might have harboured about Karzai gravitating towards Islamabad. These covert assets, in the wake of the Kabul embassy bombing, could have been utilised (if they were not already being put to use) to target Pakistan. While it is unclear, or at least not provable, that India (and Afghanistan) succeeded in achieving such objectives, the reasons for India to continue supporting Karzai persisted, and even multiplied. Karzai's attraction among partisans such as Narayanan was reflected in Musharraf's mirroring but misplaced belief (demonstrating anti-India partisanship in Pakistani policy circles) that Karzai, despite being a Pashtun, favoured the Panjsheris (mostly Tajik) and was thus alienating the Pashtuns in south and east Afghanistan.[117]

As talks about reconciling with the Taliban began in 2008, and were concretised in 2010, Karzai's relations with the West reached an all time low.

Worried that the US and the UK were plotting against him (a claim corroborated by Narayanan), Karzai had begun reaching out to various insurgents such as Hekmatyar as well as some Afghan Taliban leaders such as Mullah Zaeef, Mullah Muttawakil, Arsullah Rahmani (even though the Taliban, especially Zaeef, had little confidence in Karzai's true intentions).[118] Uneasy with Kabul's links with such elements, Narayanan claimed (in conversations with US officials in 2008) that a Pashtun-only solution may not be possible in Afghanistan, and advocated political space for non-Pashtun leaders (despite his desire to rekindle the Kabuliwallah connection and focus on Karzai).[119] However, by 2010 (after the second year of the Obama administration), with the reconciliation process having begun in earnest, such concerns became acute. Karzai was now genuinely worried that the US may replace him with someone else. Aware that Karzai's success was critical for the future of Afghanistan and India's continuing presence therein, both Narayanan and Menon were willing to part ways with the US. According to Narayanan, this was not the moment for India 'to pull the rug from under his [Karzai's] feet'.[120] Worried that Karzai may cut rash political deals with the Taliban or Pakistan to ensure his survival, Narayanan repeatedly assured him that India was with him and 'if he [Karzai] needs anything he should come to us [India]'.[121] As Bhadrakumar, a retired conciliator active in New Delhi's policy commentariat, noted, at a time when Karzai was being 'vilified and demonised, ridiculed and snubbed alternatively by Washington', New Delhi demonstratively held his hand in solidarity.[122] The strength of India's support to Afghanistan in light of such political balancing within Kabul was tested when Karzai demanded from New Delhi a wish list of military hardware.

Military wish list

In May 2013, with the spectre of NATO withdrawal looming large and skirmishes between the Afghan and Pakistani forces along the Durand Line at an all-time high, Karzai visited India and handed New Delhi a 'wish list' of military hardware. Not the first of its kind, the list included combat helicopters, 105-mm artillery, An.32 medium-lift aircraft, bridge-laying equipment, and trucks.[123] This hardware would not have propelled a qualitative shift in Afghanistan's military disparity vis-à-vis Pakistan, but it was a powerful signal to Islamabad as to where Karzai stood. India, however, remained hesitant, buttressing the perception of its half-hearted support for Afghanistan.[124] In fact, in 2003, Afghanistan had an open offer from New Delhi to seek lethal light weaponry for the ANSF. Kabul, however, was not keen to seek military assistance from India at that point in time and wanted to coordinate 'anything' in that sector with the US. That India was vacillating on its offer a decade later fed into Kabul's doubts about New Delhi's reliability as a regional security provider.[125] Afghan foreign minister Zalmai Rassoul stated in 2013 that 'a decade ago the BJP government wanted to help us [Afghanistan] militarily but we refused, due to Pakistani sensitivities. This time, we are keen, but India is hesitant.' Responding to Rassoul's statement the MEA gave an elusive response that, 'there was a discussion on political and security issues [with Rassoul], without going into specifics. But India is ready to stand by Afghanistan as a close, friendly and historic neighbour through these transitions and will play a due and responsible role in this regard.'[126] India's reluctance to arm Kabul, according to some, was a 'strategic volte-face' by New Delhi.[127]

India had vacillated tremendously before gifting four Mi-25 attack helicopters to Kabul in December 2015, which was also treated as a 'one-off' arrangement in light of Afghanistan's evolving political and security situation.[128] Popular analyses emphasise Pakistan's sensitivities as the causal factor for India's reluctance in supplying such weaponry.[129] While it is true that Pakistan's perceptions about such an arms transfer was not lost on Indian policymakers, this geopolitical angle was not critical in restricting India from supplying weapons to Kabul.[130] India dithered mostly due to the other two drivers of its Afghanistan policy, i.e. domestic Afghan politics and international posture towards Kabul coupled with India's own capacity constraints. Before detailing the exact operational and systemic causes that delayed India's supply of lethal weaponry to Afghanistan, the following paragraphs outline the contours of debate between partisans and conciliators on this issue. Despite holding different policy core beliefs on how to engage with Afghanistan, the partisans and conciliators agreed on the legitimacy of India's arms transfer to Kabul. But Afghanistan's domestic political situation, worsening of relations with Pakistan, and the drastic reduction among NATO member's political will to continue fighting India's complicated options.

The motivations for partisans and conciliators to supply weapons to Kabul were radically different. The partisan's logic was rooted in their belief that Pakistan-sponsored groups should be actively contained in Afghanistan. Such advocacy had three angles to it. Firstly, India should call Pakistan's bluff and not be scared that supplying weapons to Kabul would destabilise the region. Secondly, providing weapons to the Afghan forces would allow India to buttress Kabul's capacity to keep the Taliban at bay. Thirdly, India needed to step up to the occasion as a regional power and secure its interests in Afghanistan. Though few policymakers categorically stated that India should equip Afghanistan as a counter-weight to Pakistan, the hope of pulling Pakistan into a military quagmire in Afghanistan remained potent.[131] The lack of ordnance factories in Afghanistan only made it imperative for India, the partisans argued, to increase Kabul's military capacities.[132] Though such support would not allow Afghanistan to effectively trade artillery fire with the Pakistan army at the border, it would allow the former to patrol the border better. Moreover, with NATO troops withdrawing from active combat roles, the nature of engagement was changing from the Taliban fighting an 'occupying force' to the Afghan army fighting 'anti-state insurgents'.

India actively reached out to Moscow in April 2014 to discuss the supply of heavy weaponry to Afghanistan for which New Delhi could pay for.[133] India's traditional ally who gave the partisans muscular agency in the 1990s, Russia favoured the deal for security and economic reasons. From a security perspective a strong Afghan army would help keeping the Taliban away from the Central Asian Republics whereas money generated from arms sales would bolster, in whatever little way, Moscow's defence production. Indo-Russian cooperation, however, was contingent on continued Western military presence that entailed Karzai signing the BSA with the US. Both New Delhi and Moscow were convinced about the futility of arming the ANSF without a comprehensive security infrastructure that only the US and the NATO could provide. A *Times of India* editorial on this issue reflected the dominance of partisan narratives:

> Short of putting military boots on the ground, New Delhi shouldn't be niggardly in helping in this regard. Karzai's wish list includes, reportedly, hand-me-down howitzers, helicopters and bridge-laying equipment. While it features nothing that would break New Delhi's bank, fulfilling the wish list carries the risk of offending Pakistan. On that score, however, New Delhi can go all out to assuage Islamabad's anxieties. Once we are willing to move beyond policies designed to cut off one's own nose in order to spite one's neighbour, it ought to be abundantly clear that Afghan security is as much, or even more, in Pakistan's interest as it is in India's.[134]

The conciliators argued that there is no reason why India should not supply weapons to Afghanistan. After all they were both sovereign nations and strategic partners. Nonetheless, unlike the partisans, the conciliators were reluctant to proactively seek a defence partnership with Kabul. This reservation had two aspects. Firstly, the supply of weapons to Kabul would indeed antagonise Pakistan, and India should not be seen as supporting territorial revisionism. Secondly, an arms transfer could have a destabilising effect if the weapons fall into the wrong hands, those being, the anti-government elements. This was compounded by the fact that India and its regional allies including Russia and Iran could not offer the security umbrella in Afghanistan that NATO did. Lack of confidence in the ANSF to hold ground under military pressure and little clarity about the post-2014 Afghan political landscape gave credence to this argument. According to a high-ranking MEA official, 'Kabul's wish list keeps on growing every time and before committing to anything we have to keep the larger regional interest and peace in mind.'[135] Differences existed between Manmohan Singh, a conciliator, and Narayanan, a partisan, on issues related to Pakistan and, by corollary, Afghanistan.[136] But as the PM, Singh reigned supreme. India's political leadership as well as the MEA, despite accepting the need to develop Afghanistan's capacities to counter Pakistan-sponsored anti-state actors, was comfortable with soft power decisions. This was because, as the conciliators argued, a soft power approach may not help achieving certain goals in Afghanistan, but it would surely not jeopardise India's long-term interests in the region.

The conciliators were derided as 'peace-*wallahs*' (peacenicks). Such terms reverberated with the old British debates where the closed border school was disparaged as 'masterly inactivity' and the forward school was ridiculed as 'mischievous activity'. In 2013, allegedly, these 'peace-*wallahs*' pushed the PMO to not supply weapons to Afghanistan. They argued that if stabilising relations with Pakistan was India's strategic aim then engagement with Afghanistan should be reduced, especially as the latter is not even in New Delhi's immediate strategic circuit. An editorial in the *Indian Express* advocated a conciliatory position (as opposed to the *ToI's* partisan stand) as such:

> While Delhi has offered to enhance its contribution to Afghan reconstruction, it must move forward more carefully on arms supply. India needs to balance its stakes in Afghanistan against the potential reaction from Pakistan and the NATO. The Pakistan army is indispensable for peace in Afghanistan—it is also the problem. Moreover, Karzai's visit to India coincided with increased skirmishes along the Durand Line.[137]

The powerful former Editor-in-Chief of the *Indian Express*, Shekhar Gupta, who had actively reported from Afghanistan in the early 1990s, was even more blunt in saying, 'get out, leave Af to Pak'.[138] Scathing in his critique of the partisans, Gupta stated that 'engaging in a policy that puts us [India] permanently and, inevitably, violently at odds with the Pakistanis is an idea that is being accepted much too readily. As if this is our destiny, part of an ongoing blood feud. As if we have no choice. All of this, frankly, is lazy, self-serving rubbish, dished out by a strategic establishment that suffers terminally from a cold war mindset, and does not quite know, like all bigger powers [the US included], when to declare victory, and when to cut its losses'.[139] There were legal aspects to undertaking arms transfers as well. Indian law did not allow the export of lethal weapons to other countries—one reason why India 'gifted' the four Mi-25 helicopters in 2015.

Compounding this debate on whether, to what extent, of what kind, and when New Delhi should provide lethal weapons to Kabul were India's defence and financial capacity constraints. In 2012, India did not have the finances to either supply weapons or pay for the same to Russia. The government, in fact, was facing a massive resource crunch with extremely high levels of budgetary cuts. 'We did not know where the money would come from for such [armed] support to Afghanistan. We fought tough battles with the ministry of finance, at times with the NSA's support, but it still did not work out', says a senior diplomat.[140] Despite reservations about the political fallout of arming Afghanistan, officials engaged in decision-making, including Menon, contend that there was no deliberate attempt to scuttle the delivery of weapons.[141] In fact, the other option India discussed was to refurbish old Soviet weaponry. But these discussions took longer than expected for bureaucratic reasons. Not all weapons could be refurbished from India, and opening maintenance factories in Afghanistan was too much of a political issue.[142]

Lack of clarity among Afghan officials about the kind of weapons they required and the kind of army they were planning to build compounded this delay. There were several lists that kept changing depending who was asking for the weapons. Bismillah Khan Mohammadi, Afghanistan's defence minister, reached out to Menon seeking one set of weapons whereas other officials had put forth a separate list, confusing the Indian leadership. The ANSF had been trained in using American weaponry whereas the Indian armed forces were still more comfortable with Russian or indigenously produced weapons systems, raising questions about the compatibility of Indian arms in the Afghan army. During one of Karzai's many visits to New Delhi, Menon informed the president that the two countries needed a detailed conversation about what kind of force Kabul wanted to build.[143] Once that was clear, India could tell them what it can do and what it cannot do. Without such conceptual clarity on the Afghan side, Menon argued, India could do little. Communicating specifics about the nature of the Afghan security forces and their requirements took a long time.

The question, however, remains—why did India not tell Afghanistan what kind of force they 'should' build, instead of waiting to hear from them? Conciliators to the core, Singh and Menon were cautious of not coming across as being intrusive with Kabul. For X, such caution was unwarranted.[144] If anything, X argued, India should have openly communicated to Karzai as to what kind of army Afghanistan needed and provided them the relevant technology to build it. Finally, Obama's 2015 declaration that US troops will remain in Afghanistan (and may even fight on occasion, which they do until today) made it easier for India to supply lethal weapons to Kabul without much concerns about technology disparity or capacity constrains. The ANSF critically required helicopters for close air support (CAS) to effectively counter the Afghan Taliban offensives. By January 2016, under the presidency of Ashraf Ghani, the ANSF inducted the four Mi-25 helicopters supplied by India. Soon after, in 2016, Russia also gave 10,000 AK-47s to Kabul.[145]

Conclusion

His adversaries envied (and detested) his manipulations whereas his allies considered him schizophrenic. But no one doubted that Karzai was the most effective politician in post-2001 Afghanistan. In 2016, when Ghani made failed attempts to reconcile differences with Pakistan, people in Afghanistan began to look at Karzai for leadership as their *rahbar* (leader). Almost every Indian diplomat posted in Afghanistan appreciated Karzai's political acumen even if they saw the political dangers of his manipulative behavior. In his own way, Karzai had reconciled the partisans and the conciliators to a considerable extent. He was an internationally recognised figure whom India could engage with, and not earn the label of being overtly anti-Pakistan. It suited the US that India actively asked Karzai's opponents to accept his authority for the sake of Afghan unity and stability. Given the general international consensus on the need for a Pashtun candidate as president, the political value of non-Pashtun candidates including Abdullah and Qanooni was relatively diminished in New Delhi after the Bonn conference. Karzai's victory in the 2004 national elections played a decisive role in tilting India towards Karzai as opposed to his opponents. Soon after the elections, India replaced Katju with Rakesh Sood as ambassador to Kabul with a mandate to deepen engagement with Karzai and invest more in Pashtun leaders (such as Gul Agha Sherzai, the governor of Nangarhar) and communities. India's outreach to political personalities in Pashtun-dominated areas had begun in earnest.

Unlike previous Afghan presidents such as Karmal and Najibullah, who were widely considered Soviet stooges, Karzai demonstrated a fiercely independent streak with his Western benefactors. This was especially visible on issues such as reconciling with the Taliban and talking to Pakistan. Such independence made him even more attractive in New Delhi. For, if his outreach to Pakistan in the initial years of his presidency appealed to the conciliators, his anti-Pakistan activism instilled faith among the partisans in later years. Traditional partisans like Katju and R continued to nurture suspicions about Karzai, but conciliators such as Singh, Menon, Prasad, Rakesh Sood, Mukhopadhaya, and even home minister P. Chidambaram viewed his novelty and political dexterity as a blessing to reconnect with Afghanistan's Pashtun communities. Even those partisans without the political baggage of the 1990s Afghan civil war, such as Narayanan, viewed Karzai as an ally and an asset. Such convergence of ideas within India's power circles about supporting Karzai, made Indian policymakers accept the cost of such support (i.e. irritating, if not alienating, former UF leaders). Not only was Karzai sensitive to Indian interests in Afghanistan, he also wanted to develop strategic parity with Pakistan on his own will, and thus addressed India's political desire of striking a strategic balance between Afghanistan and Pakistan.

Indian calculations about Karzai was correct on each count. He welcomed India in a big way despite the West and Pakistan's reservations. Well aware of the multiple levers at work in the India-Pakistan relationship, Karzai had learnt to willfully and skillfully exploit them. His offer to Jaswant Singh, in early 2002, to mediate between India and Pakistan (scoffed at by Abdullah as being naïve), thus, was as much a gesture of goodwill as much it was a failed Machiavellian ploy to shape India-Pakistan rivalry to Afghanistan's advantage. His adept diplomacy in South Asia reached its peak when Afghanistan signed its first ever Strategic Partnership Agreement with India in October 2011, paving the way for New Delhi to support Kabul in the security sector among other areas. The catch about this agreement lay in the fact that Karzai had rejected Pakistan's offer of signing a similar document months before going ahead with India. Though Kabul's aversion to, and mistrust of, Pakistan was apparent, many senior Afghan officials including former interior minister and current NSA Hanif Atmar viewed this as a mistake on Karzai's part.[146] Though Pakistan's response to the India-Afghanistan SPA was muted, the move had fed into the impression that Karzai, the maximum leader, was too close to India.

8

NO GOOD TALIBAN?

INDIA'S TALIBAN LEARNING CURVE

'We favour neither India nor Pakistan ... We are not saying that India should get out of Afghanistan. Nor can India be completely expelled from Afghanistan. The Taliban aren't in any direct conflict with India. Indian troops aren't part of NATO forces, they haven't occupied Afghanistan ... It's possible for the Taliban and India to reconcile with each other. Our complaint is that India backed the NA [Northern Alliance], and is now supporting the Karzai government.'

Zabiullah Mujahid, Spokesperson of the Taliban, April 2010[1]

'New Delhi has come around to accepting dialogue with those Taliban elements who are prepared to renounce violence ... But New Delhi is wary of those who, under Pakistani tutelage, might pretend to be reborn constitutionalists, but seize the first opportunity after the American withdrawal to devour the regime that compromises with them.'

Shashi Tharoor, MoS External Affairs (2009–10), Congress Lok Sabha MP, and Chairman of Parliamentary Standing Committee on External Affairs.[2]

No good Taliban?

India's understanding of and approach towards the Afghan Taliban evolved considerably over the course of the war after 2002. Though New Delhi remained wary of legitimising the Afghan Taliban, it grew conscious of the hazards of viewing it as a monolithic entity subservient to Pakistan's interests and political directions. The powerful combination of political conservatism, epistemic limitations (related to knowledge about the Taliban), and the polarisation of regional political equations in the 1990s had hindered India from reaching out to the Taliban regime. By 2015, however, out of necessity if not want, Indian policymakers had begun making critical conceptual distinctions about the place of the Taliban in Afghanistan's sociopolitical landscape. The Taliban constituted a diverse and loosely held-together band of militants fighting Western forces and the Afghan government, and were not a monolithic entity. This view gained appreciation among Indian policymakers. Imbuing a complex set of grievances and ambitions, these insurgents had varying degrees of piety, and most of them were rooted in rural Pashtun cultures. To be clear, no Indian policymaker ever wants the Taliban to return. But the impossibility of militarily defeating such a heterogeneous group made it necessary for India to reconsider its policy. Thus, instead of being blindly opposed to the Taliban, New Delhi began viewing those political outfits and figures that were 'dependent' on Pakistan for political and financial sustenance as the problem entities.

The reason for this was the logic that dependence on Pakistan promised reduction in the sovereign agency of such groups in a way that may harm Indian interests. An important distinction here is India's acceptance of the fact that any Afghan government would be dependent on external financial and military support. The source of such support, however, should not be from Pakistan. For in that scenario, the Afghan government would be expected to do Pakistan's bidding in Afghanistan either willingly or by force. An important, if not the only or even the most critical aspect of Pakistan's Afghanistan policy was to reduce the Indian presence in that country (especially the four Indian consulates that Islamabad alleged were being used to forment violence and separatism within Pakistan). The IC-814 hijacking incident was a perfect example of an Afghan regime getting caught between India-Pakistan tensions against its wishes. Despite wanting to help India secure the lives of the hostages, the Taliban was unable to openly criticise Pakistan for using Afghan territory to execute the negotiations phase of the hijacking. The incident also underlined the costs that India had to bear by not engaging with the Taliban. The only difference in 2015 was the increasing degree of pragmatism wherein India began to distinguish between the nature of relationship that Afghan groups enjoyed with Pakistan than the character and composition of the group itself. From this logic, non-engagement with even those Afghan political outfits that were indeed dependent on Pakistan was unviable. Isolating such groups would only increase their dependence on Pakistan (like the Taliban regime in the 1990s), and push them into a direct standoff with both the Afghan government as well as India. The realisation that most Afghans harbored goodwill for India, and even the Pakistan-dependent factions did not nurture ill will, helped in coming to terms with the possibility to cautiously reconcile with the Afghan Taliban.

Engaging with select Afghan Taliban factions, the conciliators argued, would reduce the risk of misunderstanding, help India secure its assets and interests in the region, and ensure that the Taliban does not become hostile to India. Additionally, India's conciliatory approach would help the Kabul government in its reconciliation (however unsuccessful) with the Afghan Taliban, and to exploit the political ruptures that were visible within the insurgent groups. True, given the tormented history of India's relations with the Taliban, any engagement whatsoever would be of a limited nature. But the costs of non-engagement were higher than those of engagement. While groups like the Haqqani network elicited unambiguous hostility from the partisans and the conciliators alike (for attacking the Indian embassy and consulates), the Quetta shura (and its subfactions) were acceptable to engage with. Plus, all those Afghan Taliban figures that were ready to reconcile with the Kabul government could be engaged with. Such a nuanced and conciliatory approach, however, did not go unchallenged. The partisans continued advocating active containment of any and all militant factions along the Afghanistan-Pakistan border using force (in different forms) if necessary. For them, there was little difference between the various Taliban factions (both Afghan and Pakistani) and the only credible partners that India could have in Afghanistan were either the former United Front leaders or the Kabul government.

India's conciliatory outlook was in stark contrast with New Delhi's derision of Western categorisations such as 'good' and 'bad' Taliban (with the argument that all Taliban were unsavoury). At an operational level, indeed, Indian spies and diplomats in Afghanistan had begun engaging with the militant and political *shuras* of different Taliban factions.[3] According to T, an intelligence analyst who worked for the Joint Intelligence Committee (JIC) and analysed strategic intelligence on J&K, Pakistan, and Afghanistan from all Indian spy agencies as well as the MEA: 'The MEA took a much more lenient approach when it came to Afghanistan. At the international level they said there should no distinction between the Al Qaeda and the Taliban, or between good and bad Taliban. But at the same time when it came to internal discussions they used to have a milder approach and said "listen, if the current government in

Kabul is not being [able to deliver] then we should look for other options. We are not saying directly talk to the Afghan Taliban, but at least try to engage some other elements".[4] Though such conciliatory advocacy was viewed with scepticism by security hardliners, many officials were keen on assessing the new generation of Afghan Taliban on its military strength, political resolve, social composition, financial linkages, and attitudes towards India. Though regressive in their social customs, deeply entrenched in illicit drug networks and extortion rackets, and violently exclusive in their approach to governing a multilingual, multiethnic, and multi-religious country like Afghanistan, it became apparent to the Indian leadership that the Afghan Taliban was not fundamentally at odds with India or insensitive to Indian interests. If anything, various Afghan Taliban leaders were determined not to be, or be seen as, subservient to Pakistan. Thus, given India's vision of a united, democratic, and inclusive Afghanistan, the Taliban could never be New Delhi's favoured partners, but boycotting them came to be viewed as strategically unsound. Engagement, however distasteful, promised the possibility of positive change among Taliban ranks or their marginalisation in a democratic polity. As the following sections show, New Delhi began seeking 'good-behavior' from different Afghan insurgents soon after reopening its embassy in November 2001, and embarked on a slow, bloody, learning curve about how to deal with and how not to deal with the Afghan Taliban. After years of such engagement and policy learning, India officially accepted an Afghan-led reconciliation with the Taliban in October 2011.

Kidnap and kill

'This is not India or America. Indians should go out [of Afghanistan]', said the message in crisp English.[5] Pinned to the almost decapitated body of Maniappan Raman Kutty, the Taliban had delivered India with a 48-hour ultimatum to halt work on the Zaranj-Delaram highway and withdraw all Border Roads Organisation (BRO) personnel. A truck driver from Kerala working with the BRO (that was building the highway in Nimroz), Kutty was kidnapped on 19 November 2005, along with three others, and, as promised by the abductors, killed on 21 November. India had refused to budge under pressure.[6] Still, the promptness with which the Taliban killed Kutty was puzzling. It was unusual that the Taliban would demand the shutting of an Indian infrastructural project without allowing scope for negotiations. Even though the ultimatum was extended by 24-hours, the unreasonable demand did not change.

Within an hour of the kidnapping, India's ambassador to Kabul, Rakesh Sood, established a channel with Karzai and the Afghan national security advisor Zalmai Rassoul, and called upon his American, Iranian, and Italian counterparts seeking support. Sood also reached out to Sigbatullah Mojaddedi, former president and head of the reconciliation commission who had contacts with moderate Taliban figures, P. S. Gailani, head of the Qadari sect and a prominent religious leader, and Arif Moorjai, a tribal chief and former minister of tribal affairs, in the hope that they would be able to make contact with the kidnappers. Nothing came out of it. In a last-ditch effort India opened an informal channel with Pakistan asking for help (not a surprising development given the ongoing composite dialogue between the two countries since January 2004). Nothing emerged from that either. Pakistan flatly denied that it had any links with the Taliban since its ouster in 2001. From that moment on, instead of preparing a negotiations team or finding the kidnappers, India directed all its efforts towards securing Kutty's release (and failed).[7] Four days after Kutty's death, the MEA's joint secretary on the Pakistan-Afghanistan-Iran desk, Dilip Sinha, informed Robert O. Blake, the US political counselor in New Delhi, that blaming Pakistan for Kutty's murder was 'entirely media speculation', and India will not stop its developmental work in the country.[8] American diplomats were worried that India might pull the plug on its aid to Afghanistan at a time when the US itself had shifted most of its resources to Iraq and was requesting both NATO and non-NATO allies for support in Afghanistan.

Kutty's murder stood in contrast with what India had experienced in December 2003, when Mullah Sabir Momim of the Taliban kidnapped two Indian workers.[9] P. Murali, a lab technician, and G. Varda Rao, a plant operator, worked with a US company on the Kandahar-Kabul road project in Zabul. Accusing them of being Indian spies, Momin threatened assassination unless Kabul released fifty imprisoned militants.[10] Katju, then India's ambassador to Kabul, was able to secure their release with help from Afghan tribal elders who negotiated with the Taliban. The motive for the 2003 kidnappings was rooted in local politics and financial interests of the Taliban instead of targeting Indians per se. Neither of the two hostages was mistreated.[11] Kutty's case, however, became a fiery political issue because an Indian government employee was killed on duty. Adding fuel to fire, and in contrast to what Sinha told Blake, Narayanan candidly linked the incident to Pakistan (only to retract the statement later) as the opposition criticised the government for mishandling the situation.[12]

Questions about the efficacy of India's Afghanistan policy, the effectiveness of its intelligence and ITBP personnel deployed to protect Indian workers, the utility of not engaging with the Taliban, and countering of Pakistan's obstructionist role in Afghanistan, were raised in the parliament.[13] If this was not enough, an Indian telecommunications engineer, K. Suryanarayana, who worked for a Bahraini company in Zabul, was abducted in April 2006 and killed within two days.[14] In clockwork fashion, as Indian and Afghan agencies went about locating the kidnapper's coordinates, Narayanan reached out to his Pakistani counterpart Tariq Aziz in a back-channel effort to secure Suryanarayana's release and was met with denial.[15] Suryanarayana was beheaded without any talks, leading to a national outcry. Opposition leaders such as Advani criticised the government for not valuing national interests, adopting a 'kid-glove approach to jihadi terrorism', and for not taking the threat to Indians in Afghanistan seriously.[16] A furious and frustrated India directly blamed Pakistan for sponsoring the attack this time around. Even Sinha, who had downplayed Pakistan's role in Kutty's killing, blamed Pakistan in confidential meetings with US diplomats.[17]

Though overshadowed by attacks on the Indian embassy and consulates after 2008, these kidnappings were formative in India's understanding of the neo-Taliban. Deeply concerned about the robustness of India's crisis response mechanisms in Afghanistan, where nearly 2,000 Indians were residing in those years, gaining knowledge about the Taliban became imperative for Indian policymakers.[18] Narayanan remembers Manmohan Singh asking him often about what India was doing to ensure the safety of its citizens and projects in Afghanistan, and whether adequate contingency plans were in place in case of a crisis.[19] Kutty and Suryanarayana's killing had rankled Indian policymakers, who began highlighting changes in the Taliban's modus operandi of swiftly killing the captives. As senior Congress MP Santosh Bagrodia pointed out that, 'on earlier occasions, they [Taliban] held protracted negotiations before releasing the captives', so what could be the inherent motive for change in the *modus operandi* of the Taliban in this case?[20] Various Left parties sought similar clarifications. The CPM, otherwise staunchly anti-Taliban, pressed the government to directly reach out to the abductors. For domestic political reasons, and to gain sympathy among families of Keralite workers abroad, the communists questioned the necessity and logic behind India's prompt statement that the highway construction would continue unabated.[21] Without actually changing its policy, India could have let the 48-hour deadline pass before reaffirming its commitment towards Afghanistan. The salience of this question increased in the wake of an ostensible shift in the Taliban's tactics.

There was no shift in the Taliban's *modus operandi* per se. Different Taliban factions with divergent interests and aims had undertaken the kidnappings. One faction was rooted in Afghanistan and had linkages with local political leaders and tribal elders, while the other operated out of Pakistan and was allegedly sustained by Pakistan's security establishment. Kidnapping-for-ransom and extortion were ways by which the former survived financially, whereas it was simply a tool of coercion used by the latter with little accruing financial benefits. In such a scenario, it was easy to deal with those Taliban elements that operated from within Afghanistan and could be engaged with via tribal elders and other governmental and religious figures. Within six months of the kidnapping of Indian workers, for instance, Mullah Sabir Momin denounced Mullah Omar and formed the Jaish-ul-Muslimeen (JuM) under the leadership of Syed Akbar Agha.[22] The high-profile split within the Taliban was followed by kidnapping of three UN personnel by the JuM, and Agha's subsequent arrest and torture in, and by, Pakistan. A year later, in 2013, Agha told this author about his warmth for India as a friendly neighbouring country, unlike Pakistan, for which he had nurtured a special grouse.[23]

India also found an unexpected ally in Mullah Abdal Salam Rocketi, another senior Taliban commander from south Afghanistan, who had been close to Mullah Omar, but began participating in mainstream Afghan politics after the Taliban's rout. According to R&AW officials, Rocketi was paid by private contractors employing Indian (and other) citizens to gather real-time intelligence and sending armed men to save kidnapped Indian (and other) workers.[24] Tactical collaboration with active or ex-Taliban figures was relatively easy for India. But opening a political channel with those Taliban factions that operated from Pakistan's territory and were dependent on Pakistan's support was operationally difficult. For example, Qari Muhammad Yusuf Ahmedi, the Taliban spokesman who called international press agencies informing about the Taliban's demands in Kutty and Suryanarayana's case, actively shuttled between Pakistan and Afghanistan. Indian parliamentarians, who used the term 'Taliban' as a monolith, were not aware of these operational, but critical, distinctions. Eleven Indians and twenty-nine Afghans were killed during the construction of the Zaranj-Delaram highway (one life lost for every 1.5 km) whereas more Indians were kidnapped and/or killed over the years.[25]

These kidnappings did not force a policy rethink, but surely initiated a policy learning process whereby India started distilling different Afghan Taliban factions based on their operational linkages, organisational interests, political aims and ideologies (if any), and strategic dependencies. Non-engagement on ideological or human rights lines (such as the Afghan Taliban was a misogynistic Islamist outfit inherently hostile to India) ceased to be the operational dictum, even though it dominated popular discourse. Memories of the IC-814 hijacking and Bamiyan Buddha destruction, which were fresh among policymakers and analysts alike, did not stop Indian spies and diplomats from engaging with various Taliban factions. According to Benoy Khare, Assistant Director at the Joint Intelligence Committee (2005–11), tactical links with the likes of Rocketi 'impacted our [India's] understanding of the situation on the ground, and we started exploring ways to engage more with these figures'.[26] Most such on-the-ground links were established by the military intelligence (and some MEA officers), according to Khare, but not the R&AW. Shivshankar Menon categorically says that though the conciliatory thread of understanding and accommodating the Afghan Taliban ran through India's policy circles even before 2001, 'it [engagement with the Afghan Taliban] became much more necessary after 2003–04 ... because it was clear by then that the Taliban had not really been wiped out ... so it was worth finding out what explains their longevity, their survival, and what kind of prospects they had'.[27]

For Sahgal, a retired senior Indian army officer, India's Afghanistan policy did not witness any abrupt, radical, shifts, but New Delhi was determined about testing waters and building relations with all Afghan factions. As early as 2002, he says, Indian diplomats including Katju were 'going around [Afghanistan] spending a huge amount of money and talking to these Taliban people for good behavior'.[28] Despite being a partisan against Pakistan-supported Afghan groups, and very close to the former UF leaders, Katju was directed by his bosses to ascertain the extent to which India could engage with the Afghan Taliban without getting tied down to the movement or risk losing legitimacy over its actions. Such engagement often, allegedly, included giving briefcases full of cash to both mainstream and insurgent Afghan leaders.[29] The aim of such covert financial deals could range from ensuring safety of Indians working in Afghanistan and gaining hard intelligence about Pakistan-supported groups, to reducing the Taliban's financial dependence on Rawalpindi by out-financing Pakistan. This aspect of out-matching and out-funding Pakistan in hiring militant 'mercenaries' operating along the Afghanistan-Pakistan border was publicly articulated by India's current national security advisor Ajit Doval in 2014.[30] Whether Indian intelligence agencies cultivated the Afghan Taliban or other freelance armed militants in the region, however, remains unknown (though actively alleged by the Pakistani media).

These kidnap-and-kill incidents highlighted (at a high human cost) that not all Taliban factions were anti-India, not all Taliban were ideologues, and internal divisions within the Afghan Taliban were real and could be capitalised upon. Though Shyam Saran says that, 'the sense was that it is extremely important that in Afghanistan we [India] should make every effort so that the possibility of the Taliban coming back is obviated', Indian policymakers were acutely aware of their limitations to contain the Taliban's resurgence.[31] If the coalition military juggernaut failed at the task, no other country, or group of countries, would be able to achieve that in the short and medium term, and especially not using military means. In such a scenario, outside the media's glare, Indian officials started debating the merits of engaging with select sections of the Afghan Taliban and Hekmatyar (with whom India had a history of covert engagement). The consulates helped in facilitating such engagement that led to policy learning. Apart from monitoring the distribution of India's developmental aid and scholarships, the consulates became intelligence outposts that were meant to monitor Pakistan's activities in Afghanistan, and to harness political differences between the Afghan Taliban and Pakistan. As Sahgal articulated, 'apart from the soft power, there was a concerted effort made [by India] to penetrate the south and the east [of Afghanistan]. In Kabul, Kandahar, Jalalabad, and [in] all those areas, the consulates were opened up. The main job of the consulates was to keep track of what the Pakistani activities are. And this is the time [when] the Pakistanis started objecting and started making a hue and cry'.[32] Sameer Patil, Assistant Director at the JIC (2008–13), confirms Sahgal's point: 'In Afghanistan our [Indian intelligence] assets were everywhere, and we were able to get a good sense of what is happening'.[33]

Leave or die

Tipped off in advance by the Afghan and US intelligence services, India had been preparing for a big attack on its embassy in Kabul. HESCO barriers were set up outside the embassy compound and a 24x7 security team made of ITBP soldiers and Afghan guards were deployed on high alert.[34] But when Hamza Shakoor rammed a car laden with 100kg explosives into the HESCO barriers at 8.30 AM on 7 July 2008, the vibrations shook Kabul and beyond. Fifty-eight people, mostly Afghan, were killed, and 141 were injured.[35] Among the dead were Indian diplomat V. Venkateswara Rao, defence attaché Brig. Ravi Dutt Mehta, and ITBP personnel H. A. S. Pathania and Roop Singh. Shakoor had been tailing Mehta and Rao's car that morning and was intent on destroying the whole embassy.[36] Mehta, however, was the prized target. Within a mere six months, he had built a strong network of contacts with a variety of Afghan political, military, and intelligence officials. Given that R&AW officers stationed in Kabul were being constantly watched, the military intelligence (MI) and the Defence Intelligence Agency (DIA) had become active in covert operations inside Afghanistan.[37] Military intelligence officers manned all Indian medical missions in Afghanistan and used them as cover to gather critical intelligence. Moreover, paying money to local power brokers to undertake its developmental projects, India (mostly through these officers) created effective information networks across the country. Khare asserts that the best intelligence in Afghanistan came from the MI, including on-the-ground information about what was actually happening. 'I never, in my five years of tenure [at the JIC] and in high level meeting with the deputy NSAs and NSAs, got any intel[ligence] from R&AW [on Afghanistan] till 2011', he says.[38] Mehta in particular was an officer who had set up a lot of networks in Afghanistan that threatened Pakistan. Khare's colleague, Patil, concurs that Indian military personnel in Afghanistan generated high quality intelligence, but asserts that most of it reached the JIC via R&AW.[39] Given that Indian military officers undergo secondment with R&AW, it is possible that both the MI (and/or DIA) and the R&AW were active on the ground. Either way, Indian military personnel were playing an important role in Afghanistan, and this fact did not go unnoticed by Pakistani agencies.

Supplementing India's activism in Afghanistan, the Tehrik-e-Taliban Pakistan (TTP) launched an insurgency against Pakistan in 2007. Though supported by Pakistan's establishment in the first place, the TTP had turned its back on Pakistan after a series of failed ceasefires (the intent of which was seriously doubted by India). The situation in Balochistan had also taken a turn for the worse since 2004. In April 2006, Pakistan banned the Balochistan Liberation Army (BLA) that had been waging an alarmingly successful sabotage campaign against the battle-hardened Pakistan army for the past seventeen months. Occurring in the middle of an ongoing composite dialogue between India and Pakistan (and Karzai's outreach to Islamabad), Pakistan was reluctant in openly saying it, but was convinced of India's perverse role in these incidents via Afghanistan (more on this below). Specifically, the resisting Bugti (and Marri) tribe, whose leader Nawab Akbar Khan Bugti had gone underground (and was later killed in an operation by the Pakistan Army), was receiving Indian armed and political support, alleged Pakistan.[40]

Though no forensic evidence exists on India's links with either the Baloch or the TTP insurgencies, Pakistan seriously suspected an Indian hand in both. Mushahid Hussain Sayed, Musharraf's right-hand man, blamed India for training 600 Baloch dissidents (with the help of former UF leaders and Karzai, against whom there was an assassination attempt in April 2008) to handle explosives, use sophisticated weapons, and engineer bomb blasts in training camps on Afghan territory.[41] The R&AW, the MI, and even Indian diplomats were blamed for using their contacts in the NDS and Afghanistan's Ministry of Tribal Affairs to recruit tribal elders from Jalalabad, Kandahar, and Pakistan's North and South Waziristan tribal agencies to destabilise Pakistan. India maintained a stony silence on Pakistan's allegations. But when pushed, New Delhi demanded evidence of its involvement that never came. Having failed to present evidence, Pakistan began resorting to techniques it was most comfortable with and recruited Shakoor for the job. It was in 'response to the [role of the] military intelligence that Pakistan decided to attack our embassy in 2008', says Khare.[42] The 324 Field Intelligence Unit attached to the Peshawar-based XI Corps of the Pakistan Army was, allegedly, involved in the bombing with the decision to undertake it having been linked to the then DG-ISI Nadeem Taj.[43] A LeT recruit trained by the ISI, and logistically supported by the Haqqani network, Shakoor was targeting Mehta, and succeeded in doing so.

An incensed Narayanan publicly called the ISI the 'villain of the piece' (a claim supported by his Afghan counterpart Zalmay Rassoul).[44] Indian intelligence agencies had been tracking increased LeT movement west of Quetta since 2006. New Delhi saw LeT's rise in FATA and Afghanistan as a move by Pakistan army to influence other militant groups in the region to toe Islamabad's line.[45] Still, with India's policy on conciliatory lines, the embassy bombing did not derail New Delhi's composite dialogue with Islamabad.[46] In order to assuage Pakistan's concerns about Indian involvement in Balochistan via Afghanistan, Menon (then India's high commissioner to Islamabad) offered to sit down with Musharraf and explain exactly what India was doing in Afghanistan, without asking for a reciprocal explanation.[47] India was also happy with Pakistan conducting 'surprise' checks on Indian consulates in Afghanistan and seeking a detailed reading of its activities if that helped.[48] Islamabad rebuffed the offer. According to Indian officials, talking about Afghanistan with New Delhi was taboo for Pakistan; as such a dialogue risked legitimising India's presence in a country where Pakistan wanted (very) limited Indian presence.

Four months later, on 28 November ten militants entered Mumbai and began a mass rampage. The 26/11 attacks were under way, resulting in the killing of 166 people and injuring more than 600.[49] While there is no corroborative evidence to link these events in Mumbai with the attack on India in Afghanistan, policymakers in New Delhi viewed these developments as direct correlation of their worsening relations with Pakistan. Over the next seven years, more attacks were planned and executed against Indians and Indian installations in Afghanistan. On 8 October 2009 the Indian embassy was bombed again, killing 17 people including three ITBP soldiers, and injuring 83.[50] On 26 February 2010, three Taliban militants stormed two Kabul guesthouses, the Park and the Hamid, which the Indian embassy had rented for its staffers and development workers. Of the eighteen killed, nine were Indians, and among them two were officers of the Indian Army Medical Corps.[51] Maj. Jyotin Singh died while preventing a suicide bomber from entering the Park, and Maj. Nitesh Roy died of 40 per cent burns three days after the attack.[52] The vice consul-general of the Kandahar consulate, which Pakistan actively blamed for fomenting the Baloch insurgency, was also among the dead. A missile attack by the Haqqani network on an Indian NGO in Kunar province killed two Indians in October 2010. In May 2011, the NDS alleged that the ISI had hired two shooters—Sher Zamin and Khan Zamin—to assassinate the Indian consul-general in Jalalabad.[53]

These attacks only reinforced India's emerging policy related learning, which was shaped by the kidnappings between 2003 and 2006, which were (1) not all Afghan Taliban factions took orders from Pakistan, and (2) the neo-Taliban was a highly diverse movement in its social composition, material capacities and capabilities, support networks, and political intent. Though they were convinced that Pakistan was behind these attacks, the Afghan Taliban came to be viewed in a more nuanced manner. If anything, said Indian officials, the Afghan Taliban either denied launching anti-India attacks, or did so under tremendous Pakistani pressure.[54] Indeed, India was highly measured in its response to the 2008 and 2009 embassy bombings. In the first case, the MEA quickly responded that 'the attack on Indian Embassy was amongst the worst of the terrorist strikes in Afghanistan. Investigations of the Government of Afghanistan as also our own evidence that the attack was planned and executed by elements based in Pakistan make it a dangerous and unacceptable situation'.[55] Prasad confirms that India knew that it was not all Taliban that was the problem. 'In fact, those were days we [India] were not very worried about being attacked ... The attack came after Pakistan started viewing that

India was getting better ratings as the most loved country in Afghanistan in 2007', he says.[56] Narayanan, who was generally averse to the Taliban regardless of where they came from, also admits that the Afghan Taliban did not directly attack India and most such attacks came from Pakistan.[57]

Though an unconvincing and logically weak explanation, some Indian officials believed that India's popularity among Afghans and excellent links with Karzai were the prime reason for Pakistan's strategic discomfort. Even after the 2009 embassy bombing, rather than blaming and criticising all Afghan Taliban factions, the MEA reported that the attack 'was carried out by elements from outside Afghanistan seeking to damage the excellent relations that exist between India and Afghanistan'.[58] Similarly, in 2010, despite the attack on the Hamid guesthouse in central Kabul that housed many Indian personnel, New Delhi refused to attack the Afghan Taliban (despite the Taliban having claimed responsibility for the attack).[59] Neither was the Afghan Taliban called obscurantist (like in the 1990s), nor were its members branded bigots. From within the Afghan Taliban umbrella, the Haqqani network came to be viewed as the primary threat. When asked whether he agreed with the popular narrative of the Afghan Taliban being a proxy outfit of Pakistan's security agencies, Menon categorically stated that 'Pakistan had unleashed hell. They attacked our [Indian] embassy in July 2008, over and over again. They had to use the Haqqani group to do it. Why could they not get the [Afghan] Taliban to do it? If, as people in India say, that the [Afghan] Taliban is just a Pakistani agent, well, they are not.'[60]

By 2015, such organisational distinctions between different Afghan Taliban outfits among Indian policymakers became even more pronounced. On 3 August 2013 for instance, three suicide attackers targeted the Indian consulate in Jalalabad killing nine Afghan civilians (including eight children) and wounding twenty-four (none of whom were Indians).[61] The Afghan Taliban immediately denied any involvement in the attack while Indian security agencies blamed the LeT. 2014 was the worst of all for India in Afghanistan. Narendra Modi, a Hindu-nationalist from the Rashtriya Swayamsevak Sangh (RSS), the ideological parent organisation of the BJP, became India's PM with a resounding parliamentary majority. Afghanistan itself was undergoing a critical transition and national elections were underway to elect Karzai's successor. In this context, just before Modi's swearing-in ceremony, on 24 May at 3.15 AM, four LeT militants heavily armed with machine guns and rocket-propelled grenades attacked the Indian consulate in Herat. It took ten hours for the ITBP soldiers and the Afghan Special Forces to neutralise the attack. Unlike previous cases where the LeT used Afghans (with the Haqqani network's support) to target Indian installations, LeT operatives from Pakistan executed this attack.[62] It was a clear signal to the Modi government on what to expect in the coming months in its engagement with Pakistan. The CIA had given four specific prior warnings to Indian and Afghan agencies, while the fifth warning came two hours after the attack commenced.[63] Within a month, the US State Department publicly acknowledged that there was 'credible evidence' that the LeT was responsible for the consulate attack.[64]

Nearly 100 LeT militants had infiltrated into Nuristan in 2014 and were trying to setup bases in the Kamdish district.[65] When met with resistance they killed eleven Afghan Taliban militants. All that were killed had refused to disrupt the ongoing national elections.[66] Occurring in the wake of an unstable National Unity Government (NUG) in Kabul under Ghani's presidency (and Abdullah as the Chief Executive), and the changing nature of the US military involvement, an inflow of battle-hardened LeT militants on Afghan soil deeply troubled the Indian and Afghan leadership. In a confidential briefing in June 2014 to the new home minister Rajnath Singh, the chief of India's Intelligence Bureau (IB), Asif Ibrahim, called the NATO withdrawal the 'biggest challenge' to India's security.[67] His concerns related to increased infiltration of militants into Indian-administered Kashmir and LeT attacks on Indian missions in Afghanistan. Indeed, throughout 2015 and 2016, various attempts were made to target Indians in Afghanistan. Four Indians were killed on 13 May 2015 in an attack on the Park guesthouse (that was attacked in 2010 as well) while Indian ambassador Amar Sinha was planning a visit there, whereas a suicide attack on the Jalalabad consulate on 21 December 2015 was prevented by the NDS just before Modi's visit to Kabul. Both incidents allegedly had origins in Pakistan.[68] Another shocker came on 3 January 2016 when four militants allegedly associated to the Jaish-e-Mohammad (JeM), founded by Masood Azhar, whom India released during the IC-814 hijacking, stormed India's consulate in Mazar-e-Sharif.[69] By now, the Afghan Taliban had become less of a worry to Indian policymakers. The LeT, the JeM, and the Haqqani network, all of which operated from Pakistan's soil, and had deep links with Pakistan's security agencies, were the threat.

'A wolf in wolf's clothing'

If the Afghan Taliban was not a direct threat to India, or to Indian interests in Afghanistan, then why was New Delhi reticent about reconciling with them?

India's tough political line on the Afghan Taliban gets pronounced in the light of ongoing international efforts towards reconciliation. Even more fascinating are the Afghan Taliban's continued proclamations of strong India-Afghanistan bilateral relations despite being cold-shouldered by New Delhi. Such a mismatch between the political attitudes of the Afghan Taliban and the Indian leadership towards each other was rooted in Afghanistan's domestic political equations, and stressful policy debates between the conciliators and the partisans within India. Having thrown its political weight behind Karzai, both for reasons of realpolitik and reigniting the Pashtun connection, India had no incentive to treat the Afghan insurgents at par with Kabul. But Karzai's own willingness to engage with them made it difficult even for the staunchest of partisans to boycott the insurgents. Though engagement with the Afghan Taliban was viewed as necessary to prevent misunderstanding, increasing the Taliban's political value was deemed unnecessary. Moreover, silent engagement suited both India and the Afghan Taliban. It assured Indian officials that the Taliban would not develop hostility against India, and mitigated risks for Afghan Taliban leaders who worried that open linkages with India would land them into trouble with Pakistan.

India was not inhibited about the idea of reconciliation with or reintegration of the Afghan Taliban per se. What concerned Indian policymakers was the way in which the coalition forces, especially the UK and the US, were going about it; seemingly at Karzai's expense, and allowing Taliban hardliners to determine the terms of negotiations. New Delhi desired an Afghan-led and Afghan-owned reconciliation without external interference. This meant that Karzai would set the terms of talks and not the Afghan Taliban or, especially, Pakistan. However, a grim security scenario, the Kabul government's structural and systemic shortcomings (corruption and cronyism being some of the many), Pakistan's determination to continue with an interventionist Afghanistan policy, and the coalition forces' military exhaustion coupled with political disinterest in Afghanistan, made Afghan-led reconciliation highly unfeasible. In a scenario where Pakistan-supported groups were influencing the terms of reconciliation, contacts with the Afghan Taliban, India calculated, would also insure against the risk of potential disintegration of the Afghan state. Plus, the Afghan Taliban's support was a prerequisite to develop economic connectivity (oil and gas pipelines) with Central Asia. The cost-benefit analysis of talking to the Taliban was similar to what India faced in late 1980s when Najibullah was secretly engaging with different Mujahideen factions. In early 2006, Karzai himself had started to secretly engage with certain

Taliban figures in an attempt to lure them away (or liberate them) from the 'clutches' of the ISI.

In this context, and given India's own outreach to Pakistan, on 15 May 2006 Fazlur Rahman, a Taliban ideologue, landed in Delhi for a four-day visit. He was to be the guest-of-honour at a reception hosted by the Deobandi political organisation, the Jamiat-i-Ulama-i-Hind (JuH). Though failing to attract many Indian Muslim clerics, the JuH had convinced former Indian foreign minister Natwar Singh and former J&K chief minister Farooq Abdullah to join the reception. Little reported by the English language press, India's Urdu press covered Rahman's message intensely. Blaming the US and its coalition partners for 'butchering Muslims', Rahman threatened eternal war in Afghanistan unless the Taliban were taken into the government.[70] Allegedly, an independent Indian MP, Lalit Suri, who was close to Uttar Pradesh' (UP) Samajwadi Party (SP) chief Mulayam Singh Yadav, had bankrolled Rahman's visit. It was a politically audacious event that angered the US for whom Rahman was 'a wolf in wolf's clothing' entertained by an Indian 'rogue's gallery'. Washington saw the visit as an anti-US and anti-UPA conspiracy hatched by the 'witches' brew' of the JuH, the Samajwadi Party, and other pro-Iran Muslim clerics in India. But then came the shocker. On 19 May 2006 Rahman was invited for a meeting with the PM. While the details of what transpired in the meeting are not known, the fact that such a meeting took place underlines PM Manmohan Singh's conciliatory credentials.

Baptising India's conciliatory approach towards the Taliban, Manmohan Singh had set the ball rolling for India to deepen engagement with all political entities in Afghanistan and Pakistan, irrespective of the militancy of their Islam and closeness with Pakistan's security agencies. By 2008 New Delhi had developed connectivity with a host of Afghan insurgents ranging from Hekmatyar to various Taliban figures linked to the Quetta shura. This shift in stance, in addition to a slow policy learning process and the kidnapping of Indian citizens, was to do with the shock of Karzai's open offer to Mullah Omar and Hekmatyar to enter talks and join the government in October 2007.[71] With the 2009 national elections in sight, Karzai had domestic political reasons to launch such public initiatives. The declaration came as a rude surprise to the US as well as India. Narayanan, a partisan who had invested tremendous political capital in Karzai, was caught in an awkward situation where his own PM was pushing for regional reconciliation and the Afghan president was openly talking to the Taliban.

Narayanan, of course, knew about these covert links between Indian and Afghan intelligence officials and the Taliban. He considered intelligence links with the Taliban necessary and thought that they did not represent government policy. But in light of India's nonexistent intelligence links with the Taliban in the 1990s, this was a marked operational departure. Narayanan never saw such contacts as an exercise in seeking a rapprochement. Though the MEA was debating whether to open channels with the Pashtun-speaking Taliban (and not the Arabic-speaking AQ), for Narayanan such links were an expedient tactic to gather intelligence and use it against Pakistan (the NDS had anyways been providing copious amounts of intelligence to India on anything related to Pakistan).[72] Under no circumstances did these links mean that India was reconsidering its partisan strategy in Afghanistan. If anything, Narayanan was convinced that not only would Pakistan hijack any reconciliation process, but Karzai's motivations were also considered highly dubious. Asking Hekmatyar and Mullah Omar to join the government for personal political survival promised further weakening of the Afghan state and polarising the polity along ethnic lines. Karzai's initiative had raised such an alarm in New Delhi that Narayanan was on a plane to Kabul within hours of Karzai's announcement.[73] In Kabul, the Afghan government fruitlessly tried convincing Narayanan that Karzai 'needed' to engage with the Taliban officially—and directly—if any progress was to be made.[74] In May 2008, Narayanan told David Mulford and a top US intelligence official that Karzai's outreach to Pashtun insurgents caused leaders of other ethnic hues to question their status in Afghanistan.[75] Karzai's 'consultations' with Hekmatyar, thus, were 'unwelcome' and any deal with the Taliban, Narayanan said, 'cannot be a Pashtun-only solution'.[76]

Throughout Narayanan's tenure as NSA, allegedly, India silently funneled unknown amounts of cash to anti-Pakistan Afghan groups.[77] Amrullah Saleh, the Panjsheri NDS chief made a formidable partner in facilitating such interactions. But Karzai's overtures to the Taliban, and the traumatic experiences of the various kidnappings and killings that had occurred over the years led both R&AW and MI operatives to test the waters with the Taliban. Rakesh Sood and his team had built friendly relations with all thirty-four provincial governors, nearly seventeen of whom were close to Hekmatyar.[78] Sood's successor, Jayant Prasad, not only continued cultivating these relations with Hekmatyar's associates, but also allowed Indian intelligence officers to develop informal links with the Afghan Taliban.[79] Karzai's openness to covertly engage with the Taliban made this process both easy and necessary for India (despite reconciliation being an emotive issue at home). Thus, between 2006 and early 2010 (when Narayanan retired and Karzai won the 2009 elections), India bolstered relations with its former UF allies in the Afghan government on one hand, and reached out to the Afghan Taliban (sometime through, and sometime despite, Karzai) on the other. Having polarised the Afghan domestic political landscape along pro-Karzai and anti-Karzai lines, with a healthy doze of ethnic politicking thrown in, Karzai had left no options for India but to engage with all stakeholders to different degrees (though keeping him as the lynchpin of its approach towards Afghanistan).

Both Narayanan and Saleh's national security-related careers came to an end in 2010. While Narayanan peacefully retired after an illustrious career in the government and was made the governor of West Bengal, Saleh was fired (along with the powerful interior minister Atmar) for failing to foil a Taliban rocket attack on the 2010 peace Jirga. Rahmatullah Nabil, Karzai's confidante, took over from Saleh, and Menon, a conciliator, took over the reigns from Narayanan.[80] Occurring in the wake of Karzai's victory in the 2009 national elections and the momentous London conference in January 2010 that pushed for reconciliation with the Afghan Taliban, Nabil and Menon's security leadership led to critical qualitative shifts in how these countries dealt with the Afghan Taliban (which had an upper hand against Kabul), and treated the issue of reconciliation. As the next section shows, the changing nature of domestic Afghan politics and the coalition forces' desire to reconcile with the Afghan Taliban shifted India's Afghanistan policy into a decisive conciliatory mode in 2010. By 2011, India stopped resisting the good-Taliban/bad-Taliban paradigm altogether.[81]

Accommodating the 'Afghan' Taliban

Appreciative of the Afghan Taliban's internal distinctions, and a conciliator who believed that not all Afghan Taliban were Pakistan's proxy warriors, Menon ordered his deputies to engage further with the Afghan Taliban.[82] The only untouchable group was the Haqqani network with whom 'there is no question [of engagement]' as they 'are quite happy to be used by the Pakistanis', said Menon.[83] Home Minister P. Chidambaram, a Congress heavyweight from Tamil Nadu who had earlier challenged Narayanan's near-total control of India's security bureaucracy, Vice President Hamid Ansari, and India's Special Envoy to Afghanistan and Pakistan Satinder K. Lambah, supported Menon in his strategic endeavour in Afghanistan.[84] Though Chidambaram was firm on using force to counter anti-India militants, the conciliatory initiative resonated with Manmohan Singh's regional strategy.[85] It contributed towards the UPA-II's vision of developing economic dependencies between India, Pakistan, and Afghanistan to reduce political turmoil in the region. Senior Indian military intelligence officers soon began to instruct their deputies in Afghanistan to build links with the Afghan Taliban.[86] While the precise nature of India's covert dealings with the Afghan Taliban remains unknown, there was a visible shift in how Indian government and business officials, who travelled extensively to Afghanistan, began viewing the Afghan Taliban. For a FICCI official, who knew the nitty-gritty of India's presence in Afghanistan, 'a true Taliban will be a true Afghan and a true Afghan will not let the country go back by destroying whatever it has built in the last decade ... But they [Afghan Taliban] are afraid of other kind of insurgencies from the neighbours [Pakistan]'.[87] T concurs that senior R&AW officers began offering inputs to the JIC from sources which they claimed were 'higher up in the [Afghan] Taliban hierarchy'.[88] Led by Menon, the conciliators steered India's Afghanistan policy after 2010.

On 29 March 2010, soon after Menon's appointment, the *Indian Express* broke a story that 'India shifts Afghan policy, ready to talk to Taliban'. At Menon's orders, India had opened channel with Hekmatyar, who was termed Pakistan's 'Frankenstein's Monster' by the Indian media in the 1990s, and even entertained feelers from the Quetta Shura, whose spokesperson Zabiullah Mujahid openly talked about reconciling with India:

> This fine-tuning of India's position on Afghanistan comes after exchange of views between top diplomats. After the February [2010] attack on Indians in Kabul, Vice-President Hamid Ansari, Pakistan-Afghanistan envoy Satinder Lambah, and former West Asia envoy Chinmaya Gharekhan wanted India to adopt a neutral position in Afghanistan. This essentially meant keeping out of [internal] Afghanistan politics but carrying on the development works in the war-torn republic[89]

Menon corroborated the report by the *Indian Express*.[90] The MEA had prepared a paper that advocated proactive measures to prevent Afghanistan slipping back into a spiral of violence similar to that in the 1990s. The *Indian Express* assessed that the sub-text of the paper was that 'Afghanistan will come under the total influence of Pakistan if New Delhi was to let matters go out of hand'.[91] The report further mentioned the unhappiness of partisans over Menon, Lambah, Ansari, and Gharekhan's conciliatory advocacy. Lambah, who had been present at the 2001 Bonn conference and was known for his back-channel prowess with Pakistan, had been appointed as PM's special envoy to Afghanistan and Pakistan in 2005 (a move to 'rationalise' India's bureaucracy) in order to bring pragmatism to relations with Pakistan.[92]

Though he could not break bureaucratic logjams, he increased the conciliators' strength within the bureaucracy. Partisans (including X) could not prevent India's policy shift, and all further diplomatic energy was focused on crafting a reconciliation strategy that would ensure Afghanistan's sovereignty and territorial integrity. Former Afghan President Burhanuddin Rabbani, who was appointed as the key negotiator with the Afghan Taliban, visited India in September 2011 at New Delhi's request, and had a long meeting with R. S. Pandey, India's principle interlocutor with the Naga separatist outfit National Socialist Council of Nagaland (NSCN).[93] Having fought various insurgencies in Kashmir, Punjab, and the northeast, New Delhi had a wealth of counterinsurgency (COIN) expertise to share with Kabul. Respecting 'red lines' such as accepting the Afghan constitution and giving-up violence were preconditions to such talks, Pandey advised Rabbani.[94] India's approach towards reconciliation was in stark contrast with how the coalition forces, especially Britain, envisaged it (leading to a standoff between London and New Delhi). In October 2011 India signed the Strategic Partnership Agreement (SPA) with Afghanistan and officially accepted an Afghan-owned, Afghan-led, and Afghan-controlled transition.[95]

The partisans challenged this conciliatory strategy vehemently. X remembers that India's 'game' was going well until the time Narayanan was NSA, but it went downhill after Menon's appointment. 'Bizarre' orders about talking to the Afghan Taliban started coming from Menon and Chidambaram's office, which X and his colleagues listened to but didn't, and couldn't, do much about. 'They were far from realities', X says disdainfully.[96] Menon used to give a patient hearing to the R&AW's assessments and debriefs about what the agency's Afghanistan and Pakistan desk officers were doing, but never gave clear directions like Narayanan or Brajesh Mishra. X remembers having many meetings with Menon, in which 'he [Menon] would listen and then at the end say, "let's try and accommodate the Taliban's line" ... but that was difficult to do as we [R&AW] did not have the contacts with them [Afghan Taliban]'.[97] Unlike what X claims, India did have links with the Afghan Taliban, with the MI (and even some R&AW) officers often facilitating such links. Despite being outside their operational ambit, the MI played an important role in opening channels on the ground with various Afghan Taliban commanders.[98]

When pushed about the inconsistency between his claim and that of what other Indian officials thought about India's outreach to the Afghan Taliban, X articulated the real reason for his disaffection with Menon. 'How could you trust them [Afghan Taliban]? They were all based out of Pakistan or had families there. They held Pakistan passports, and were Pakistanis. But Menon wouldn't agree with that,' says X.[99] It was classic anti-Pakistan partisanship. Though X agreed that the Afghan Taliban was a fractured movement and Haqqanis were the most dangerous for India, he refused to accept that an open approach towards the Afghan Taliban was worthwhile. India's focus on moderate Afghan Taliban leaders such as Tayyab Agha (Quetta Shura's spokesperson), Abdal Salam Zaeef, and Muttawakil, was pointless in his opinion. Instead, he argued, even if India wanted to engage with the Afghan Taliban, it should have reached out to the likes of Agha Jan Mutasim, Mullah Omar's son-in-law, and Abdul Ghani Baradar, both of 'whom the NDS got out of Pakistan's clutches'.[100] Mutasim and Baradar had become faces of the 'moderate' Taliban factions who were willing to reconcile directly with the Afghan government. Having opposed engagement with the Taliban in the mid-1990s, X continued opposing talks with insurgent groups based out of Pakistan. Such partisanship, however, grew increasingly marginal.

In April 2010, weeks after the Hamid guesthouse attack and the London conference, Taliban spokesperson Zabiullah Mujahid publicly responded to India's evolving policy approach. In an interview with Rahimullah Yusufzai, Mujahid stated that the Taliban did not 'believe that India will seriously oppose Karzai's policy' of reconciliation and that 'if the Taliban returns to power, we would like to maintain normal relations with all countries including India. It's possible for the Taliban and India to reconcile with each other.'[101] Mujahid reiterated that India cannot be completely expelled from Afghanistan and that the Taliban had no direct conflict with India. But neither can they ignore Pakistan for it was a neighbouring Islamic country that gave refuge to hundreds and thousands of Afghans and supported the Taliban in the 1990s. As for Indian worries of the Taliban supporting fighters in Kashmir, Mujahid clarified that there were no links between the Taliban and the LeT, and the Taliban had never taken part in any attack in India, nor will it do it at Pakistan's behest. The tone of Mujahid's message, however, was eerily similar to that of Muttawakil, Jaleel, and Zaeef's interviews describing India's Afghanistan policy in the mid and late 1990s and that of Massoud in 1992. Though India's role was different from the big powers that 'occupy' Afghanistan, it was far from neutral. Allegedly, during a battle in Khost, the Taliban found Indians in civilian clothes fighting alongside the Afghan National Army.[102] It was an old allegation that many Mujahideen (and Taliban) elements had made since mid-1980s, without evidence. The real problem, however, was India's lack of acceptance of the

Afghan Taliban as a legitimate political movement. In 2013, India responded to this specific grievance by allowing Zaeef to participate in the *Tehelka* magazine's festival in Goa called *Think*.[103] Zaeef had been introduced to Indian intelligence officials during his visit to London in 2011, where he had participated in a similar conclave at King's College London. Two years later when the question of granting him a visa for the festival emerged, the R&AW backed his case strongly.[104]

The Afghan Taliban and the Hizb-e-Islami were interested in engaging with India for domestic political reasons. Having built goodwill across Afghanistan, India was the only country that could work as a credible counterweight against Pakistan and also increase their domestic political value vis-à-vis Karzai and former United Front leaders. According to Sanaullah Tasal, an Afghan security analyst at the Bacha Khan Foundation, who worked closely with the Americans and knew the internal dynamics of the Hizb-e-Islami, the Afghan Taliban, and the Kabul government extremely well, Hekmatyar took Pakistan's support despite being frustrated and disillusioned with the ISI because no other country was willing to support him.[105] The Indians for the most part, from his standpoint, were simply afraid of opening up to Hekmatyar based on a false belief that he was still an ISI crony. 'One thing that I always blame India from [sic] when I meet with them [Indian officials in Afghanistan] is, why are you not reaching to these people [Hizb-e-Islami]? Why are you always suspicious of them? Massoud, Rabbani, Sayyaf, all of them were trained by the ISI in Peshawar [in 1970s and 1980s]. And during the [anti-Soviet] jihad all of them, including Hekmatyar, had good relations with the ISI. But when they came to Afghanistan, and changed their direction. The only one [Hekmatyar] who did not have any support [from countries other than Pakistan], did not change. He is also looking to change direction and establish relations with other countries', says Tasal.[106] The conciliators within India's policymaking circuit understood and appreciated this logic of engagement, and viewed it as a risky but necessary step to develop influence on hitherto estranged Pashtun insurgents.

Similar to Hizb-e-Islami, the Afghan Taliban also viewed India as a powerful regional actor to be engaged with in their quest to gain strategic autonomy from Pakistan, and began signaling the same. The timing of such outreach to India by the Taliban was interesting, for this is when India's former UF allies were getting slightly disillusioned by India's reluctance to support them in their domestic political battles (and were being lobbied by Pakistan). Islamabad's pressure on the Afghan Taliban and politicking between different insurgent networks had angered the Pashtun communities tremendously. The ISI had pitched the Peshawar shura against the Quetta shura, and the Haqqani network against almost every other faction. It held Mullah Omar and other Taliban figures in Pakistan and supplied fighters to the Pashtun areas of Afghanistan. Such actions had problematised Pakistan's image among the border tribes. Military actions in South Waziristan further undermined its image among Pashtuns. As Akbar Agha put it, 'Pakistan is the country that shows its back to us [Afghanistan] ... and in that situation we have India to have close and friendly relations with, because India is a country that wants, forever, to make good brotherly relations with us'.[107] Various Afghan Taliban factions sent feelers to India at different points in time. India silently entertained some of them.[108] But more often than not, after this initial interaction, the Afghan Taliban would retreat out of fear of reprisals from Pakistan. For Menon, the architect of India's conciliatory approach, the Afghan Taliban's toing-and-froing raised a pertinent question which were how far can the Taliban take its relations with India? '*Unki bhi majbooriyan hoti hain* [they also have their compulsions] ... I don't think that we [India] should put too much load on them [Afghan Taliban] so as to break the relationship ... let it evolve and see where it goes', he says.[109]

The Afghan Taliban's interest in engaging with India raises another question—is the Haqqani network necessarily opposed to India (or, as Menon says, happy to be manipulated by Pakistan)? In a testimony to the US Senate Committee on Armed Services, in September 2011, Admiral Mike Mullen, former chairman of the US Joint Chiefs of Staff, described the Haqqani network as a 'veritable arm' of the ISI.[110] Parallel to his testimony were assurances by Pakistan that it could credibly 'persuade' the Haqqani leadership to participate in talks with the Karzai government.[111] Such statements reflected the confidence that Rawalpindi had its influence over the Haqqanis, a fact that worried India considerably. However, independent scholarship shows that despite being closely linked with Pakistan's security agencies, the Haqqanis may not necessarily be totally 'dependent' on Pakistan's support.[112] Geographically focused in the border areas of Afghanistan and Pakistan, the network enjoys considerable financial, political, and military independence. Linked to the wider jihadist network the Haqqanis actively interact with Al Qaeda, the Afghan Taliban, the TTP, the LeT, and other smaller militant groups that benefit from the illicit drug economy in the region. Such linkages allow the Haqqani Network (HN) to have a transactional relationship with the ISI where both parties benefit from the other as allies instead of being subservient to Pakistan's diktats.

Though the HN helped execute the 2008 Indian embassy bombing (among other attacks on NATO installations), the precise motivations for the same are not clear. If the motivations were monetary and not ideological (a scenario that is highly probable), then the HN can be manipulated by powers other than Pakistan as well. For some Pakistan-watchers, the possibility of HN using the Pakistan's security establishment for their own strategic ends is equally high and makes the group open to engagement with extra-regional powers in south and central Asia.[113] The scenario of Indian intelligence services opening a channel with Serajuddin Haqqani, who is now second-in-command in the Taliban hierarchy, after Haibatullah Akhundzada (who became Taliban's chief after Mullah Akhtar Mansour's assassination in a US drone strike in May 2016), or counter-bribing the HN, cannot be discounted (though there is little political appetite among Indian officials to do this). Whether or not New Delhi reaches out to the HN, the evolution of its policy approach towards the Afghan insurgents remains a cause of concern for Pakistan. India's engagement with the Afghan Taliban would reduce Pakistan's indispensability for the group. In such a scenario, either Islamabad will have to increase financial support for these groups (to keep them from breaking away), or use active coercion and blackmail to prevent them from gravitating towards New Delhi. Given the history of India's support to the Baloch and Pashtunistan movements, this is an entirely credible threat.

Baloch and Pashtun cards

Somewhere between Islamabad's vehement allegations of India's role in fomenting separatism and violence in Pakistan (especially via Afghanistan), and New Delhi and Kabul's stony denials, lies the truth. Bereft of evidence, Pakistan's allegations of an omnipresent Indian hand behind its domestic troubles (in Balochistan, FATA, and Karachi) are treated, often correctly, as neuralgia of an insecure state marred by confused and conflicting nationalisms. But that does not absolve India politically, even if it has a strong legal defence to make. The buzz of India's covert successes in Balochistan is anything but subtle in Indian strategic circles, and the demand for such action is generally high. None other than Narayanan voiced such sentiments (of paying back Pakistan in the same coin) after the 2008 embassy bombing, and allegedly reached out to Saleh to seek Afghan help to target LeT assets.[114] Then foreign secretary, Menon, met with Karzai soon after the bombing and both agreed that 'the terrorist menace' should be 'rooted out from the region [read

Pakistan] by targeting bases, recruitment places, and financial links', and agreed with Narayanan to counter Pakistan using force.[115] Islamabad's use of militants against both these countries inculcated a healthy appetite to make Pakistan pay.[116] So why has this not happened if one is to believe the Indian narrative (Narayanan denies that India undertook such offensive covert action against Pakistan)? Before we proceed with examining these issues, the reader should be forewarned that this section does not necessarily offer the 'truth' or even a comprehensive overview of the complex geopolitical dynamics along the Afghanistan-Pakistan border regions and India's covert activities therein. Despite interviews with a host of Indian and Afghan security officials, systematic analysis of various US diplomatic cables, and a plethora of reports by credible media, this section provides an Indian reading of the situation, that is what Indian policymakers thought and planned for. What really happened remains a state secret and shall continue to remain so for decades to come.

For Indian security analysts the fact that former Indian PMs Narasimha Rao, I K Gujral, and Morarji Desai depleted R&AW's offensive capabilities inside Pakistan, is one reason why India never credibly threatened Pakistan using indirect means. Such proclamations of India's incapability because some PMs decades ago wrapped up its covert offensive capabilities does not match the rhetoric of Indian agencies' prowess in Balochistan. Moreover, depleting covert assets (which take years to develop) against ostensible enemies, by a conservative state and politically weak leaders is highly unlikely. That such strategic lethargy would continue even after the glaring failure of Operation Parakram to meet its objectives is even more inconceivable. This is reflected in Menon's candid assessments of India's covert infrastructure in the region. When quizzed whether India kept its promise of countering Pakistan after the 2008 embassy attacks, Menon answered: 'what goes on covertly between India and Pakistan has gone on for a long time. There is a mythology that India gave up everything during Gujral's time [but] that has never happened, and that goes on'.[117]

The differences within India's bureaucracy in its covert war with Pakistan have been 'tactical' in nature, that is who, when, and how to target, and the scale of the covert strike. There have hardly ever been fundamental differences on whether India should or not fight Pakistan because, as Menon explains, 'you are in a war. It might be a covert war or whatever, but it's there ... it's a fact of life with which we have lived for many years'.[118] Afghanistan has been adjunct to this rivalry in differing capacities across time. But just like the blow-hot-blow-cold nature of India-Pakistan bilateral relations, it has not always been used as a launchpad for anti-Pakistan operations. Former deputy NSA

Vijay Nambiar (2005–06) similarly asserts that while there is a natural convergence of interests between Afghanistan and India on the Pashtunistan and Balochistan issues, there was 'no active collaboration in any major way' other than broad political support during his tenure.[119] Though New Delhi is comfortable with using its close relationship with Kabul and the presence of its four consulates as a tool of psychological warfare against Islamabad, it allegedly practiced considerable restraint in using Afghan soil for such activities (despite Pakistan's suspicions).[120] This is because (a) evidence of Indian covert activities from Afghanistan will hurt Afghans more than India, which in turn, would undermine India's strategic aim of supporting Afghanistan in the first place, and (b) such a covert war may get difficult for India to handle without support by powers such as the US, and within the region, Iran.[121]

Though Manmohan Singh's conciliatory regional approach restrained the scale of India's covert actions after 2004, Pakistan's concerns of Indian involvement in exacerbating its domestic fault-lines, to little or large extents, cannot be discarded despite lack of evidence. Detailing the precise nature or scale of India's covert operations in Pakistan and Afghanistan during the post-9/11 era, or a comprehensive history of the Baloch conflict, is beyond the scope of this book. But highlighting aspects of India's covert approach towards the region is critical for the study of India's Afghanistan policy. Having proactively supported the UF in its anti-Taliban endeavours with Russian and Iranian support in the 1990s, it was unlikely that India would abandon effective partisanship under US pressure. Opening its embassy in Kabul in November 2001, against the wishes of US officials, was a small but potent way to demonstrate India's determination to reengage with Afghanistan along partisan lines. Spymaster Sood admits of a growing sense in India that stronger relations with Afghanistan's Pashtun leaders were critical not just to increase India's presence inside Afghanistan but also with Baloch separatists.[122]

Soon after 2002 India began developing its covert infrastructure to develop what Indian officials called their 'Baloch' and 'Pashtun' cards. Afghanistan's intelligence agency, the National Directorate of Security (NDS), then under, then under Mohammad Arif Sarwari, who had an excellent rapport with India since the civil war years, was a strong ally. With Karzai's permission, Arif began dispatching NDS officers for training to India, unlocking new and heightened levels of intelligence cooperation. Arif's successor, Amrullah Saleh, also had a close relationship with Narayanan. Though various (serving and retired) Indian intelligence officers acknowledge this relationship, Khare, who knew its nuts-and-bolts, is categorical that India remains 'very close to the

NDS'.[123] Though he denies that such links translate into joint offensive operations against Pakistan, the latter's allegation of a R&AW-NDS 'nexus', more broadly if not on specific operations, is accurate.

In 2004, a full-blown insurrection broke out in Balochistan with the Baloch Liberation Front (BLF, formerly known as the Baloch People's Liberation Front or the BPLF), the Baloch Liberation Army (BLA), and the Baloch Republican Party (BRP) undertaking attacks against the Pakistan army's installations. Nawab Akbar Khan Bugti, with support of his grandson Brahamdagh Bugti (among others), and Mir Balach Marri led the insurrection, and Musharraf openly blamed India and Afghanistan for fanning the insurgency.[124] Apart from harassing Pakistan, Indian motivations for the same were seen as linked to its geopolitical rivalry with China that began developing the Gwadar port in Balochistan. Promising to undermine India's naval and economic dominance and strengthening the China-Pakistan axis further, Gwadar's development is viewed with reservation in New Delhi.[125] Furthermore, China's policy of sending its nationals to build the port increased Baloch anxieties of becoming an exploited minority on their own land. These are powerful reasons for both India and the Baloch separatists to collaborate against China and Pakistan, if that ever happened.

There were nearly 500 Chinese nationals working at Gwadar in 2004 when the attacks on the Chinese and the Pakistan army began. On 3 May 2004, the BLA killed three Chinese engineers working on the port, and attacked the Gwadar airport on 21 May. Two Chinese engineers were kidnapped in October 2004 from South Waziristan, one of whom was later killed.[126] By December 2005 the violence had reached alarmingly high levels inviting official criticism by the MEA of Pakistan's heavy-handed counter-terrorism operations in Balochistan (eliciting angry ripostes from Islamabad).[127] Nambiar, in a meeting with the US ambassador to India in January 2006, assessed Islamabad's woes in Balochistan as a 'taste of their own medicine' similar to what India had been facing in Kashmir.[128] Whether this implied that India had adopted a similar strategy (to that of Pakistan in Kashmir) of supporting Baloch rebels covertly was left unsaid. Either way, in July 2006, Pakistan banned the BLA. Pakistan's allegations of India training Baloch insurgents in Afghanistan with Karzai's help, and the subsequent attack on Indian assets in Afghanistan, came in this context. The Zaranj-Delaram highway cut right through the Baloch-dominated Nimroz province from where Kutty had been kidnapped in 2005. The presence of Indian security personnel in that sector was a highly sensitive issue for Pakistan.[129] Rumours about India supplying 'commandos' or 'secret police' in Afghanistan that may undertake hot-pursuit of militants were rife (though incorrect).[130] India had also set up a consulate in Zahedan in Iran's Sistan-Balochistan province (with nearly two million Baloch population) to monitor the construction of the Zaranj-Delaram highway and the Chahbahar port; all of which were seen as indications by the Pakistani military of an Indian hand in the insurgency.

On 26 August 2006, when Akbar Khan Bugti was mysteriously killed in a ground operation,[131] the MEA came out with an official statement criticising the 'unfortunate killing of the veteran Baloch leader' and calling it a 'tragic loss to the people of Balochistan and Pakistan'.[132] With former foreign secretary Shyam Saran advocating a harder line on Balochistan as a pressure point against Pakistan, India also asked its high commissioner in Islamabad to visit Gilgit-Baltistan (but nothing happened given the divisions over the question within the government).[133] Pakistan sharply retorted asking India to mind its 'own business', and not interfere in the affairs of Balochistan.[134]

On 17 January 2007, an angry Musharraf told visiting US Assistant Secretary for South and Central Asian affairs, Richard Boucher, that Akbar Khan Bugti's grandson, Brahamdagh (as well as Balaach Marri) was living in Afghanistan and traveled frequently between Kabul and Kandahar planning operations against Pakistani security forces with Indian support.[135] When Boucher tried reassuring Musharraf that the US would not allow any anti-Pakistan activities from Afghan soil, the general sharply replied: 'that's bullshit'.[136] Three days later in Kabul, Boucher challenged Karzai on the issue of Brahamdagh Bugti. The Afghan president, in a candid response, admitted that Brahamdagh was operating from Afghanistan.[137] Maintaining that he did not consider the Baloch separatists as terrorists, Karzai asserted that Afghanistan was not supporting Brahamdagh militarily, as that would mean 'too much trouble' for Afghanistan, and that neither was India involved in such activities. Yet, 'turn[ing] over' Brahamdagh to Pakistan, Karzai underlined, would create tremendous 'disgust' among Afghans for Washington and Karzai.[138] While Boucher's shuttle diplomacy yielded no visible results, in September 2008 the Pakistan army and the Baloch separatists declared a ceasefire. If there ever was an India-Afghanistan axis on Balochistan, it was likely to be in full play during this time. That the NDS chief Saleh was closely engaged with the Baloch rebels as well as Narayanan was amply clear. Even if Indian intelligence agencies did not directly support the Baloch insurgents, it is unlikely that they remained aloof from the unfolding dynamic.

Khare, who followed these events on a regular and intimate basis, confirms that India had contacts with the Baloch separatists.[139] India had given (limited) protection to the sons and grandsons of most Baloch leaders, and Akbar Bugti was well known in variety of Indian circles. But still, India did not support the insurrection when the Pakistan army launched heavy counter-attacks. 'We allowed them to do that [kill Bugti] ... and didn't say much', Khare argues.[140] Despite the partisans' willingness to build pressure on Pakistan, Manmohan Singh was keen on preserving the peace process with Islamabad. Musharraf was a promising bet on that count. As Singh told the US in October 2008, 'we want our activities in Afghanistan to be an open book'.[141] No evidence emerged of India's direct, or indirect (via Afghanistan) support to the insurgency. But in January 2009, the insurgency was reignited after the three Baloch groups called-off the ceasefire. Brahmdagh threatened retaliation if Islamabad did not stop army operations in Balochistan, release political prisoners, account for alleged missing persons, and give autonomy to the province.[142] The breakdown of the ceasefire just two months after the 26/11 Mumbai attacks convinced Pakistan that Brahmdagh had India's support. Not just Pakistan, but even the UK was convinced that supporting proxies in Balochistan would be the 'minimum' India would do in response, and targeting LeT training camps in Pakistan-administered Kashmir was the 'maximum' (the US did not share British concerns).[143]

On 27 April 2009, Pakistan's interior minister Rehman Malik openly blamed India, Afghanistan, and Russia for supporting the BLA. A sharp increase in the number of rocket attacks and bombings against Pakistan's Frontier Corps pushed Islamabad to blame Indian consulates in Afghanistan for trying to dismember Pakistan.[144] To make things worse, the Marri group sought Indian (and US) support for the movement in a televised interview soon after Malik's testimony. In addition to violent attacks, a 'Long March' across Balochistan had been organised to rally support against Islamabad. The situation reached such a crescendo that soon after Malik's allegations, US senator Berman bluntly asked Narayanan what his men in Afghanistan were up to. Taken aback, Narayanan reassured the US delegation that Islamabad's worry that a handful of Indian personnel at the consulates would 'dismember' Pakistan was paranoid. After fifty years in the intelligence business he could assure them that his spies were 'not that good'. If anything, those who thought about strategic threats were focused on China and not Pakistan, a country about which people in India 'don't think much'.[145]

In July 2009, at a meeting in Sharm-el-Sheikh, Manmohan Singh met his Pakistani counterpart, Yousuf Raza Gilani, to assess the possibility of resuming dialogue. India had offered a dossier of evidence showing how the 26/11 attacks were planned and executed from Pakistan's soil and its lone survivor, Ajmal Kasab, was a Pakistani national. In return, Gilani allegedly told Singh that Pakistan had three Ajmal Kasab's to show in Balochistan and had a dossier on the same, and thus, it would be prudent for India to address Pakistan's concerns about Balochistan.[146] Gilani had been cautious and limited in his allegations, but the salvo worked. Singh agreed to discuss Balochistan and the associated role of Indian consulates in Afghanistan and issued a joint statement to that effect.[147] The move backfired domestically with the BJP, the CPM, and government allies such as the Samajwadi Party coupled with members of the Congress terming it a sell out.[148] Blaming Singh for budging under US pressure to 'allay Pakistan's anxieties in Balochistan', the opposition argued that the government had unnecessarily legitimised Pakistan's allegations.[149]

In retrospect, opposition parties failed Manmohan Singh in July 2009. The logic of 'why should we talk about Balochistan when we have nothing to do with it?' was misplaced from a historical standpoint, and went against the grain of conciliatory diplomacy. If anything, it reinforced the notion that Indian agencies were involved in Balochistan. Indian politicians had incorrectly assessed Singh's statement that India had 'nothing to hide' in Balochistan as an admission of guilt.[150] The reality was far from it. Indian intelligence had snooped onto the secret dossiers that Pakistan had prepared about India's involvement in Balochistan prior to the Sharm-el-Sheikh meeting. Khare, who analysed the dossiers (and sent his analysis to Narayanan, Menon, and Singh), was appalled by the 'low quality job' Pakistan had done. Khare notes: 'They said India is involved in Balochistan, and I remember reading ISI alerts, and they were desperately trying to fudge intelligence to prove it. And they could not do even that, because it was so difficult'.[151] Had that dossier been made public in 2009 or afterwards (it never was), it would have further cornered Pakistan and exonerated India from allegations of fomenting insurgency in Balochistan. Narayanan and Singh knew this before accepting Pakistan's challenge in Sharm-el-Sheikh. Not following up on the Sharm-el-Sheikh joint statement actually deprived India of a strategic victory on the negotiations table with Pakistan. When asked about Pakistan's allegations of India using its consulates in Afghanistan to foment the Baloch insurgency, Menon crisply responded: 'we don't have to do that. As I keep saying, if somebody [Pakistan] is committing suicide, you don't have to murder him'.[152]

The BJP, which considered the Sharm-el-Sheikh a 'shameful act', turned the tables along partisan lines giving credence to Pakistan's allegations of an Afghan-Indian nexus in Balochistan. Sometime in 2009, the Hindu-nationalist fringe group called the Bhagat Singh Kranti Sena, led by R. S. N. Singh and Tejender Singh, provided shelter to Balaach Pardili in New Delhi.[153] A Baloch from Afghanistan, Pardili represented the BLO and was linked to the Hyrbyair Marri group. His presence in India was exposed by *The Hindu* newspaper on 8 October 2015.[154] The MEA, while confirming Pardili's presence on Indian soil, categorically denied that it supported a policy of hosting Baloch separatists in India.[155] Pardili's presence in India had caught even the R&AW off-guard, with its Afghanistan-Pakistan desk/field officers wondering how and when this happened and how far the BJP government would take this issue.[156] Pushing the agenda of ending Pakistan's 'illegal occupation' of the part of Kashmir it administered, which curiously coincided with protests in Muzzafarabad, Gilgit, and Kotli, seeking 'freedom' from Pakistan, the Modi government had geared India's Afghanistan and Pakistan policy along partisan lines.[157]

India's 'Baloch card', regardless of its Afghan connection, was supplemented by what Indian security officials call their 'Pashtun card'. As previous chapters show, whether it was Daoud, Najibullah, or Karzai, there has always been a partisan desire in India to cultivate Afghan leaders of Pashtun background, who could challenge Pakistan. Whether the top Indian political leadership chooses to exercise these capacities against Pakistan is a separate matter. After 2002, despite India's links with former UF leaders, Karzai and his network was the lynchpin of India's Pashtun card. The rise of the TTP under the leadership of Baitullah Mehsud made operationalising such an enterprise horrifically real. However, given India's close links with the NDS and heavy financial aid investments in Afghanistan, R&AW had no need to dip its hands in the TTP. The TTP, as scholars have argued, was a 'parochial insurgency' with weak central processes but powerful local processes.[158] Unlike the Baloch insurgency where a small population spread over a large geographical mass was fighting a battle-hardened army (and needed external help), the TTP could sustain itself with little financial and moral support from outside, making it dangerous and difficult to contain. The TTP could, however, benefit from external tactical support, that is, providing safe havens and some funds. The NDS, in unknown capacities and at different points in time, did just that.

Pakistan's allegations of Indian and Afghan agencies funding the TTP, especially its leader Mullah Fazlullah, who was responsible for the December 2014 attack on the Army Public School in Peshawar, emerges from this perceived NDS-R&AW nexus.[159] India denies such allegations more strongly than those of supporting the Baloch insurgency. But Afghan intelligence services have not been secretive about this project. In October 2013 the US arrested Latif Mehsud, a senior TTP commander, in the middle of a sensitive NDS operation to recruit Mehsud and potentially use him against Pakistan.[160] The incident vindicated Pakistan's allegations that Karzai was supporting the TTP, and left Kabul both embarrassed and red-faced. That the NDS worked closely with India and received financial support from New Delhi led Islamabad to conclude of an Indian hand in the ploy, albeit indirectly. UAE intelligence officials, interestingly, were equally convinced of India's financial support to the TTP. Being a fund-raising hub for the Taliban, AQ and the Haqqanis, the UAE had been proactive in tracing money-laundering networks in Dubai and regularly shared intelligence with their Western counterparts.[161] Based on this author's interviews on the ground in Afghanistan as well as in India, whose details cannot be divulged, it seems clear that more than one faction of the TTP reached out to India for financial and material support at different points in time. While it is possible that such interactions took place in Dubai, many of them also happened at Indian consulates across Afghanistan. Whether this led to any direct or indirect support from India to the TTP remains unknown (though not implausible).

Indian security officials were not averse to offering such support in principle. Reasons for their reticence lay elsewhere. Were these alleged TTP members genuine, or were they ISI agents planted to frame India? What if the US and British intelligence agencies, who were proactive in Afghanistan, found out about such covert dealings? India would lose its credibility as a responsible regional power if it became directly linked with the TTP. More than the Americans, India worried about British Secret Intelligence Service (SIS), also known as MI6, for London had taken the baton of facilitating a dialogue between the Afghan Taliban and the Kabul government on one hand, and Pakistan and Afghanistan on the other. 'The SIS would not let [India] breathe easy' if it found out that India was using Afghan territory for ops against Pakistan, says Khare.[162] Mistrust between the UK and India about each other's role in Afghanistan persists till today. Hence, more than its own will, the presence of international troops tempered India's covert activities in Afghanistan. But the NDS, some of whose officials were trained in India (as well as the US and other Western countries) and were keen on sending a tough message to the ISI, did not shy away.

Another unverified (and perhaps unverifiable) dimension of India's covert actions against Pakistan was its association with the robust Afghan immigrant community in New Delhi (and the various Afghans who visit Indian hospitals such as Max and Apollo for medical treatment).[163] Mostly settled in south Delhi's Lajpat Nagar, Jung Pura, and Saket areas, these Afghan exiles, according to various interviewees speaking on condition of strict anonymity, provided a pool of recruits for Indian intelligence agencies. Trained in spy-craft, sabotage, and other lethal skills, these recruits, or their networks on the ground in the Afghanistan-Pakistan border areas, were utilised to gather intelligence and even undertake targeted killings of anti-India militants based in Pakistan. While there is no easy way to authenticate this aspect of India's covert actions, confidential assertions of the very existence of such programmes highlight how New Delhi may have engaged with Afghan diaspora settled in India. T, for instance, confirms that the R&AW was making 'efficient use' of the Afghan students in India for intelligence gathering purposes.[164] Though unaware of offensive covert operations undertaken by India as alleged by Pakistan, he does not reject all Pakistani allegations (even if he would temper down some such allegations).

Pakistan's uncontrolled spiral into violence elicited curious responses from Indian security officials. If the conciliators worried about the deteriorating situation, it was *schadenfreude* for the partisans. Similar to the early and mid-1990s' discourse of turning Afghanistan into Pakistan's Vietnam, the partisans viewed the TTP and its NDS links as an effective tool to bog down the Pakistan military. As Sahgal put it, 'the assessment we had was that Pakistan would require close to about 32 Brigades, which means about 10 Divisions plus for counter-insurgency operations. We were also trying to look at what kinds of operations were going on over there, which in turn created a void on the east [LoC]. So the perception was that if push came to shove, can we utilise that void for [strikes in Pakistan], because of post-Mumbai options?'[165] Indeed, on 15 June 2014, Pakistan launched Operation *Zarb-e-Azb* in North Waziristan.[166] While India never conducted any strikes against Pakistan after 26/11, its security planners had, quite unsurprisingly, thought of different possible scenarios of containing Pakistan's military and use that as a tool to set the terms of talks with Pakistan on Kashmir and other bilateral issues.[167]

As for Afghanistan, India was confident that it would not slip back to the 1990s where one (or more) Pakistan-supported group(s) would dominate in Afghanistan's political space. True, Afghanistan may not be safe, and often stable, but it will not be under Pakistan's influence either. If it were to happen that any specific Afghan Taliban faction began to dominate the battle then it 'should not be a Pashtun [versus] non-Pashtun front line. It should be Pashtuns fighting reactionary Pashtuns backed by radicalism and Pakistan with the support of the rest', says Mukhopadhaya.[168] By supporting Karzai, talking to his domestic opponents to accept his authority, cautiously opening channels with the Afghan Taliban and Hekmatyar, accepting an Afghan-led reconciliation in 2011, and silently influencing its contours by facilitating meetings between Afghan COIN specialists with their Indian counterparts, India was trying to obviate the possibility of a Taliban takeover on one hand, and keeping its presence robust in Afghanistan's Pashtun-dominated regions on the other.

Conclusion

India went through a steady policy learning curve on the issue of dealing with the Afghan Taliban after 2002. Adopting a dual approach of publicly criticising the Taliban but privately engaging with some factions, India learnt to differentiate between groups who were actually linked to Pakistan and those who, despite their links to Pakistan, sought political independence. This policy learning process, as this chapter detailed, evolved upon an interplay between the three drivers of India's Afghanistan policy, that is, changing Afghan domestic politics, New Delhi's desire to strike a balance between Afghanistan and Pakistan, and evolving international postures towards Afghanistan. The resurgence of the Afghan Taliban after 2003, Karzai's covert dealing with the insurgents (for domestic political reasons), and the various attacks on Indian installations and personnel pushed a partisan-dominated India to reconsider its approach towards the Afghan Taliban. Having invested tremendous financial and political capital in Karzai, it became difficult even for staunch partisans such as Narayanan to avoid the realities of a changing Afghanistan. Already at odds with the conciliators on their outreach to Pakistan, Narayanan refused to entertain serious talks with the Afghan Taliban. On the ground in Afghanistan, however, in their own capacities, Indian intelligence and diplomatic officials had begun engaging with select Afghan Taliban and Hizb-e-Islami figures in the wake of reconnecting with the Pashtuns. Supplementing Karzai's own outreach to the Afghan Taliban, international posture against the Taliban began evolving by 2008 as the idea of reconciliation took roots. Such international changes, which had resonance even in Moscow and Tehran, only increased the value of the conciliators within India's policymaking circuit.

The ultimate policy shift, however, occurred in 2010 with the rise of Menon as NSA and Chidambaram as home minister. Instead of offering blanket opposition to the idea of reconciling with the Afghan Taliban, India developed a nuanced approach to negotiations, with the hope of influencing the terms of these talks. The 2011 India-Afghanistan Strategic Partnership Agreement (SPA) and subsequent interaction between Kabul and New Delhi were steps in that direction. The rise of the conciliators in 2010 within India's policy bureaucracy did not mean that the value of coercion (either overt or covert) was lost upon India. The criticism that Manmohan Singh and Menon often face is that they were too soft on Pakistan and Afghanistan. Narayanan, some argue, was better at playing hardball with Pakistan and the 'great game' in Afghanistan.[169] This assessment is misplaced. Conciliators such as Menon resorted to force when required without hesitation. What they did not do was make it public. India's covert war with Pakistan, or support to the NDS in its strategic endeavours, was not called off under Menon's watch. If anything, silently but surely, India had ensured that (1) Pakistan continued to remain politically marginalised in Afghanistan, (2) such marginalisation did not impede New Delhi's talks with Islamabad, and (3) India is not viewed as an obstructionist regional power. The next and final chapter of this book shows how changing international dynamics influenced change in India's Afghanistan policy towards a more conciliatory direction.

9

FIRST AS TRAGEDY, THEN AS FARCE

MANAGING THE US WITHDRAWAL

'U.S. and its partners must recognise that they are in Afghanistan for the long haul and that if the U.S. did not persevere, Islamist groups would be even further emboldened ... [and] until the Pakistan military had made this commitment [eliminating all terror groups on its territory], the U.S. would be fighting a losing battle in Afghanistan.'

Manmohan Singh, PM of India to US Senator John Kerry, December 2008[1]

'One of our regrets has been that India was a passive player with regards to America's intervention in Afghanistan. I just couldn't believe that there wasn't that much strategic consultation and interaction between India and the US on Afghanistan. In fact, I was the one who facilitated the first trilateral engagement between the three countries [in 2012] and I realised in that meeting how distant the two countries were.'

Jawed Ludin, former deputy foreign minister of Afghanistan, 2013[2]

A mismatch made in heaven

It was a peculiar situation. Despite witnessing the worst historical lows in its bilateral relationship with the US, Pakistan was the most critical player in Afghanistan. In the aftermath of the 9/11 attacks the White House, the department of defense, and the state department, considered Pakistan as the linchpin for any strategy to fight against Al Qaeda and the Taliban.[3] NATO and the US needed Islamabad's support to enter Afghanistan, to halt the

Taliban insurgency (that was covertly being supported by Pakistan), and to talk to the Taliban to ensure a honourable exit.[4] Pakistan received nearly US$ 19 billion since 2002 as economic and military assistance and an additional US$13 billion as reimbursements from the Coalition Support Fund in order to allow transit to Afghanistan and the use of Pakistan's naval and airport facilities for coalition troops and equipment transfers.[5] India on the other hand, despite having positively overhauled its relationship with the US during the Bush presidency, figured marginally in Washington's 'Af-Pak' canvass.

Despite regular consultations, neither New Delhi nor Washington knew how to work together in Afghanistan.[6] When India had expressed interest in training the Afghan National Army in 2001–02, Washington balked in order to secure Pakistan's support. By the time the US realised that Pakistan was an unreliable ally in Afghanistan, India had lost interest to step in militarily given its ongoing peace talks with Islamabad. Though the two countries tried hard to find common ground for promoting democracy in Afghanistan and helping in the reconstruction of the war-torn country, this trend of political bad timing continued throughout the war.[7] The political mismatch between New Delhi and Washington would have been highly comic had Afghanistan's situation not been as scary and tragic as it was. But more than the initial US-Pakistan alliance, it was the US withdrawal that worried India. Just like the Soviet case, premature drawdown of the coalition forces from Afghanistan had the potential to put Pakistan in the driving seat in Kabul. India was worried that the tragedy of 1992 might repeat itself as a farce in 2014, and Karzai (and later Ghani) might meet with Najibullah's fate.

Similar to its 1987 request to Moscow, New Delhi asked Washington to go slow with the withdrawal. But much like the 1980s, when Pakistan mattered more to the Soviet Union despite India being the bigger South Asian partner, the same was the case with the US. India was important, but not critical. This chapter highlights how, given its limited strategic importance in Afghanistan, India managed the early phases of the war, its slow-motion unraveling, and subsequent Western attempts towards reconciliation with the Taliban. Though the coalition military umbrella offered India a security blanket to reengage with Afghanistan, and helped bringing down the levels of infiltrations in Indian-administered Kashmir, there was little in common between Indian and American perceptions about Afghanistan. Beginning with the ISAF's efforts to rebuild Afghanistan (an endeavour that had full support of US president Bush especially after 9/11), and Washington's decision to invade Iraq in 2003, to the reconciliation drive launched by London in 2010, India had political and conceptual differences on nearly all these issues. Focused on defeating Al Qaeda, the US had little intention to undertake serious nation building in Afghanistan. The 'Light Footprint' model or 'Nation-Building Lite', as it was called, required few boots on the ground and even less money.[8] In the first donor's conference in Tokyo, for instance, Washington pledged a meager US$ 290 million in aid and was outbid by Iran that pledged US$ 540 million.[9] In February 2002, the then US secretary of defence Donald Rumsfeld stated that a large peacekeeping force outside Kabul was not necessary. Soon after, in 2003 the US declared war on Iraq and shifted most of its resources to the Middle East.

Such neglect of Afghanistan was dangerous from an Indian perspective. It meant that the US involvement in Afghanistan would be marred by failures and would eventually pave the way for Pakistan to influence domestic Afghan politics. The situation evolved along expected lines. Within a short span, the Taliban had unleashed a potent insurgency against the coalition forces. In 2006, despite building pressure to counter the Taliban, then US secretary of defense Robert Gates (Rumsfeld's successor) asserted that the NATO/ISAF would not conduct long-term counter-insurgency (COIN) operations in Afghanistan. The new US President Barack Obama ordered a troop surge in 2008 and began looking for a way out. The US decision to withdraw by 2014 was formally announced in 2011.[10] According to a senior Western official posted in Kabul in 2008, 'the idea of the surge was not really to fight an insurgency, but to put pressure on the Taliban and secure a honourable exit'.[11] India was unimpressed. Even staunch partisans, to whom alignment with the US seemed like the 'correct' response in the shadow of 9/11, grew wary.[12] Former Afghan deputy foreign minister Jawed Ludin ruefully recalled that 'one of our [Afghanistan's] regrets has always been that India was a passive player with regards to America's intervention in Afghanistan. I just couldn't believe that there wasn't that much strategic consultation and interaction between India and the US on Afghanistan. In fact, I was the one who facilitated the first trilateral engagement between the three countries [in 2012] and I realised in that meeting how distant the two countries were.'[13]

The changing Western approach towards Afghanistan impacted India's foreign policy calculus. As the previous two chapters showed, India had increased its support for Karzai and began appreciating differences between the various Taliban factions and the complex nature of their relationship with Pakistan. This policy learning was as much an outcome of India's own desire to better understand Afghanistan's internal dynamics, as much it was steered by the realisation that the West lacked the political will to counter the Taliban on a long term basis. A decisive shift towards reconciliation at the 2010 London conference merely confirmed what India feared the most, which was a format of talks that could give Pakistan strategic leeway to set the terms of talks (one of which was reduced Indian presence in Afghanistan). As this chapter shows, immediately after the London conference, India began hectic behind-the-scenes lobbying with various Afghan, regional, and international stakeholders to steer the reconciliation initiative away from Pakistan. Quickly adjusting to the fact that talks with the Afghan Taliban was inevitable, India signed the Strategic Partnership Agreement with Kabul in October 2011 and endorsed an Afghan-led reconciliation. New Delhi's conciliatory policy shift, led by Manmohan Singh, Menon, and Lambah, thus, was an exercise to dilute the so-called 'Western model' of reconciliation, and to make it an Afghan-owned enterprise, however difficult it may be.[14]

India's statements at the UN reflected its changing stance on reconciliation. From blaming the UN for not terming all Afghan militants as 'terrorists', India developed a nuanced terminology of whom to blame and how when debating the Afghan situation at the UN. It eventually accepted that the Afghan Taliban were not terrorists even if they were not to be valued at par with the Afghan government. Evolving regional advocacies by China, Russia, and Iran also pushed India into adopting a conciliatory stand. Worried about a spillover of Islamist militancy within its borders both China and India saw increasing convergence whereas Russia, which had never really viewed India as the strategic lynchpin in Afghanistan, began tilting towards Pakistan and eventually tactically collaborated with the Taliban to counter the rise of ISIS in Afghanistan.[15] Throughout this phase, Iran continued with its own interventionist approach towards Afghanistan. Similar to Pakistan (though of a limited nature) Iran supported certain Afghan Taliban elements.[16] Ironically, unlike its political outbursts against Pakistan, India decided to remain quiet about Iran's interventionism in Afghanistan. The following sections outline these issues in turn. However, they should be read with a note of caution. The following sections are essentially an Indian reading of the situation on the ground in Afghanistan rather than how the (various) reconciliation process(es) actually panned out. The US, British, French, and German advocacy and practice of reconciling with the Taliban, and attempting the same between the Kabul government and Taliban factions, for instance, was highly complicated in nature and character.[17] The diversity, depth, and changing political and military rhythms of these processes will not be captured in this chapter. The idea, instead, is to show how Indian policymakers perceived (correctly or incorrectly) the idea of reconciling with the Taliban depending on who advocated it.

Iraq versus Afghanistan

India witnessed an unprecedented foreign policy debate related to the US invasion of Iraq in 2003. Should US actions be supported or condemned? Relishing an increasingly close relationship with Washington, especially under President Bush, many Indian policymakers supported the invasion despite parliamentary and popular opposition. Similar to the November 2001 request regarding Afghanistan, the US asked for an Indian military contingent in Iraq in 2003. Home minister Advani, a partisan who favoured deeper defence collaboration with the US, was willing to offer such support.[18] But PM Vajpayee, a conciliator, was unconvinced. Initially agreeing to consider the US request for Indian troops in Iraq if there was 'an explicit UN mandate' for the invasion, New Delhi ended up 'deploring' the invasion.[19] Splitting India's body politic and civil society, the Iraq invasion invited strong cross-country protests. While the decision-making processes on this issue is narrated in detail elsewhere, the Iraq war raised concerns among Indian strategists about its potential negative impact on Afghanistan.[20] US focus on Iraq meant that Afghanistan may not receive the financial, political, and security attention that it deserved. In a heated parliamentary debate, communist MP Nilotpal Basu highlighted that despite committing funds towards the reconstruction of Afghanistan in the initial years of war, the US 'had not kept a single penny for the reconstruction of Afghanistan'.[21]

Though US$ 300 million had been allocated to Afghanistan in the first four days of the Iraq invasion, the US economy was running on daily deficit of US$1.5 billion, with the total budgetary deficit standing at US$437 billion—most of which was being financed by the surplus economies of Europe and Japan.[22] Even the aid projects that the coalition partners had initiated, argued Indian diplomats, were like 'Band-Aid' focused on short-term curative aspects rather than long-term capacity development.[23] It was a horrifying economic scenario that only became worse during the 'great recession' of 2007–09.[24] From the very beginning of the Afghan war, the US had advocated a 'light footprint' model instead of a 'Marshall Plan' for Afghanistan. Moreover, according to Indian policymakers, there was a false impression in the US that the Taliban had been defeated.[25] Formal US military operations against the Taliban had ceased in March 2002, and only 18,000 American and 4,500 ISAF soldiers were stationed in the provincial reconstruction teams (PRTs) in 2003. Indian concerns (like those of many other countries) were highly accurate.

Mukhopadhaya, who was in Kabul as a liaison officer at the time and participated in many closed-door meetings with top Indian and US officials, argued that India's 'greater interest [was] Afghanistan rather than Iraq, so therefore our [Indian] focus should be on Afghanistan. Not only should we not get engaged in Iraq, we should work in order to try and prevent the Americans being distracted from Afghanistan to Iraq'.[26] Top Indian military generals as well as Narayanan were of a similar view.[27] They argued that Washington's focus on Baghdad would make it impervious to Kabul, allowing Islamabad to make inroads by supporting the Taliban's revival. There was considerable skepticism even within US policy circles about the negative fallout of the Iraq invasion on the Afghan situation.[28] By 2004 Karzai made appeals for robust COIN measures while the insurgency was still in infancy, whereas Abdullah conceded with India that he was 'very worried' about the Taliban's activity.[29] But their appeals went unheeded. In June 2006, Karzai bitterly complained that 'for two years, I have systematically, consistently and on a daily basis warned the international community of what was developing in Afghanistan and of the need for a change of approach in this regard ... the international community [must] reassess the manner in which this war against terror is conducted'.[30] More than 669 Afghan civilians were killed in 2006 in about 350 armed attacks by the Taliban that were intentionally aimed at non-combatants.[31]

In December 2006, the US released the Baker-Hamilton Report on Iraq (also known as the Iraq Study Group Report).[32] Calling for the people of Iraq to take responsibility of their future, the report recommended an increase in the US military and diplomatic resources in Iraq to facilitate a credible transition as an external catalyst. Having invaded Iraq on the false pretense of Saddam Hussein's acquisition of weapons of mass destruction, the US had begun losing control over the situation on the ground in Afghanistan. Now it was intent on cutting its losses. Already uncomfortable with how the West had conducted itself in Afghanistan, the report further watered down India's hopes for sustained US presence in Afghanistan. Narayanan baldly asked US Under Secretary of State for Political Affairs, William J. Burns, 'after reading the Baker Hamilton Report on Iraq, we [India] want to know if the U.S. is going to stay the course in Afghanistan'.[33] Narayanan warned that if the US falters in Afghanistan, international jihadists would raise the same cry the

Mujahideen had raised after the Soviet defeat.[34] India did not want to see a friendly neighbouring country become 'almost hostile' due to US mistakes. Burns promised Narayanan that the US would stay the course 'and more'.[35]

The combination of partisan advocacy of sending Indian troops to Iraq, a shift of US resources to the Middle East, and Indian reservations about the negative impact of the Iraq war on Afghanistan's security, had an interesting spinoff on how the US began viewing India's role in Afghanistan. In 2004, Washington took a U-turn on its decision to keep India out of Afghanistan's security sector and asked New Delhi if it would be interested in taking charge of a PRT. Involving both developmental and security management of a designated geographical area, a PRT would allow India to considerably expand its political presence in Afghanistan. With its GDP growth rates soaring at 8.5 per cent (2003–04) and 7.5 per cent (2004–05), finances were not a problem, but a PRT in Afghanistan risked India being bracketed as an 'occupying' force.[36] From the US perspective, an Indian PRT in Afghanistan had multiple benefits. Firstly, it would have filled a resource void that had been created by the Iraq invasion. Secondly, it would reduce pressure on the ISAF and NATO to provide security to Indian workers. The partisans in India had been blaming Washington's reluctance to allow Indian 'boots on the ground' for the deaths of Indian workers in Afghanistan (a misplaced blame given India's own reluctance to send troops). Soon after the killing of Kutty in November 2005, for instance, US diplomat in New Delhi, Richard O. Blake, took the opportunity to push for an Indian PRT in west Afghanistan in Washington.

Though the ultimate decision lay with India, Blake highlighted that an Indian PRT would be a first from the developing world (and would join South Korea and Australia as the third non-NATO PRT), would benefit from India's long-standing experience in development and peacekeeping, buttress Afghanistan's fledgling democracy, embed India in Afghanistan's reconstruction, and deepen US-India relations.[37] Additionally, routing Indian assistance via US channels would give the latter a better handle (if not control) over Indian actions in Afghanistan, and use the 'India card' with Pakistan effectively and at will. Blake had argued with his bosses in the US that an Indian PRT in west Afghanistan, far from the Pakistan border, would not raise objections from Islamabad (it was a naïve hope at best). By 2005 India was being proactively pushed to take charge of the PRT in west Afghanistan and get involved in counter-terrorism operations like other US allies.[38] Narayanan confirms that 'a lot of offers were made [by the US]. Holbrooke spent many hours discussing with me and asking us to send people [to Afghanistan] to help out. Not exactly boots on the ground. But we were very clear that we don't want to go beyond anything than the area of development. That's how our mind was working at that time.'[39] Having witnessed the IPKF fiasco in Sri Lanka first-hand, India was not willing to risk the lives of its citizens in Afghanistan.

India refused the offer. Giving priority to improving relations with Pakistan, concerned about getting militarily involved in Afghanistan (and not knowing where it would stop), India was wary of sending troops to Afghanistan or routing India's developmental assistance through the US. It was also not keen on being seen as part of an international 'occupying' force. Under strain from communal Hindu-Muslim tensions, siding with the West by sending troops to Afghanistan ran the risk of getting branded that India was participating in the 'killing [of] Muslims all over the world'.[40] Both the NDA and the UPA governments wanted to avoid this. The Gujarat riots in February–March 2002, which witnessed one of the worst carnage of Muslim minorities in the history of independent India, had accentuated the need for India to ensure that it did not make enemies in the Muslim world. Only a strict bilateral and non-military relationship with Afghanistan could ensure such diplomatic balancing. Shyam Saran, who was foreign secretary at the time, dealt with the issue and confirms that India's 'response always used to be that whatever is required by Afghanistan, we will respond to a request from the Afghan government ... there was always a very conscious effort on our part to keep a very distinct personality for India dealing with Afghanistan [and] not be seen as part and parcel of an American led effort'.[41] India was anyways highly skeptical of the forty countries doing counter-insurgency and the US focused on Al Qaeda.[42]

Indian and US political cycles were not conducive for a meaningful strategic partnership in Afghanistan either. As Shashank, India's foreign secretary (2003–04), says, not just Washington, 'most NATO countries said that we don't want India anywhere, because Pakistan is our best bet. Pakistan does not want India, so we also don't want India. Only Germans said, all right, in our area of responsibility, we don't mind Indians coming and helping. And these were all civilian projects, these had nothing to do with defence, law, and order'.[43] When the US shifted its focus to Iraq in 2003 and required more international assistance in Afghanistan (including by regional allies such as India), India was not keen. Pakistan's unreliability in the Afghan war had become apparent by then. In a secret cable sent to Washington in 2005 by the then US ambassador to Afghanistan, Ronald E. Neumann, the Taliban's resurgence was attributed to the 'four years that the Taliban has had to reorganise and think about their approach in a sanctuary beyond the reach of either government'.[44]

The Iraq war had distracted Western political attention and shifted military resources to such an extent that little hope existed for a rerun of the initial successes of Operation Enduring Freedom by the time the US revisited Afghanistan in 2008–09. While the coalition forces ensured that the Taliban remained militarily contained, it had lost the appetite to obviate the possibility of the Taliban's return in totality (as India wanted). The US drone strike campaign in Pakistan's tribal areas (from where the Afghan Taliban operated), which began in 2004, was limited in its ambition. Only ten strikes were executed in a span of four years (2004–07) killing 116 people, of whom 101 were civilians.[45] Despite Narayanan's excellent rapport with the US, India found it difficult to convince Washington (and the UN), as to how difficult the situation on the ground was in its view. This is indicative in a meeting of the India-US counter-terrorism (CT) joint working group on 2 March 2007. From the Indian side, K. C. Singh, assistant secretary on the MEA's CT desk, and Sharad Kumar, joint secretary at the CT desk of R&AW, participated in the meeting, whereas David Mulford, the US ambassador to India, and Frank Urbancic, acting coordinator for CT, represented the US. Presenting a bleak picture of Afghanistan's ground situation, Kumar assessed that the Taliban insurgency was gaining strength, the Kabul government was weak and divided (unable to expand its influence outside of Kabul), and Pakistan was not sincere about uprooting 'terrorist infrastructure' on its soil. Kumar flatly told Urbancic that India knew that Mullah Omar was 'under Pakistani protection'.[46]

Differences between NATO and ISAF over how to deal with the Taliban attacks and their unwillingness to engage in direct combat 'was the wrong approach for the current situation in Afghanistan' according to India. Occurring long before the Indian embassy came under attack in 2008, this India-US Counter-terrorism Joint Working Group (CT JWG) meeting also reflected India's reservations about talking to the Taliban. In a move to pacify the insurgency, the coalition forces had launched political drives to reconcile local and regional political differences in different provinces. The various PRTs were critical for supporting local political processes that involved talking with Afghan tribal leaders who knew the Taliban elements. While such engagement with the moderate Taliban was acceptable for tactical reasons, 'any agreement with the tribes would provide temporary relief, at best' India argued. Speaking to Taliban hardliners also sent a 'wrong message to these leaders about their status and ability to influence the situation in Afghanistan'. None of this meant, however, that India would give up on talks with Pakistan, whom New Delhi held responsible for the Taliban's resurgence. Guided by

Manmohan Singh's conciliatory approach, India went ahead with the India-Pakistan Joint Counterterrorism Mechanism, whose first meeting occurred on 6 March 2007, four days after the India-US CT JWG meeting (where India would present evidence about the July 2006 Mumbai blasts to Pakistan).[47] Interestingly, in 2007 the US did not share India's pessimism on Afghanistan's security situation, the adverse impact of an intensely corrupt Afghan government, and the futility of talking to the Taliban, or Pakistan's CT collaboration with the US. Narayanan delivered a similar message to US senators John Kerry, Joe Biden, and Chuck Hagel in February 2008, calling an early US withdrawal and talking to the Taliban 'disasterous' for the region.[48] In a couple of years though, the US approach in Afghanistan changed considerably.

On 1 December 2009, in a historic speech from the US Military Academy at West Point after months of intense internal policy debate,[49] US President Barack Obama officially announced that after an initial surge of 30,000 troops, US soldiers will start 'coming home' after 18 months.[50] The focus would be on unified training of the Afghan army and the Afghan police. Though 'fully backed' by Narayanan, the US decision to train Afghans was too late and too little.[51] For serious COIN the US required close to 450,000 soldiers as against the maximum of 142,000 in 2009 after the surge.[52] The troop surge was not meant to counter the Taliban effectively, but to pave the way for a honourable exit—which, in turn, required Pakistan's cooperation. Obama's rise to power in January 2009 had already set alarm bells ringing in New Delhi as Indian officials started thinking that Washington would intervene on Kashmir in order to seek Pakistan's help in Afghanistan. Holbrooke's initial appointment as US special representative to 'Afghanistan, Pakistan, and Kashmir' confirmed these fears (leading to proactive 'stealth lobbying' by India to get Kashmir removed from his portfolio).[53] From that very moment, Indian diplomats began pressuring the US to stay the course in Afghanistan. This is reflected in a series of meetings between Indian, American, and British officials throughout 2009.

In February, EAM Pranab Mukherjee told Holbrooke that India favoured an integrated 'Af-Pak' approach, but wanted greater political commitment from the US.[54] Menon informed Holbrooke that India had a 'huge stake' in the latter's success in Afghanistan.[55] At the mid-level, MEA joint secretary T. C. A. Raghavan told his US counterpart that the US decision to bring the Taliban to the negotiating table had 'greatly muddied the waters' for Afghanistan's reconstruction, and created a corrosive sentiment among Afghan people who thought the system was allowing the Taliban 'in through the back door'.[56] In April, Manmohan Singh urged US Senator Howard Berman to push Obama to 'stay the course in Afghanistan', an endeavour in which India was happy to support by offering large-scale training to the Afghan National Police (ANP).[57] Raghavan and Singh's requests did not cut any ice with the White House.[58] Increment in India's training of the ANP, Washington argued, would put more strain on India-Pakistan relations, and make it difficult for the US to move forward with its Af-Pak policy (Holbrooke pushed this issue strongly with Narayanan and asked India to stick to Afghanistan's agricultural sector).[59] In June, US National Security Advisor James Jones told Singh (and other top Indian leadership including Narayanan and defence minister A. K. Antony) that despite the deteriorating of the security situation since 2007 (as India had correctly warned), military options were no longer dominant in the new US approach towards Afghanistan.[60] There were reasons for India's diplomatic activism. Patil, at the JIC, had begun receiving troubling intercepts from Kashmir-centric militants. Obama's announcement, as he puts it: 'changed the rhetoric coming from groups like Lashkar-e-Taiba and Jaish-e-Mohammad. I saw multiple intercepts saying "our Taliban brothers have been successful in defeating the US in Afghanistan, and we will do the same to India in Kashmir .... [and] that the Taliban are coming, and Afghanis are coming, so we should step up the fight". Eventually we realised that this was just pep-talk. However, our initial concern was that if such is the rhetoric when the US has not withdrawn, then what will happen when one year later?'[61]

On 27–28 October 2009, during an official visit to London, foreign secretary Nirupama Rao met with her British counterpart FCO permanent under-secretary Peter Ricketts. Behind the glare of the media, Rao politely but forcefully expressed India's 'strong reservations' about the UK policy of reconciliation with the moderate Taliban elements.[62] With a timeline for withdrawal taking rounds, Rao argued that the moderate Taliban would engage in negotiations with the strategic objective of waiting for the West to leave and then the radical elements would assert themselves. Ricketts rubbished Rao's concerns. He countered that the UK had a great deal of experience dealing with insurgencies, and 'there comes a point when you need to engage by political means'. Soon after the disastrous meeting, the FCO requested the US to urge a 'pragmatic' Manmohan Singh to 'support reconciliation with moderate Taliban elements ... and Pakistan'.[63] To buttress the reconciliation process with economic incentives, the West brokered meetings between Kabul and Islamabad to sign the Afghanistan-Pakistan Transit Trade

Agreement (APTTA) and increase bilateral trade that stood at US$832 million in 2006. The agreement had gone through several stages of negotiations and entailed duty-free trade between the two countries. The thorn in the agreement, expectedly, was India. The Afghans wanted access to Indian markets but Pakistan would not allow that.[64] All Afghan trucks would have to unload at the India-Pakistan border at Wagah, and reload the goods into Indian trucks for onward passage. It made little economic sense for Afghanistan to sign an agreement that would not connect them with the 'jackpot' of South Asia's largest market.[65] Still, with reconciliation and withdrawal in view, London (and Washington) lobbied hard in December 2009 for the accord to be signed (only to be met with staunch rebuttals from Kabul). It was 'perfidy' lamented an Indian diplomat closely following the events from Kabul.[66]

'The second deception'

On 28 January 2010, representatives from more than seventy countries convened at the Lancaster House in London for a conference on Afghanistan. Co-hosted by Afghan President Hamid Karzai, UN Secretary General Ban Ki-Moon, and British PM Gordon Brown, the conference marked the beginning of the Afghan war's end. Focusing on security, development and governance, and regional cooperation, the conference sought to influence the Taliban to shun violence and start a dialogue with Kabul.[67] Just a one-day affair, the conference was pivotal in the history of the Afghan war. It did not change the course of the war, as the Taliban continued with its strategy of coercion, but it changed the calculus of all other regional and global actors involved in Afghanistan, as well as that of the Afghan government. Just like Gorbachev had decided in the fateful November 1986 politburo meeting that the USSR was to prepare for an exit from Afghanistan, the West agreed on a similar course of action in London that day. The idea of talking to the Taliban was anything but new (James Jones had informed Singh already). Informally, all fighting parties were in touch in some form or the other. Having challenged the US approach of talking to the Taliban, India had been expecting such a turn of events since the very first Taliban attack in 2003. What it had not hoped for, however, was the ready acceptability of the West's advocacy of reconciliation.

On 29 January 2010, the *Times of India* reported: the 'World Rejects India's Taliban Stand' that there are no degrees of Talibanism.[68] The report resented the conference's lack of focus on accommodating former UF leaders including

Abdullah (an absurd statement given that Abdullah was well entrenched in Afghanistan's mainstream politics). Nonetheless, it reflected India's discomfort with the changing political tide in Afghanistan. Complicating India's position further, soon after the London conference, Turkey hosted the first political meeting of the 'Heart of Asia' process (also called the Istanbul conference), from which New Delhi was excluded at Pakistan's request.[69] Initiated by the Ministry of Foreign Affairs of Afghanistan (MoFA), the Istanbul process marked the thrust of Afghanistan's foreign policy imperatives in the region seeking cooperation between Kabul and its neighbours on security and economic issues.[70] India took offense to Ankara's decision to keep India out of the process under Pakistan's pressure. On 2 February 2010, just before John Kerry's visit to New Delhi, Roemer told Washington that 'India was kept out of the Istanbul regional conference on Afghanistan (based on Pakistan's veto) and New Delhi was the odd man out at the London conference over reintegration.'[71] As the *Times of India* stated, despite 'being the biggest regional aid-giver to Afghanistan with a commitment of $1.3 billion ... Turkey, an ally of Pakistan, did not even bother to invite India to a confabulation on Afghanistan'.[72]

Top Indian strategist K. Subrahmanyam called the London conference and Pakistan's role therein as 'the second deception'.[73] Widely portrayed as a 'victory for Pakistan' and a 'setback' for New Delhi by the Indian press, the conference was accompanied by a crackdown by the Pakistan army on the leadership of the Quetta *shura* and detention of 124 Taliban militants, whose existence Pakistan had denied throughout.[74] The suddenness of Pakistan's crackdown and appreciation of the same by the US persuaded India's 'strategic community that the Obama administration has decided to make use of the services of Pakistan to partly neutralise and partly buy up the Afghan Taliban and leave Afghanistan at the mercy of Pakistan in 2011, when the American forces plan to withdraw from Afghanistan'.[75] Adding credibility to India's concerns were official US assessments of the threat emanating from Pakistan. In February 2009, then Director of National Intelligence (DNI) Dennis Blair had informed the Senate Intelligence Committee that Islamabad was convinced that militant groups are an important part of its strategic arsenal to counter India.[76] Blair asserted that Islamabad maintained relationships with other Taliban-associated groups including the Haqqani Network, the Gul Bahadur group and the Commander Nazir group that conducted operations against the US and ISAF forces in Afghanistan.[77] Though these reports adversely impacted US-Pakistan relations (which became worse in May 2011 when Washington carried out the Abbottabad raid against Osama bin Laden),

Indian perceptions about the West's desire to cut its losses in Afghanistan persisted. Katju, a key partisan (but no more part of the policymaking setup) lamented that 'such is the measure of America's strategic desperation that it has accepted the Taliban's vague assurances and gone to great lengths to accommodate the outfit.'[78]

Why was India averse to the Western forces negotiating with the Afghan Taliban if it had developed a nuanced understanding of the movement? There are two aspects to this puzzle. Firstly, the conference occurred at a critical juncture in India's bureaucratic shuffle. Narayanan, a partisan, retired as NSA in January 2010, while Menon and Chidambaram, both conciliators, took charge of India's security and foreign policy. In February 2010, hardly a month after Narayanan's exit, top US diplomats expressed hope that India's Kashmir policy had 'become consolidated under the more forward leaning Home Minister P.C. Chidambaram after the exit of National Security Advisor M.K. Narayanan, who played a dominant, conservative and often obstructive role in GOI policy on Kashmir'.[79] Under the new setup, the powers of the NSA were diluted with Chidambaram responsible for all issues related to domestic and foreign intelligence.[80] This meant that India was entering a phase of constructive engagement with Pakistan and Kashmiri separatists that would bode well for the region as well as the reconciliation process in Afghanistan. New Delhi had accepted 'reintegration' of mid-level Taliban fighters and commanders in mainstream Afghan social and political life. Menon and Chidambaram made sure that India did not lag behind, and orchestrated a pragmatic pro-reconciliation policy shift soon after the London conference. Aware of its limitation of going alone in Afghanistan, this shift was in keeping with India's multi-stakeholder strategy in Afghanistan.

Secondly, there was a clash between India's desire to be seen as a responsible international player in Afghanistan and its intent to strike a balance between Afghanistan and Pakistan. Menon and Chidambaram's conciliatory shift did not mean that India endorsed the London conference. There was a key conceptual difference between India's approach towards reconciliation from the one advocated by London. New Delhi accepted the reconciliation to occur on Kabul's terms and not those set by the Taliban or Pakistan. For this, it was imperative to frontload preconditions for the talks to commence. One such condition included accepting the 2004 Afghan constitution by the Taliban. Setting precondition was not possible according to British policymakers. Accepting the Afghan constitution could only be an 'outcome' of talks, London argued.[81] Then Foreign Secretary David Miliband and British ambassador to

Kabul, Sherard Cowper-Coles, advocated the latter perspective forcefully among Western policy circles.[82] India's differences with the British (in particular) were so strong that Holbrooke had to clarify to Narayanan days before the conference that Cowper-Coles' thinking on the issue of talking to the Taliban did not reflect US policy.[83] Distinguishing between reconciliation and reintegration, Holbrooke reasserted that the US would not have a 'power sharing' arrangement with the Taliban to foreign secretary Rao on the day of the conference.[84] Indeed, former US secretary of state (2005–09) Condoleezza Rice had sent multiple directives in 2008 to all US diplomats in the region clarifying Washington's differences with the British approach on reconciliation. The US had been clear that the reconciliation process had to be Afghan-led and Afghan-owned.[85] Holbrooke, however, made it clear to both Narayanan and Rao that the US disagreed with Indian assessment that reintegration of Taliban fighters would lead to a Taliban takeover of parts of Afghanistan.

Refusing to accept the outcomes of the London conference (no matter whether the NSA was Narayanan or Menon), India crafted a dual approach to reconcile the evolving international postures on Afghanistan with its desire to balance Afghanistan and Pakistan. Publicly, India began supporting the international community's efforts in finding a political solution to the Afghan conflict, but privately, Indian diplomats began to pressure the US not to leave Afghanistan in a rush or get tricked by Pakistan. On 22 February 2010, MEA joint secretary Yash K. Sinha told his US counterpart to beware of Pakistan's 'game' of enlisting US government support to 'drive India out of Afghanistan'.[86] Sinha warned that Pakistan was treating Indian presence in Afghanistan as a 'zero-sum' game, and was likely to present Washington with 'fabricated' evidence of alleged Indian misbehavior in Afghanistan and in the FATA (a claim that was corroborated by Afghan NSA Rassoul and foreign minister Rangin Dafdar Spanta in a separate meeting with US officials in July 2009).[87] Agreeing that some form of political process was required with the Taliban, Sinha contested that a precipitate US exit would embolden 'fanatics' to think that they had defeated both the USSR and the US—the result of which would be catastrophic for the region.[88]

Three days later, on 25 February 2010, Menon told US senator Claire McCaskill that he may be a 'minority of one', but thought there was more potential for success in Afghanistan than most observers in India think. 'The British were convinced the coalition would lose because they lost three wars there, but others had been able to tame the country', said Menon.[89] The very next day, an unusually 'candid' General V. K. Singh (then in transition from being the Indian army's chief of eastern command to becoming the COAS), met with the US consul-general in Kolkata and offered Indian expertise in counterinsurgency warfare to help the US efforts in Afghanistan (catching the US embassy in New Delhi by surprise).[90] Such unsubtle Indian attempts to shape the contours of the reconciliation process had limited impact.

Menon confirms that India never accepted the idea the way it was presented by Britain. 'The idea that reconciliation per se, as reconciliation qua reconciliation, is good, we never accepted that idea. We have always accepted the idea that reconciliation [should happen] on certain basic terms such as accepting the Afghan constitution. And that they [Taliban] will have to come back to the mainstream, and that the fighting had to stop', he says.[91] There was a chicken-and-egg problem. Were these aspects to be outcomes or preconditions? For a diverse country riddled by multiple separatist insurgencies such as India, whose policymakers were trained to be constitutionalists, this was a precondition. For the UK, which had fought the Irish for decades, these were outcomes of talks. Menon asked British policymakers, how could they reconcile with somebody who is still carrying weapons, waging war against a state, does not accept the constitution or the legality of the government, and disenfranchises half the country [all the women]? What were they reconciling with? 'We are not saying he [Taliban] has to do it all today, but he has to say today that he will do these in an agreed time frame. [If not], then it's not reconciliation, then its capitulation. Or it's just an agreement that you both negotiated some arrangement amongst yourself and you can give it nice names like reconciliation, but it isn't.'[92]

Manmohan Singh, Prasad, Mukhopadhaya, Chidambaram, and Rakesh Sood were in agreement with Menon. 'We did not accept the British approach towards reconciliation, and still don't think that it will work', said Prasad.[93] Citing examples of Tajikistan and Nepal, both countries with a history of violent insurgencies and where he worked as a diplomat, Prasad thought that the British format of reconciliation did more harm than good. 'Unlike the British who come up with detailed timelines, we [India] don't put pressure on other governments. We let the process take its own time and develop to a position where an internal agreement is reached between fighting parties'.[94] India's position on reconciliation came from its own COIN experience where legitimising the Indian constitution has always been a precondition that kept India together. According to Sahgal, the British had more political space to manuevre the coalition approach towards Afghanistan after 2009, and it was London's 'understanding that they can't have an antagonistic Pakistan till the time they pull out'.[95] This was not it, even top MI and R&AW officials viewed British involvement in Afghanistan with suspicion.[96] Most Indian policymakers interviewed for this book attributed British advocacy of reconciliation as (1) a colonial bias in favour of Pakistan, and (2) a quid pro quo with Pakistan, whose help was needed by the UK government to keep a check on radicalisation of the one million plus Pakistani diaspora in the UK (especially the Mirpuri community from Pakistan-administered Kashmir).

Two FCO officials working on Afghanistan and South Asia counter that India misunderstood London's political intent in Afghanistan and the situation on ground. 'The US-Afghanistan SPA had sent out the signal that the West is not going anywhere. That US, UK, and their allies will not cut funding and that the situation will not be as bad as it was after Soviet financial support to Najibullah dried out in 1990s,' they say.[97] The strong Indian perception of Afghanistan slipping into civil war after 2014, they worried, might lead New Delhi to reignite its military links with former UF delegates leading to 'sure shot confrontation' with Pakistan.[98] Underlining this point was H, a senior Western official posted in Kabul until 2009. 'There was a sense in India that the UK is more sympathetic to Pakistan. The London conference was perceived wrongly. That conference was inevitable as the decision was taken way before. India's non-accommodation or lack of acceptance of the idea of reconciliation was more of an embarrassment to its leadership than any sort of diplomatic disaster for India or diplomatic victory for Pakistan. The accusation was that reconciliation was not possible. I think that there was slow-footedness from India's side to adapt' he says.[99] Bifurcating India's Afghanistan diplomacy into two angles which were official and unofficial, H argued that in his unofficial interactions with Indian diplomats he could tell that there were people who supported the idea of taking sides and supporting factions (partisans) in case the security situation deteriorated, or even otherwise.[100]

Such partisan advocacy, however, H concurred, was different from the formal conciliatory policy line. Recognising a shift in India's staunch anti-Taliban policy stance in 2010, H mentioned that some Indian officials understood the rationale of the West's dialogue with the Taliban and also sympathised with it to an extent. However, they remained 'very cautious about being part of the reconciliation process, and simply refused to engage.'[101] Rakesh Sood confirms that India was in disagreement with H and other Western officials working on the reconciliation agenda and deliberately kept away from it. Though heavily clued into the discussions, Rakesh Sood decided not to jump on the Western bandwagon but instead support the Afghan government to set its own terms for talks. 'The British and other Western officials were trying to get ahead of the Afghans themselves in terms of saying ... irrespective of any terms and conditions we should have dialogue', but this what not how India was guiding its Afghanistan policy.[102] He told his British (and some US) counterparts that India was 'quite sure that any lasting reconciliation will be one that is led by the Afghans, negotiated by the Afghans, and takes into account their [Afghan] concerns, rather than deadlines of exit and withdrawal which are dictated by domestic public opinion in Western capitals.'[103] Taking into account Karzai's attitude towards reconciliation and that of other Afghan politicians such as Abdullah, India decided not to get involved with London on Afghanistan. Instead, it would try and undercut any format of reconciliation that would undermine the Afghan government or treat the two sides which were, Kabul and the Taliban, at par.

Competing models of reconciliation

The London conference significantly impacted India's approach towards Afghanistan. On one hand New Delhi criticised the UK and the US for giving Pakistan a major role in the reconciliation. But on the other hand, it nuanced its stance on reconciliation by highlighting the 'red lines' for such talks to move ahead and introducing preconditions that would allow the talks to be Afghan-led and Afghan-owned. Kabul supported India's stance. Concerned that London's attempt at a time-bound withdrawal would allow Pakistan to determine the terms of reconciliation, senior Afghan politicians began pushing India take a hard line on the issue as they were not in a position to do the same.[104] Forced to play his hand in London, Karzai too became disillusioned by London's initiatives. To steer the initiative away from the UK (and Islamabad), Karzai organised the Afghan Peace Jirga in April 2010 with support from India. On 5 September 2010, the Afghan High Peace Council (HPC) was inaugurated, and in November the same year, India was seen working closely with Kabul at the Heart of Asia conference from which it had been excluded on Pakistan's behest earlier.[105] In May 2011, Manmohan Singh paid a visit to Kabul to set the ball rolling on the India-Afghanistan bilateral Strategic Partnership Agreement that was signed in New Delhi five months later in October 2011. Though Burhanuddin Rabbani, the first head of the HPC was assassinated on 20 September 2011, allegedly by militants belonging to the Quetta *shura*, the reconciliation process continued.[106] In November 2011 New Delhi extensively contributed to the Istanbul process with Karzai publicly praising Kabul's deepening friendship with India and Turkey as a model for how Afghanistan sought its future relationships with other regional partners'.[107]

India's diplomatic activism on Afghanistan was accompanied by increasingly worsening relations between the US and Pakistan. 2011 was one of the worst years in the history of US-Pakistan relations. On 27 January, a former US army officer and CIA contractor Raymond A Davis shot two people dead in the middle of a street in Lahore, unleashing a diplomatic storm.[108] Adding insult to injury, on 2 May a team of US Navy SEALS conducted a successful raid in Abbottabad, killing Al Qaeda chief Osama bin Laden. Though the debate on whether Pakistan's security agencies knew of bin Laden's presence on their soil is far from settled, the incident marked a historical low in US-Pakistan bilateral relations. If this was not enough, two NATO Apache helicopters, an AC-130 gunship, and two F-15E Eagle fighter jets entered Pakistan's territory in the Salala sector of the Mohmand agency at 2 AM on 26 November 2011, and destroyed two Pakistani army check-posts 'Volcano' and 'Boulder' killing 28 Pakistani soldiers and wounding 12 others.[109] An enraged Pakistan responded by closing all NATO supplies to Afghanistan via its territory and refused to participate in the December 2011 Bonn Conference. Though Islamabad's position was communicated throughout the conference, the diplomatic boycott undermined the effectiveness of the conference (but was highly appreciated by India).

It was a 'remarkable rebound' says Mukhopadhaya. As Pakistan's relations with the US took a downturn, India, with Karzai's support, successfully muddied the waters on reconciliation as envisioned by London. 'Being a very clever politician and someone capable of thinking very well on his feet and doing things about it, the moment they [London] said reconciliation, he [Karzai] said yes, Loya Jirga. And he took, to some extent, the initiative away from them', says Mukhopadhaya who actively engaged with Karzai and his team on this issue.[110] India continued to create parallel political constituencies in Afghanistan and the region to ensure that the London reconciliation plan failed. Though popular demand for reconciliation had strengthened the conciliators over the partisans, India continued to fight diplomatic battles in Washington and in the Istanbul process to counter the British line. 'We found the French [Chantilly process] to be much more sensible about this than the British, but a lot of Indian diplomats say that Britain has no longer any strategic thinking left outside the EU. They have just given it all up', says Pramit Pal Chaudhuri.[111]

Much like it had done in the pre-1996 phase by using the UN to advocate its stance on Afghanistan, India had adopted an internationalist multi-stakeholder strategy in 2010 to strike a strategic balance between Afghanistan and Pakistan. Though political ground for partisans remained strong in 2010 just like in the 1990s, India's regional partners were not in the mood for muscular intervention in Afghanistan. Neither Iran nor Russia had the appetite to get militarily entangled in Afghanistan. A cooperative regional approach, thus, was the only way forward. Partisan advocacy of marginalising Pakistan or building extra-governmental politico-military alliances in Afghanistan did not fit this paradigm. Resultantly, similar to the 1992 Rao Doctrine, building international consensus for an Afghan-led and Afghan-owned peace process was India's conciliatory response to the evolving geopolitical dynamics. Surely, Pakistan was to be part of this process, but not as a dominating power. As Bhadrakumar, an old-time conciliator said, 'it was an aberration that a civilisation like India with such insight into the shades of political Islam had a mental bloc about the Taliban. No country today questions the wisdom of reconciling with the Taliban.'[112] Not only did New Delhi accept reconciliation, but, by not blocking Pakistan out of regional conferences (like Islamabad was doing with India), New Delhi hoped to assuage Pakistan's concerns about India's attempts to strategically encircle its neighbours.

India's diplomatic rebound, however, was met with a setback when a secret document titled 'Roadmap to Peace 2015' was leaked in December 2012. Drafted sometime in early 2012, the document said that by 2015, the Taliban, the Hizb-e-Islami and other armed groups will have 'given up armed opposition, transformed from military entities into political groups, and are actively participating in the country's political and constitutional processes, including national elections'.[113] For this to happen, however, it was imperative that Pakistan facilitated 'direct contact between the HPC/Government of Afghanistan and identified leaders of the Taliban and other armed opposition groups' through Salahuddin Rabbani, Burhanuddin's son who had taken over as the chief of the HPC.[114] Giving space to almost every armed group including the Haqqani network, the roadmap was received with disdain by India. What worried India more than the document itself was the fact that it had come from Karzai's palace, and had been drafted by none other than Jawed Ludin, Afghanistan's charismatic deputy foreign minister, and a good friend of Mukhopadhaya. The document belied efforts New Delhi had made in the recent months to keep Pakistan from setting the terms of reconciliation. Drafted sometime in early 2012, practical implementation of the roadmap's recommendation required sustained US military presence in Afghanistan after 2015. Even if different factions in Kabul would have accepted the roadmap, continued US military presence was a no-go, especially for the conservative section of Karzai's palace officials. Karzai's chief of staff, Karim Khurram, for instance, bitterly opposed a bilateral security agreement with the US.[115] The roadmap was leaked amidst a series of failed talks between Kabul and the Taliban in Qatar, Islamabad, Chantilly, and Ashgabad.

Shocked, Mukhopadhaya personally informed Karzai, Ludin, and Rabbani that he didn't think they knew what they were doing with the roadmap to peace.[116] He asserted that Kabul's faith in Pakistan was misplaced and Islamabad would surely sabotage the peace process. Arguing that India was averse to what it called the 'Western model' of reconciliation (however straightjacketed and under-appreciative this term is about the complexity of the ongoing dialogue), Mukhopadhaya tried to push for a return to the 'Afghan model' of reconciliation. The basic idea of the 'Afghan Model' was to get the Taliban 'out of the clutches' of the ISI.[117] This was to be done by bringing Taliban figures to a third country (Turkey, Saudi Arabia, or Qatar) where they can talk to the government Afghan-to-Afghan without Pakistan looking over their shoulders. The Taliban's office in Doha, which hosted many members of the Quetta shura, was an exercise to this effect. In this setting the Karzai administration was willing to give them some things they wanted, which were security, immunity, and livelihood. On the other hand, the Western model was understood as having little to do with Afghanistan's interests. It had more to do with Western interests in which 'they' present 'themselves' as the saviours of peace and exit from Afghanistan. In that scenario, if talks broke down at a later stage, then the West can say that they gave the Afghans a good 'present but they [Afghans] squabbled amongst themselves and tore it up,' he argued.[118] India was skeptical about either of the two models succeeding, but favoured the Afghan model over the Western one.

Ludin was surprised by India's pushback on the roadmap. 'Gautam [Mukhopadhaya] argued with me [and] said, "I am sorry but then you're wrong about this thing [roadmap], the whole timeline [of transition of Taliban to a political entity] and elections"'. In February 2013, soon after the Chantilly process and the leaking of the Roadmap, Afghan and Pakistani officials met for the UK-Afghanistan-Pakistan trilateral. Ludin was hoping that his political gamble would pay off and Pakistan would cooperate in intensifying the peace process (at least in stopping the Taliban from disrupting the 2014 elections). As Mukhopadhaya had warned him, nothing came out of it. 'We realised after the London trilateral in early February that the Indian analysis was right' conceded Ludin.[119] Convincing the Taliban not to disrupt the elections, and to become a political party was too ambitious a plan. Especially 'when everything really hinges on Pakistan, then it is not something that is in my control, in India's control, or even in America's control. I think if any country that plays a big role is Pakistan', he argued.[120] But Pakistan was unwilling and/or unable to deliver. By 2013 all hope faded for reconciliation to proceed either on Afghan terms or those set by Pakistan. Washington had decided to wrap up its mission by the end of 2014 and initiated an independent dialogue with the Afghan Taliban, incensing both Kabul and Islamabad.

Persian disconnect

A gateway to Afghanistan and Central Asia for India, political differences between Iran and India on Afghanistan are not emphasised in popular discourse. On the ground, however, these differences have a life and dynamism of their own, and not all of them had to do with the US-Iran rivalry. To begin with, having played a critical role in keeping the partisans thriving in India during the 1990s, Iran's strategic calculus in wake of the US military intervention put Tehran and New Delhi in an awkward situation. India was supporting the US-led NATO intervention and saw it as an opportunity to reengage with Afghanistan, but Iran, after initial tactical convergence with Washington at the 2001 Bonn Conference, grew increasingly averse to the US military presence in its neighbourhood. India's vote against Iran's nuclear programme at the International Atomic Energy Agency (IAEA) in November 2009 created tremendous tension between the two countries. Moreover, New Delhi's deepening ties with Israel and Saudi Arabia underlined Iran's marginalisation in the Indian strategic calculus (this began changing after the US-Iran nuclear deal, and the signing of the deal that gave India rights to develop the Chabahar port). Though diplomatic attempts were made to bridge this gap given India's trade and energy links with Iran, political differences persisted. Within Afghanistan, for instance, Iranian intelligence agencies began developing links with and financially supporting factions of the Afghan Taliban and other anti-US factions regardless of their Sunni orientation.[121] It was a big loss for India's partisans who needed Iran's logistical and political support to see their anti-Taliban and anti-Pakistan advocacy bear fruit. A closer examination of Iran's approach towards Afghanistan shows that it was very similar to that of Pakistan, but focused more in west Afghanistan as opposed to Pakistan's dominance in the south and east. Undermining Iran's popular image as a constructive partner of India in Afghanistan, many Afghans found Tehran's foreign policy highly interventionist.[122]

Like Pakistan, Iran also cultivated its own proxy groups to influence Afghan politics. Former governor of Herat, Daud Saba, considers this strategy 'crazy' and wanted Iran to treat Afghanistan as an independent country. 'We are land-locked country [and] we have certain rights recognised by the international community i.e. [access to] ports [and] transit routes. And what we have seen in the past years [is that] there were breaches of these international laws by both our neighbours—Pakistan and Iran' says Saba.[123] True, the fact that India and Iran cooperated on many issues in Afghanistan cannot be underestimated. Indian investment in Iran's Chahbahar Port, building of the Zaranj-Delaram highway that connects Iran and Afghanistan, and use of Iranian territory to supply goods to Afghanistan impart a critical strategic dimension to the India-Iran-Afghanistan trilateral relationship. Beneath this larger strategic convergence, however, there were divergences on the ground. For instance, the Salma Dam, built by Indian companies and managed by the Water and Power Consultancy Services Ltd. (WAPCOS), was a source of bitter rivalry between Kabul and Tehran, and often dragged India into the dispute.

Being the lower riparian on the Hari Rud River on which the dam is built, Iran stands to lose from its construction. Unlike the Chahbahar port that would make Afghanistan dependent on Iran, the dam would give Kabul power over east Iran's water supplies, which is an unacceptable proposition for Tehran (the Hari Rud goes on to Turkmenistan after crossing Iran). Not without reason. The two countries have a history of mutual mistrust over water sharing. The question of sharing Helmand River's water during the drought hit year of 1971, animated diplomatic duels and political mud-slinging between Tehran and Kabul.[124] In 1998 when Iran threatened to attack Afghanistan in retaliation for the killing of Iranian diplomats in Mazar-e-Sharif, the Taliban diverted the Helmand's flow southwards into the Gowd-e-Zerrah depression, drying up Iran's Hamun-e-Helmand Lake and nearly destroying Sistan-Baluchistan's farming, flora, fauna, and wildlife. More recently, Afghan politicians have often threatened cutting water supplies to Iran (and Pakistan) in response to the latters' interventionism. In 2009, for instance, Afghan parliamentarian Najibullah Kabuli vehemently protested against Tehran's interference in the completion of the dam and argued that 'we [Afghans] want to stop water flowing into Iran and Pakistan. Every Iranian is benefitting from the water but not the Afghans who have the right to it.'[125] Even for Ismael Khan, the powerful warlord-cum-politician from Herat, the possibility of storing water (an act that will give Afghanistan leverage over the supply of this water to Iran) is of paramount importance.[126] Without fail, when Iran refused India permission to ferry dynamites to the Chest-e-Sharif district where the dam was to be built (in order to blow up the nearby mountains to build the dam), Khan arranged for the explosives from a Central Asian country.[127]

Having agreed to build the dam at Karzai's request, India was caught in the bilateral rivalry. On 28 February 2005, then Iranian foreign minister Kamal Kharazi officially complained to Manmohan Singh about India's decision to build the dam, only to be told to discuss the matter with Kabul rather than drag India into it.[128] Indeed, in April 2007, Tehran pressured visiting Afghan foreign minister Rangin Dafdar Spanta to reach an acceptable water sharing agreement, only to be deflected by the latter.[129] While nothing changed for the coming years, reports of Iranian attempts to sabotage the project occasionally hit the local Herati newswires. Then, in 2011, Khare came across highly specific intelligence inputs that members of Iran's Islamic Revolutionary Guard Corps (IRGC) were determined to destroy the dam using proxy forces.[130] He refused to believe that Tehran would give such a direction against a project built by India. But soon afterwards, in 2012, Iran's ambassador to Afghanistan undertook a protest march to the Indian embassy in Kabul demanding a halt in construction of the dam.[131] On the ground, allegedly, Iran had begun to manipulate local powerbrokers in Herat to slow down, if not sabotage, the construction of the dam. In October of same year, for instance, the battalion commander of the Herat Police testified that local anti-government commander Mullah Mustafa (of the nearby Ghor province who operated in Chest-e-Sharif), who had strong support from Ismael Khan, was being financed by Iran to oppose the construction of the dam.[132]

A double game was on. On the one hand, Mullah Mustafa and other local Herati power brokers wanted the dam to be built, but on the other hand, they threatened peaceful construction as a stick to negotiate power and patronage with Herat. Not surprisingly, Indian consular officials got along well with Mullah Mustafa, but were equally wary of him (were he to decide on sabotaging the construction of the dam). On one occasion, in fact, Mullah Mustafa had secured the release of a kidnapped Indian worker from a local Taliban unit within two days.[133] But, in order to maintain his power in Chest-e-Sharif, he pushed Ahmad Yusuf Nuristani, the then governor of Heart, in March 2009 to change the district governor of Chest-e-Sharif, or else he would not allow peaceful construction of the dam.[134] That Ismael Khan supported Mullah Mustafa complicated things further. Khan did not always get along well with Nuristani, and neither with his successor Daud Saba. But more than Saba and

Nuristani, it was Maulvi Khodaidad, a powerful cleric of the Herati *ulema* who had Karzai's support from Kabul, who opposed Khan. Khodaidad had his own favoured strongmen, who took on Mullah Mustafa's men on the ground, and helped keeping Khan politically marginal in Herat.

Open to the continuation of the NATO forces in Afghanistan for years to come, Khodaidad criticised Khan for making Herat unstable. 'During the Jihad he [Ismael Khan] fought against Russia. Because of that people respected him. But after that, when he was governor of Herat, all things were destroyed, and he started bothering people' complains Khodaidad.[135] The rivalry is ongoing and tested India's diplomatic skills to a considerable extent. Mandated to ensure the timely and peaceful construction of the dam and other Indian aid projects in West Afghanistan, managing these local rivalries was part of the consul-general's job (in addition to keeping an eye on the Pakistani consulate nearby). And the success of it was visible in India's close relationship with both Khodaidad and Khan. Offering regular visas to Khodaidad for annual medical trips to New Delhi was part of this diplomacy that convinced the cleric that India could genuinely bring peace to Afghanistan as both the government and the insurgents liked Indians.[136]

But at the same time, threats against Indians working at the dam site, and to the dam itself, despite India's skillful diplomacy, were real (in 2009 a senior WAPCOS official was nearly kidnapped on the road to Salma Dam).[137] In light of these politics, the charge against Mustafa of trying to destroy the dam in 2012 had to be taken seriously. In order to settle the situation, Mukhopadhaya visited the project site with Ludin in November 2012. Instead of halting work on the dam, India disbursed more funds for its timely completion. When asked if he was concerned about Iranian meddling in the project by a local Afghan journalist, Mukhopadhaya diplomatically replied that there was more than one reason for the delay in the completion of the project, not all of which were security related. Throwing the mantle on the Afghan government he added that 'the issue of security must be managed by the Afghan government because we cannot control it'.[138] In March 2013, Afghan security forces captured about 1,300 kg of high-grade explosives en-route to the dam.[139] Allegedly, the Quetta *shura* had given orders to blow the dam, and the explosives had come from Iran.[140]

The then serving governor of Herat, Saba confirmed that Iran was bent on destroying the dam.[141] Not just the Salma Dam, Iran was also opposed to the Badkhshabad hydroelectric facility in the Farah province, which Indian engineers surveyed in 2008.[142] When asked why, he wryly (though unconvincingly) replied, 'you should ask the Iranians why they do this'.[143] To underplay differences Mukhopadhaya ruled out that India was siding with Kabul in its dispute with Iran.[144] However, according to senior FICCI official deeply involved in coordinating India's trade and development activities in Afghanistan, New Delhi's differences with Iran on the Salma Dam 'is a very controversial political topic' that no one talks much about.[145] Menon agrees that the Salma dam was a project with which Iran had a problem, but these differences were sorted out at a working level and never allowed to blow out of proportion. Despite Afghan accusations of the IRGC funding the anti-government elements to destroy the dam, Menon, just like Khare, was skeptical about it. There were a host of loose militants and criminals in that part of Afghanistan making it difficult to point a finger on any one entity regarding the discovery of explosives. In fact, according to Menon, *Jundullah*, a Sunni militant organisation based out of Balochistan in Pakistan but operating on both sides of the Pakistan-Iran border might have been behind the act. It was a hint that instead of Iran doing such activities against Indian projects, it is possible that the origin of the plot lay in Pakistan, and the intent of the plan was to drive a wedge between India and Iran by bombing the dam. Tehran had no problems with other Indian projects in Afghanistan and was supportive of India's engagement in the country by and large.[146] Though India-Iran relations within Afghanistan are much deeper and complex than a hydro-project (and the Salma dam is not a big enough issue to spark bilateral discord), it does indicate that India and Iran's vision of an Afghanistan that is stable, sovereign, and capable, may not always match.[147]

The impact of these differences was visible. By 2006, Indian diplomats had started worrying that a breakdown in bilateral relations with Iran (over the nuclear issue) may jeopardise India's access to Afghanistan and Central Asia.[148] Tehran already used India's dependence for connectivity to Afghanistan and Central Asia as a diplomatic pressure point by making it logistically difficult for Indian convoys to cross into Afghanistan.[149] Such irritants often pushed Indian diplomats to complain to US diplomats about Iran's complicated posture on Afghanistan, and how the US-Iran rivalry was limiting India-Iran collaboration (like in the 1990s) 'to ensure that the Taliban do not return to power'.[150] Tehran and New Delhi were at odds even on the question of US military presence in Afghanistan after 2014 (until the 2015 Iran-US nuclear deal resolved such issues). Iran wanted the US to leave, whereas India wanted to delay the withdrawal. In order to maintain influence on Afghan affairs, Iran not only supported Taliban factions but also allegedly funneled substantial funds into Islamic religious and educational institutions.[151] The Khatam-al Nabyeen Islamic University in Kabul, for instance, has the same curriculum as Iranian madrassas.[152] Staff members of the Academy of Sciences of Afghanistan have been accused of being Iranian spies. Iran's payment to the Taliban militants for killing Americans or destroy US military vehicles has been estimated between US$ 1,000 and US$ 6,000. Much like Islamabad, Tehran ensured that the cost of the US military presence in Afghanistan remained high.[153] Often termed as a marriage of convenience, Iran-Taliban links have not worked in India's favour.[154] India could not, however, 'dump Iran' as put by a senior Indian journalist and retired military personnel in private conversations with Western diplomats.[155] Iran's tactical alliance with the Afghan Taliban raised the question: if born-rivals like Shia Iran and Sunni Afghan Taliban can engage and reach an understanding, then why can India not do the same?

Bleeding heart of Asia

The uncertainty of the Afghan situation after 2010 was reflected in the complex web of regional and international conferences: Berlin (2004), London (2006), Rome (2007), Paris (2008), Moscow and The Hague (2009), and London (2010), the 'Heart of Asia' or Istanbul Process (2011), Bonn Conference (2011), UK-Afghanistan-Pakistan trilateral (2012), and the US-India-Afghanistan trilateral (2012). In India, the MEA and the Confederation of Indian Industries (CII) jointly hosted the Regional Economic Cooperation Conference on Afghanistan (RECCA) and the Delhi Investment Summit in June 2012. The only India-Pakistan-Afghanistan trilateral was the Track-II arranged by the Delhi Policy Group.[156] Disconnected from the political and security dynamics on the ground, most such conferences were a series of failed promises. Translating into a collective decline of hope around the prospects for peace and stability in Afghanistan, persistent uncertainty pushed Afghanistan's neighbours into hedging their bets.

Unlike the late-1990s when Russia, Iran, and India coalesced into a strategic embrace against the Taliban, regional political equations were very different this time around. Not just Iran, even Moscow was no longer militantly opposed to the Taliban by 2014. Though Moscow shared India's concerns on reconciliation in 2010, as the NATO-Russia rivalry focused on Ukraine and Syria, the question of militarily containing the Afghan Taliban lost saliency in Russia.[157] The rise of ISIS in Afghanistan gave the Taliban and Russia a platform for tactical collaboration in fighting against a common enemy.[158] Building and sustaining such operational linkages with the Taliban required Moscow to develop ties with Pakistan. Not surprisingly, the two countries signed a landmark defence deal in August 2015 that allowed the sale of four Mi-35 'Hind-E' attack helicopters.[159] Russia's opening-up to Pakistan came in context of India's pro-US tilt. Not worried about militancy in Chechnya, Moscow's threat perception from Afghanistan in 2015 was different from that in 1996. Though India's lack of criticism during Russia 2014 annexation of Crimea helped alleviating differences, Russia had little appetite to form a 1990s-style similar Russia-Iran-India axis.[160]

If Russia and Iran's evolving postures gave the conciliators a fillip, China's political participation in Afghanistan by 2015 gave them a boost. China had been silently engaging with both Russia and India within the Russia-India-China (RIC) trilateral to enhance a multipolar world. In October 2007, foreign ministers of the three regional powers met in Harbin, China, and reached an agreement that they work together to counter the rise of the Taliban in Afghanistan (among other issues). While the Russians saw the meeting as 'pivotal',[161] the Chinese viewed it as a vehicle to emphasise multilateral diplomacy rather than getting substantive results.[162] To this effect, in 2006, Beijing had floated the idea of launching a China-US-India trilateral in order to discuss issues of 'mutual concerns' such as 'terrorism', 'separatism', and 'religious extremism'.[163] But India (under Narayanan) didn't trust China on Afghanistan-Pakistan, and refused to engage.[164] Though having gained rights over the strategic Aynak copper mine in Afghanistan's Logar province, China was not interested in enhancing its political and security profile in the country.[165] But soon after, Beijing began to exert its influence on Pakistan as Afghanistan's security situation worsened (raising fears of unrest in China's Uighur-dominated Xinjiang province).[165] China had pronounced the 'one belt, one road' development strategy that entailed connecting Europe and China via the Middle East and Central Asia—and stability in Afghanistan was central for the strategy to succeed.[167] Within a couple of years, in May 2015, China facilitated secret talks between the Taliban and the Afghan government in the city of Urumqi (with Pakistan's officials as observers).[168] Interestingly, the spy agencies of Afghanistan and Pakistan, enemies for decades, signed a Memorandum of Understanding (MoU) on intelligence sharing during these talks, sending a shock wave within and outside Afghanistan. In July of the same year, another round of talks took place in Murree (in Pakistan),[169] followed by the Doha Dialogue in January 2016, and creation of the quadrilateral coordination group (QCG) wherein the US, China, Pakistan, and

Afghanistan engaged in dialogue to resolve bilateral differences between Afghanistan and Pakistan.[170]

Given India's concerns about China's growing regional influence, Beijing's entry into Afghan politics should have raised suspicions in India. The truth was far from it. China's entry had been made easy by the same vehicle of multilateral diplomacy that had taken shape in Harbin. India sought another RIC meeting in February 2013 to discuss the situation in Afghanistan. The aim was to isolate Pakistan and reduce its strategic value in Afghanistan—that received positive reception from Iran as well. Common ground between India, Russia, China and Iran coupled with a willing Washington meant that Pakistan's value would get confined to becoming a tactical catalyst in bringing the Taliban to the talking table. In this context, India began to view China's separate trilateral with Russia and Pakistan as a way to coerce or persuade Islamabad into 'convincing' the Taliban to engage in negotiations. Tight-lipped on the exact nature of India's collaboration with China on Afghanistan, Menon says: 'I don't think people talk about that [India-China cooperation in Afghanistan] ... because it goes on ... it is quiet ... and to be effective, it has to be quiet'.[171] Though such RIC coordination did not translate into worthy strategic outcomes, it helped ensuring that New Delhi, Beijing, and Moscow did not sleepwalk into a regional quagmire of their own in Afghanistan.

Conclusion

India's policy approach towards Afghanistan is determined as much by its desire to strike a strategic balance between Kabul and Islamabad as it is by evolving international postures and shifting regional alignments. This was visible in its careful handling of the post-2010 phase of the Afghan war wherein the coalition countries were intent on reconciling with the Taliban in a way that directly threatened India's core policy aim of striking a balance between Afghanistan and Pakistan. India's decision to keep a low security profile in the light of Western and (at times) Pakistan's sensitivities meant that its policy was being shaped by keeping the comfort levels of international actors on the ground. Despite high decibel partisan advocacy in the wake of NATO withdrawal, the conciliators began to chart India's policy course and succeeded in sustaining a general international consensus on Afghanistan. Both partisans and conciliators were concerned that a full withdrawal of the US forces and drying up of funds would lead to a political meltdown in Kabul. But to avoid such an eventuality, all Indian officials pushed Washington not to walk out on Afghanistan.

On 15 October 2015 Obama reversed his decision to withdraw from Afghanistan.[172] The decision came in light of failed talks between Pakistan and Afghanistan and the steadily deteriorating security scenario. In August 2015, despite having decided to move ahead with the reconciliation process, news broke that the Taliban leader Mullah Omar was dead. He had been dead since April 2013.[173] The new leader, Mullah Akhtar Mansour, had been passing orders in the name of Omar ever since. To assert his authority and overcome internal splits in the light of Omar's death, Mansour needed to deliver results on the ground. In late September 2015, the Taliban did just that. After months of heavy fighting around the city, Kunduz fell to a Taliban assault in early October 2015. It took the Afghan and US forces nearly two weeks to jointly recapture Kunduz.[174] Two months later, in December, the Taliban attacked the fortified Kandahar airfield and ended up killing twenty-two Afghan soldiers.[175] Though failing militarily, the Kandahar airfield attack succeeded in splitting the Afghan government. NDS chief Rahmatullah Nabil put in his resignation and openly criticised the government's resistance to dialogue.[176] A Karzai confidante, Nabil's differences with Ghani and Atmar over reconciliation with Pakistan had become irreparable. Further complicating the situation was the rise of a splinter group that pledged support to Daesh/ISIS in Syria and Iraq, but was made of second-rung disgruntled and/or ambitious Taliban commanders.[177] Though concerned about Afghanistan's deteriorating security situation and Ghani's proactive outreach to Islamabad, India warmed up to the new Afghan government as well as the US decision to reverse the withdrawal.

There was a key difference in how India dealt with the NATO drawdown and the Soviet withdrawal. Instead of holding on to Afghan leaders such as Karzai (like it did with Najibullah), India used its increased diplomatic weight to proactively shape the situation in a way that a general post-2001 consensus would be preserved against the Taliban and Pakistan.[178] Adjusting to Russia and Iran's growing convergences with both the Taliban and Pakistan was acceptable in these changing circumstances. But the masterstroke was Menon's decision to involve China and use Beijing's leverage over Islamabad and Rawalpindi to convince or coerce the Taliban to the talking table (Narayanan had little engagement with China on Afghanistan and Pakistan during his tenure as NSA). India's determination was also visible in its support to Karzai at a time when the world was criticising him for heading a corrupt government, taking an unnecessarily hardline against Pakistan, and becoming an obstacle to peace. Knowing well that Kabul was not in a position to set the terms of talks given its capacities limitations relative to Pakistan, New Delhi accepted the challenge to build diplomatic pressures that would push Washington and other international actors to exercise their capacities on the ground in a way that strengthened Kabul's hand at the negotiation table. Combined with a steadily worsening security situation and rise of the Islamic State of Iraq and the Levant (ISIS), also known as *Wilayat Khorasan*, the idea of reconciliation between Afghanistan and Pakistan as 'equals' and between Kabul and the Afghan Taliban came to be readily accepted by the West as well as India and other regional powers. The conciliators' active chaperoning of India's Afghanistan policy after 2010 seemed to have been successful.

EPILOGUE

A BLESSING

The taboo was broken. After refusing to talk about Afghanistan for years, Pakistan invited India's external affairs minister, Sushma Swaraj, to deliberate upon Afghanistan at the 'Heart of Asia' conference in Islamabad on 8 December 2015.[1] Though unexpected, the invitation was politically astute. The two South Asian rivals had not been talking for over a year at India's insistence.[2] While their diplomats had been engaging regularly throughout the politically frosty year of 2015, there was no ministerial level dialogue. India wanted to set the terms of talks on Kashmir, and wanted Kabul to push for the same on reconciliation with the Taliban. Displeased by Afghan president Ashraf Ghani's outreach to Pakistan and temporary distancing from India, Swaraj had allegedly snubbed Afghanistan at the 6th RECCA meet held in Kabul in September 2015.[3] In this scenario, if India refused to take up Islamabad's offer, it would come across as being hardline under a Hindu nationalist government, and give Pakistan the moral high ground as a conciliator. But if it accepted the offer, then doors for talks on other potent bilateral disputes such as Kashmir would open up. It was a win-win situation for Pakistan. Contrary to expectations, Swaraj accepted the invitation. There had been a surprise breakthrough in Bangkok where India and Pakistan's national security advisors met shortly after their PMs spoke in Paris in early December 2015.[4] The backchannel paved the way for a comprehensive bilateral dialogue that Swaraj formally announced in Islamabad along with a beaming Sartaj Aziz, her Pakistani counterpart.[5]

Afghanistan was central to this (temporary) thaw in India-Pakistan ties—both as a curse and a potential blessing. It had been a curse because of the powerful but unimaginative trope that Afghanistan is a proxy battlefield. Pakistan's support to the Taliban in the 1990s, and India's counter-balancing strategy of arming the anti-Taliban United Front, was perhaps the peak of such shadow boxing. But it had also been a potential blessing because resolving differences on Afghanistan required little political capital from both sides, and cleared the way for communicating about other ostensibly intractable issues such as Kashmir, Balochistan, and cross-border terrorism. Unending conflict in Afghanistan only fed into the existing mistrust between the two countries. Pakistan's media and retired civilian and military officials, for instance, continued to allege that India and Afghanistan's intelligence agencies covertly support TTP and Baloch insurgents.[6] Though no corroborative evidence was offered in support of such claims, Islamabad's allegations cannot be discarded in the light of popular Indian (and Afghan) rhetoric of targeting Pakistan. Indian intelligence officials, for instance, admitted in off-the-record conversations that both TTP and Baloch elements seek covert military and financial support from India and have reached out to Indian officers posted in Afghanistan.[7] India may not be the cause of Pakistan's troubles in Afghanistan, but its presence in Afghanistan did exacerbate Pakistan's political anxieties. India, in contrast, offers evidence (even if limited) of Pakistan's complicity in a series of attacks on Indian nationals, consulates, and embassy in Afghanistan via the Haqqani network, select Afghan Taliban factions, and the LeT.

But why talk about Afghanistan in December 2015 after not engaging in dialogue for over a year? Arguably, Pakistan's unflinching support to the Afghan Taliban made Islamabad's goodwill indispensable to ensure stability, if not peace, in Afghanistan, and that too on terms that it deemed favourable. Whether it could deliver the Afghan Taliban to the negotiating table both timely and effectively is a separate, but not unrelated, matter. India on the other hand, despite its heavy economic and political involvement, remained marginal, if not inconsequential, in influencing Afghan politics, making it a seemingly unimportant player. Yet, instead of being a strategic genius, Pakistan had been caught in a dangerous vortex of fire fighting that it could not sustain. Islamabad, for instance, may not be in a position to curb the various militant proxies that it nurtured over the years even if it wants to, given the expected blowback. But it also could not just continue nurturing these groups given the proactive regional pushback. The recent failures of the Afghan Taliban to credibly capture Kunduz or Helmand (or to gain control of the Kandahar airfield), and that of the LeT to substantially infiltrate into India-administered Kashmir, then, only increased Pakistan's operational costs of cultivating and sustaining these so-called strategic assets. In such a scenario, where the cost of supporting proxies seemed higher than the accruing benefits, talking to India on traditional bilateral disputes, but also on Afghanistan, was an attractive option. Pakistan's treatment of Afghanistan as a taboo topic (with India) only toughened New Delhi's resolve to maintain its presence in Kabul and contain Pakistan's influence.

The timing suited India as well. Already under pressure from the US to open talks with Pakistan, New Delhi employed a variety of coercive methods ranging from no talks and heavy firing along the border to, allegedly, increasing covert funding and support to various anti-government elements in Karachi, Balochistan (via Afghanistan), and Pakistan-administered Kashmir (big protests were held in Muzzafarabad, Gilgit and Kotli seeking 'freedom' from Pakistan), to pressurise Islamabad.[8] Responding to Islamabad's overtures for talks was imperative to reap the benefits of its proactive Pakistan policy on the negotiation table. Indian PM Narendra Modi's strong mandate and the Pakistan military's consolidation of power after the 16 December 2014, Army Public School massacre (that resulted in the death of 141 people of whom 132 were children) made it viable for such talks to succeed.[9] Ghani's steadfast engagement with Pakistan also helped India's quest for resolving differences with Islamabad by creating a conciliatory environment across the region, instead of being stuck in a dangerous cold-peace/hot-war dynamic that only promised instability and insecurity. Not surprisingly, within a week of the official launch of the comprehensive bilateral dialogue, the Turkmenistan-Afghanistan-Pakistan-India (TAPI) pipeline was inaugurated.[10] Such were the hopes that Modi, in his address to the Afghan parliament two weeks later said: 'I hope that Pakistan will become a bridge between South Asia and Afghanistan and beyond'.[11] Indian policymakers also reluctantly welcomed the Quadrilateral Coordination Group (QCG) wherein the US and China facilitated a dialogue between Afghanistan and Pakistan, and pushed Islamabad to bring the Afghan Taliban to the talking table.[12] It was a marked departure from India's unkind reaction to the six plus two process in the 1990s or the London conference in 2010. New Delhi was not feeling left out from Afghanistan anymore.

The bonhomie was short-lived. On 2 January 2016, four militants belonging to the United Jihad Council, a militant organisation based out of Pakistan-administered Kashmir (and allegedly supported by the Pakistani intelligence services), attacked the Pathankot Air Force Station, part of the western air command of the Indian Air Force, killing seven Indian security personnel, one civilian, and the four attackers.[13] Resulting in national outcry, and severe criticism of the government in mishandling the defence of the air base, the attack derailed the India-Pakistan thaw. Complicating the situation further, a former Indian naval officer, Kulbhushan Jadhav, was caught, allegedly, entering Pakistan via Iran. He gave a video recorded confession, parts of which were made publicly available by Pakistan, and declared that he was commissioned to the R&AW from the navy in 2003 and had opened a small business in Chabahar, Iran, from where he undertook subversive activities in Karachi and Balochistan.[14] Pakistan cried foul, for it had finally produced evidence of Indian covert involvement in attacks on its soil. India firmly rejected the video as a doctored enterprise, and rejected that Jadhav was a spy (though they accepted that he was an Indian naval officer and demanded consular access to him which was denied by Pakistan).[15] Whether Jadhav is indeed a spy who undertook subversive activities in Pakistan is yet to be established, but the incident raised many questions about the R&AW's operations in Pakistan, and threatened to compromise India's moral high ground vis-à-vis Pakistan.

More worryingly for India, failed deliberations over the Pathankot attack and the Kulbhushan Jadhav case, were accompanied by popular unrest in Kashmir. On 8 July 2016, the Indian army had killed a young Kashmiri militant belonging to the Hizbul Mujahideen (and social media icon) Burhan Wani in an operation.[16] The Kashmir valley erupted in protests, leading to more police firing, and even more deaths and injuries. More than fifty protestors, and two policemen were killed, whereas pellets and rubber bullets wounded nearly 674 persons in a single day, many of whom (mostly teenagers) were blinded by the pellets.[17] Instead of initiating a serious political dialogue, India began to blame Pakistan, a peripheral actor in the protests, for causing the unrest in the first place. In response, on 15 August 2016, the seventieth independence day of India, Modi articulated a shift in India's approach towards Pakistan from the ramparts of the historic Red Fort as such: 'I want to express my gratitude to the people of Balochistan, Gilgit, and Pakistan-occupied Kashmir, for the way they wholeheartedly thanked me, the way they expressed gratitude to me ... people of a distant land I haven't even seen ... when they thank the Indian prime minister, it's an honour for the 125 crore people of the country'.[18]

What for, and how, the people of these regions had thanked Modi was left unsaid. The implicit message was that India was capable of, and perhaps already exercising (both via Afghanistan and otherwise), covert intervention in Pakistan's internal troubles. The mention of Pakistan's domestic fault-lines at the Independence Day celebrations in response to unrest in Kashmir, among other issues, was unprecedented. Whether this was empty rhetoric, as in the 1960s when Indian parliamentarians sought to support the Pashtun and Baloch insurgencies in the wake of the 1965 war, or a true shift in India's security practices like the early 1970s when Indira Gandhi proactively supported the Baloch insurgency, is yet to be seen. But if one is to go by optics, India was now intent on exploiting Pakistan's fear of strategic encirclement and India's role in exerting diplomatic pressure on Pakistan's human rights violations in Balochistan and Gilgit-Baltistan. That this statement came at a time of high toxicity in Afghanistan-Pakistan relations made it even more potent.

Parallel to worsening India-Pakistan relations, Kabul's relations with Islamabad also took a nosedive after December 2015. Afghan outreach had been dependent on Pakistan's willingness and capacity to bring different Afghan Taliban factions to the table, not all of which were interested in talking. The gambit failed. Instead of expecting to meet the Taliban at the negotiating table, on 10 August 2015, a massive bomb blast rocked Kabul, killing scores of people.[19] This blast was one of the many that had come to wreak havoc in Afghanistan, but its intensity shocked most Afghans. The attack underlined that if Pakistan was expecting to convert Mullah Omar's death into an opportunity to consolidate its control over the Afghan Taliban and then get them to talk to Kabul, it was failing miserably. Soon after becoming the chief, Mansour made a statement seeking a continuation of armed attacks in Afghanistan.[20] The intensity of the blast and the high number of casualties broke the fragile but developing Afghanistan-Pakistan bilateral relationship. In a public address, Ghani caustically told his eastern neighbour:

> In the middle of the night, at 1:30 a.m., doomsday descended upon our people. It wasn't an earthquake, it wasn't a storm, it was human hand ... I ask the people and the government of Pakistan: If a massacre such as the one that occurred in Shah Shaheed had happened in Islamabad and the perpetrators had sanctuaries in Afghanistan, had offices and training centers in our major cities, how would you react?[21]

Was there an implicit threat in Ghani's statement? The answer to this question will become clearer in the coming months or years. Having (strategically and patiently) waited for Ghani's outreach towards Pakistan to fail, New Delhi proactively stepped in. To underline support for Afghanistan, Modi launched the much-awaited and long-delayed Salma Dam in June 2016 (called the India-Afghanistan Friendship Dam). In a powerful speech marking the timelessness of India-Afghanistan relations, Modi made his intent about Pakistan, without naming the country, amply clear. 'It was a war not of Afghan making, but it was one that stole the future of an entire generation of Afghans ... India will not forget you or turn away ... your friendship is our honour, your dreams our duty'.[22] Conciliation had not worked to secure India's security interests in Afghanistan, or to strike a balance between Afghanistan and Pakistan. The conditions for a partisan comeback were ripe, and Modi, with support from his advisors, had done just that by raking up human rights violations in Balochistan and Pakistan-administered Kashmir.

India's approach towards Afghanistan is not simply about fighting proxy wars with Pakistan. Yes, India finds it expedient to politically harass Pakistan via Afghanistan (and vice versa), but this is not the long-term goal. The aim is to ensure balance between its two neighbours wherein neither of them has an overbearing influence on the domestic polity of the other. Despite its close relations with Daoud Khan in the 1970s, for instance, India was wary of his forward policy on Pashtunistan and refused him support for fear of dividing Pakistan. Though New Delhi did not substantially criticise the Soviet intervention, it looked upon the event with extreme disdain. The ensuing civil war in Afghanistan fundamentally altered the structural balance in Pakistan's favour. Afghanistan today is arguably among the weakest states in the world constituting a highly divided society susceptible to external interference. This makes India nervous that Afghan territory may be used for training militants to foment violence in Kashmir (and elsewhere), often leading policymakers in New Delhi to incorrectly blame Afghan groups for supporting anti-India militancy. It is in this context that India advocates a strong, stable, inclusive, and sovereign Afghanistan that is not dependent on Pakistan for its economic and political survival. Addressing, if not correcting, this structural imbalance between Afghanistan and Pakistan lies at the heart of India's current policy approach towards Kabul.

As this book shows, India's foreign policy is a dynamic process of constant interaction between the agent and the structure. The evolving global order and India's material and economic capacities set the structural confines within which foreign policy options are debated. Within these structural limits, Indian policymakers have the agency to choose between a conformist or revisionist policy approach. On issues such as nuclear power and climate change, India adopted a revisionist course that ended up changing the global nuclear order and climate change debates. Within South Asia, India prefers status quo in order to preserve its dominance (to be challenged by Pakistan). Though critical in influencing India's foreign policy, such structural factors do not adequately explain policy change. To understand why India choses a particular policy path in Afghanistan or other areas, there is a need to highlight the interplay between India's political objectives and the various policy beliefs held by different Indian policymakers. For example, India's rising economic and political power does not explain the numerous shifts in India's Afghanistan policy between 1979 and 2015.

Theoretical constructs such as the Advocacy Coalition Framework (ACF) help teasing out the complexity of India's foreign policy debates. It helps explaining the interplay between policy beliefs held by different Indian policymakers across bureaucratic and political lines, and changing regional and global geopolitical dynamics. All factions standing at odds with Pakistan and/or who are not under the influence of, or dependent upon, Islamabad, should be India's natural partners according to the partisans. Conciliators on the other hand argue that India should focus on whoever comes to power in Kabul without fear or favour. Building goodwill among the people of Afghanistan and politically engaging with every entity, including the Afghan Taliban and its various factions, is the way forward. Highly pragmatic, conciliators believe that non-engagement with factions dependent on Pakistan is not a viable option for India. While the final decision of whom Kabul wants to reconcile with is a decision that only Afghans can take, conciliators are not opposed like the partisans are if Kabul talks with groups New Delhi views as vehemently anti-India. Such a conciliatory approach was visible when New Delhi accepted Karzai's outreach to hardline Taliban elements in the final years of his presidency. The commonalities between the partisans and the conciliators is that both view Pakistan as a source of instability in Afghanistan, neither wants Afghanistan to be strategically dependent on Islamabad, and both reject a political process where Kabul does not influence the terms of talks (at least to an extent).

Apart from delineating policy advocacies, the ACF also helped assessing how and why partisans and conciliators influenced India's Afghanistan policy at different points in time. Their debate was driven by three core and intertwined factors such as (a) striking a balance between Afghanistan and Pakistan, (b) international political posture towards Afghanistan, and (c) domestic Afghan politics. How these sources of policy change interact with each other determined whether the conciliators or the partisans influenced India's Afghanistan policy. In December 1979 India's strategic dependence on the Soviet Union undermined genuine neutrality, whereas Najibullah's fall in April 1992, which occurred in light of India's economic woes and the disintegration of the Soviet Union, pushed the conciliators to the fore. By 1996, regional actors such as Iran and Russia had reemerged as credible partners to counter the rise of the Taliban that had Pakistan, Saudi Arabia, and the UAE's support. The US-led

NATO intervention in 2001 allowed India to continue with its partisan approach. However, Afghanistan's changing domestic politics paved the way for conciliators to orchestrate tactical shifts in India's approach towards reconciliation after 2010. Equipped with better knowledge and economic resources, India underwent steady policy learning about the Afghan Taliban and the myriad interests and ideas the insurgent movement embodied.

This policy learning allowed the conciliators to chart a nuanced policy approach until early 2016 allowing India to secure its interests in Afghanistan, ensuring a balance between Afghanistan and Pakistan, and preventing New Delhi from getting isolated in Afghanistan as it had been after the Soviet withdrawal. Following these sources driving India's foreign policy is crucial to understand which way India's Afghanistan policy will evolve in future. Guided by an enduring vision for the region that requires a stable balance of power across the Durand Line, India will react strongly to any event or process that allows excessive strategic weight to Pakistan in Afghan affairs. However, depending on international and regional geopolitical equations, if there were a balance between Afghanistan and Pakistan, then the conciliators would remain influential. Thus, Pakistan's attempts to push India out of Afghanistan will only increase New Delhi's political will to deepen its footprint in that country. If India can be an enemy across the Hindu Kush, it can also be a friend who understands Pakistan's territorial insecurities, and has little interest in exacerbating them. This is not to say that talking about Afghanistan is a sufficient condition for sustaining an India-Pakistan dialogue, for India-Pakistan talks are highly accident-prone. But discussing the situation in Afghanistan surely is a necessary condition that will impart credibility to such India-Pakistan talks.

APPENDIX

INTERVIEWS CONDUCTED BY THE AUTHOR

1. 'A', senior Indian Military Intelligence officer, 2013, (details of interview withheld on the interviewee's request)
2. Abdullah Abdullah, current Chief Executive of the Islamic Republic of Afghanistan, Kabul, May 02, 2013
3. Ahmad Wali Massoud, younger brother of Ahmad Shah Massoud, now leading the *Hizb-e Nahzat-e Melli-ye Afghanistan* [or National Movement of Afghanistan], Kabul, April 29, 2013
4. Arun Sahgal [Brig. [Retd.], Director, Office of Net Assessment, Integrated Defence Staff of India (2001–03), New Delhi, February 18, 2013
5. Aunohita Mojumdar, Indian journalist, New Delhi, January 30, 2013
6. 'B', former top military intelligence official of India, (details of interview withheld on the interviewee's request)
7. Benoy Khare, Assistant Director (2005–11), Joint Intelligence Committee, National Security Council Secretariat (NSCS), Bengaluru, January 14, 2015.
8. 'C', aide to Ahmad Shah Massoud, Kabul, April 09, 2013, details of interview withheld on interviewee's request.
9. Chander D Sahay, Chief of R&AW (2003–05), September 2016 (via email)
10. C. V. Ranganathan, India's ambassador to China (1987–89), who was earlier posted to Moscow (1985–87), February 08, 2016 [Via email]
11. Chinmaya Gharekhan, former Indian Permanent Representative to the UN, New Delhi, March 06, 2013

12. 'D' serving senior security official of India, (details of interview withheld on the interviewee's request)
13. Daud Saba, former governor of Herat, Afghanistan, Kabul, April 17, 2013
14. David Sedney, former Deputy Assistant Secretary of Defense for Afghanistan, Pakistan and Central Asia, talk at the *Afghanistan Studies Group*, King's College London, May 12, 2014, organised by the author in capacity of chairperson of the group.
15. 'E', serving official of the Ministry of Defence of India, (details of interview withheld on the interviewee's request)
16. Ershad Ahmadi, former Deputy Foreign Minister of Afghanistan (2013–14), Kabul, April 07, 2013
17. 'F', senior FICCI official, New Delhi, 2013, (details of interview withheld on the interviewee's request)
18. 'G', serving Indian diplomat with expertise on Afghanistan and Pakistan. (Details of interview withheld on interviewees' request).
19. Gautam Mukhopadhaya, former Indian Ambassador to Afghanistan (2010–13), Kabul, April 11, 2013
20. 'H', senior Western official posted in Afghanistan. Details of the interview withheld on interviewee's request.
21. Haji Mohammad Mohaqiq, current deputy Chief Executive of Afghanistan and leader of the Hizb-e-Wahdat, Kabul, May 03, 2013
22. Hakimullah Mujahid, former Taliban representative to the UN, Kabul, May 06, 2013
23. Hanif Atmar, current NSA and former Interior Minister of Afghanistan, Kabul, April 13, 2013.
24. 'I', mid-ranking MEA official, 2016, details of interview withheld on interviewee's request.
25. 'J', two UK Foreign and Commonwealth Office (FCO) officials. Details of the interviews withheld on interviewees request.
26. Janan Musazai, current Afghan Ambassador to Pakistan, Kabul, April 07, 2013
27. Jawed Ludin, former Deputy Foreign Minister of Afghanistan, Kabul, April 22, 2013
28. Jayant Prasad, Former Indian Ambassador to Afghanistan (2008–2010), New Delhi, January 24, 2015
29. 'K', senior Indian diplomat, New Delhi, 2015 (details of interview withheld on interviewee's request).

30. K Raghunath, former Foreign Secretary of India (1997–99), New Delhi, March 19, 2013
31. Krishnan Srinivasan, Foreign Secretary of India (1994–95), Via telephone, September 23, 2016
32. 'L', serving senior Indian diplomat, December 2014 (details of interview withheld on the interviewee's request)
33. 'M' Indian consular officials in Herat, Afghanistan, 2013 (details of interview withheld on the interviewee's request)
34. Lalit Mansingh, Foreign Secretary of India (1999–2001), New Delhi, January 25, 2013
35. M. K. Bhadrakumar, former director and joint secretary (Pakistan, Afghanistan, Iran) desk, 1990–92, Ministry of External Affairs, June 03, 2013 [Via telephone]
36. M. K. Narayanan, Former Director of Intelligence Bureau (1987–1990), chairman of Joint Intelligence Committee (1987–1992), and National Security Advisor of India (2005–2010), Chennai, January 11, 2016
37. Mahmood Khan, Member of Parliament (Wolesi Jirga) of Afghanistan, April 07, 2013 [Via email]
38. Mahmoud Saikal, former Afghan Deputy Foreign Minister for Economic Affairs (2005–06), current Afghan ambassador to the US, Kabul, May 02, 2013
39. Maulvi Khodaidad, Senior Cleric in the Ulema Council of Herat, Herat, April 15, 2013
40. Mohammad Fahim Dashty, Founder of Kabul Weekly and former aide of Ahmad Shah Massoud, Kabul, April 08, 2013.
41. Mohammad Halim Fidai, former Governor of Wardak Province in Afghanistan, Kabul, April 27, 2013
42. Mohammad Tariq Ismati, former deputy minister at the Ministry of Rural Rehabilitation and Development (MRRD, at the Afghanistan Studies Group, King's College London, December 14, 2013, talk organised by the author in capacity of chairperson of the group.
43. Nader Nadery, current Chief Advisor to the President of Afghanistan on Public and Strategic Affairs, Kabul, May 07, 2013.
44. Nandan Unnikrishnan, Vice President of the Observer Research Foundation (ORF), and former journalist with the Press Trust of India, New Delhi, February 21, 2013
45. Omar Sharifi, former director, Afghan-American Institute for Research, Kabul, April 25, 2013

46. 'P', a serving Indian intelligence official, 2015 (details of interview withheld on the interviewee's request)
47. Pramit P. Chaudhuri, Foreign Editor of the Hindustan Times and Member National Security Advisory Board (NSAB), New Delhi, June 14, 2013
48. Pranab D. Samanta, Bureau Chief, Indian Express, New Delhi, January 28, 2013
49. Rajiv Sikri, Former Additional Secretary, Strategic Policy and Research, MEA, New Delhi, January 23, 2013
50. Rakesh Sood, India's Ambassador to Afghanistan (2005–2008), New Delhi, June 17, 2013
51. 'R', former Special Secretary R&AW, New Delhi, March 07, 2013
52. Salman Haider, former Foreign Secretary of India (1995–97), New Delhi, February 13, 2013
53. Sameer Patil, Assistant Director (2008–13), Joint Intelligence Committee, National Security Council Secretariat (NSCS), May 05, 2017 [Via Skype]
54. Samir Saran, Vice President of the Observer Research Foundation (ORF), New Delhi, March 14, 2013
55. Sanaullah Tasal, Afghan security analyst, Bachcha Khan Foundation, Kabul, April 19, 2013
56. Sanjar Sohail, Editor, 8 AM Daily News, Kabul, April 24, 2013
57. Satinder Lambah, India's Special Envoy to Afghanistan, New Delhi, March 26, 2013
58. Shashank, Foreign Secretary of India (2003–04), New Delhi, March 19, 2013
59. Shivshankar Menon, former foreign secretary and national security advisor of India (2010–2014), London, November 24, 2014
60. Shyam Saran, former Foreign Secretary (FS) of India (2004–06), New Delhi, March 12, 2013.
61. Syed Akbar Agha, close aide of Taliban leader Mullah Omar and former chief of the Jaish-ul-Muslimeen, Kabul, April 30, 2013
62. T, former intelligence analyst at the Joint Intelligence Committee, National Security Council Secretariat (NSCS). Details of this interview withheld on the interviewee's request.
63. Vijay Nambiar, India's ambassador to Kabul (1990–92), former deputy NSA (2005–06), currently United Nation's special envoy to Myanmar, New York, August 21, 2016. [Via telephone]
64. Vikram Sood, Chief of R&AW (2001–03), New Delhi, March 20, 2013

65. Waheed Omar, former Spokesperson at the Office of the President of Afghanistan (Hamid Karzai), Kabul, April 11, 2013
64. Walter Andersen, former Chief of South Asia Division in the Office of Analysis for the Near East and South Asia, US Department of State, London, August 26, 2014
65. 'X', former high-ranking R&AW officer (details of interview withheld on interviewee's request).

NOTES

PROLOGUE: A CURSE

1. Abdul Waheed Wafa and Carlotta Gall, 'Ex-Afghan Spy Chief is Sentenced to Death', *NYT*, 26/02/2006
2. Ibid.
3. Afghan Death List, Openbaar Ministerie, https://www.om.nl/onderwerpen/kopie-international/zie/afghanistan-death/death-lists/ (Accessed 28 March 2017)
4. On Assadullah Sarwari, the 'gang of four' and Amin's assassination see Diego Cordovez and Selig Harrison, *Out of Afghanistan: The Inside Story of the Soviet Withdrawal* (New York: Oxford University Press, 1995).
5. Malcolm Byrne and Vladislav Zubok, 'The Intervention in Afghanistan and the Fall of the Détente: A Chronology', *National Security Archives:* http://nsarchive.gwu.edu/carterbrezhnev/docs_intervention_in_afghanistan_and_the_fall_of_detente/fall_of_detente_chron.pdf (Accessed 28 March 2017)
6. Wafa and Gall, 'Ex-Afghan Spy Chief is Sentenced to Death'.
7. Henry S. Bradsher, Afghan C*ommunism and Soviet Intervention* (Karachi: Oxford University Press, 2002) 161.
8. Steve Coll, 'In Afghanistan, Dinner and Then a Coup', *The New Yorker*, 28/11/2012.
9. Sabina Sehgal, 'Afghan Leader Languishing in Jail', *ToI*, 10/04/1991.
10. Ibid.
11. Sehgal, 'Afghan Leader Languishing in Jail'.
12. Ibid.
13. 'Afghan ex-dy. PM to be deported', ToI, 15/07/1991; Amnesty International appealed to India in 1991: 'Forcible Repatriation and Fear of Torture/Execution: Mr. Assadullah Sarwari', Amnesty International, 14/10/1991.
14. Sehgal, 'Afghan Leader Languishing in Jail'.

1. IN PURSUIT OF FRIENDSHIP: INDIA'S QUEST IN AFGHANISTAN

1. Kautilya, *The Arthashastra* (New Delhi: Penguin Books, 1992) 505.

2. Interview with Lalit Mansingh, Foreign Secretary of India (1999–2001), New Delhi, 25/01/2013.
3. The term 'great game' came into mainstream in Rudyard Kipling's famous novel *Kim*. Rudyard Kipling, *Kim*, (Hertfordshire: Wordsworth Classics, 1994).
4. Hillary R Clinton, 'The Way Forward in Afghanistan,' *Senate Foreign Relations Committee*, Washington, 2011, https://2009-2017.state.gov/secretary/2009 2013clinton/rm/2011/12/178306.htm (Accessed 28 March 2017)
5. Text of the 1907 Hague Convention: http://www.opbw.org/int_inst/sec_docs/1907HC-TEXT.pdf (Accessed 28 March 2017)
6. Daniel Domby and Matthew Green, 'US aims to turn Afghanistan into Neutral Zone,' *Financial Times*, 27/06/2011, http://www.ft.com/cms/s/0/de0bcfc8-a0ff-11e0-adae-00144feabdc0.html (Accessed 28 March 2017)
7. On Pakistan's Afghanistan policy see Khalid Homayun Nadiri, 'Old Habits, New Consequences: Pakistan's Posture Towards Afghanistan Since 2001', *International Security*, 39:2, 132–68, Fall 2014.
8. Hamid Ansari and Chinmaya Gharekhan, 'Another Approach to Afghanistan,' *The Hindu*, 24/12/2013.
9. Harsh Pant, *India's Afghan Muddle: A Lost Opportunity* (New Delhi: HarperCollins, 2014); Sandra Destradi, 'India: A Reluctant Partner for Afghanistan', *Washington Quarterly*, 25/06/2014.
10. 'Government Clears Rs. 540 crore development aid for Afghanistan,' *NDTV*, 08/11/2012, http://www.ndtv.com/india-news/government-clears-rs-540-crore-development-aid-for-afghanistan-504088 (Accessed 28 March 2017)
11. Cable: 06ISLAMABAD16962_a, [CONFIDENTIAL], *Wikileaks*, 29/08/2006, https://wikileaks.org/plusd/cables/06ISLAMABAD16962_a.html; Marianna Baabar, 'RAW is training 600 Balochis in Afghanistan (interview with Mushahid Hussain Sayeed)', *Outlook*, 24/04/2006, http://www.outlookindia.com/article/raw-is-training-600-balochis-in-afghanistan/231032 (Accessed 28 March 2017)
12. Niccolo Machiavelli, *The Prince*, (London: Penguin Classics, 2009).
13. Matthieu Aikins, 'India in Afghanistan: Nation Building or Proxy War?', *The Caravan—A Journal of Politics and Culture*, 01/10/2010
14. William Dalrymple, 'A Deadly Triangle: Afghanistan, Pakistan, and India', *The Brookings Institution* (Washington DC: Brookings Institution, 2013).
15. Peter John Brobst, *The Future of the Great Game: Sir Olaf Caroe, India's Independence, and the Defense of Asia* (Ohio: University of Akron Press, 2005).
16. C Raja Mohan, 'Beyond U.S. Withdrawal: India's Afghan Options,' *The American Interest*, 06/04/2012.
17. Text of the India-Afghanistan Treaty of Friendship: http://www.commonlii.org/in/other/treaties/INTSer/1950/3.html (Accessed 28 March 2017)
18. Harsh Pant, 'India in Afghanistan: A test case for a rising power', *Contemporary South Asia*, 18 (2), 133–53, June 2010

19. On ACF see Paul A. Sabatier and Christopher M. Weible eds., *Theories of the Policy Process* (Colorado: Westview Press, 2014); Paul A. Sabatier and Hank Jenkins-Smith eds. *Policy Change and Learning: An Advocacy Coalition Approach* (Colorado: Westview, 1993).
20. Sabatier and Wieble, *Theories of Policy Process*, 195–8.
21. Ibid 200.
22. Christopher M Weible et al., 'A Quarter Century of the Advocacy Coalition Framework: An Introduction to the Special Issue,' *Policy Studies Journal*, 39 (3), 349–60, 2011, 352.
23. The term policy narrative was enunciated in the Narrative Policy Framework, which lies within the bracket of ACF and treats narratives as a method of 'structuring and communicating (one's) understanding of the world'. Elizabeth A Shahnahan, Michael D Jones and Mark K McBeth, 'Policy Narratives and Policy Processes,' *The Policy Studies Journal*, 39 (3), 2011, 535–61.
24. Ibid.
25. Ibid., 544.
26. Oxford Dictionaries, meaning of 'conciliator': http://www.oxforddictionaries.com/definition/english/conciliator (Accessed 28 March 2017)
27. Oxford Dictionaries, meaning of 'partisan': http://www.oxforddictionaries.com/definition/english/partisan (Accessed 28 March 2017)
28. Ramachandra Guha, *India After Gandhi: The History of the World's Largest Democracy* (London: Picador, 2008) xxv.
29. National Security Archive, 'Electronic Briefing Books': http://nsarchive.gwu.edu/NSAEBB/index.html (Accessed 28 March 2017)
30. Most of these interviews were conducted as part of the author's doctoral research at King's College London.

2. KABULIWALLAH: A BRIEF HISTORY OF INDIA-AFGHANISTAN RELATIONS

1. 'Tagore's 'Kabuliwala' has given us a brand: Afghan President Ashraf Ghani', *Indian Express*, 28/04/2015.
2. Rabindranath Tagore, 'The Cabuliwallah (The Fruitseller from Kabul)', (translated by the Sister Nivedita), *Modern Review*, 11 (1), January, 1912, 50–51
3. Ibid., 55.
4. Ibid., 53.
5. FAR, 21 (3), 10/03/1975, 80.
6. Interview with M K Narayanan, Former Director of Intelligence Bureau (1987–90), chairman of Joint Intelligence Committee (1987–92), and National Security Advisor of India (2005–10), Chennai, 11/01/2016.
7. Interview with Brig. (Retd.) Arun Sahgal, Director, Office of Net Assessment, Integrated Defence Staff of India (2001–03), New Delhi, 18/02/2013

8. Nancy Dupree, *A Historical Guide to Afghanistan* (Kabul: Afghan Tourist Organisation, 1977) 45–94.
9. Irfan Habib and Vivekanand Jha, *Mauryan India: A People's History of India* (New Delhi: Tulika Books, 2004) 189–95.
10. For a history of ancient India see Romila Thapar, *Penguin History of India, Volume 1* (London: Penguin Books, 1990).
11. Irfan Habib, *Medieval India: A Study of Civilizations* (New Delhi: National Book Trust, 2008).
12. Tim Smith and Irna Qureshi, *The Grand Trunk Road: From Delhi to the Khyber Pass* (Devi Lewis Publishers, 2001).
13. Ainsley T. Embree ed., 'Frontiers into Boundaries' in *Imagining India: Essays on Indian History* (Oxford: Oxford University Press, 1990) 154.
14. Buffer Zone is 'a neutral area serving to separate hostile forces or nations', says Oxford Dictionaries: http://www.oxforddictionaries.com/definition/english/buffer-zone (Accessed 28 March 2017)
15. Bijan Omrani, 'The Durand Line: History and Problems of the Afghan-Pakistan Border', *Asian Survey*, 40 (2), 177–195, 2009.
16. Ashley Tellis, 'Securing the Barrack: The Logic, Structure and Objective of India's Naval Expansion—Part I' *Naval War College Review*, XLIII/3, (Sequence 331) 1990, 77–97.
17. Ibid, 85–91.
18. Sarvepalli Gopal ed., 'India-Afghanistan Relations', *SWJN*, Second Series, 1 (New Delhi: Jawaharlal Nehru Memorial Fund, 1984) 583–4.
19. Sarvepalli Gopal ed., 'Conversations with John F Dulles', *SWJN*, 32, February 01–April 30, 1956, (New Delhi: Jawaharlal Nehru Memorial Fund, 2003) 379.
20. B N Mullik, *My Years With Nehru—1948–1964* (New Delhi: Allied Publishers, 1972) 81.
21. Ibid.
22. On the Bandung Conference and its legacy see Seng Tan and Amitav Acharya eds. *Bandung Revisited: The Legacy of the 1955 Asian-African Conference for International Order* (Singapore: National University of Singapore Press, 2008).
23. Srinath Raghavan, *War and Peace in Modern India* (New Delhi: Palgrave Macmillan, 2010) 20–21.
24. *FAR*, 1 (12), 246, 1955.
25. Ibid.
26. Ibid 97–160.
27. *FAR*, 11 (1), January 1965, 5–6.
28. Quoted in R. D. Pradhan, *1965 War The Inside Story: Defence Minister Y B Chavan's Diary of the India-Pakistan War* (Delhi: Atlantic Publishers, 2007) 82.
29. Farhan Hanif Siddiqi, *The Politics of Ethnicity in Pakistan: The Baloch, Sindhi, and Mohajir Ethnic Movements* (Abingdon: Routledge, 2012) 52–74.

30. 'Call for concrete help for Pakhtoon movement,' *ToI*, 10/10/1965.
31. *FAR*, 11 (11), November 1965, 325–6.
32. William Spengler to Department of State, [CONFIDENTIAL], *National Archives and Records Administration*, RG 58, Central Files, 09/10/1965.
33. 'Kabul's Concerns', *ToI*, 16/09/1965.
34. *FAR*, 11 (11), November 1965, 325–6.
35. Sumit Ganguly and Nicholas Howenstein, 'India-Pakistan Rivalry in Afghanistan', *Journal of International Affairs*, 63 (1), Fall/Winter 2009, 127.
36. Interview with Chinmaya Gharekhan, former Indian Permanent Representative to the UN, New Delhi, 06/03/2013.
37. J. N. Dixit, *An Afghan Diary: Zahir Shah to Taliban* (Delhi: Konark Publishers, 2000) 19–20.
38. William Spengler to Department of State, [CONFIDENTIAL], *National Archives and Records Administration*, RG 58, Central Files, 09/10/1965.
39. Ibid.
40. 'Anschluss' was the Nazi propaganda term for the annexation of Austria into Nazi Germany in March 1938.
41. Spengler to Department of State, 09/10/1965.
42. *Lok Sabha*, Starred question 663, 06/12/1965.
43. 'Kabul reminds UN, Pindi, of Pakhtoon's demands', *ToI*, October 15/10/1965.
44. DO133/181, [SECRET], CRO to Commonwealth Secretary, 10/01/1966, *Foreign Office Files for India, Pakistan and Afghanistan, 1947–1980*, 92.
45. *FAR*, 12 (7), July 1966, 10–15.
46. *FAR*, 18 (4), April 1971, 81–2.
47. M Rashiduzzaman, 'The National Awami Party of Pakistan: Leftist Politics in Crisis', *Pacific Affairs*, 43 (3). Autumn, 394–409, 1970.
48. Ibid 395–402.
49. FCO 37/899, [SECRET], Kabul to Department of State, 27/08/1971, *Foreign Office Files for India, Pakistan and Afghanistan, 1947–1980*, 154.
50. FCO 37/898, [SECRET], Kabul to Department of State, 25/08/1971, *Foreign Office Files for India, Pakistan and Afghanistan, 1947–1980*, 2.
51. Quoted in Timothy Nunan, *Humanitarian Invasion: Global Development in Cold War Afghanistan* (Cambridge: Cambridge University Press, 2016) 33–4.
52. Cable: 1974NEWDE13474_b, [CONFIDENTIAL], 08/10/1974, *Wikileaks*, https://wikileaks.org/plusd/cables/1974NEWDE13474_b.html (Accessed 28 March 2017)
53. 'Balochistan Insurgency: Fourth Conflict', *Global Security*, http://www.globalsecurity.org/military/world/war/balochistan-1973.htm (Accessed 28 March 2017)
54. Ibid.
55. Ibid.
56. 'Waldheim's reply to Kabul annoys Pindi,' *ToI*, 14/04/1975.

57. FCO 37/11416, [CONFIDENTIAL], Kabul to FCO, 03/01/1974, *Foreign Office Files for India, Pakistan and Afghanistan, 1947–1980*, 22.
58. M S Rajan, 'The Indo-Soviet Treaty and India's non-alignment policy', Australian Outlook, 27 (2), 1972, 204–15.
59. B. Raman, Kaoboys of R&AW: Down Memory Lane (New Delhi: Lancer Publishers, 2007) 40–41.
60. Rajiv Sikri, Challenge and Strategy: Rethinking India's Foreign Policy (New Delhi: Sage Publishers, 2013) 134.
61. Cable: 1974KABUL06445_b, [CONFIDENTIAL], 09/10/1974, Wikileaks, https://www.wikileaks.org/plusd/cables/1974KABUL06445_b.html (Accessed 28 March 2017)
62. Interview with serving Indian intelligence official P, 2015 (details of interview withheld on the interviewee's request).
63. 'Balochistan Insurgency: Fourth Conflict', Global Security.
64. Jumma Khan Sufi, Faraib-e-Na-Tamam (Lahore: Pak Book Empire, 2016) originally published in Urdu, the title of the book translates to 'The Unending Deception'. In his autobiography Sufi, a Pashtun revolutionary agent in the 1970s, corroborates Pakistani allegations of Indian support to the Pashtunistan and Baloch movements.
65. 'Balochistan Insurgency: Fourth Conflict', Global Security.
66. Ibid.
67. P N Haksar Papers [III], 'Indian Ambassador to Tehran', March 02, 1975, [SECRET]—TEH/Pol/103/274, Nehru Memorial Museum and Library (NMML).
68. Harold Saunders and Henry Appelbaum to Henry Kissinger, [SECRET], National Security Archives, 17/07/1973, http://nsarchive.gwu.edu/NSAEBB/NSAEBB59/ (Accessed 28 March 2017)
69. Cable: 1974KABUL02504_b, [CONFIDENTIAL], Kabul to Secretary of State, 25/04/1974, Wikileaks:, https://wikileaks.org/plusd/cables/1974KABUL02504_b.html (Accessed 28 March 2017)
70. Cable: 1974ISLAMA10317_b, [SECRET], Byorade to Secretary of State, Wikileaks, 01/11/1974, https://wikileaks.org/plusd/cables/1974ISLAMA10317_b.html
71. Dixit, An Afghan Diary, 19.
72. Ibid.
73. FAR, 19 (12), December 1973, 506–7.
74. Cable: 1973NEWDE08429_b, [LIMITED OFFICIAL USE], 21/07/1973, Wikileaks: https://wikileaks.org/plusd/cables/1973NEWDE08429_b.html (Accessed 28 March 2017)
75. FAR, 19 (12), 506–7.
76. Mansingh interview.
77. Cable: 1975NEWDE03600_b, [LIMITED OFFICIAL USE], 14/03/1975,

Wikileaks:, https://wikileaks.org/plusd/cables/1975NEWDE03600_b.html (Accessed 28 March 2017)

78. FAR, 21 (3), March 1975, 82–3.
79. Cable: 1975STATE071657_d, [SECRET], Kissinger to Kabul, Wikileaks, 29/03/1975: https://wikileaks.org/plusd/cables/1975STATE071657_b.html (Accessed 28 March 2017)
80. FAR, 21 (3), March 1975
81. Mansingh interview. As an observant US diplomat in Kabul noted, Gandhi's visit to Kabul lacked substance despite the 'hoopla' around it. Cable: 1976 KABUL05267_b, [CONFIDENTIAL], Eliot to Secretary of State, 14/07/1976, Wikileaks: https://wikileaks.org/plusd/cables/1976KABUL05267_b.html (Accessed 28 March 2017)
82. Kabul embassy to Department of State, Airgram A-33, [CONFIDENTIAL], National Security Archive, 22/05/1973: http://nsarchive.gwu.edu/NSAEBB/NSAEBB59/zahir13.pdf (Accessed 28 March 2017)
83. Thomas Ruttig, 'Islamists, Leftists, and a void in the Centre: Afghanistan's political parties and where they come from', Konrad Adenauer Stiftung, 9–10.
84. Srinath Raghavan, 1971: A Global History of the Creation of Bangladesh (Harvard: Harvard University Press, 2013) 268–9.
85. 'Documentation: Soviet-Afghan Treaty of Friendship', Survival, 21 (2), 1979.
86. Girijalal Jain, 'Coup in Afghanistan: Many unanswered questions', ToI, 03/05/1978.
87. Cable: 1978STATE211561_d, [CONFIDENTIAL], Department of State to Kabul and New Delhi, Wikileaks, 21/08/1978: https://wikileaks.org/plusd/cables/1978STATE211561_d.html (Accessed 28 March 2017)
88. FAR, 24 (9), September 1978.
89. Cable: 1978KABUL06203_d, [CONFIDENTIAL], Kabul to Secretary of State, 01/08/1978, Wikileaks: https://wikileaks.org/plusd/cables/1978KABUL06203_d.html (Accessed 28 March 2017)
90. Quoted in A S Abraham, 'Afghanistan Since the Coup: Consolidation of Soviet Influence', ToI, 18/12/1978.
91. Ibid.
92. 'Kabul unhappy with Delhi: stand on neutrals', ToI, 23/09/1978.
93. Cable 1978NEWDE07475_d, [SECRET], Goheen to Secretary of State, Wikileaks, 11/05/1978: https://wikileaks.org/plusd/cables/1978NEWDE07475_d.html (Accessed 28 March 2017)
94. Cable: 1978NEWDE08321_d, [SECRET], Goheen to Secretary of State, Wikileaks, 27/05/1978: https://wikileaks.org/plusd/cables/1978NEWDE08321_d.html
95. Cable: 1978KATHMA02367_d, [SECRET], Kathmandu to Secretary of State, Wikileaks, 05/05/1978: https://wikileaks.org/plusd/cables/1978KATHMA02367_d.html (Accessed 28 March 2017)

96. Cable: 1978KABUL07600_d, [CONFIDENTIAL], Kabul to Secretary of State, Wikileaks, 21/09/1978: https://wikileaks.org/plusd/cables/1978KABUL07600_d.html (Accessed 28 March 2017)
97. Cable 1978NEWDE07475_d
98. Cable 1978NEWDE06878_d, [SECRET], Goheen to Secretary of State, Wikileaks, 02/05/1978: https://wikileaks.org/plusd/cables/1978NEWDE06878_d.html (Accessed 28 March 2017)
99. Cable: 1978KABUL07187_d, [CONFIDENTIAL], Kabul to Secretary of State, Wikileaks: 07/09/1978, https://wikileaks.org/plusd/cables/1978KABUL07187_d.html (Accessed 28 March 2017)
100. Cable: 1978NEWDE12751_d, [CONFIDENTIAL], New Delhi to Secretary of State, Wikileaks, 22/08/1978, https://wikileaks.org/plusd/cables/1978NEWDE12751_d.html (Accessed 27 March 2017)
101. Christopher Andrew and Vasili Mitrokhin, The World Was Going Our Way—The KGB and the Battle for the Third World (New York: Basic Books, 2006) 396.
102. Partha S. Ghosh and Rajaram Panda, 'Domestic Support for Mrs. Indira Gandhi's Afghan Policy: The Soviet Factor in Indian Politics', Asian Survey, 23 (3), March 1983, 261–79.
103. Raman, Kaoboys of R&AW, 256.

3. LEANING TOWER OF DELHI: MANAGING THE SOVIET INVASION AND WITHDRAWAL

1. 'No Meddling in Kabul: Says India', ToI, 13/01/1980.
2. Lok Sabha, 01/02/1980, 328–9.
3. Quoted in Raman, Kaoboys of R&AW, 186.
4. Special Correspondent, 'No Meddling: India', ToI, 28/12/1979.
5. Dixit, An Afghan Diary, 20–21.
6. I K Gujral, 'Oral History: India's Response to the Soviet Military Intervention in Afghanistan', Indian Foreign Affairs Journal, 1 (1), January–March 2006, 123–31.
7. Ghosh and Panda, 'Domestic Support for Mrs. Indira Gandhi's Afghan Policy' 265.
8. On Soviet role in Balochistan see Selig Harrison, In Afghanistan's Shadow: Baluch Nationalism and Soviet Temptations (Washington D.C.: Carnegie Endowment for International Peace, 1981).
9. Arvind Panagriya, 'India in the 1980s and 1990s: A Triumph of Reforms', International Monetary Fund, 06/11/2003, https://www.imf.org/external/np/apd/seminars/2003/newdelhi/pana.pdf
10. 'No Meddling: India', ToI.
11. Dixit, An Afghan Diary, 21.

12. 'Delhi concern conveyed to Carter envoy', ToI, 30/01/1980.
13. Robert C. Horn, 'Afghanistan and the Soviet-Indian Influence Relationship', Asian Survey, 23 (3), March 1983, 246.
14. 'No Meddling in Kabul: Says India', ToI.
15. '7 Pak divisions on Afghan border', ToI, 17/01/1980.
16. Ibid.
17. Ibid; Rajya Sabha, 17/12/1981.
18. FCO37/228, [CONFIDENTIAL], Kabul to FCO, 03/01/1980, Foreign Office Files for India, Pakistan and Afghanistan, 1947–1980, 127.
19. Inder K Gujral, Matters of Discretion: An Autobiography (New Delhi: Hay House Publishers, 2011) 171.
20. Quoted in M K Rasgotra, A Life in Diplomacy (New Delhi: Penguin, 2016) 301–28.
21. Editorial, 'A Wide Gap', ToI, 15/02/1980.
22. FCO 37/2255 [CONFIDENTIAL], Ewans to FCO, 23/05/1980, Foreign Office Files for India, Pakistan and Afghanistan, 1947–1980, 29.
23. Rajya Sabha, Session 114, 18/06/1980, 206–24.
24. Dixit, An Afghan Diary, 22–23.
25. Ibid.
26. Ibid.
27. Email interview with C. V. Ranganathan, India's ambassador to China (1987–89) and who was earlier posted in Moscow (1985–87), 08/02/2016.
28. Horn, 'Afghanistan and Soviet-Indian Influence Relationship', 246.
29. Rajya Sabha (Questions), Session 113, 14/03/1980.
30. US Library of Congress, 'Pakistan', http://countrystudies.us/india/123.htm
31. Girijalal Jain, 'Zia provokes Indira', ToI, 10/08/1980 (Accessed 28 March 2017)
32. J N Dixit, Across Borders: 50 years of Indian Foreign Policy (New Delhi: Picus Books, 1998) 156–7.
33. Dixit, An Afghan Diary, 66.
34. Quoted in Horn, Afghanistan and Soviet-India Influence Relationship', 246.
35. FCO 37/2228, [CONFIDENTIAL] White to Braithwaite, 07/02/1980, Foreign Office Files for India, Pakistan and Afghanistan, 1947–1980, 139.
36. FCO 37/2229, [CONFIDENTIAL] April 1980, Foreign Office Files for India, Pakistan and Afghanistan, 1947–1980, 67
37. FCO 37/2228
38. Rajya Sabha (Questions), Session 117, 20/02/1981, 40–41.
39. Special Correspondent, 'Soviets may tarry in Afghanistan: Rao', ToI, June 17/06/1980.
40. Dennis Kux, The United States and Pakistan, 1947–2000: Disenchanted Allies (Baltimore: JHU Press, 2001) 380–82.
41. Rajya Sabha, Session 112, 24/01/1980, 28–29.

42. Andrew and Mitrokhin, The World Was Going Our Way, 336–9.
43. Gujral, Matters of Discretion, 171.
44. Andrew and Mitrokhin, The World Was Going Our Way, 331–2.
45. Raman, Kaoboys of R&AW, 40–41.
46. US Library of Congress, 'Pakistan', http://countrystudies.us/india/123.htm (Accessed 28 March 2017)
47. Pran Chopra, 'Pakistan's 'Afghan Crisis': I—Rejection of Indian Offer', ToI, 12/12/1985.
48. Ibid.
49. Claire Provost, 'Sixty Years of US aid to Pakistan: Get the data', Guardian, 11/07/2011.
50. Rajya Sabha (Questions), Session 114, 13/06/1980.
51. Pran Chopra, 'Pakistan's 'Afghan Crisis: II—Fear of Indo-Iranian Friendship', ToI, 13/12/1985.
52. Rajya Sabha, Session 114, 18/06/1980.
53. Raman, Kaoboys of R&AW, 124–5.
54. Cable: 1978NEWDE19468_d, [Limited Official Use], New Delhi to Secretary of State, 19/12/1978, Wikileaks: https://wikileaks.org/plusd/cables/1978 NEWDE19468_d.html (Accessed 28 March 2017)
55. 'Gujral, 'Oral History', 130.
56. Horn, 'Afghanistan and the Soviet-Indian Influence Relationship', 249.
57. Gujral, 'Oral History', 127.
58. Maloy Krishna Dhar, *Open Secrets: India's Intelligence Unveiled* (New Delhi: Manas Publishers, 2005), 248.
59. Ibid.
60. Ghosh and Panda, 'Domestic Support for Mrs. Indira Gandhi's Afghan Policy' 262.
61. Election Commission of India, 1981: http://eci.nic.in/eci_main/Statistical Reports/LS_1980/Vol_I_LS_80.pdf (Accessed 28 March 2017)
62. T. P. Sreenivasan, 'A diplomat ahead of his times', Rediff News, 10/03/2014.
63. Jagat S. Mehta, March of Folly in Afghanistan, 1978–2001 (New Delhi: Manohar Publishers, 2002) 162.
64. Rajya Sabha, Session 112, 24/01/1980, 28–32.
65. Dixit, An Afghan Diary, 67.
66. Rajya Sabha, Session 112, 24/01/1980, 54.
67. Rajya Sabha, Session 114, 18/06/1980, 225.
68. Rajya Sabha, Session 112, 24/01/1980, 104–14
69. 'Indira's stand on Kabul irks Desai', ToI, 13/01/1980.
70. Quoted in Ghosh and Panda, 'Domestic Support for Mrs. Indira Gandhi's Afghan Policy' 264.
71. Lok Sabha, 01/02/1980, 328–9.

72. A M Zaidi, ed., The Annual Register of Indian Political Parties: Proceedings and Fundamental Texts, 1980 (New Delhi: S. Chand and Co., 1981) 650.
73. Ibid.
74. Quoted in Ghosh and Panda, 'Domestic Support for Mrs. Indira Gandhi's Afghan Policy', 264.
75. Quoted in P. B. Sinha, 'Impact of Afghan Developments', Strategic Analysis, 5:5–6, 1981, 211–12.
76. Quoted in Ghosh and Panda, 'Domestic Support for Mrs. Indira Gandhi's Afghan Policy', 265.
77. 'Masani raps Indira: pro-Soviet stand', ToI, 16/01/1980.
78. Election Commission of India, 1981: http://eci.nic.in/eci_main/Statistical Reports/LS_1980/Vol_I_LS_80.pdf (Accessed 28 March 2017)
79. 'CPM Defends Soviet Step in Afghanistan', ToI, 02/01/1980.
80. Zaidi, The Annual Register of Indian Political Parties, 485.
81. Rajya Sabha, Session 112, 24/01/1980, 89–90.
82. Ibid., 92–3.
83. Ibid., 89.
84. Dixit, An Afghan Diary, 22–3.
85. Ibid. 59–61.
86. J. D. Singh, 'Common man in Kabul critical of Delhi', ToI, 13/02/1980.
87. Serge Schmemann, 'Mrs. Gandhi, on Soviet visit, affirms Indian nonalignment', NYT, 23/09/1982.
88. National Security Decision Directive (NSDD) 147, 11/10/1984, Ronald Reagan Presidential Library and Museum: https://reaganlibrary.archives.gov/archives/reference/Scanned%20NSDDs/NSDD147.pdf (Accessed 28 March 2017)
89. Praveen Swami, 'India's Language of Killing', The Hindu, 01/05/2014.
90. Raman, Kaoboys of R&AW, 193.
91. Peter J S Duncan, 'The Soviet-Indian Model: Continuity in a Changing Environment', in Margot Light ed., Troubled Friendships: Moscow's Third World Venture (London: Royal Institute of International Affairs, 1993) 40–41.
92. Then Congress General Secretary Srikant Verman quoted in Sergey Radchenko, 'India and the End of the Cold War', in Artemy M. Kalinovsky and Sergey Radchenko eds, The End of the Cold War and the Third World: New Perspectives on Regional Conflict (London: Routledge, 2011) 178.
93. United States Government, 'India's Position on Afghanistan: Prospects for Change', *Directorate of Intelligence*, April 19, 1985 [CIA Archives].
94. 'PM keen on to solve Afghan issue', ToI, 12/06/1985.
95. John Gunther Dean's Oral History, Jimmy Carter Presidential Library and Museum, 377, http://www.jimmycarterlibrary.gov/library/oralhistory/clohproject/India.pdf
96. John Gunther Dean, Oral History, 348–9.

97. John Gunther Dean, Oral History, 342.
98. Quoted in Kalinovsky, A Long Goodbye, 79–80.
99. John Gunther Dean, Oral History, 377.
100. Ibid.
101. Ibid.
102. Anatoly Cherniav's Diary, National Security Archives: http://nsarchive.gwu.edu/NSAEBB/NSAEBB57/r18.pdf (Accessed 28 March 2017)
103. 'Session of CC CPSU Politburo, November 13, 1986', Cold War International History Project Bulletin, 8–9, Winter 1996/1997, National Security Archives: http://nsarchive.gwu.edu/NSAEBB/NSAEBB57/r18.pdf (Accessed 28 March 2017)
104. Ranganathan interview, and quoted in Mehta, March of Folly, 29.
105. Ranganathan interview.
106. 'Minutes of the Politburo of the CC CPSU Session of February 23–26, 1987', National Security Archives.
107. NSDD 270, 01/05/1987, Ronald Reagan Presidential Library and Museum: https://www.reaganlibrary.archives.gov/archives/reference/Scanned%20NSDDS/NSDD270.pdf (Accessed 28 March 2017)
108. John Gunther Dean, Oral History, 378–9.
109. John Gunther Dean, Oral History, 381.
110. NSDD 270.
111. 'Moscow Summit: Joint Document, 'Realistic approach' to reducing nuclear risk', NYT, 02/06/1988.
112. John Gunther Dean, Oral History, 385.
113. Raman, Kaoboys of R&AW, 185.
114. Riaz M. Khan, Untying the Afghan Knot: Negotiating Soviet Withdrawal (Duke University Press, 1991).
115. Radchenko, 'India and the End of the Cold War' 173.
116. 'India's Stakes in Kabul', ToI, 08/03/1988.
117. Pranay Gupte, Mother India: A Political Biography of Indira Gandhi (New Delhi: Penguin, 2009) 32.
118. Amin Saikal, Modern Afghanistan: A History of Struggle and Survival (London: I B Tauris, 2004) 190–92.
119. Anthony Arnold, 'The Ephemeral Elite: The Failure of Socialist Afghanistan' in Myron Weiner and Ali Banuazizi eds, The Politics of Social Transformation in Afghanistan, Iran, and Pakistan (New York: Syracuse University Press, 1994) 45–6.
120. I. P. Khosla 'Oral History: Last days of the Soviet Troops in Afghanistan', Indian Foreign Affairs Journal, 6 (1), January–March 2011, 96–7; Interview with Mohammad Halim Fidai, former Governor of Wardak Province in Afghanistan, Kabul, April 27, 2013.

121. 'Drama in Kabul', ToI, 24/07/1980.
122. FCO 37/2231, [CONFIDENTIAL], 25/06/1980, Foreign Office Files for India, Pakistan and Afghanistan, 1947–1980, 146–50.
123. Amstutz, J. Bruce, Afghanistan: The First Five Years of Soviet Occupation (Darby: Diane Publishing, 1986) 388.
124. Dixit, An Afghan Diary, 23.
125. Dixit, An Afghan Diary, 97.
126. Artemy M. Kalinovsky, A Long Goodbye: The Soviet Withdrawal from Afghanistan (Cambridge, Massachusetts: Harvard University Press, 2011) 95–7.
127. Ibid., 96.
128. Khosla, 'Oral History', 87–103.
129. Steven Weisman, 'On India's Border, A Huge Mock War', NYT, 06/03/1987: http://www.nytimes.com/1987/03/06/world/on-india-s-border-a-huge-mock-war.html (Accessed 27 March 2017)
130. Natwar Singh, One Life is Not Enough: An Autobiography (New Delhi: Rupa & Co., 2014) 276.
131. Ibid.
132. Editorial, 'Mr. Gandhi, on Four Fronts', NYT, June 07/06/1987.
133. B. Raman, 'Was there an intelligence failure?', *Frontline*, 16 (15), July 17–30, 1999, http://www.frontline.in/static/html/fl1615/16151170.htm
134. Dhar, *Open Secrets*, 277.
135. Raman, Kaoboys of R&AW, 193.
136. Rajya Sabha, Session 146, 29/04/1988, 206–14.
137. Rajya Sabha, Session 140, 1986, 204.
138. Rajya Sabha (Questions), Session 150, 03/05/1989.
139. Interview with X, former high-ranking R&AW officer. Details of interview withheld on interviewees request.
140. Rajya Sabha (Questions), Session 150, 03/05/1989, 77–8.
141. 'A Bizarre Invitation', ToI, 27/02/1988.
142. 'A Daring Invitation', ToI, 07/05/1988.
143. 'India assures all help to Kabul', ToI, 06/05/1988.
144. 'A Daring Invitation' ToI.
145. Khosla, 'Oral History', 102.
146. Vappala Balachandran, National Security and Intelligence Management: A New Paradigm (Mumbai: Indus Source Books, 2014) 16.
147. Vappala Balachandran, 'What made AK Verma a great intelligence officer', DailyO, 04/09/2016.
148. Telephone interview with Vijay K. Nambiar, India's ambassador to Kabul (1990–92), deputy national security advisor (2005–06), 21/08/2016.
149. Coll, 'In Afghanistan, Dinner and Then a Coup'.
150. Quoted in Radchenko, 'India and the End of the Cold War' 186.
151. Rajya Sabha, Session 142, 24/04/1987, 270–71.

152. Rajya Sabha (Questions), Session 149, 15/03/1989, 76–7.
153. Rajya Sabha (Questions), Session 154, 23/05/1990, 65–6.
154. Saikal, Modern Afghanistan, 172–8.
155. Quoted in Raman, Kaoboys of R&AW, 186.

4. THE TALIBAN DILEMMA: PARTISANS VERSUS CONCILIATORS

1. Quoted in John Gunther Dean, Oral History, 390.
2. Phillip Corwin, Doomed in Afghanistan: A UN Officer's Memoir of the Fall of Kabul and Najibullah's Failed Escape, 1992 (New Brunswick: Rutgers University Press, 2003) 95.
3. Rahimullah Yusufzai, 'India Must Not Treat The Taliban As Enemy,' Outlook, 11/06/1996.
4. Corwin, Doomed in Afghanistan, 33–125. Corwin was one of the UN officers with Najibullah that night.
5. Nambiar interview.
6. M.K. Bhadrakumar, 'Manmohan Singh resets Afghan policy', The Hindu, 15/05/2011.
7. Shekhar Gupta, 'Najibullah: No Escape', India Today, 15/05/1992.
8. Nambiar interview.
9. Ibid.
10. 'Afghan Guerillas order Afghan Army to Surrender City', NYT, 18/04/1992.
11. Corwin, Doomed in Afghanistan, 114.
12. Shekhar Gupta and Sharad Saxena, 'Ominous Future', India Today, 15/05/1992.
13. Nambiar interview.
14. Ibid.
15. Lok Sabha, Session 3, 11 (35), 21/04/1992.
16. Nambiar interview.
17. Gupta, 'Najibullah: No Escape'.
18. Nambiar interview.
19. Subhash Kirpekar, 'India ready to shelter Najib', ToI, 30/04/1992.
20. Rajya Sabha (Questions), Session 163, 04/05/1992.
21. Lok Sabha, Session 3, 11 (35), 21/04/1992.
22. Lok Sabha, Session 3, 11 (37), 23/04/1992.
23. Nambiar interview.
24. Ibid.
25. Ibid.
26. Ibid.
27. X interview.
28. Nambiar interview.
29. X interview.
30. Gupta and Saxena, 'Ominous Future'.

31. Telephone interview with Krishnan Srinivasan, Foreign Secretary of India (1994–95), 23/09/2016.
32. M K Bhadrakumar, 'How India reached out to the Afghan Mujahideen', Rediff News, 14/09/2016.
33. Srinivasan interview.
34. Nambiar interview.
35. For Fatana Najib's views see: 'Exclusive Interview with F. Najibullah, the wife of former Afghan president' BBC Afghanistan, 26/09/2016, https://soundcloud.com/bbcafghanistan/y98glekc8kju [Translated by Hameed Hakimi, Chatham House, 28/09/2016] (Accessed 27 March 2017)
36. Interview with Jayant Prasad, Indian Ambassador to Afghanistan (2008–10), New Delhi, 24/01/2015.
37. Interview with C, aide to Ahmad Shah Massoud, Kabul, 09/04/2013.
38. Valerie Cerra and Sweta C. Saxena, 'What caused 1991 currency crisis in India?' IMF Working Paper, WP/00/157, International Monetary Fund, 2000, 395–425.
39. World Bank Data: http://data.worldbank.org/indicator/NY.GDP.MKTP.KD.ZG?page=4 (Accessed 27 March 2017)
40. Vinay Sitapati, Half Lion: How P V Narasimha Rao transformed India (New Delhi: Penguin Books, 2016).
41. Interview with Vikram Sood, former Chief of R&AW (2001–03), New Delhi, 20/03/2013. Dixit confirms the dominance of the conciliators in New Delhi till 1996. PM Rao was categorical in his shift of approach from that of Rajiv Gandhi. See J. N. Dixit, My South Block Years: Memoirs of a Foreign Secretary (New Delhi: UBS Publishers, 1996) 108.
42. Bhadrakumar, 'Manmohan Singh resets Afghan policy'.
43. Dixit, My South Block Years, 108.
44. Rajya Sabha (Questions), Session 164, 09/07/1992.
45. Nambiar interview.
46. Bhadrakumar, 'How India reached out to the Afghan Mujahideen'.
47. Bhadrakumar, 'Manmohan Singh resets Afghan policy'.
48. Srinivasan interview.
49. Ibid.
50. Bhadrakumar, 'Manmohan Singh resets Afghan policy'.
51. Nambiar interview.
52. Dixit, My South Block Years, 109.
53. MEA Annual Report, 1993.
54. Lok Sabha (Questions), 25/11/1992.
55. Rajya Sabha, Session 149, 13/03/1989.
56. Ibid.
57. 'How Amitabh Bachchan floored the Mujahideen', Indian Express, 04/10/2012.

58. Ibid.
59. Interview with L, Indian diplomat, December 2014 (details of interview withheld).
60. Lok Sabha, 20 (21–30), 29/03/1993.
61. Ibid.
62. Rajya Sabha, Session 156, 08/01/1991.
63. Ibid.
64. Ibid, 534.
65. Lok Sabha, Session 3, 11 (35), 21/04/992.
66. Lok Sabha, Session 3, 11 (36), 22/04/1992.
67. 'BJP cautions govt. on Afghanistan', ToI, 04/05/1992.
68. Lok Sabha, Session 3, 11 (36), 22/04/1992.
69. 'BJP cautions govt. on Afghanistan,' ToI, 04/05/1992.
70. Ibid.
71. Rajya Sabha, Session 142, 27/04/1987.
72. Ausaf Saied Vasifi, 'India cannot gain by ignoring the Mujahideen', ToI, 02/06/1989.
73. Ibid.
74. MEA Annual Report, 1991, 5–6.
75. MEA Annual Report, 1992, 24.
76. Rajya Sabha (Questions), Session 166, March 1993, 96–7.
77. MEA Annual Report, 1994, 12.
78. 'Mujahideen role in Kashmir alleged', ToI, 18/09/1989.
79. Narayanan interview.
80. Quoted in Adrian Levy and Catherine Scott-Clarke, Nuclear Deception: The Dangerous Relationship Between the United States and Pakistan (New York: Walker and Co., 2008) 182.
81. Rajya Sabha, Session 154, 03/05/1990.
82. Lok Sabha (Questions), Session 4, 15 (21), 05/08/1992.
83. P interview. This Indian intelligence official was posted on the border in late 1980s and arrested Kashmiri men trained by Hekmatyar. Rajya Sabha, Session 164, 1992.
84. 'Rabbani for talks on Kashmir', ToI, 28/09/1992.
85. 'Mojaddedi rakes up border issue,' ToI, 29/05/1992.
86. L interview.
87. Raman, Kaoboys of R&AW, 258.
88. Ibid., 193.
89. Ibid.
90. Kamal Matinuddin, The Taliban Phenomenon: Afghanistan 1994–1997 (Karachi: Oxford University Press, 1999) 179–80.
91. Sood interview.
92. Ibid.
93. 'Recruited by RAW, trained by Army: LTTE,' IBNlive, 07/07/2006.

94. Sitapati, Half Lion, 225–57.
95. Amir Mir, 'Mast Gul, a freedom fighter turned terrorist attacks Peshawar', Dawn.com, 07/02/2014.
96. Email interview with C D Sahay, Chief of R&AW (2003–05), September 2016.
97. Rajya Sabha, Session 173, 15/05/1995.
98. Ibid., 512.
99. Rajya Sabha (Questions), Session 170, 23/02/1994.
100. Rajya Sabha (Questions), Session 166, March 1993, 76.
101. Rajya Sabha (Questions), Session 166, 31/03/1993.
102. Rajya Sabha (Questions), Session 166, March 1993, 76; and Rajya Sabha (Questions), Session 173, 10/05/1995.
103. Islamabad to Washington, [SECRET], 06/12/1994, National Security Archives: http://nsarchive.gwu.edu/NSAEBB/NSAEBB97/tal5.pdf (Accessed 27 March 2017)
104. Srinivasan interview.
105. Srinivasan interview; Bhadrakumar, 'How India reached out to the Afghan Mujahideen'.
106. 'Guerillas take Afghan capital as troops flee', NYT, 28/09/1996.
107. Sood and Mansingh interviews.
108. UNSC Resolution 1076: http://unscr.com/en/resolutions/1076 (Accessed 27 March 2017)
109. Interview with K Raghunath, former Foreign Secretary of India (1997–99), New Delhi, 19/03/2013.
110. Interview with Aunohita Mojumdar, Indian journalist, New Delhi, 30/01/2013.
111. Interview with Shyam Saran, former Foreign Secretary (FS) of India (2004–06), New Delhi, 12/03/2013.
112. M. D. Nalapat 'India has no option but to help Rabbani', ToI, 01/10/1996.
113. Islamabad to Washington, [CONFIDENTIAL], 26/11/1996, National Security Archives: http://nsarchive.gwu.edu/NSAEBB/NSAEBB227/19.pdf
114. CIA [SECRET], August 1996, National Security Archives: http://nsarchive.gwu.edu/NSAEBB/NSAEBB227/10.pdf (Accessed 28 March 2017)
115. Islamabad to Washington, [CONFIDENTIAL], 09/03/1998, National Security Archives: http://nsarchive.gwu.edu/NSAEBB/NSAEBB97/talib6.pdf (Accessed 28 March 2017)
116. Sahay interview.
117. Tara Kartha, 'Pakistan and Taliban: Flux in an Old Relationship?' Institute for Defence Studies and Analyses, 07/10/2000.
118. Mukhopadhaya interview.
119. Islamabad to Washington [CONFIDENTIAL], 10/03/1997, National Security Archives: http://nsarchive.gwu.edu/NSAEBB/NSAEBB227/21.pdf (Accessed 28 March 2017)
120. Prakash Nanda, 'India seeks to open channel with Taliban,' ToI, 28/05/1997.

121. Bhadrakumar, 'Manmohan Singh resets Afghanistan policy'.
122. 'Indians Flee Afghanistan,' ToI, 09/07/1992.
123. MEA Annual Report, 1993, 8–9.
124. MEA Annual Report, 1995, 8–9.
125. Dixit, My South Block Years, 113.
126. Ibid.
127. Seema Guha, 'India's strange silence on the recent events in Afghanistan is baffling,' ToI, 08/10/1996.
128. Ibid.
129. Islamabad to Washington [CONFIDENTIAL], 10/03/1997, National Security Archives: http://nsarchive.gwu.edu/NSAEBB/NSAEBB227/21.pdf (Accessed 27 March 2017)
130. Kartha, 'Pakistan and the Taliban—Flux in an old relationship?'.
131. Islamabad to Washington, [CONFIDENTIAL] 19/02/1996, National Security Archives: http://nsarchive.gwu.edu/NSAEBB/NSAEBB227/9.pdf (Accessed 27 March 2017)
132. 'U.S. govt. to receive Taliban delegation,' ToI, 05/02/1997.
133. Sunil Narula, 'India Still Hesitant,' Outlook, 16/10/1996.
134. Prakash Nanda, 'India seeks to open channel with Taliban,' ToI, 28/05/1997. Srinivasan, who had retired as foreign secretary, though not in the know of specifics of these debates, thinks that it is 'highly likely' that they took place.
135. Ibid.
136. Yusufzai, 'India Must Not Treat The Taliban As Enemy'.
137. Ibid.
138. Rahimullah Yusufzai, 'India Must Not Treat The Taliban As Enemy,' Outlook, 11/06/1997.
139. Raghunath interview.
140. Nanda, 'India seeks to open channel with Taliban'.
141. Ibid.
142. Raghunath interview.
143. I K Gujral, 'We'll discuss all issues hampering ties,' Outlook, 13/03/1997.
144. Ibid.
145. Ibid.
146. J. N. Dixit, 'Making Sense of Afghanistan,' Outlook, 26/06/1997.
147. 'New Afghan Crisis,' ToI, 21/02/1995.
148. Aabha Dixit, 'Taliban Factor in Afghan Civil War', ToI, 24/01/1995.
149. K. Subrahmanyam, 'Pakistan disputes U.N, report on drugs,' ToI, 19/12/1994.
150. Srinivasan interview.
151. Aabha Dixit, 'India's Possible Role in Afghan Conflict,' ToI, 21/10/1994.
152. Dixit, 'Taliban Factor in Afghan Civil War'.
153. US Department of State, [CONFIDENTIAL] 'Discussing Afghan Policy with

the Pakistanis,' 22/12/1995, National Security Archives: http://nsarchive.gwu.edu/NSAEBB/NSAEBB227/7.pdf (Accessed 28 March 2017)

154. 'Reaping the Whirlwind,' ToI, 25/05/1995.
155. Rajya Sabha, Session 179, 03/12/1996.
156. Ibid.
157. Raghunath interview.
158. Mahendra Ved, 'Gujral Supports efforts to prevent Afghanistan from being Balkanised' ToI, 13/09/1997.
159. Raghunath interview.
160. X interview.
161. Interview with Salman Haidar, former Foreign Secretary of India (1995–97), New Delhi, 13/02/2013.
162. Ibid.
163. Shyam Saran interview.
164. Mansingh interview.
165. Ibid.
166. Khosla 'Oral History', 87–103.
167. Haidar, Sood, Mansingh, and Gharekhan interviews.
168. Lok Sabha, Session 3, 27/11/1996.
169. Nambiar interview.
170. Ibid.
171. Lok Sabha, Session 3, 27/11/1996.
172. Ibid.
173. Ibid.
174. Shyam Saran and C interviews.
175. Praveen Swami 'India's new language of killing,' The Hindu, 01/05/2014.
176. 'Seizing Success: Ignoring the media and renewing our commitment in Afghanistan,' Talk by David Sedney, former Deputy Assistant Secretary of Defense for Afghanistan, Pakistan and Central Asia, at the Afghanistan Studies Group, King's College London, 12/05/2014.
177. Interview with A, a senior Indian Military Intelligence officer, identity undisclosed on official's request.
178. Ibid.
179. Ibid.
180. Interview with B, former top military intelligence official of India (contemporary of A), identity undisclosed on interviewee's request.
181. Sood interview.
182. Ibid.
183. Ibid.
184. Steve Coll.,Ghost Wars: The Secret History of the CIA, Afghanistan, and Bin Laden from Soviet invasion to September 10, 2001 (London: Penguin, 2004) 292–3.

185. Haidar interview.
186. X interview.
187. Chris Ogden, 'Tracing the Pakistan-Terrorism Nexus in Indian Security Perspectives: From 1947 to 26/11,' India Quarterly: A Journal of International Affairs, 69 (1) (New Delhi: ICWA, Sage Publishers, 2013) 35–50.
188. Nambiar interview.

5. FRIENDS FROM NORTH, FOES FROM SOUTH: INDIA, UNITED FRONT, AND THE HIJACKING OF FLIGHT IC-814

1. X interview.
2. Interview with Syed Akbar Agha, close aide of Taliban leader Mullah Omar and former chief of the Jaish-ul-Muslimeen, Kabul, 30/04/2013.
3. Coll., Ghost Wars, 352.
4. Nalapat 'India has no option but to help Rabbani'.
5. Ibid.
6. Coll, Ghost Wars, 352.
7. Manoj Joshi, 'India kept Northern Alliance Afloat', ToI, 16/10/2001.
8. Mukhopadhaya interview.
9. Ahmed Rashid, Taliban: Militant Islam, Oil, and Fundamentalism in Central Asia (New Haven: Yale University Press, 1998).
10. Islamabad to Washington, [CONFIDENTIAL] 30/11/1995, National Security Archives: http://nsarchive.gwu.edu/NSAEBB/NSAEBB227/6.pdf (Accessed 27 March 2017)
11. 'India offers aid to Kabul,' ToI, 01/05/1992.
12. Gupta, 'Najibullah: No Escape'.
13. Nambiar interview.
14. 'Mujahideen may help J&K Ultras,' ToI, 28/05/1992.
15. Praveen Sawhney, 'Pak-Afghan Nexus bodes ill for India,' ToI, 31/05/1992.
16. Ibid.
17. 'Indians Flee Afghanistan,' ToI, 09/07/1992.
18. Interview with 'R', former Special Secretary R&AW, New Delhi, 07/03/2013.
19. Sood interview.
20. S. Iftikhar Murshed, Afghanistan: The Taliban Years (London: Bennett and Bloom, 2006) 248.
21. Sood and X interviews.
22. Mojumdar interview.
23. Seema Guha, 'Pakistan got Taliban in, it should take them out: Khalili,' ToI, 17/10/1996.
24. Hamid Ansari in J N Dixit ed., External Affairs: Cross-Border Relations (India: Roli Books 2003) 183.
25. Mojumdar interview.

26. Ibid.
27. Interview with Pranab Dhal Samanta, former bureau chief, Indian Express, New Delhi, 28/01/2013.
28. Mukhopadhaya interview.
29. Interview with Nandan Unnikrishnan, VP at Observer Research Foundation, and formerly with the Press Trust of India, New Delhi, 21/02/2013.
30. Gupta and Saxena, 'Ominous Future'.
31. X interview.
32. Ibid.
33. 'Today We Shall all Die: Afghanistan's Strongmen and the Legacy of Impunity', Human Rights Watch, 03/03/2015: https://www.hrw.org/report/2015/03/03/today-we-shall-all-die/afghanistans-strongmen-and-legacy-impunity (Accessed 28 March 2017)
34. Samanta interview.
35. Mojumdar interview.
36. A. S. Dulat and Aditya Sinha, Kashmir: The Vajpayee Years (New Delhi: HarperCollins, 2015) 290.
37. Ibid.
38. Interview with Rajiv Sikri, Former Additional Secretary, MEA, New Delhi, 23/01/2013.
39. X interview.
40. Ibid.
41. Ibid.
42. 'Key commander and Dostum close aide killed', Afghan Islamic Press, 28/12/1999.
43. Seymour M Hersh, 'The Getaway: Questions Surround a Secret Pakistani Airlift,' The New Yorker, 28/01/2002.
44. Mahendra Ved, 'Afghan trouble is seen as Pakistan's Vietnam,' ToI, 14/10/1996.
45. Ibid.
46. DIA to Washington, [CONFIDENTIAL] 07/11/1996 National Security Archives: http://nsarchive.gwu.edu/NSAEBB/NSAEBB227/17.pdf (Accessed March 28 2017)
47. Interview with Pramit P Chaudhuri, Foreign Editor of the Hindustan Times and former member National Security Advisory Board (NSAB), New Delhi, 14/06/2013.
48. Saran interview.
49. C. and Sikri interviews.
50. Interview with Ahmad Wali Massoud, brother of Ahmad Shah Massoud, Kabul, 29/04/2013.
51. Saikal, Modern Afghanistan, 230; X confirms this.
52. Yusufzai, 'India must not treat the Taliban as enemy'.
53. Ibid.

54. Rajya Sabha (questions), Session 173, 16/05/1995.
55. Yusufzai, 'India must not treat the Taliban as enemy'.
56. Matinuddin, The Taliban Phenomenon, 180.
57. Sitapati, Half Lion, 257–78.
58. Srinivasan interview.
59. Ibid.
60. Praveen Swami, 'The Terror Trajectory,' Frontline, 18 (1), 13–26/10/2001.
61. Rajya Sabha (Questions), Session 179, 11/12/1996.
62. Lok Sabha, Unstarred Question 2521, 12/12/2001.
63. Coll., Ghost Wars, 410.
64. CIA [SECRET] National Security Archive: http://www2.gwu.edu/~nsarchiv/NSAEBB/NSAEBB227/8.pdf (Accessed 27 March 2017)
65. C interview.
66. Ibid.
67. Inderfurth to US State Department', [CONFIDENTIAL], National Security Archive: http://www2.gwu.edu/~nsarchiv/NSAEBB/NSAEBB227/33.pdf (Accessed 28 March 2017)
68. X interview.
69. Interview with Samir Saran, Vice President of the Observer Research Foundation (ORF), New Delhi, 14/03/2013.
70. X interview.
71. Ibid.
72. Satinder K Lambah, 'Graveyard of Empires, Crucible of Coalitions,' Outlook, 26/12/2011.
73. UNSC Resolution 1076: http://nsarchive.gwu.edu/NSAEBB/NSAEBB227/10.pdf (Accessed March 28 2017)
74. MEA Annual Report, 1992.
75. MEA Annual Report, 1991.
76. Ibid.
77. Afghan Information Centre Monthly Bulletin, Nos. 123–4, June–July 1991.
78. MEA Annual Report, 1992.
79. Ibid.
80. UN, Progress Report of the Special Mission to Afghanistan, A/49/208, 01/07/1994.
81. MEA Annual Report, 1994.
82. Srinivasan interview.
83. Ibid.
84. Saikal, 'The UN and Afghanistan', 23.
85. Ibid., 24.
86. Ibid.
87. Islamabad to Washington, [CONFIDENTIAL], 18/10/1995, National Security

Archives: http://nsarchive.gwu.edu/NSAEBB/NSAEBB227/4a.pdf (Accessed 28 March 2017)

88. MEA Annual Report, 1995.
89. Saikal, 'The UN and Afghanistan', 24.
90. Ibid., 31.
91. UNSC SC/6203, 09/04/1996: http://www.un.org/News/Press/docs/1996/19960409.sc6203.html (Accessed March 28 2017)
92. Dixit, My South Block Years, 112.
93. UNSC SC/6203.
94. MEA Annual Report, 1993.
95. Raghunath and Saran interviews.
96. 'India will attend meeting on Afghanistan in Iran,' ToI, 29/10/1996.
97. MEA Annual Report 1996.
98. Haidar interview.
99. Ibid.
100. Raghunath interview.
101. MEA Annual Report 1996.
102. 'Iran sees Taliban as American creation,' ToI, 10/11/1985.
103. 'Rafsanjani urges co-operation to maintain peace in region,' ToI, 17/04/1995.
104. Ibid.
105. K Subrahmanyam, 'Dangerous Liaisons: U.S.-Pak containment of Iran,' ToI, 26/09/1995.
106. Ibid.
107. M. B. Naqvi, 'Taliban remains a thorn in Iran-Pakistan ties,' ToI, 08/11/1995.
108. 'India has no reason to accuse Iran of terrorism: Gujral,' ToI, 24/02/1997.
109. Mansingh interview.
110. Rajya Sabha (Questions), Session 193, 02/08/2001.
111. Text of Tehran Declaration: http://news.bbc.co.uk/1/hi/world/middle_east/3211036.stm (Accessed 28 March 2017)
112. 'Russia charges the U.S. with helping Taliban,' ToI, 13/10/1996.
113. A K Dhar, 'Russia warns of action if Taliban moves North,' ToI, 20/12/1996.
114. CIA, [SECRET], October 09/10/1996, National Security Archives, http://nsarchive.gwu.edu/NSAEBB/NSAEBB295/doc03.pdf (Accessed 28 March 2017)
115. Ibid.
116. MEA Annual Report, 1996.
117. Joshi, 'India kept Northern Alliance Afloat'.
118. MEA Annual Report, 1996.
119. Ibid.
120. Sudha Ramachandran, 'India's Foray into Central Asia,' Asia Times Online, 12/08/2006.

121. A interview.
122. X interview.
123. Ibid.
124. Saikal, Modern Afghanistan, 225.
125. 'China urges Pakistan to curb Taliban's plans: Janes Weekly,' ToI, 10/04/1997.
126. Lok Sabha, Session 3, 27/11/1996.
127. 'Russia, CIS nations plan to raise forces against Taliban,' ToI, 10/03/1997.
128. Rashid, Taliban, 122–45.
129. Lok Sabha, 03/03/2000.
130. Alex Strick van Linschoten and Felix Kuehn, An Enemy We Created: The Myth of the Taliban-Al Qaeda Merger in Afghanistan (Oxford: Oxford University Press, 2012) 199.
131. Jaswant Singh, A Call to Honour: In Service of Emergent India (Indiana: Indiana University Press, 2007) 199–210.
132. Sahay interview.
133. Ibid.
134. Interview with Benoy Khare, Assistant Director (2005–11), Joint Intelligence Committee, National Security Council Secretariat (NSCS), Bangalore, 14/01/2015.
135. Ibid.
136. 'What we did was correct—We had no relations with the Taliban: Brajesh Mishra,' India Today 17/01/2000.
137. Ansari in Dixit ed., External Affairs, 183.
138. 'Did Advani know about Kandahar?' NDTV, 28/08/2009.
139. J N Dixit, India-Pakistan in War and Peace (India: Konark Publishers, 2002) 142.
140. Singh, A Call to Honour, 235.
141. GoI, 'Suo Moto Statement by the EAM Jaswant Singh', 28/02/2000.
142. Lok Sabha, 13/03/2000.
143. Mansingh interview.
144. Dixit, India-Pakistan in War and Peace, 145.
145. Samir Saran interview.
146. Ibid.
147. Sood interview.
148. Ibid.
149. X interview.
150. Raghunath and Sood interviews.
151. Singh, A Call to Honour, 240.
152. Lok Sabha, 10/05/2000.
153. Sood interview.
154. Nirupama Subramaniam, 'IC-814 hijacking: New Taliban chief Mullah Akhtar

Mansour escorted Maulana Masood Azhar, says ex-RAW Officer', Indian Express, 03/08/2015.

155. Sahay interview.
156. Interview with 'D', top Indian security official (details of interview withheld).
157. Raghunath interview.
158. 'Pakistan's nexus with Taliban cannot be ignored: Advani,' The Hindu, 15/09/2001.
159. Dulat and Sinha, Kashmir: The Vajpayee Years, 53–4.
160. Ibid.
161. Samir Saran interview.
162. 'Ajit Doval's speech as Sastra University', Sastra University, 22/04/2015, http://www.dailymotion.com/video/x2njwui
163. Balraj Puri, 'Deoband to Taliban: Fall of a Once Symbol of Nationalism', ToI, 04/10/2001.
164. Lok Sabha, Unstarred Question 3952, 19/04/2000.
165. Jaswant Singh, Suo Moto Statement in Lok Sabha and Rajya Sabha.
166. Jyoti Malhotra, 'India appreciates Taliban's role in hijacking drama,' Express India, 28/12/1999.
167. Ibid.
168. Singh, A Call to Honour, 242.
169. Lok Sabha, Unstarred Question 943, 01/03/2000.
170. Linschoten and Kuehn, An Enemy We Created, 197–200.
171. Akbar Agha interview.
172. Ibid.
173. Interview with Hakimullah Mujahid, former Taliban representative to the UN, Kabul, 06/05/2013.
174. Rajya Sabha (Questions), Session 192, 01/03/2001.
175. Barbara Crossette, 'Tough sanctions imposed on Taliban Government Split UN', NYT, 20/12/2001.
176. Mujahid interview.
177. 'Taliban planning to expel Indian hijacked plane from Afghanistan', Afghan Islamic Press, 26/12/1999.
178. Dulat and Sinha, Kashmir: The Vajpayee Years, 290–1.
179. Ibid.
180. Peshawar to Washington [CONFIDENTIAL] 02/10/1996, National Security Archives: http://nsarchive.gwu.edu/NSAEBB/NSAEBB227/12.pdf (Accessed March 28 2017)
181. Raghunath interview.
182. 'CBI zeroes in on key player in IC-814 hijack,' The Economic Times, 10/11/2003; Rajya Sabha (Questions), Session 200, 17/12/2003.
183. Cable: 05NEWDELHI2266_a, [CONFIDENTIAL], Mulford to unknown,

Wikileaks, 24/03/2005: https://wikileaks.org/plusd/cables/05NEWDELHI2266_a.html (Accessed March 28 2017)

184. Quoted in Jyoti Malhotra, 'India should recognise the Taliban,' Business Standard, 07/12/2009.
185. Lok Sabha, Unstarred question 943, 01/03/2000.
186. Sahay interview.
187. Rajya Sabha (Questions), Session 194, 11/12/2001.
188. Quoted in Malhotra, 'India should recognise the Taliban'.
189. X interview.
190. Sahay interview.
191. Quoted in Malhotra, 'India should recognise the Taliban'.
192. Ibid.
193. Nambiar interview.
194. Ibid.
195. Raja Mohan, 'Taliban wants to Engage India,' The Hindu, 12/02/2001.
196. Ibid.
197. Sood interview.
198. X interview.
199. Dulat and Sinha, Kashmir: Vajpayee Years, 290.
200. Ibid.
201. Swami, 'The Terror Trajectory'.
202. Ibid.
203. 'Govt. plans unified command against terrorism,' ToI, 18/01/2000.
204. Swami, 'The Terror Trajectory'.
205. Ibid.
206. I. K. Gujral, A Foreign Policy for India (New Delhi: Ministry of External Affairs, 1998).
207. Text of the Lahore Declaration: http://mea.gov.in/in-focus-article.htm?18997/Lahore+Declaration+February+1999 (Accessedd 28 March 2017)
208. Dixit, 'Making Sense of Afghanistan'.

6. WAR AND TERROR: DESTRUCTION IN BAMIYAN AND THE AFTERMATH OF 9/11

1. Rajya Sabha, Session 192, 02/03/2001.
2. Strobe Talbott, Engaging India: Diplomacy, Democracy and the Bomb (Washington DC: Brookings Institution, 2004) 119.
3. Rajya Sabha, Session 194, 27/11/2001.
4. Pierre Centlivres, 'The Controversy over the Buddhas of Bamiyan', South Asia Multidisciplinary Academic Journal, 31/12/2008.
5. Nasir Behzad and Daud Qarizadah, 'The man who helped blow up the Bamiyan Buddhas', BBC, 12/03/2015.

6. Census of India: censusindia.gov.in/Census_And_You/religion.aspx (Accessed 28 March 2017)
7. Dixit, An Afghan Diary, 510.
8. Rajya Sabha, Session 180, 02/05/1997.
9. Lok Sabha, 02/03/2001.
10. Rajya Sabha, Session 192, 02/03/2001.
11. Ibid.
12. Lok Sabha, 09/03/2001.
13. 'Imam's conditional offer', The Hindu, 07/03/2001.
14. UNGA Press Release, 09/03/2001: https://www.un.org/press/en/content/general-assembly/press-release (Accessed 28 March 2017)
15. Lok Sabha, Starred Question 442, 18/04/2001.
16. Abdul Salam Zaeef, My Life with the Taliban (London: C Hurst & Co., 2010) 127.
17. Barbara Crosette, 'Taliban Explains Buddha Demolition', NYT, 19/03/2001.
18. Zaeef, My Life with the Taliban, 127.
19. Lok Sabha, Starred Question 60, 25/07/2001.
20. 'Rabbani govt. condemns Taliban decree against Hindus', ToI, 22/05/2001.
21. Rajya Sabha, Session 193, 28/08/2001.
22. Lok Sabha, Unstarred question 40, 20/02/2001.
23. Rajya Sabha, Session 194, 22/11/2001.
24. Akshaya Mukul, 'India less tolerant of Afghan refugees: UNHCR report', ToI, 06/11/2000.
25. UNHCR India: http://www.unhcr.org.in/index.php?option=com_content&view=article&id=8&Itemid=130
26. Lok Sabha, Starred Question. 351, 21/03/2001.
27. Lok Sabha, Unstarred Question. 4534, 17/04/2001.
28. Felix Kuehn and Alex Strick van Linschoten, Missed Opportunities: Lessons from the West's talks with the Taliban pre-2001 (Unpublished paper) 67.
29. UNSC SC/6743, 22/10/1999: https://www.un.org/en/sc/meetings/records/1999.shtml (Accessed 28 March 2017)
30. UNIS/SG/2666, 18/09/2000: https://www.un.org/en/sc/meetings/records/1999.shtml (Accessed March 28 2017)
31. 'Taliban, Iran hold talks,' CNN, 03/02/1999.
32. Coll, Ghost Wars, 410–11.
33. Rashid, Taliban, 134.
34. Unknown to DIA Washington [CONFIDENTIAL], 07/11/1996, National Security Archives: http://nsarchive.gwu.edu/NSAEBB/NSAEBB227/17.pdf (Accessed 27 March 2017)
35. Ibid., 118.
36. Raghunath and Haidar interviews.

37. MEA Annual Report 1999.
38. Rajya Sabha, Session 194, 22/11/2001.
39. Rajya Sabha, Session 194, 26/11/2001.
40. Kuehn and Linschoten, Missed Opportunities, 68.
41. Ibid.
42. Singh, A Call to Honour, 270.
43. Inderfurth to the Secretary of State, [CONFIDENTIAL], National Security Archives: http://www2.gwu.edu/~nsarchiv/NSAEBB/NSAEBB227/33.pdf (Accessed 28 March 2017)
44. Ibid.
45. Kuehn and Linschoten, Missed Opportunities, 68–72.
46. Ibid, 69–70.
47. Rajya Sabha, Session 193, 16/08/2001.
48. R Bedi, 'India Joins anti-Taliban coalition,' Janes Security News, 15/03/2001.
49. Ibid.
50. 'India in anti-Taliban military plan,' Public Affairs Magazine, 26/06/2001.
51. Raghunath and Haidar interviews.
52. Singh, A Call to Honour, 277.
53. Islamabad to Washington [CONFIDENTIAL], 12/11/1996, National Security Archives: http://www2.gwu.edu/~nsarchiv/NSAEBB/NSAEBB227/18.pdf
54. Ibid.
55. Interview with Walter Andersen, former Chief of South Asia Division in the Office of Analysis for the Near East and South Asia, US Department of State, London, 26/08/2014.
56. Quoted in Talbott, Engaging India, 119.
57. Ibid, 120.
58. Ibid.
59. UN Resolution 50/245, 17/09/1996: https://www.un.org/documents/ga/res/50/a50r245.htm (Accessed 27 March 2017)
60. Prakash Nanda, 'India reacts cautiously to U.S. air strikes in Afghanistan, Sudan,' ToI, 22/08/1998.
61. Ibid.
62. 'Jihad against Jews and Crusaders World Islamic Front Statement', South Asia Terrorism Portal, 23/02/1998, http://www.satp.org/satporgtp/usa/IIFstatement.htm (Accessed 27 March 2017)
63. Murshed, Afghanistan: The Taliban Years, 249–50.
64. Ibid.
65. Talbott, Engaging India, 119.
66. Inderfurth to the Secretary of State.
67. Ibid..
68. Pervez Musharraf, In the Line of Fire: A Memoir (New York: Simon and Schuster, 2008) 10–68.

69. Peter R. Lavoy ed., Asymmetric Warfare in South Asia: The Causes and Consequences of the Kargil Conflict (New York: Cambridge University Press, 2009).
70. Singh, A Call to Honour, 190–3.
71. X interview.
72. Singh, A Call to Honour, 320.
73. Inderfurth to Department of State, [SECRET], National Security Archives: http://nsarchive.gwu.edu/NSAEBB/NSAEBB227/34.pdf (Accessed 28 March 2017)
74. 'Indo-Russian meeting will draw up strategy on Afghanistan', ToI, 18/06/2001.
75. MEA Annual Report 2000.
76. Sukumar Muralidharan, 'A recognition of India's "new status"' Frontline, 17 (3), 05–18/02/2000.
77. Venkitesh Ramakrishnan, 'For a new Orientation,' Frontline, 17 (3) 05–18/02/2000.
78. 'The Taliban Formally Recognises Chechnya,' The Jameson Foundation, 18/01/2000.
79. 'Taliban Foe Hurt and Aide Killed by Bomb', NYT, 10/09/2001.
80. Interview with Mohammad Fahim Dashty, former aide of Massoud, Kabul, 08/04/2013.
81. 'Militants attack Kashmir Assembly,' BBC, 01/10/2001.
82. Rajya Sabha (Questions), Session 194, 22/11/2001.
83. Rajya Sabha (Questions), Session 194, 29/11/2001.
84. Rajya Sabha, Session 194, 27/11/2001.
85. Ibid.
86. Rajya Sabha (Questions), Session 194, 29/11/2001.
87. 'Mumbai endorses airstrikes against Afghanistan', ToI, 10/10/2001.
88. Bob Woodward, Bush at War (London: Pocket Books, 2003) 42–8.
89. Ibid., 59.
90. Donald Rumsfeld, Known and Unknown: A Memoir (New York: Sentinel Press, 2011) 397.
91. Rajya Sabha (Questions), Session 194, 20/11/2001.
92. Ibid, 209–10.
93. Rajya Sabha, Session 194, 26/11/2001.
94. Rajya Sabha, Session 194, 27/1//2001.
95. Rajya Sabha, Session 194, 26/11/2001.
96. UNDP Annual Report, 2001: http://www.undp.org/content/dam/undp/library/corporate/UNDP-in-action/2001/English/complete.pdf (Accessed 28 March 2017)
97. Rajya Sabha, Session 194, 26/11/2001.
98. 'CPM opposes U.S. plan to extend action beyond Afghanistan', ToI, 10/10/2002.
99. 'Protest Actions Against US War', People's Democracy, 25 (42), 21/10/2001.

100. USA PATRIOT Act: http://www.gpo.gov/fdsys/pkg/BILLS-107hr3162enr/pdf/BILLS-107hr3162enr.pdf (Accessed 28 March 2017)
101. POTO 2001: http://www.satp.org/satporgtp/countries/india/document/actandordinances/POTO.htm
102. Ben Smith and Arabella Thorpe, 'The legal basis or invasion of Afghanistan', House of Commons, 26/02/2010.
103. Rajya Sabha, Session 194, 26/11/2001.
104. Lok Sabha, Unstarred Question 1686, 28/11/2001.
105. Rajya Sabha, Session 194, 26/11/2001.
106. Ibid., 210.
107. Rajya Sabha, Session 194, 26/11/2001.
108. Ibid.
109. Chidanand Rajghatta, 'Afghan war brings strategic shift in Indo-U.S. relations', ToI, 07/11/2001.
110. Sahgal interview.
111. Rajghatta, 'Afghan war brings strategic shift in Indo-U.S. relations'.
112. Josy Joseph, 'Post-9/11, US sought India's military help for Afghan ops,' ToI, 11/09/2011.
113. Rajya Sabha, Session 194, 19/12/2001.
114. Ibid.
115. Rajya Sabha, Session 194, 18/12/2001.
116. Rajya Sabha, Session 195, 17/05/2002.
117. Srinath Raghavan, 'A Coercive Triangle: India, Pakistan, the United States and the Crisis of 2001–2002,' Defence Studies, 9 (2), 2009, 242–60.
118. James Dobbins, After the Taliban: Nation Building in Afghanistan (Washington DC: Potomac Books, 2008) 112.
119. Satinder Lambah, 'The US Needs to Change its Attitude Towards Indo-Afghan Relations', TheWire.in, 11/12/2015.
120. Mark Sedra, 'Afghanistan: Assessing the Progress of Security Sector Reform, One Year After the Geneva Conference,' Bonn International Centre for Coversion (BICC), 2003, 2–15.
121. Dobbins, After the Taliban, 142; Developing the Afghan army was important for India to ensure a potent counter-balance to Pakistan, and dominated New Delhi's strategic thinking even before the war; Rajya Sabha (Questions), Session 195, 18/04/2002.
122. Gharekhan interview.
123. Sood interview.
124. Saran interview.
125. Sahgal interview.
126. Sikri interview.
127. Ibid.
128. Mukhopadhaya interview.

129. Ibid.
130. Celia W Dugger, 'Gunmen Kill 30, Including 10 Children, in Kashmir', NYT, 15/05/2002.
131. Rajya Sabha, 17/05/2002.
132. Khare interview.
133. 'Task force constituted', The Hindu, 05/11/2005.
134. Khare interview.
135. Narayanan interview.
136. 'Bonn Again? India kept out of the Afghan peace process', ToI, 23/11/2001.
137. Satinder K. Lambah, 'India at the United Nations Talks on Afghanistan, 2001,' Indian Foreign Affairs Journal, 1 (1) January–March (India: Foundation Books, 2006) 76.
138. Andersen interview.
139. UN: http://www.un.org/News/dh/latest/afghan/afghan-agree.htm
140. Lambah, 'Graveyard of Empires, Crucible of Coalitions'.
141. Lambah, 'India at the United Nations Talks on Afghanistan, 2001', 75.
142. X interview.
143. Lambah, 'India at the United Nations Talks on Afghanistan, 2001', 82.
144. Lambah, 'Graveyard of Empires, Crucible of Coalitions'.
145. Mark Fields and Ramsha Ahmed, 'A Review of the 2001 Bonn Conference: An Application to the Road Ahead in Afghanistan,' Strategic Perspectives, Institute for National Strategic Studies (Washington DC: National Defence University, 2011) 6.
146. X interview.
147. 'Bonn Homie', ToI, 06/12/2001.
148. Interview with Satinder Lambah, India's Special Envoy to Afghanistan, New Delhi, 26/03/2013.
149. Dobbins, After the Taliban, 72.
150. Ibid., 73. Former US envoy to Afghanistan Zalmay Khalizad confirms this point in his biography. Zalmay Khalilzad, The Envoy: From Kabul to the White House, my Journey Through a Turbulent World (New York: St. Martins Press, 2016) 177.
151. Fields and Ahmed, 'A Review of the 2001 Bonn Conference', 8.
152. Lambah, 'India at the United Nations Talks on Afghanistan, 2001', 82.
153. Dobbins, After the Taliban, 112.
154. Interview with 'E', Ministry of Defence of India, details withheld.
155. Interview with Abdullah Abdullah, current Chief Executive of Afghanistan, Kabul, 02/05/2013.
156. X interview.
157. 'R' interview.
158. Saran interview.

159. Narayanan interview.
160. Mukhopadhaya interview.
161. Lok Sabha, Unstarred Question 2521, 05/12/2001.
162. Lok Sabha, Unstarred Question 4619, 19/12/2001.
163. Ibid.
164. Aunohita Mojumdar, 'Who gagged Afghan minister, MEA or Hamid Karzai?', ToI, 19/12/2001.
165. Mukhopadhaya interview.
166. Massoud interview.
167. Abdullah interview.
168. Fields and Ahmed, 'A Review of the 2001 Bonn Conference', 7–9.
169. G. Parthasarthy, 'Pakistan ISI and role of their Taliban in Afghanistan,' Securing Asia 2013, https://www.youtube.com/watch?v=ABxqzeZj7lY
170. Sood interview.
171. Islamabad to Wasington [CONFIDENTIAL] National Security Archives: http://nsarchive.gwu.edu/NSAEBB/NSAEBB295/doc09.pdf (Accessed 28 March 2017)
172. Barfield, Afghanistan, 240–71.
173. National Security Archive Electronic Briefing Book 295, [CONFIDENTIAL]: http://nsarchive.gwu.edu/NSAEBB/NSAEBB295/doc13.pdf (Accessed 27 March 2017)

7. 'MAXIMUM LEADER': HAMID KARZAI, INDIA, AND THE KABUL DURBAR

1. Quoted in Robert Kaplan, Monsoon: The Indian Ocean and the Future of American Power (US: Random House, 2011) 213.
2. Vivek Katju, 'In Afghanistan, back to the future,' The Hindu, 24/06/2013.
3. Mukhopadhaya interview.
4. Lok Sabha, Unstarred question 2436, 05/12/2001.
5. Hersh, 'The Getaway'.
6. Michael Moran, 'The Airlift of Evil', Council on Foreign Relations, 29/11/2001.
7. Hersh, 'The Getaway'.
8. Rajya Sabha, Session 194, 06/12/2001.
9. Ibid.
10. Rajya Sabha, Session 197, 12/12/2002.
11. Rajiv Bhatia, India-Myanmar Relations: Changing Contours (New Delhi: Routledge, 2016) 105.
12. Abdullah interview.
13. Hersh, 'The Getaway'.
14. 'Ground broken: TAPI project no more in pipeline', ToI, 14/12/2015.
15. X interview.

16. Manoj Joshi, 'Indian team sets up liaison office in Kabul', ToI, 23/11/2001.
17. Ibid.
18. Cable: 08KABUL2938_a [FOR OFFICIAL USE], Wikileaks, 05/11/2008: https://wikileaks.org/plusd/cables/08KABUL2938_a.html (Accessed March 27 2017)
19. MEA A Development Partnership: http://www.mea.gov.in/Uploads/PublicationDocs/176_india-and-afghanistan-a-development-partnership.pdf (Accessed 28 March 2017)
20. MEA, India-Afghanistan Relations, 2012: http://www.mea.gov.in/Portal/ForeignRelation/afghanistan-aug-2012.pdf; and Gareth Price (2013) 2–10
21. Cable: 05NEWDELHI3746_a, [CONFIDENTIAL], Wikileaks, 18/05/2005: https://wikileaks.org/plusd/cables/05NEWDELHI3746_a.html (Accessed 28 March 2017)
22. Saran interview; '52 Afghan Army cadets to pass out of IMA today,' The Hindu, November 13/11/2013.
23. Lok Sabha, Unstarred Question 1532, 13/03/2002.
24. Rajya Sabha, Session 199, 24/07/2003.
25. Jyoti Thottam, 'Afghanistan: India's Uncertain Road,' Time, April 11/04/2001.
26. Indian Development Cooperation Research (IDCR): http://idcr.cprindia.org/blog/india-afghanistan-partnership (Accessed 28 March 2017)
27. Cited in Rani D Mullen, 'India-Afghan Partnership', IDCR and Centre for Policy Research (CPR), 16/05/2013: http://idcr.cprindia.org/blog/india-afghanistan-partnership (Accessed 27 March 2017)
28. Cable: 05NEWDELHI6797_a, [CONFIDENTIAL], Mulford to unknown, Wikileaks, 02/09/2005, https://wikileaks.org/plusd/cables/05NEWDELHI6797_a.html (Accessed 28 March 2017)
29. Rajya Sabha, Session 206, 08/12/2005.
30. Meeta Parti, 'India and US to strengthen livelihoods of over 3,000 Afghan women', US Aid, 08/05/2015.
31. Rajya Sabha, Session 204, 02/05/2005.
32. Lok Sabha, Unstarred Question 580, 04/03/2002.
33. MEA A Development Partnership
34. Rajya Sabha, Session 204, 24/03/2005; Session 203, 09/12/2004; Session 199, 24/07/2003.
35. Rajya Sabha, Session 198, 24/04/2003.
36. Aman Malik, 'ITBP wants more forces and better weapons in Afghanistan,' LiveMint, 02/10/2014.
37. Interview with F, FICCI official, New Delhi, 2013.
38. A, X, and Khare interviews.
39. Mukhopadhaya interview.
40. Interview with 'M', various Indian consular officials in Herat, Afghanistan, April 2013.

41. MEA ICCR Scholarships: http://eoi.gov.in/kabul/?0359?000
42. Saran and Mukhopadhaya interviews,
43. Email interview with Mahmood Khan, Member of Parliament (Wolesi Jirga) of Afghanistan, 07/04/2013.
44. Ludin, Ahmadi, and Musazai interviews.
45. Talk by Tariq Ismati, former deputy minister at the Ministry of Rural Rehabilitation and Development (MRRD, at the Afghanistan Studies Group, KCL, 14/12/2013.
46. Abdullah interview.
47. Akbar Agha interview.
48. Rahimullah Yusufzai, 'The Taliban And India Can Be Reconciled', Outlook, 05/04/2010.
49. Interview with G, Indian diplomat, details of interview withheld.
50. On Karzai family's role in the Afghan war, see Joshua Partlow, A Kingdom of Their Own: The Family Karzai and the Afghan Disaster (London: Simon and Schuster, 2016).
51. Narayanan interview.
52. Mukhopadhaya interview.
53. Saran interview.
54. MEA Annual Report 2004.
55. Samanta interview.
56. MEA Annual Report 2005.
57. Cable: 06NEWDELHI7870_a, [CONFIDENTIAL], Roemer to Secretary of State, Wikileaks, 20/11/2006, https://wikileaks.org/plusd/cables/06NEWDELHI7870_a.html (Accessed March 28 2017)
58. Chaudhuri interview.
59. Cable: 08NEWDELHI3165_a, [SECRET], Mulford to Secretary of State, Wikileaks, 16/12/2008, https://wikileaks.org/plusd/cables/08NEWDELHI3165_a.html (Accessed March 28 2017)
60. MEA Annual Report 2007.
61. Cable: 07NEWDELHI1051_a, [SECRET], Wikileaks, 02/03/2007, https://wikileaks.org/plusd/cables/07NEWDELHI1051_a.html (Accessed March 28 2017)
62. Cable: 08NEWDELHI270_a, [CONFIDENTIAL] Wikileaks, 28/01/2008: https://wikileaks.org/plusd/cables/08NEWDELHI270_a.html (Accessed March 28 2017)
63. Interview with Rakesh Sood, India's Ambassador to Afghanistan (2005–2008), New Delhi, 17/06/2013.
64. Mukhopadhaya interview.
65. Cable: 09NEWDELHI2396_a, [CONFIDENTIAL], Roemer to Secretary of State, Wikileaks, 27/11/2009, https://wikileaks.org/plusd/cables/09NEWDELHI2396_a.html (Accessed March 28 2017)

66. Interview with Waheed Omar, former Spokesperson at the Office of the President of Afghanistan, Kabul, 11/04/2013.
67. Interview with Shivshankar Menon, National Security Advisor of India (2010–2014), London, 24/11/2014.
68. Ibid.
69. Akbar Agha and Mujahid interviews.
70. Mukhopadhaya interview.
71. Prasad interview.
72. Mukhopadhaya interview.
73. X interview.
74. Telephone interview with M K Bhadrakumar, former director and joint secretary MEA, 1990–92, 03/06/2013.
75. Abdullah interview.
76. 'President Karzai's Interaction with Press & think-tanks in New Delhi, India', Arg 1880, 14/12/2013, https://www.youtube.com/watch?v=LZ5AqYtE0OA (Accessed March 28 2017)
77. Ibid.
78. Quoted in Bob Woodward, Obama's Wars: The Inside Story (London: Simon and Schuster, 2010) 163.
79. Chaudhuri interview.
80. Samir Saran interview.
81. UK Home Office, 'Afghanistan: persons supporting or perceived to support the government and/or international forces', Country Information and Guidance, February 2015, 21–2.
82. Cable: 10KABUL408_a, [CONFIDENTIAL], Eikenberry to Secretary of State, Wikileaks, 03/02/2010: https://wikileaks.org/plusd/cables/10KABUL408_a.html (Accessed March 28 2017)
83. Saran interview.
84. Interview with Shashank, Foreign Secretary of India (2003–04), New Delhi, 19/03/2013.
85. Fidai interview.
86. Massoud interview.
87. Interviews with Omar Sharifi, Sanjar Sohail, Fahim Dashty, and C, Kabul, 2013.
88. Interview with Haji Mohammad Mohaqiq, leader of Hizb-e-Wahdat, Kabul, 03/05/2013.
89. Abdullah interview.
90. Ibid.
91. Wali Massoud interview.
92. C interview.
93. Wali Massoud interview.
94. Ibid.

95. UNAMA, 06/05/2013, http://unama.unmissions.org/Default.aspx?ctl=Details&tabid=12329&mid=15870&ItemID=36778 (Accessed March 28 2017)
96. Interview with Hanif Atmar, Kabul, current National Security Advisor of Afghanistan, 27/04/2013.
97. Mukhopadhaya interview.
98. Prasad interview.
99. Ibid.
100. Sood interview.
101. Interview with Jawed Ludin, former Deputy Foreign Minister of Afghanistan, Kabul, 22/04/2013.
102. Ibid.
103. Interview with Ershad Ahmadi, Deputy Foreign Minister of Afghanistan (2013–14), Kabul, 07/04/2013.
104. Interview with Janan Musazai, former Afghan Ambassador to Pakistan, Kabul, 07/04/2013.
105. Ibid.
106. Interview with Mahmoud Saikal, Afghan Deputy Foreign Minister for Economic Affairs (2005–06), Kabul, 02/05/2013.
107. Cable: 08NEWDELHI1433_a, [CONFIDENTIAL] Mulford to CIA, 27/05/2008, Wikileaks: http://www.wikileaks.org/plusd/cables/08NEWDELHI1433_a.html (Accessed March 28 2017)
108. Katju, 'In Afghanistan, back to the future'.
109. 'R' interview.
110. Ibid.
111. X interview.
112. Ibid.
113. A interview.
114. Narayanan interview.
115. Swami, 'India's New Language of Killing'.
116. Menon interview' Cable: 08NEWDELHI1957_a, [SECRET], Mulford to Washington, 15/07/2008, Wikileaks: https://wikileaks.org/plusd/cables/08NEWDELHI1957_a.html (Accessed March 28 2017)
117. Cable: 07ISLAMABAD1583_a, [SECRET], Bodde to Secretary of State, Wikileaks, 10/04/2007: https://wikileaks.org/plusd/cables/07ISLAMABAD1583_a.html (Accessed March 28 2017)
118. Narayanan interview (regarding concerns of a coup against Karzai); and Cable: 10KABUL503_a, [SECRET], Wikileaks, 09/02/2010: https://wikileaks.org/plusd/cables/10KABUL503_a.html
119. Cable: 08NEWDELHI1433_a.
120. Narayanan interview.
121. Ibid.

122. M. K. Bhadrakumar, 'India resets its Afghan policies,' Russia and India Report, 16/12/2013.
123. Praveen Swami, 'Why India is concerned about supplying arms to Afghanistan', Firstpost, 23/05/2013.
124. Ludin interview.
125. Cable: 06KABUL1977_a, [CONFIDENTIAL], Neumann to Secretary of State, 02/05/2006, Wikileaks: https://wikileaks.org/plusd/cables/06KABUL1977_a.html (Accessed March 28 2017)
126. Indrani Bagchi, 'Wary of Pakistan, India hesitant over Karzai wish list for military hardware,' ToI, 23/05/2013.
127. Shanthie Mariet D'Souza, 'President Karzai's Wishlist and New Delhi's Strategic Volte-Face in Afghanistan,' Georgetown Journal of International Affairs, 11/06/2013.
128. 'India to provide helicopters to Afghanistan soon,' NDTV, 15/02/2014.
129. Bagchi, 'Wary of Pakistan, India hesitant over Karzai wish list for military hardware'.
130. Menon and L interviews.
131. Chaudhuri interview.
132. Sahgal Interview.
133. Chaudhuri interview.
134. 'Karzai's visit: New Delhi should help Kabul in all respects, except military boots on the ground', ToI, 24/05/2013.
135. Quoted in Sanjay Kumar, 'Why India Can't fulfill Afghanistan's Wish List,' The Diplomat, 31/05/2013.
136. 'Ex-NSA Narayanan had differences with PM: Wikileaks', ANI News, 03/09/2011.
137. 'Karzai's Wishlist,' Indian Express, 23/05/2013.
138. Shekhar Gupta, 'Get out, leave Af to Pak,' Indian Express, 21/11/2011.
139. Ibid.
140. L interview.
141. L and Menon interviews.
142. L interview.
143. Menon interview.
144. X interview.
145. 'Russia sends 10,000 automatic rifles to Afghanistan as a gift to fight insurgency', ABC News, 24/02/2016.
146. Atmar interview.

8. NO GOOD TALIBAN? INDIA'S TALIBAN LEARNING CURVE

1. Yusufzai, 'The Taliban and India Can Be Reconciled'.

2. Shashi Tharoor, Pax Indica—India and the World of the 21st Century (New Delhi: Allen Lane, 2012) 96.
3. Menon interview.
4. Interview with T, former intelligence analyst at the Joint Intelligence Committee, National Security Council Secretariat (NSCS). Details of this interview have been withheld on the interviewee's request.
5. Pranay Sharma, 'Dead Driver's boss on security recce: Border Roads chief set for Afghanistan', The Telegraph, 25/11/2005.
6. Rajya Sabha, Session 206, 01/12/2005.
7. Ibid.
8. Cable: 05NEWDELHI8933_a.
9. Rajya Sabha, Session 200, 12/12/2003.
10. 'Terrorist attacks and threats on Indians in Afghanistan since 2003', South Asia Terrorism Portal (SATP), http://www.satp.org/satporgtp/countries/india/database/afganistanindianattack.htm
11. Paul Watson, 'Afghan Abductors Free Two Indians,' Los Angeles Times, 25/12/2003.
12. 'M K Narayanan sees Pakistan's hand in the killing of Maniappan,' The Hindu, 27/11/2005.
13. Rajya Sabha, Session 200, 12/12/2003.
14. 'Terrorist attacks and threats on Indians in Afghanistan since 2003', SATP.
15. Cable: 06NEWDELHI2967_a, [CONFIDENTIAL], Blake to Director National Intelligence, Wikileaks, 01/05/2006: https://wikileaks.org/plusd/cables/06NEWDELHI2967_a.html (Accessed March 28 2017)
16. Cable: 06NEWDELHI2967_a.
17. Cable: 05NEWDELHI9771_a, [CONFIDENTIAL], 28/12/2005, Wikileaks: https://wikileaks.org/plusd/cables/05NEWDELHI9771_a.html (Accessed March 28 2017)
18. Rajya Sabha, Session 200, 12/12/2003.
19. Narayanan interview.
20. Rajya Sabha, Session 200, 12/12/2003.
21. Ibid.
22. Saeed Ali Achakzai, 'Taliban splits', Reuters, 10/08/2004.
23. Akbar Agha interview.
24. X interview.
25. Cable: 09NEWDELHI413_a, [CONFIDENTIAL], White to Secretary of State, Wikileaks, 05/03/2009, https://wikileaks.org/plusd/cables/09NEWDELHI413_a.html (Accessed March 28 2017)
26. Khare interview.
27. Menon interview.
28. Sahgal interview. Vivek Katju was unavailable for an interview for this book.

29. This information is based on this author's confidential interviews with Indian, Afghan, and Western officials. The details of these interviews, unfortunately, cannot be divulged. Thus, little evidence can be offered to prove that such dealings actually did take place. However, given the history of India's covert engagement with insurgents both within and outside India (in places such as Kashmir, Myanmar, Northeast, Sri Lanka, Nepal, and Tibet), the possibility of such deals, for whatever purpose they were undertaken, remains within the realm of possibility.
30. 'Strategic Response to Terrorism: NSA Ajit Doval's full speech', Sastra University, 26/11/2014, https://www.youtube.com/watch?v=v4RaCJrT51w
31. Saran interview.
32. Sahgal interview.
33. Interview with Sameer Patil, Assistant Director (2008–13), Joint Intelligence Committee, National Security Council Secretariat, May 05, 2017 [Via Skype].
34. Menon and Prasad interviews; ATTACK THREAT RPT Kabul, 'TB Threat to Indian embassy', 01/07/2008, POLISH NIC THREAT REPORT: Wikileaks: https://warlogs.wikileaks.org/id/7C4503CB-2219–0B3F-9FF7098AB77A6582/ (Accessed March 28 2017)
35. Mark Mazzetti and Eric Schmitt, 'Pakistanis aided attack in Kabul, U.S. officials say', NYT, 01/08/2008.
36. Menon and Prasad interviews.
37. Khare interview.
38. Ibid.
39. Patil interview.
40. Mariana Baabar, 'Got The Bla-Hs', Outlook India, 24/04/2006.
41. Baabar, 'RAW is training 600 Balochis in Afghanistan'.
42. Khare interview.
43. V K Shashikumar, 'The India factor in Afghanistan', India Defence Review, 23 (3), July–September 2008; Andrew Small, The China-Pakistan Axis: Asia's New Geopolitics (London: C Hurst & Co., 2015) 114.
44. Shashikumar, 'The India factor in Afghanistan'.
45. Khare interview.
46. Saran interview.
47. Cable: 09NEWDELHI288_a, [CONFIDENTIAL] Mulford to Secretary of State, Wikileaks, 17/02/2009, https://wikileaks.org/plusd/cables/09NEWDELHI288_a.html (Accessed March 28 2017)
48. Saran interview.
49. Sandeep Unnithan, Black Tornado: Mumbai 26/11 (New Delhi: HarperCollins, 2015).
50. 'Afghan blast targets Indian embassy', Al Jazeera, 08/10/2009.
51. 'Terrorist attacks and threats on Indians in Afghanistan since 2003', SATP.
52. Dalrymple, 'A Deadly Triangle: Afghanistan, Pakistan, and India'.

53. 'Terrorist attacks and threats on Indians in Afghanistan since 2003', SATP.
54. G interview.
55. MEA Annual Report 2008.
56. Prasad interview.
57. Narayanan interview.
58. MEA Annual Report, 2009.
59. Yusufzai, 'The Taliban And India Can Be Reconciled'.
60. Menon interview.
61. 'Afghanistan: Devastation after botched attack on Indian consulate', The Telegraph, August 03/08/2013.
62. 'Terrorist attacks and threats on Indians in Afghanistan since 2003', SATP.
63. Ibid.
64. Department of State, Office of the Spokesperson, 25/06/2014, http://www.state.gov/r/pa/prs/ps/2014/06/228431.htm (Accessed March 28 2017)
65. 'Terrorist attacks and threats on Indians in Afghanistan since 2003', SATP.
66. Ibid.
67. Vijaita Singh, 'IB told Rajnath: NATO troops withdrawal from Afghan will up infiltration, terror activities', Indian Express, 06/06/2014.
68. 'Terrorist attacks and threats on Indians in Afghanistan since 2003', SATP.
69. Praveen Swami, 'Indian consulate attack: Before dying, Afghan attackers scrawled "Afzal Guru avenged" on walls', Indian Express, 06/01/2016.
70. Cable: 06NEWDELHI3506_a, [CONFIDENTIAL], Mulford to DNI, 19/05/2006, Wikileaks, https://wikileaks.org/plusd/cables/06NEWDELHI3506_a.html (Accessed March 28 2017)
71. Jyoti Malhotra, 'MK on Kabul recce mission,' The Telegraph, 04/10/2007.
72. Khare and Narayanan interviews.
73. Malhotra, 'MK on Kabul recce mission'.
74. Ludin and Ahmadi interviews.
75. Cable: 08NEWDELHI1433_a.
76. Ibid.
77. X interview and other confidential interviews with top Indian security officials.
78. Rakesh Sood interview.
79. Prasad interview.
80. Carlotta Gall, 'New Intelligence Chief Aims to Earn Afghan's Trust', NYT, 19/08/2010.
81. Khare interview.
82. Menon interview (confirmed by X).
83. Ibid.
84. X interview.
85. Patil interview.
86. B interview.

87. F interview.
88. T interview.
89. Shishir Gupta, 'India Shifts Afghanistan Policy, ready to talk to the Taliban,' Indian Express, 29/03/2010.
90. Menon interview.
91. Ibid.
92. Cable: 05NEWDELHI1073_a, [CONFIDENTIAL], Mulford to unknown, Wikileaks, 10/02/2005, https://wikileaks.org/plusd/cables/05NEWDELHI 1073_a.html
93. Samanta interview.
94. Samanta interview.
95. Text of India-Afghanistan SPA: http://mfa.gov.af/Content/files/Agreement%20 on%20Strategic%20Partnership%20Between%20The%20Islamic%20 Republic%20of%20Afghanistan%20and%20Republic%20of%20India.pdf
96. X interview.
97. Ibid.
98. Khare and B interviews.
99. X interview.
100. Ibid.
101. Yusufzai, 'The Taliban And India Can Be Reconciled'.
102. Ibid.
103. Mullah Zaeef, 'Think', Tehelka, Goa, 2013, http://thinkworks.in/speakers/ mullah-abdul-salam-zaeef/
104. 'Indian visa granted to Taliban leader after suggestions from intelligence agencies', DNA India, 12/11/2013.
105. Interview with Sanaullah Tasal, security analyst, Bachcha Khan Foundation, Kabul, 19/04/2013.
106. Ibid.
107. Akbar Agha interview.
108. Menon interview.
109. Ibid.
110. Senate Committee on Armed Services, 22/09/2011: http://www.armed-services.senate.gov/imo/media/doc/11–70%20 %209–22–11.pdf
111. Vahid Brown and Don Rassler, Fountainhead of Jihad—The Haqqani Nexus, 1973–2012 (New Delhi: Hachette India, 2013) 152–6.
112. Syed Saleem Shahzad, Inside Al-Qaeda and the Taliban: Beyond Bin Laden and 9/11 (London: Pluto Press, 2013).
113. Ibid., 6–10.
114. Cable: 08NEWDELHI1957_a
115. Ibid; Menon interview.
116. Swami, 'India's new language of killing'.

117. Menon interview.
118. Menon interview.
119. Nambiar interview.
120. Cable: 06ISLAMABAD11311_a, [SECRET], Crocker to Secretary of State, 15/06/2006, Wikileaks: https://wikileaks.org/plusd/cables/06ISLAMABAD11311_a.html (Accessed March 28 2017)
121. Nambiar interview.
122. Sood interview.
123. Khare interview.
124. 'Balochistan Insurgency: Fourth Conflict', Global Security.
125. Anurag Kotoky and A Ananthlakshmi, 'India "concerned" by China role in Pakistan's Gwadar port', Reuters, 16/02/2013.
126. Balochistan Insurgency: Fourth Conflict', Global Security.
127. Cable: 06NEWDELHI163_a, [CONFIDENTIAL], Mulford to Secretary of State, Wikileaks, 09/01/2006: https://wikileaks.org/plusd/cables/06NEWDELHI163_a.html (Accessed March 28 2017)
128. Ibid.
129. Cable: 06ISLAMABAD16962_a.
130. Cable: 06NEWDELHI1230_a, [CONFIDENTIAL], Mulford to Secretary of State, 16/02/2006, Wikileaks: https://wikileaks.org/plusd/cables/06NEWDELHI1230_a.html (Accessed March 28 2017)
131. Cable: 06ISLAMABAD18929_a, [SECRET], Bodde to Secretary of State, 25/09/2006, Wikileaks:, https://wikileaks.org/plusd/cables/06ISLAMABAD18929_a.html (Accessed March 28 2017)
132. MEA Statement 28/08/2006: https://www.indianembassy.org/archives_details.php?nid=647 (Accessed March 28 2017)
123. Quoted in Suhasini Haidar, 'In policy shift, Modi brings up Balochistan again', The Hindu, 16/08/2016.
134. Rajya Sabha, Session 217, 2009.
135. Cable: 07ISLAMABAD256_a, [SECRET], Crocker to Secretary of State, 17/01/2007, Wikileaks:, https://wikileaks.org/plusd/cables/07ISLAMABAD256_a.html
136. Ibid.
137. Cable: 07KABUL185_a, [SECRET], Neumann to Secretary of State, 20/01/2007, Wikileaks:, https://wikileaks.org/plusd/cables/07KABUL185_a.html (Accessed March 28 2017)
138. Ibid.+++
139. Khare interview.
140. Ibid.
141. Cable: 08PARTO100603_a, [CONFIDENTIAL], US Delegation to NSC, Cablegate: Wikileaks, 06/10/2008, https://wikileaks.org/plusd/cables/08PARTO100603_a.html (Accessed March 28 2017)

142. Cable: 09KARACHI73_a, [CONFIDENTIAL], Kaachi to Secretary of State, 06/03/2009, Wikileaks: https://wikileaks.org/plusd/cables/09KARACHI73_a.html (Accessed March 28 2017)
143. Cable: 08ISLAMABAD3716_a, [SECRET], Islamabad to Secretary of State, 28/11/2008, Wikileaks:, https://wikileaks.org/plusd/cables/08ISLAMABAD3716_a.html (Accessed March 28 2017)
144. Cable: 09KARACHI145_a, [CONFIDENTIAL], Karachi to Secretary of State, April 27/04/2009, Wikileaks: https://wikileaks.org/plusd/cables/09KARACHI145_a.html (Accessed March 28 2017)
145. Cable: 09NEWDELHI797_a, [CONFIDENTIAL], Burleigh to Secretary of State, 22/04/2009, Wikileaks: https://wikileaks.org/plusd/cables/09NEWDELHI797_a.html (Accessed March 28 2017)
146. Hamid Mir, 'India and the Baloch insurgency', The Hindu, 28/07/2009.
147. MEA Statement 16/07/2009: http://mea.gov.in/bilateral-documents.htm?dtl/4855/Joint+Statement+Prime+Minister+of+India+Dr+Manmohan+Singh+and+the+Prime+Minister+of+Pakistan+Syed+Yusuf+Raza+Gilani
148. Lok Sabha, 29/07/2009.
149. Ibid.
150. Siddharth Vardarajan, 'No 'sell-out' at Sharm-el-Sheikh; Pakistan forced to admit terror link', The Hindu, 18/07/2009.
151. Khare interview.
152. Menon interview.
153. Kallol Bhattacherjee and Suhasini Haidar, 'Pakistan outraged at presence of Baloch activist in India', The Hindu, 09/10/2015.
154. Kallol Bhattacherjee and Suhasini Haidar, 'After PoK, India turns focus on Balochistan', The Hindu, 08/10/2015.
155. Ibid.
156. Author's confidential interviews with serving Indian intelligence officials in 2015 and 2016.
157. Haidar, 'After PoK, India turns focus on Balochistan'.
158. Paul Staniland, Networks of Rebellion: Explaining Insurgent Cohesion and Collapse (Ithaca: Cornell University Press, 2014) 7–10.
159. Rohan Joshi, 'Pakistan's Terrorism Accusation Against India: Bizarre But Calculated', The Diplomat, 03/03/2015.
160. 'Pakistan Taliban leader Latif Mehsud seized by US military forces', The Telegraph, 12/10/2013.
161. Cable: 10ABUDHABI9_a, [SECRET], Olson to CIA, 07/01/2010, Wikileaks:, https://wikileaks.org/plusd/cables/10ABUDHABI9_a.html (Accessed March 28 2017)
162. Khare interview.
163. Nilanjana Bhowmick, 'Indian Hospitals Are Doing a Roaring Trade in Medical Tourists from Afghanistan', Time, 03/03/2014.

164. T interview.
165. Ibid.
166. Zahir Shah Sherazi, 'Zarb-e-Azb operation: 120 suspected militants killed in N Waziristan', Dawn, 16/06/2014.
167. On Indian decision-making after 26/11 see Shivshankar Menon, Choices: Inside the Making of India's Foreign Policy (Washington DC: Brookings Institution, 2016) 60–81.
168. Mukhopadhaya interview.
169. X interview.

9. FIRST AS TRAGEDY, THEN AS FARCE: MANAGING THE US WITHDRAWAL

1. Cable: 08NEWDELHI3165_a.
2. Ludin interview.
3. Woodward, Bush at War, 58–61.
4. Cable: 09STATE131801_a, [SECRET], Secretary of State to Department of Treasury, 30/12/2009, Wikileaks: https://wikileaks.org/plusd/cables/09STATE131801_a.html (Accessed March 28 2017)
5. Saeed Shah, Adam Entous, and Gordon Lubold, 'U.S. Threatens to Withold Pakistan Aid', Wall Street Journal, 21/08/2015.
6. Cable: 10NEWDELHI263_a, '[FOR OFFICIAL USE], Roemer to Secretary of State, 09/02/2010, Wikileaks: https://wikileaks.org/plusd/cables/10NEWDELHI263_a.html
7. Cable: 05NEWDELHI395_a, [CONFIDENTIAL], Mulford to unknown, Wikileaks, 14/01/2005, https://wikileaks.org/plusd/cables/05NEWDELHI395_a.html (Accessed March 28 2017)
8. Alex Marshall and Tim Bird, Afghanistan: How the West Lost its Way (Yale: Yale University Press, 2011) 112–13.
9. Dobbins, After the Taliban, 120–21.
10. 'Obama announces Afghanitsan troop withdrawal plan', CNN, 23/06/2011.
11. Interview with H, senior Western official posted in Afghanistan. Details of interview withheld.
12. Saran interview.
13. Ludin interview.
14. Mukhopadhaya interview.
15. Javid Ahmad, 'Russia and the Taliban Make Amends: Moscow's New Ally in Afghanistan', Foreign Affairs, 31/01/2016.
16. Margherita Stancati, 'Iran Backs Taliban With Cash and Arms', Wall Street Journal, 11/06/2015.
17. On the Afghan reconciliation process, see Michael Semple, Reconciliation in Afghanistan (Washington DC: United States Institute for Peace Press, 2009); and

Sherard Cowper-Coles, Cables from Kabul—The Inside Story of the West's Afghanistan Campaign (London: Harper Press, 2012); On the Chantilly process, see Saba Imtiaz, 'The Outcomes of the 'Taliban/Paris Meeting on Afghanistan', Al Jazeera, January 24/01/2013.

18. Sahgal interview.
19. Amit Baruah, 'No troops for Iraq Without Explicit UN Mandate: India', The Hindu, 15/07/2003; for more on this see Rudra Chaudhuri, Forged in Crisis: India and the United States Since 1947 (New York: Oxford University Press, 2014).
20. Chaudhuri, Forged in Crisis, 175–212.
21. Rajya Sabha, Session 198, 09/04/2003.
22. 2003 US Federal Budget, http://federal-budget.insidegov.com/l/106/2003
23. Interview with I, mid-ranking MEA official, 2016, details of interview withheld.
24. World Economic and Financial Surveys, 'World Economic Outlook: April 2009', International Monetary Fund, 2009, 2–9.
25. Rajya Sabha, Session 198, 09/04/2003.
26. Mukhopadhaya interview.
27. Quoted in Kaplan, Monsoon, 213.
28. Robert Grenier, 88 Days to Kandahar: A CIA Diary (New York: Simon and Schuster Paperbacks, 2015), 21–3.
29. Cable: 05NEWDELHI5117_a, [CONFIDENTIAL], 15/07/2005, Wikileaks:, https://wikileaks.org/plusd/cables/05NEWDELHI5117_a.html (Accessed March 28 2017)
30. Alastair Liethead, 'Frustrated Karzai toughens stance' BBC, 26/06/2006.
31. 'Afghanistan: Civilians bear cost of escalating insurgent attacks', Human Rights Watch, 16/04/2007.
32. James Baker and Lee Hamilton et al. Authorised Ed., The Iraq Study Group Report: The Way Forward—A New Approach. (New York: Vintage Books, 2006).
33. Cable: 06NEWDELHI8278_a, [SECRET], Pyatt to DNI, 11/12/2006, Wikileaks:, https://wikileaks.org/plusd/cables/06NEWDELHI8278_a.html (Accessed March 28 2017)
34. Cable: 07ISLAMABAD1583_a.
35. Cable: 06NEWDELHI8278_a.
36. 'India's GDP booms at 7.5% in 2004–05', Rediff News, 31/01/2006.
37. Cable: 05NEWDELHI8933_a, [CONFIDENTIAL], 25/11/2005, Wikileaks, https://wikileaks.org/plusd/cables/05NEWDELHI8933_a.html (Accessed March 28 2017)
38. Saran interview.
39. Narayanan interview.
40. Chaudhuri interview.

41. Saran interview.
42. Ibid.
43. Shashank interview.
44. Lalit K Jha, 'Pakistan safe havens helped Taliban regroup: US documents,' Pajhwok News, 14/09/2010.
45. International Security Program, 'Drone Wars Pakistan: Analysis', New America Foundation, http://securitydata.newamerica.net/drones/pakistan-analysis.html (Accessed March 28 2017)
46. Cable: 07NEWDELHI1051_a.
47. Ibid.
48. Cable: 08NEWDELHI560_a, [CONFIDENTIAL], Mulford to Secretary of State, 22/02/2008, Wikileaks: https://wikileaks.org/plusd/cables/08NEWDELHI560_a.html (Accessed March 28 2017)
49. On insider accounts on US decision-making see Woodward, Obama's Wars; Robert Gates, Duty: Memoirs of a Secretary at War (London: Alfred Knopf, 2014) 335–86; Hillary Rodham Clinton, Hard Choices: A Memoir (London: Simon and Schuster, 2014) 129–69.
50. The White House, 01/12/2009: https://www.whitehouse.gov/the-press-office/remarks-president-address-nation-way-forward-afghanistan-and-pakistan (Accessed March 28 2017)
51. Cable: 09NEWDELHI797_a.
52. C Christine Fair, 'The Other Drawdown in Afghanistan', Current History: A Journal of Contemporary World Affairs, April 2015, 137–43.
53. Laura Rozen, 'India's stealth lobbying against Holbrooke's brief', Foreign Policy, 24/01/2009.
54. Cable: 09NEWDELHI413_a.
55. Cable: 09NEWDELHI288_a.
56. Cable: 09NEWDELHI283_a, [CONFIDENTIAL], Mulford to Secretary of State, 13/02/2008, Wikileaks:, https://wikileaks.org/plusd/cables/09NEWDELHI283_a.html (Accessed March 28 2017)
57. Cable: 09NEWDELHI782_a, [UNCLASSIFIED], Burliegh to Secretary of State, 21/04/2009, Wikileaks:, https://wikileaks.org/plusd/cables/09NEWDELHI782_a.html (Accessed March 28 2017)
58. Cable: 09NEWDELHI1339_a, [SECRET], Burliegh to CIA, 29/06/2009, Wikileaks: https://wikileaks.org/plusd/cables/09NEWDELHI1339_a.html
59. Cable: 10NEWDELHI162_a, [CONFIDENTIAL], Roemer to Secretary of State, 28/01/2010, Wikileaks:, http://wikileaks.org/cable/2010/01/10NEWDELHI162.html (Accessed March 28 2017)
60. Cable: 09NEWDELHI1338_a, [SECRET], Burliegh to Secretary of State, 29/06/2009, Wikileaks:, https://wikileaks.org/plusd/cables/09NEWDELHI1338_a.html (Accessed March 28 2017)

61. Patil interview.
62. Cable: 09LONDON2557_a, [CONFIDENTIAL], Sussman to Secretary of State, 13/11/2009, Wikileaks: https://wikileaks.org/plusd/cables/09LONDON 2557_a.html
63. Ibid.
64. Cable: 09KABUL3814_a, [UNCLASSIFIED], Eikenberry to Secretary of State, 30/11/2009, Wikileaks:, https://wikileaks.org/plusd/cables/09KABUL3814_a. html (Accessed March 28 2017)
65. Cable: 09KABUL3974_a, [CONFIDENTIAL], Ricciardone to Secretary of State, 09/12/2009, Wikileaks:, https://wikileaks.org/plusd/cables/09KABUL 3974_a.html (Accessed March 28 2017)
66. I interview.
67. Paul Reynolds, 'Aims of the London conference on Afghanistan,' BBC, 28/01/2010.
68. Ashis Ray, 'World Rejects India's Taliban Stand,' ToI, 29/01/2010.
69. Cable: 10ANKARA154_a, [UNCLASSIFIED], Jeffrey to Secretary of State, 29/01/2010, Wikileaks:, https://wikileaks.org/plusd/cables/10ANKARA154_a. html (Accessed March 28 2017)
70. Ludin interview.
71. Cable 248366, [CONFIDENTIAL], Roemer to Secretary of State, 11/02/2010, Wikileaks:, http://www.thehindu.com/news/the-india-cables/the-cables/article2042827.ece (Accessed March 28 2017)
72. Ray, 'World Rejects India's Taliban Stand'.
73. K Subrahmanyam, 'The Second Deception,' Indian Express, 03/03/2010.
74. Ray, 'World rejects India's Taliban stand'.
75. Ibid.
76. DNI Dennis Blair, 2009: http://www.intelligence.senate.gov/090212/blair.pdf (Accessed March 28 2017)
77. Ibid.
78. Katju, 'In Afghanistan, back to the future'.
79. Cable: 10NEWDELHI201_a, [CONFIDENTIAL], Roemer to Secretaries of State, 01/02/2010, Wikileaks: https://wikileaks.org/plusd/cables/10NEW DELHI201_a.html (Accessed March 28 2017)
80. Cable: 10NEWDELHI77_a, [CONFIDENTIAL], Roemer to Secretary of Defence, 15/01/2010, Wikileaks:, https://wikileaks.org/plusd/cables/10NEW DELHI77_a.html (Accessed March 28 2017)
81. Cowper-Coles, Cables from Kabul, 209–32.
82. 'Talk to the Taliban, Miliband urges,' BBC, 27/07/2009.
83. Cable: 10NEWDELHI162_a.
84. Cable: 10NEWDELHI163_a, [CONFIDENTIAL], Roemer to Secretary of State, 28/01/2010, Wikileaks:, https://wikileaks.org/plusd/cables/10NEW DELHI163_a.html (Accessed March 28 2017)

85. Cable: 08STATE18079_a, [CONFIDENTIAL], State Department, 05/11/2008, Wikileaks:, https://wikileaks.org/plusd/cables/08STATE118079_a.html (Accessed March 28 2017)
86. Cable: 10NEWDELHI334_a, [CONFIDENTIAL], Roemer to Secretary of State, 23/02/2010, Wikileaks: https://wikileaks.org/plusd/cables/10NEWDELHI334_a.html
87. Cable: 09KABUL1912_a, [SECRET], Eikenberry to Secretary of State, 18/07/2009, Wikileaks:, https://wikileaks.org/plusd/cables/09KABUL1912_a.html
88. Cable: 10NEWDELHI334_a
89. Cable: 10NEWDELHI355_a, [CONFIDENTIAL], Roemer to Secretary of State, 25/02/2010, Wikileaks:, https://wikileaks.org/plusd/cables/10NEWDELHI355_a.html (Accessed March 28 2017)
90. Cable: 10KOLKATA29_a, [CONFIDENTIAL], Payne to Secretary of State, 26/02/2010, Wikileaks: https://wikileaks.org/plusd/cables/10KOLKATA29_a.html (Accessed March 28 2017)
91. Menon interview.
92. Ibid.
93. Prasad interview.
94. Ibid.
95. Sahgal interview.
96. B interview.
97. Interview with two UK Foreign and Commonwealth Office (FCO) officials collectively termed J. Details of the interviews withheld.
98. Ibid.
99. H interview.
100. Ibid.
101. Ibid.
102. Rakesh Sood interview.
103. Ibid.
104. I interview.
105. Mukhopadhaya interview.
106. 'Former Afghanistan president Burhanuddin Rabbani killed in Kabul blast', The Telegraph, 20/09/2011.
107. Indrani Bagchi, 'India upbeat after Istanbul Conference on Afghanistan,' ToI, 07/11/2011.
108. Mark Mazzetti, The Way of the Knife: The CIA, a Secret Army, and a War at the Ends of the Earth (London: Penguin Books, 2014).
109. Saeed Shah and Luke Harding, 'Taliban may have lured NATO forces to attack Pakistani outpost: US', Guardian, 29/11/2011.
110. Mukhopadhaya interview.

111. Chaudhuri interview; Erich Schmidt-Eenboom, 'German intelligence in Afghanistan from the 1950's to the present day', NISA Intelligence: http://www.nisa-intelligence.nl/PDF-bestanden/NISAcongresSchmidtEenboom.pdf (Accessed March 28 2017)
112. Bhadrakumar, 'Manmohan Singh resets Afghan policy'.
113. Afghan Peace Process Roadmap 2015: http://www.foreignpolicy.com/files/121213_Peace_Process_Roadmap_to_2015.pdf (Accessed March 28 2017)
114. Ibid.
115. Qais Azimi and Mujib Mashal, 'Karzai's team clash over relations with US', Al Jazeera, 21/03 2012.
116. Mukhopadhaya interview.
117. Ibid.
118. Mukhopadhaya interview.
119. Ludin interview.
120. Ibid.
121. Emma Graham-Harrison, 'Afghan Taliban send delegation to Iran,' Guardian, 03/06/2013.
122. Interview with Daud Saba, former Herat governor, Afghanistan, Herat, 17/04/2013; Interview with Nader Nadery, Former Director, Free and Fair Elections Foundation of Afghanistan, Kabul, 07/05/2013.
123. Saba interview.
124. United States Government, 'Iran-Afghanistan: Trouble over the Helmand River Waters', Intelligence Note, *Bureau of Intelligence and Research*, November 18, 1971 [CIA Archives].
125. Shapoor Saber, 'Iran Again accused of trying to halt Afghan dam', Institute for War and Peace Reporting, 19/02/2010.
126. Quoted in Devirupa Mitra, 'The Amazing Indian Story Behind Herat's Salma Dam', The Wire, 04/06/2016.
127. Ibid.
128. Cable: 05NEWDELHI1521_a, [CONFIDENTIAL], Mulford to N/A, 28/02/2005, Wikileaks:, https://wikileaks.org/plusd/cables/05NEWDELHI1521_a.html (Accessed March 28 2017)
129. Cable: 07KABUL1327_a, [SECRET], Richard Norland to the CIA, 18/04/2007, Wikileaks:, https://wikileaks.org/plusd/cables/07KABUL1327_a.html (Accessed March 28 2017)
130. Khare interview.
131. 'Iran threatening peace prospects for war-ravaged Afghanistan,' Khaama Press, 11/02/2013.
132. Saber, 'Iran Again accused of trying to halt Afghan dam'.
133. Mitra, 'The Amazing Indian Story Behind Herat's Salma Dam', The Wire.
134. Cable: 09KABUL624_a, [FOR OFFICIAL USE], 17/03/2009, Wikileaks:,

https://wikileaks.org/plusd/cables/09KABUL624_a.html (Accessed March 28 2017)

135. Interview with Maulvi Khodaidad, senior cleric in the Ulema Council of Herat, Herat, 15/04/2013.
136. Ibid.
137. Mitra, 'The Amazing Indian Story Behind Herat's Salma Dam', The Wire.
138. Ibid.
139. J and M interviews.
140. Ibid.
141. Saba interview.
142. Saber, 'Iran Again accused of trying to halt Afghan dam'.
143. Saba interview.
144. Ibid.
145. F interview.
146. Menon interview.
147. Menon and Khare interviews.
148. Cable: 06NEWDELHI553_a, [CONFIDENTIAL], Mulford to Secretary of State, 25/01/2006, Wikileaks:, https://wikileaks.org/plusd/cables/06NEWDELHI553_a.html (Accessed March 28 2017)
149. M interview.
150. Cable: 09NEWDELHI2388_a, [CONFIDENTIAL], White to Secretry of State, 25/11/2009, Wikileaks: https://wikileaks.org/plusd/cables/09NEWDELHI2388_a.html (Accessed March 28 2017)
151. Cable: 10ABUDHABI9_a
152. Zarif Nazar and Charles Recknagel, 'Controversial Madrasah Builds Iran's Influence in Kabul,' Radio Free Europe, 06/11/2010.
153. 'Iran Pays Bounties to Taliban for Dead Americans', The Weekly Standard, 06/09/2010.
154. Shanthie Mariet D'Souza, 'Iran, US and the Afghan Conundrum', ISAS Insights,132, 01/09/2011.
155. Cable: 07NEWDELHI1488_a, [CONFIDENTIAL], Mulford to Secretary of State, 28/03/2007, Wikileaks: https://wikileaks.org/plusd/cables/07NEWDELHI1488_a.html (Accessed March 28 2017)
156. Radha Kumar and Kailash K Prashad, 'Afghanistan 2012: Looking to the Future', Delhi Policy Group, 1–50.
157. Cable: 10NEWDELHI334_a.
158. Ahmad, 'Russia and the Taliban Make Amends'.
159. Mateen Haider, 'Pakistan, Russia sign landmark defence deal', Dawn, 20/08/2015.
160. Chaudhuri interview. Without a larger security infrastructure that only the US could provide, there was no point of having Russian or Indian arms, as they risked falling into wrong hands.

161. Cable: 07MOSCOW5869_a, [CONFIDENTIAL], Burns to Secretary of State, 19/12/2007, Wikileaks:, https://wikileaks.org/plusd/cables/07MOSCOW5869_a.html (Accessed March 28 2017)
162. Cable: 07BEIJING6976_a, [CONFIDENTIAL], Randt to Secretary of State, 05/11/2007, Wikileaks: https://wikileaks.org/plusd/cables/07BEIJING6976_a.html (Accessed March 28 2017)
163. Cable: 06BEIJING16162_a, [CONFIDENTIAL], Randt to Secretary of State, 07/08/2006, Wikileaks: https://wikileaks.org/plusd/cables/06BEIJING16162_a.html (Accessed March 28 2017)
164. Khare interview.
165. Cable: 09BEIJING3287_a, [CONFIDENTIAL], Huntsman to Secretary of State, 09/12/2009, Wikileaks: https://wikileaks.org/plusd/cables/09BEIJING3287_a.html (Accessed March 28 2017)
166. Andrew Small, 'Why is China Talking to the Taliban?' Foreign Policy, 21/06/2013.
167. Jeremy Page, 'China to Contribute $40 Billion to Silk Road Fund', Wall Street Journal, 08/11/2014.
168. Margherita Stancati, 'Afghan Peace Envoy Met Taliban in Secret China Talks', Wall Street Journal, 25/05/2015.
169. Ismail Khan, 'Afghan govt., Taliban resume peace talks in Murree on Friday,' Dawn, 29/07/2015.
170. Department of State, 11/01/2016: http://www.state.gov/r/pa/prs/ps/2016/01/251105.htm
171. Menon interview.
172. Matthew Rosenberg and Michael D. Shear, 'In Reversal, Obama Says U.S. Soldiers Will Stay in Afghanistan Till 2017', NYT, 15/10/2015.
173. 'Taliban admit covering up death of Mullah Omar', BBC, 31/08/2015.
174. Obaid Ali, 'The fall and recapture of Kunduz,' Afghanistan Analysts Network, 16/10/2015.
175. 'Taliban attacks heavily fortified Kandahar airport', Al Jazeera, 09/12/2015.
176. Jessica Donati and Habib Khan Totakhil, 'Afghan Intelligence Chief Nabil Resigns; clashed with President Ghani Over Pakistan', WSJ, 10/12/2015.
177. Emma Graham-Harrison, 'Taliban fears over yung recruits attracted to Isis in Afghanistan', Guardian, 07/05/2015.
178. Mukhopadhaya interview.

EPILOGUE: A BLESSING

1. 'Pakistan invites India for key Afghan conference' The Hindu, 09/11/2015.
2. Suhashini Haidar, 'India-Pak talks are off', The Hindu, 19/08/2014.
3. Suhashini Haidar, 'India rebuffs Afghanistan on strategic meet', The Hindu, 29/08/2015.

4. 'India, Pakistan NSAs hold breakthrough talks in Bangkok', Hindustan Times, 06/12/2015.
5. Irfan Haidar, 'Pakistan, India agree to restart 'comprehensive' dialogue process', Dawn, 10/12/2015.
6. 'Peshawar: As India mourns with Pakistan, Musharraf blames New Delhi, Kabul', Dawn, 18/12/2014.
7. Interviews with serving Indian intelligence officials during 2013–16—details withheld.
8. 'Massive protests erupt in PoK as people demand freedom from Pakistan, raise pro-India slogans', DNA India, 30/09/2015.
9. 'Pakistan Taliban: Peshawar school attack leaves 141 dead', BBC, 16/12/2015.
10. Barnett Rubin, 'The TAPI Pipeline and Paths to Peace in Afghanistan', New Yorker, 20/12/2015.
11. 'Full Text of Prime Minister Narendra Modi's Speech at the Afghan Parliament', NDTV, 25/12/2015.
12. 'India Not Sidelined in Afghanistan for Staying Out of Taliban Peace Talks', Outlook India, 23/02/2016.
13. Peerzada Ashiq, 'United Jihad Council Claims Responsibility for Pathankot Attack', The Hindu, 04/01/2016.
14. The confessional video is available here: 'Govt airs video of Indian spy admitting involvement in Balochistan insurgency', Dawn, 31/03/2016.
15. 'MEA rejects 'confession of spy', asks Pak. To give consular access', The Hindu, 30/03/2016.
16. 'Hizbul Mujahideen 'poster boy' Burhan Wani killed in joint encounter', Indian Express, 08/07/2016.
17. Nasir Ganai, '674 wounded in a single day as pellets, tear gas rain in on Kashmir protestors', India Today, 06/08/2016.
18. For full text of Modi's speech: http://indianexpress.com/article/india/india-news-india/pm-narendra-modis-speech-on-independence-day-2016-here-is-the-full-text/ (Accessed March 28 2017)
19. 'Afghanistan: Taliban Suicide Bomb Attack Near Kabul,' BBC, 10/08/2015.
20. Jibran Ahmed, 'Taliban Leadership Struggle Fuels Wave of Attacks in Afghanistan,' Reuters, 12/08/2015.
21. Mujib Mashal, "After Kabul Attack, Afghan Leader Points Finger at Pakistan for Failing to Stop Taliban", NYT, 10/08/2015.
22. Full speech by Modi at Salma Dam inauguration: https://www.youtube.com/watch?v=HJ4NtBKvOY0

SELECT BIBLIOGRAPHY

Archives

- National Security Archives, George Washington University.
- UK Foreign Office Files for India, Pakistan and Afghanistan 1947–1980.
- P N Haksar Papers, The Nehru Memorial Museum and Library, India.
- Foreign Relations of the United States, Historical Documents.
- John Gunther Dean's Oral History, Jimmy Carter Presidential Museum and Library.
- Foreign Affairs Records, Ministry of External Affairs of India.
- United States National Security Decision Directives (NSDD), Reagan Administration.
- Parliament of India, Lok Sabha Debates.
- Parliament of India, Rajya Sabha Debates.
- Ministry of External Affairs of India Annual Reports.
- Amnesty International Reports.
- US Senate Foreign Relations Committee Reports.
- US Senate Intelligence Committee Reports.
- Speeches by the President of the United States, White House.
- US Library of Congress.
- UK House of Commons, International Affairs and Defence Section.
- International Crisis Group Reports.
- Human Rights Watch Reports.
- Ministry of Foreign Affairs of Russia Reports.

Wikileaks

- Carter Cables.
- Carter Cables 2.
- PlusD.

- CableGate.
- Kissinger Papers.
- Global Intelligence Files.

Select Official Documents.

- Text of the India-Afghanistan Treaty of Friendship, 1950, http://www.commonlii.org/in/other/treaties/INTSer/1950/3.html.
- Text of the US-Afghanistan Bilateral Security Agreement, http://mfa.gov.af/en/news/bsa.
- Text of the Treaty of Peace and Friendship (with Nepal), http://mea.gov.in/bilateral-documents.htm?dtl/6295/Treaty+of+Peace+and+Friendship.
- Treaty of Friendship and Cooperation (with Bhutan), http://mea.gov.in/Portal/ForeignRelation/Bhutan-February–2012.pdf.
- International Monetary Fund (IMF) and World Bank reports.
- UNSC Resolution 1076 full text: United Nations Security Council, 'Situation in Afghanistan', October 22, 1996.
- http://daccess-dds-ny.un.org/doc/UNDOC/GEN/N96/284/26/PDF/N9628426.pdf?OpenElement.
- United Nations General Assembly, 'Resolution 49/60: Measures to eliminate international terrorism', December 09, 1994, http://www.un.org/documents/ga/res/49/a49r060.htm.
- United National Security Council, 'Foreign interference major obstacle to negotiated peace in Afghanistan', *Press Release SC/6203*, April 09, 1996, http://www.un.org/News/Press/docs/1996/19960409.sc6203.html.
- 'Text of the Lahore Declaration', *Ministry of External Affairs*, February 02, 1999 http://mea.gov.in/in-focus-article.htm?18997/Lahore+Declaration+February+1999.
- United Nations General Assembly, 'General Assembly 'appalled' by edict on destruction of afghan shrines; strongly urges Taliban to halt implementation', *UN Press Release*, March 09, 2001, http://www.un.org/press/en/2001/ga9858.doc.htm.
- United Nations Security Council, 'Resolution 1267', October 15, 1999, http://www.un.org/ga/search/view_doc.asp?symbol=S/RES/1267(1999).
- Presidential Statement, 'President Condemns Afghanistan's 'Taliban' for the July military offensive, sheltering terrorists', *United Nations Security Council SC/6743*, October 22, 1999, http://www.un.org/News/Press/docs/1999/19991022.sc6743.doc.html.
- UN Information Service, 'Secretary-General Says "Six plus Two" Group Remains Essential Forum For Solution of Afghan Question', *UNIS/SG/2666*, September 18, 2000, http://www.unis.unvienna.org/unis/pressrels/2000/sg2666.html.

- United Nations, 'Comprehensive Test Ban Treaty', *Resolution 50/245*, September 17, 1996, http://www.un.org/documents/ga/res/50/ares50–245.htm.
- United Nations Development Program (UNDP), 'Partnerships to Fight Poverty', *Annual Report*, 2001, http://www.undp.org/content/dam/undp/library/corporate/UNDP-in-action/2001/English/complete.pdf.
- USA PATRIOT Act: http://www.gpo.gov/fdsys/pkg/BILLS-107hr3162enr/pdf/BILLS-107hr3162enr.pdf.
- Full text of the POTO 2001, http://www.satp.org/satporgtp/countries/india/document/actandordinances/POTO.htm.
- 'Agreement on provisional arrangements in Afghanistan pending the re-establishment of permanent government institutions', *United Nations*, http://www.un.org/News/dh/latest/afghan/afghan-agree.htm.
- UK Home Office, 'Afghanistan: persons supporting or perceived to support the government and/or international forces', *Country Information and Guidance*, February 2015, 21–22.
- United States Government (USG), 'Amendments to the Terrorist Designations of Lashkar-e-Tayyiba', *Department of State*, Office of the Spokesperson, Washington D.C., June 25, 2014, http://www.state.gov/r/pa/prs/ps/2014/06/228431.htm.
- Full text of India-Afghanistan Strategic Partnership Agreement.
- 2003 United States Federal Budget: http://federal-budget.insidegov.com/l/106/2003.
- Full text of the Afghan Peace Process Roadmap 2015:, http://www.foreignpolicy.com/files/121213_Peace_Process_Roadmap_to_2015.pdf. For the full speech by Modi at Salma Dam inauguration see PM Modi's speech at the Joint Inauguration of Salma Dam in Afghanistan, https://www.youtube.com/watch?v=HJ4NtBKvOY0.
- Foreign and Commonwealth Office of India, *The Transfer of Power 1942–7*, Volume VIII, 'The Interim Government, Letter from Sir O. Caroe (NWFP) to Field Marshall Viscount Wavell', (Governor's Camp, Parachinar) October 23, 1946.
- The Transfer of Power 1942–7, Volume VIII, *The Interim Government*, Letter from Pandit Nehru to Sir O. Caroe (NWFP) Enclosure to No. 520, New Delhi, October 24, 1946.
- 'Documentation: Soviet-Afghan Treaty of Friendship', *Survival*, 21 (2), 1979.

Media Outlets

- Times of India.
- New York Times.
- Associated Press.
- Kuwait News Agency.
- The New Yorker.

- The Hindu.
- NDTV.
- Outlook.
- BBC News.
- The Caravan—A Journal of Politics and Culture.
- The American Interest.
- Foreign Policy.
- Indian Express.
- Hindustan Times.
- Dawn.
- Global Security Project.
- The Guardian.
- Rediff News.
- DailyO.
- India Today.
- IBNLive.
- Reuters.
- Frontline Magazine.
- Afghan Islamic Press.
- Press Information Bureau of India.
- Asia Times Online.
- Express India.
- The Economic Times.
- Business Standard.
- CNN.
- Public Affairs Magazine.
- Janes Security News.
- South Asia Terrorism Portal.
- The Jameson Foundation.
- People's Democracy (Weekly Organ of the Communist Party of India, Marxist).
- TheWire.in.
- Time Magazine.
- US Aid.
- Live Mint.
- ABC News.
- UNAMA News Articles.
- Russia and India Report.
- Firstpost.
- The Diplomat.
- ANI News.
- The Telegraph.

- Los Angeles Times.
- India Defence Review.
- Al Jazeera.
- Tehelka.
- DNA India.
- Afghan Analysts Network.
- Wall Street Journal.
- Foreign Affairs.
- Pajhwok News.
- New America Foundation.
- NISA Intelligence.
- Khaama Press.
- Radio Free Europe.
- Op-ed News.
- The Weekly Standard.
- Delhi Policy Group.

Books and Articles:

Aikins, Matthieu. 'India in Afghanistan: Nation Building or Proxy War?', *The Caravan—A Journal of Politics and Culture*, October 01, 2010.

Amstutz, J Bruce. *Afghanistan: The First Five Years of Soviet Occupation* (Darby: Diane Publishing, 1986).

Andrew, Christopher and Vasili Mitrokhin, *The World Was Going Our Way—The KGB and the Battle for the Third World* (Newly Revealed Secrets from the Mitrokhin Archive) (New York: Basic Books, 2006).

Baker, James and Lee H. Hamilton et al. Authorised Ed., *The Iraq Study Group Report: The Way Forward: A New Approach*. (New York: Vintage Books, 2006).

Balachandran, Vappala. *National Security and Intelligence Management: A New Paradigm* (Mumbai: Indus Source Books, 2014).

Bhatia, Rajiv. *India-Myanmar Relations: Changing Contours* (New Delhi: Routledge, 2016).

Bradsher, Henry S. *Afghanistan and the Soviet Union* (North Carolina: Duke University Press, 1983).

Brobst, Peter John. *The Future of the Great Game: Sir Olaf Caroe, India's Independence, and the Defense of Asia* (Ohio: University of Akron Press, 2005).

Centlivres, Pierre. 'The Controversy over the Buddhas of Bamiyan', *South Asia Multidisciplinary Academic Journal*, December 31, 2008.

Chaudhuri, Rudra. *Forged in Crisis: India and the United States Since 1947* (New York: Oxford University Press, 2014).

Clinton, Hillary Rodham. *Hard Choices: A Memoir* (London: Simon and Schuster, 2014).

Coll, Steve. *Ghost Wars: The Secret History of the CIA, Afghanistan, and Bin Laden from Soviet invasion to September 10, 2001* (London: Penguin, 2004).

Cordovez, Diego and Selig Harrison, *Out of Afghanistan: The Inside Story of the Soviet Withdrawal* (New York: Oxford University Press, 1995).

Corwin, Phillip. *Doomed in Afghanistan: A UN Officer's Memoir of the Fall of Kabul and Najibullah's Failed Escape, 1992* (New Brunswick: Rutgers University Press, 2003).

Cowper-Coles, Sherard. *Cables from Kabul: The Inside Story of the West's Afghanistan Campaign* (London: Harper Press, 2012).

D'Souza, Shanthie Mariet. 'President Karzai's Wishlist and New Delhi's Strategic Volte-Face in Afghanistan,' *Georgetown Journal of International Affairs*, June 11, 2013.

D'Souza, Shanthie Mariet. 'Iran, US and the Afghan Conundrum', *ISAS Insights*, 132, September 01, 2011.

Dalrymple, William. 'A Deadly Triangle: Afghanistan, Pakistan, and India', *The Brookings Institution* (Washington DC: Brookings Institution, 2013).

Dhar, Maloy Krishna, *Open Secrets: India's Intelligence Unveiled* (New Delhi: Manas Publishers, 2005).

Destradi, Sandra. 'India: A Reluctant Partner for Afghanistan', *Washington Quarterly*, June 25, 2014 (online version).

Dixit, J. N. *An Afghan Diary: Zahir Shah to Taliban* (Delhi: Konark Publishers, 2000).

——— *My South Block Years: Memoirs of a Foreign Secretary* (New Delhi: UBS Publishers, 1996).

——— ed., *External Affairs: Cross-Border Relations* (India: Roli Books 2003).

——— *India-Pakistan in War and Peace* (India: Konark Publishers, 2002).

——— *Across Borders: 50 years of Indian Foreign Policy* (New Delhi: Picus Books, 1998).

Dobbins, James. *After the Taliban: Nation Building in Afghanistan* (Washington DC: Potomac Books, 2008).

Dulat, Amarjit S. and Aditya Sinha, *Kashmir: The Vajpayee Years* (New Delhi: HarperCollins, 2015).

Dupree, Nancy. *A Historical Guide to Afghanistan* (Kabul: Afghan Tourist Organisation, 1977).

Embree, Ainsley T. *Imagining India: Essays in Indian History* (Oxford: Oxford University Press, 1990.

Fair, Christine. 'The Other Drawdown in Afghanistan', *Current History: A Journal of Contemporary World Affairs*, April 2015, 137–143.

Fields, Mark and Ramsha Ahmed, 'A Review of the 2001 Bonn Conference: An Application to the Road Ahead in Afghanistan,' *Strategic Perspectives*, Institute for National Strategic Studies (Washington DC: National Defence University, 2011).

Ganguly, Sumit and Nicholas Howenstein. 'India-Pakistan Rivalry in Afghanistan', *Journal of International Affairs*, 63 (1), Fall/Winter 2009.

Gates, Robert. *Duty: Memoirs of a Secretary at War* (London: Alfred Knopf, 2014).

Ghosh, Partha S. and Rajaram Panda, 'Domestic Support for Mrs. Indira Gandhi's Afghan Policy: The Soviet Factor in Indian Politics', *Asian Survey*, 23 (3), March 1983, 261–279.

Gopal, Sarvepalli ed. 'India-Afghanistan Relations', *Selected Works of Jawaharlal Nehru*, Second Series, 1 (New Delhi: Jawaharlal Nehru Memorial Fund, 1984).

Guha, Ramachandra. *India After Gandhi: The History of the World's Largest Democracy* (London: Picador, 2008).

Gujral, Inder K. 'Oral History: India's Response to the Soviet Military Intervention in Afghanistan', *Indian Foreign Affairs Journal*, 1 (1), January–March 2006.

Gujral, Inder K. *Matters of Discretion: An Autobiography* (New Delhi: Hay House Publishers, 2011).

Gujral, Inder K. *A Foreign Policy for India* (New Delhi: Ministry of External Affairs, 1998).

Gupte, Pranay. *Mother India: A Political Biography of Indira Gandhi* (New Delhi: Penguin, 2009).

Habib, Irfan. *Medieval India: A Study of Civilizations* (New Delhi: National Book Trust, 2008).

——— *Post-Mauryan India 200BC-AD300: A Political and Economic History* (New Delhi: Tulika Books, 2013).

Harrison, Selig. *In Afghanistan's Shadow: Baluch Nationalism and Soviet Temptations* (Washington D.C.: Carnegie Endowment for International Peace, 1981).

Horn, Robert C. 'Afghanistan and the Soviet-Indian Influence Relationship', *Asian Survey*, 23 (3), March 1983, 244–260.

Kalinovsky, Artemy M. *A Long Goodbye: The Soviet Withdrawal from Afghanistan* (Cambridge, Massachusetts: Harvard University Press, 2011).

Kalinovsky, Artemy M. and Sergey Radchenko eds, *The End of the Cold War and the Third World: New Perspectives on Regional Conflict* (London: Routledge, 2011).

Kaplan, Robert. *Monsoon: The Indian Ocean and the Future of American Power* (US: Random House, 2011).

Kartha, Tara. 'Pakistan and Taliban—Flux in an Old Relationship Relationship?' *Institute for Defence Studies and Analyses (IDSA)*, October 07, 2000.

Kautilya, *The Arthashastra* (New Delhi: Penguin Books, 1992).

Khalilzad, Zalmay. *The Envoy: From Kabul to the White House, my Journey Through a Turbulent World* (New York: St. Martins Press, 2016).

Khan, Riaz M. *Untying the Afghan Knot: Negotiating Soviet Withdrawal* (Duke University Press, 1991).

Khosla, I. P. 'Oral History: Last days of the Soviet Troops in Afghanistan', *Indian Foreign Affairs Journal*, 6 (1), January–March 2011.

Kipling, Rudyard. *Kim*, (Hertfordshire: Wordsworth Classics, 1994).

Kux, Dennis. *The United States and Pakistan, 1947–2000: Disenchanted Allies* (Baltimore: Johns Hopkins University Press, 2001).

Lambah, Satinder K. 'India at the United Nations Talks on Afghanistan, 2001,' *Indian Foreign Affairs Journal*, 1 (1) January–March (India: Foundation Books, 2006).

Lavoy, Peter R. ed. *Asymmetric Warfare in South Asia: The Causes and Consequences of the Kargil Conflict* (New York: Cambridge University Press, 2009).

Levy, Adrian and Catherine Scott-Clarke, *Nuclear Deception: The Dangerous Relationship Between the United States and Pakistan* (New York: Walker and Co., 2008).

Light, Margot ed. *Troubled Friendships: Moscow's Third World Venture* (London: Royal Institute of International Affairs, 1993).

Linschoten, Alex Strick van and Felix Kuehn, *An Enemy We Created: The Myth of the Taliban-Al Qaeda Merger in Afghanistan* (Oxford: Oxford University Press, 2012).

Linschoten, Alex Strick van and Felix Kuehn, *Missed Opportunities: Lessons from the West's talks with the Taliban pre-2001* (Unpublished paper. The author was granted access to this document for this study on request, 2013).

Machiavelli, Niccolo. *The Prince*, (London: Penguin Classics, 2009).

Marshall, Alex and Tim Bird, *Afghanistan: How the West Lost its Way* (Yale: Yale University Press, 2011).

Matinuddin, Kamal. *The Taliban Phenomenon: Afghanistan 1994–1997* (Karachi: Oxford University Press, 1999).

Mazzetti, Mark. *The Way of the Knife: The CIA, a Secret Army, and a War at the Ends of the Earth* (London: Penguin Books, 2014).

Mehta, Jagat S. *March of Folly in Afghanistan 1978–2001* (New Delhi: Manohar Publishers, 2002).

Menon, Shivshankar. *Choices: Inside the Making of India's Foreign Policy* (Washington DC: Brookings Institution, 2016).

Mullik, B N. *My Years With Nehru, 1948–1964* (New Delhi: Allied Publishers, 1972).

Murshed, S. Iftikhar. *Afghanistan: The Taliban Years* (London: Bennett and Bloom, 2006).

Musharraf, Pervez. *In the Line of Fire: A Memoir* (New York: Simon and Schuster, 2008).

Nadiri, Khalid Homayun. 'Old Habits, New Consequences: Pakistan's Posture Towards Afghanistan Since 2001', *International Security*, 39:2, 132–168, Fall 2014.

Nunan, Timothy. *Humanitarian Invasion: Global Development in Cold War Afghanistan* (Cambridge: Cambridge University Press, 2016).

Ogden, Chris. 'Tracing the Pakistan-Terrorism Nexus in Indian Security Perspectives: From 1947 to 26/11,' *India Quarterly: A Journal of International Affairs*, 69 (1) (New Delhi: ICWA, Sage Publishers, 2013) 35–50.

Omrani, Bijan. 'The Durand Line: History and Problems of the Afghan-Pakistan Border', *Asian Survey*, 40 (2), 177–195, 2009.

Paliwal, Avinash. 'Securing Afghanistan—Historic Sources of India's Contemporary Challenge', *Observer Research Foundation*, Occasional Paper Number 43, August 2013 http://www.orfonline.org/cms/export/orfonline/modules/occasionalpaper/attachments/occasionalpaper47_1378805497092.pdf.

Pant, Harsh V. *India's Afghan Muddle: A Lost Opportunity* (New Delhi: HarperCollins, 2014).

——— 'India in Afghanistan: A test case for a rising power', *Contemporary South Asia*, 18 (2), 133–153, June 2010.

Partlow, Joshua. *A Kingdom of Their Own: The Family Karzai and the Afghan Disaster* (London: Simon and Schuster, 2016).

Pradhan, R. D. *1965 War The Inside Story—Defence Minister Y B Chavan's Diary of the India-Pakistan War* (Delhi: Atlantic Publishers, 2007).

Raghavan, Srinath. *War and Peace in Modern India* (New Delhi: Palgrave Macmillan, 2010).

——— 'A Coercive Triangle: India, Pakistan, the United States and the Crisis of 2001–2002,' *Defence Studies*, 9 (2), 2009, 242–260.

——— *1971—A Global History of the Creation of Bangladesh* (Harvard: Harvard University Press, 2013).

Rajan, M. S. 'The Indo-Soviet Treaty and India's non-alignment policy', *Australian Outlook*, 27 (2), 1972, 204–215.

Raman, B. *Kaoboys of R&AW: Down Memory Lane* (New Delhi: Lancer Publishers, 2007).

Rasgotra, M. K. *A Life in Diplomacy* (New Delhi: Penguin, 2016).

Rashid, Ahmed. *Taliban: Militant Islam, Oil, and Fundamentalism in Central Asia* (New Haven: Yale University Press, 1998).

Rashiduzzaman, M. 'The National Awami Party of Pakistan: Leftist Politics in Crisis', *Pacific Affairs*, 43 (3). Autumn, 394–409, 1970.

Rumsfeld, Donald. *Known and Unknown: A Memoir* (New York: Sentinel Press, 2011).

Ruttig, Thomas. 'Islamists, Leftists—and a void in the Centre. Afghanistan's political parties and where they came from (1902–2006), *Konrad Adenauer Stiftung*, http://www.kas.de/wf/doc/kas_9674-544-2-30.pdf.

Sabatier, Paul A. and Christopher M. Weible eds., *Theories of the Policy Process* (Colorado: Westview Press, 2014).

Sabatier, Paul A. and Hank Jenkins-Smith eds. *Policy Change and Learning: An Advocacy Coalition Approach* (Colorado: Westview, 1993).

Saikal, Amin. *Modern Afghanistan: A History of Struggle and Survival* (London: I. B. Tauris, 2004).

Sedra, Mark. 'Afghanistan: Assessing the Progress of Security Sector Reform, One Year After the Geneva Conference,' *Bonn International Centre for Conversion (BICC)*, 2003, 2–15.

Semple, Michael. *Reconciliation in Afghanistan* (Washington DC: United States Institute for Peace Press, 2009).

Shahnahan, Elizabeth A., Michael D Jones and Mark K McBeth, 'Policy Narratives and Policy Processes,' *The Policy Studies Journal*, 39 (3) 535–561 (Washington D.C.: Policy Studies Organisation, 2011).

Shahzad, Syed Saleem. *Inside Al-Qaeda and the Taliban: Beyond Bin Laden and 9/11* (London: Pluto Press, 2013).

Siddiqi, Farhan Hanif. *The Politics of Ethnicity in Pakistan: The Baloch, Sindhi, and Mohajir ethnic movements* (Abingdon: Routledge, 2012).

Sikri, Rajiv. *Challenge and Strategy: Rethinking India's Foreign Policy* (New Delhi: Sage Publishers, 2013).

Singh, Jaswant. *A Call to Honour: In Service of Emergent India* (Indiana: Indiana University Press, 2007).

Singh, Natwar. *One Life is Not Enough: An Autobiography* (New Delhi: Rupa & Co., 2014).

Sinha, P. B. 'Vajpayee's Visit to Kabul', *Strategic Analysis*, 2:7, 236–241, 1978.

Sitapati, Vinay. *Half Lion: How P V Narasimha Rao transformed India* (New Delhi: Penguin Books, 2016).

Small, Andrew. *The China-Pakistan Axis—Asia's New Geopolitics* (London: C Hurst & Co., 2015).

Smith, Tim and Irna Qureshi. *The Grand Trunk Road: From Delhi to the Khyber Pass* (Devi Lewis Publishers, 2001).

Staniland, Paul. *Networks of Rebellion: Explaining Insurgent Cohesion and Collapse* (Ithaca: Cornell University Press, 2014).

Sufi, Jumma Khan. *Faraib-e-Na-Tamam* (Lahore: Pak Book Empire, 2016).

Tagore, Rabindranath. 'The Cabuliwallah (The Fruitseller from Kabul)', (translated by the Sister Nivedita), *Modern Review*, 11 (1), 50–56, January, 1912.

Talbott, Strobe. *Engaging India: Diplomacy, Democracy and the Bomb* (Washington DC: Brookings Institution, 2004).

Tan, Seng and Amitav Acharya eds. *Bandung Revisited: The Legacy of the 1955 Asian-African Conference for International Order* (Singapore: National University of Singapore Press, 2008).

Tellis, Ashley. 'Securing the Barrack: The Logic, Structure and Objective of India's Naval Expansion—Part I' *Naval War College Review*, XLIII/3, (Sequence 331) 1990, 77–97.

Thapar, Romila. *Penguin History of India, Volume 1* (London: Penguin Books, 1990).

Tharoor, Shashi. *Pax Indica: India and the World of the 21st Century* (New Delhi: Allen Lane, 2012).

Unnithan, Sandeep. *Black Tornado: Mumbai 26/11* (New Delhi: HarperCollins, 2015).

Weible, Christopher M. et al., 'A Quarter Century of the Advocacy Coalition

Framework: An Introduction to the Special Issue,' *Policy Studies Journal*, 39 (3), 349–360, 2011.

Weiner, Myron and Ali Banuazizi eds. *The Politics of Social Transformation in Afghanistan, Iran, and Pakistan* (New York: Syracuse University Press, 1994).

Woodward, Bob. *Bush at War* (London: Pocket Books, 2003).

Zaeef, Abdul Salam. *My Life with the Taliban* (London: C Hurst & Co., 2010).

Zaidi, A. M. ed., *The Annual Register of Indian Political Parties: Proceedings and Fundamental Texts, 1980* (New Delhi: S. Chand and Co., 1981).

INDEX